Reading the Thread

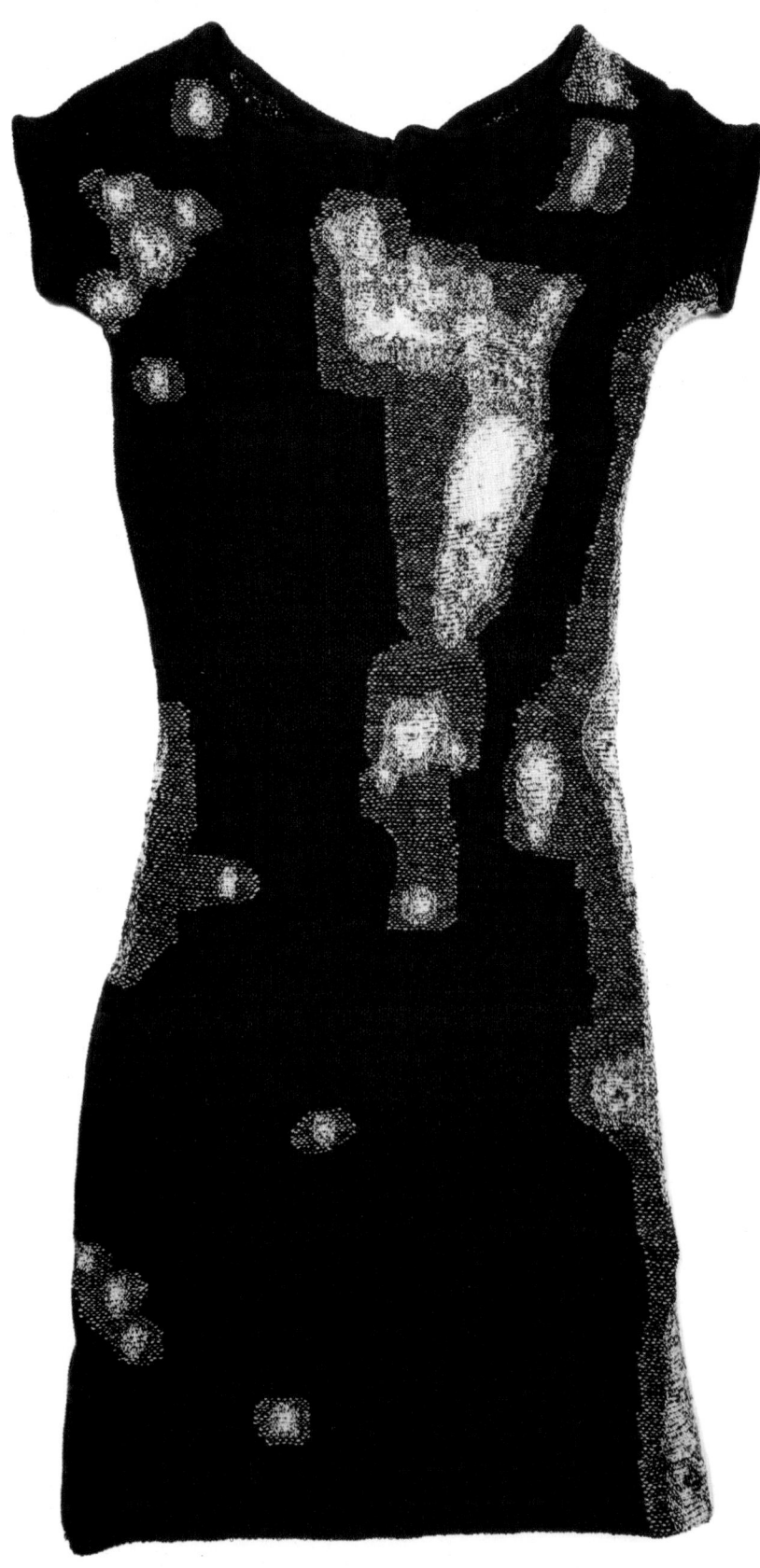

Figure 0.1 *Vivienne Leigh's dress*, 2021. © Celia Pym. Photography: © Michele Panzeri.

Reading the Thread

Cloth and Communication

Edited by
LESLEY MILLAR and ALICE KETTLE

BLOOMSBURY VISUAL ARTS
LONDON · NEW YORK · OXFORD · NEW DELHI · SYDNEY

BLOOMSBURY VISUAL ARTS
Bloomsbury Publishing Plc
50 Bedford Square, London, WC1B 3DP, UK
1385 Broadway, New York, NY 10018, USA
29 Earlsfort Terrace, Dublin 2, Ireland

BLOOMSBURY, BLOOMSBURY VISUAL ARTS and the Diana logo are trademarks of Bloomsbury Publishing Plc

First published in Great Britain 2024

Selection, editorial matter, Introductions © Lesley Millar and Alice Kettle, 2024
Individual chapters © their Authors, 2024

Lesley Millar and Alice Kettle have asserted their right under the Copyright, Designs and Patents Act, 1988, to be identified as Editors of this work.

For legal purposes the Acknowledgments on p. xiii constitute an extension of this copyright page.

Cover image © DCano/iStock Images

All rights reserved. No part of this publication may be reproduced or transmitted in any form or by any means, electronic or mechanical, including photocopying, recording, or any information storage or retrieval system, without prior permission in writing from the publishers.

Bloomsbury Publishing Plc does not have any control over, or responsibility for, any third-party websites referred to or in this book. All internet addresses given in this book were correct at the time of going to press. The author and publisher regret any inconvenience caused if addresses have changed or sites have ceased to exist, but can accept no responsibility for any such changes.

A catalogue record for this book is available from the British Library.

A catalog record for this book is available from the Library of Congress.

ISBN:	HB:	978-1-3503-2049-9
	PB:	978-1-3503-2048-2
	ePDF:	978-1-3503-2050-5
	eBook:	978-1-3503-2051-2

Typeset by RefineCatch Limited, Bungay, Suffolk
Printed and bound in India

To find out more about our authors and books visit www.bloomsbury.com
and sign up for our newsletters.

CONTENTS

List of Illustrations vii
Notes on Contributors ix
Acknowledgments xiii

Introduction 1
LESLEY MILLAR AND ALICE KETTLE

PART ONE
READING THE RECORD 15

1. Tenapi: Markers of Clan Identity of the Alurung, East Indonesia 17
   LINDA S. MCINTOSH

2. The *Powerful Whispers* Project: A Reimagined Story of Mills, Menders, and Archived Family Memories 29
   ROBERT BURTON

3. Drapery and Napery: Lace War Memorials 39
   CAROL QUARINI

4. Cloth, Nationalism, and Cultural Identity: The Symbolism of Traditional Attire in Defining Nigeria's Diverse Ethnic Indigenism 51
   CLEMENT EMEKA AKPANG

Artist Maria Nepomuceno in conversation with Alice Kettle, Part 1 63

PART TWO
FOLLOWING THE THREAD 67

5. Robe à la Grand'mère—The Reuse of Eighteenth-Century Silks in Romantic-Era Fashion 69
   RUBY HODGSON

6. Layers of Comfort: Shetland Taatit Rugs 81
   CAROL CHRISTIANSEN

7. Making of Kediyun: A Conscious Approach to Cloth 93
   LOKESH GHAI

8. Transformations in the Making and Meaning of Bark Cloth in Uganda 103
   VENNY MARY NAKAZIBWE

Artist Maria Nepomuceno in conversation with Alice Kettle, Part 2 113

PART THREE
CHALLENGING THE READING 117

9 Small Acts of Refusal: Suffragette-Embroidered Cloths Worked in Holloway Prison 119
DENISE JONES

10 Stitching Justice: Textiles as a Means for Contemporary Social Justice 131
ALICIA DECKER AND SUSAN T. AVILA

11 Film as Fabric: Textile Practice as Feminist Critique in Expanded Cinema 143
MARY STARK

12 Cuttings 1820–2020 155
PIPPA HETHERINGTON

Artist Celia Pym in conversation with Lesley Millar, Part 1 165

PART FOUR
DRAFTING THE FUTURE 169

13 Portraying a Practice: Communicating E-Textiles 171
HANNAH PERNER-WILSON, BECCA ROSE, IRENE POSCH, LAURA DEVENDORF

14 Cloth, Techné, and Traces in Digital Fashion 181
KATHARINA SAND

15 The Coded Lab 195
SONJA ANDREW

16 Piñatex®, A New Material for a New World 207
CARMEN HIJOSA

Artist Celia Pym in conversation with Lesley Millar, Part 2 217

Index 220

ILLUSTRATIONS

0.1 *Vivienne Leigh's dress*, 2021. ii
0.2 *The Procession (figure 86)*, 2022. 3
0.3 GROUND, 2018 (one of three works, Ground, Sea and Sky), Thread Bearing Witness project. 4
0.4 *Cuttings #2*, 2019. 6
0.5 *Warp and Weft, Cloth and Memory* (2), 2013. 7
0.6 Video stills from *The Last Yarn, Cloth and Memory* (2), 2013. 8
0.7 *Haiku*, 1961. 9
0.8 *The Plants That Hold Us*, 2021. 11
0.9 *Rice Dreams*, 2013. 13
1.1 Alurung women wearing various types of tenapi while attending the Al Quran Festival held in Alor Besar, Alor Regency, East Indonesia, in 2020. 19
1.2 The Alurung man on the left has a patola draped over his shoulder to indicate his patrilineage, while the two other men wear tenapi in the traditional manner or as sarongs. 25
2.1 *Doris Hainsworth née Wilson*, 2017. Materials: cotton yarn, found object, starch glue, dye sublimation print construction, 42 × 40 cm. 33
2.2 *Powerful Whispers*, 2018. Materials: Silk shantung fiber, glues, dye sublimation print with embedded electronics, 4 × 70 × 140 cm. 35
3.1 Battle of Britain commemorative lace panel made by Dobson and Browne of Nottingham, 1946. 40
3.2 Queen Elisabeth's needlelace tablecloth completed in 1919 as part of the Belgian war lace initiative. 41
4.1 Onyonyo dress of the Efiks. 55
4.2 Onyonyo dress as worn by a cultural dance troupe, Yenago, Nigeria. 56
5.1 T.854-1974. © Victoria and Albert Museum, London. 73
5.2 T.1-1967. © Victoria and Albert Museum, London. 75
6.1 Taatit rug with center circle, border, and central field all containing crosses. Some areas of the central field have cross-like forms which join to form checkerboards, delineated by color. 83
6.2 The non-pile side of a marriage rug, laid as it was in use. The hearts, divided circle, crosses, and checkerboards were visible from outside the bed. 84
7.1 The incorporated character of making the kediyun is seen here in Jamnaben's use of her big toe, legs, and hands in stitching of the cloth. 96
7.2 Jamnaben Karna Hungla Ahir, with her husband wearing a kediyun made by the author. 99
8.1 Coronation of Kabaka Muwenda Mutebi II. 106
8.2 *All Things Fashion: Fashionista Catwalk—Runway*, London Fashion Week, September 2022, Jose Hendo. 111
9.1 *Embroidered panel*, 1912. 121
9.2 *Suffragette signatures*, embroidered panel, undated. 122
10.1 *I want Great Climate*. 136
10.2 Installation view of Protest Banner Lending Library. 140

11.1 "Sorting, Examining and Joining the Strips of Film" (Talbot 1914: 156). The cutting room at the Pathé Frères Production Studios, 1912. Paris. 146

11.2 *Film as Fabric*, 2016. Expanded cinema performance at Radio Revolten International Festival of Radio Art. 149

12.1 *Cuttings 1820–2020* #7, 2019. Textile, cyanotype, wire, 40 cm x 140 cm. 161

12.2 *Cuttings 1820–2020*. Clay #2, 2020 Pigmented denim, cotton twill, embroidery. 123 × 82 cm. 162

13.1 A participant mounting their swatches as part of the E-Textile Swatchbook Exchange. 174

13.2 Interested Swatch #2, 2020. 175

14.1 *Work in Progress*, 2022. 185

14.2 Judith Brachem in the *Puffed spacewalk.jumpsuit* by Caste.less in the Warburg Haus Hamburg, bought via DressX; altered by Judith Brachem. 187

15.1 Above: detail from St John's Ambulance printed textile sling (First World War). Below: detail from "We've Come a Long Way", 1 × 1 meter square reactive dye digital prints on silk twill. 198

15.2 Experiments with digital color adaptions and overprinting incorporating William Astbury's photomicrographs of hair cortical cells and X-ray crystallography images of silk, wool and rubber, 2019. 203

16.1 *No. 1 Piñatex® production line in Acabados Gonzalez*, 2019. 212

16.2 *Piñatex, Charcoal* (colour) 213

MN1 *Untitled,* 2010, ropes and beads, 440 × 170 × 1230 cm, 173 1/4 × 66 7/8 × 484 1/4 in. 64

MN2 Installation view. 114

CP1 *Freddie's rug*, 2022. 166

CP2 *Fraser's jacket* (detail), 2022. 219

NOTES ON CONTRIBUTORS

Lesley Millar is Emerita Professor of Textile Culture at the University for the Creative Arts, Farnham, Surrey, UK. She has been responsible for many international textile exhibitions since 1996 including "Textural Space" (2001), "21:21—the textile vision of Reiko Sudo and NUNO" (2005–7), "Cloth & Culture NOW" (2008), "Lost in Lace" (2011), "Cloth & Memory {2}" (2013), "Here & Now: Contemporary tapestry" (2016–17), "Weaving New Worlds" (2018) and, with Alice Kettle, "Fabric: Touch and identity" (2020). She writes regularly about textile practice including co-editing, with Alice Kettle, the book, *The Erotic Cloth* (Bloomsbury, 2018). Her work is much concerned with the transition from traditional practice to contemporary outcomes.

Alice Kettle is a contemporary textile/fiber artist in the United Kingdom. She is Professor in Textile Arts at Manchester School of Art, Manchester Metropolitan University. Her work is represented in various international public collections. Her major exhibition "Thread Bearing Witness" (2019) at the Whitworth Art Gallery used stitch to address issues of migration and people displacement. She has co-edited various publications including *Collaboration Through Craft* (Bloomsbury, 2014) and *The Erotic Cloth* (Bloomsbury, 2018) with Professor Lesley Millar.

Linda S. McIntosh specializes in the study of Southeast Asian textiles. Receiving her Ph.D. from Simon Fraser University, Canada, McIntosh has written extensively about textiles of numerous Southeast Asian cultures including the volume on the Tilleke & Gibbins Textile Collection and *Thread and Fire: Textiles and Jewellery of the Islands of Indonesia and Timor* (2012). Her chapter on Southeast Asian Ikat entitled "Ikat in Monsoon Asia" is in the book, *Global Ikat: Roots and Routes of a Textile Technique* (2023). McIntosh was awarded a grant from the Endangered Material Knowledge Project in 2022 to document textile production of the Alurung ethnic group, Alor Regency, Indonesia using audio and video recordings.

Robert Burton is a visual artist and academic who explores themes of memory, loss, and transformation in cloth, print, and visual image making. As an artist theorist, Burton questions how material objects speak to us as signifiers connecting an evocative experience of the "things" of material culture that reframe the mythic narratives of communities, society, and culture. He examines how material thinking through cloth employs experience as a dynamic framework that unites the empirical, critical, and interpretive in dialogic creative practice. He exhibits his textile art internationally in solo, group exhibitions, biennials, and triennials.

Carol Quarini is a researcher and artist specializing in lace. She undertook her practice-based Ph.D. at the University for Creative Arts, Farnham, UK, and her postdoctoral research focuses on lace history, manufacture, and design. Her practice is inspired by nineteenth-century gothic fiction, veiling, domesticity, women's history, and subversive stitching. In 2016 she was commissioned to produce a contemporary response to the

Battle of Britain commemorative lace panel and its associated archive material. Her new textile panels and installation of paper spirals, recording those who died in the battle, were exhibited in three UK venues in 2018–19.

Clement Emeka Akpang is a contemporary artist and theoretician of African art. He is an associate professor and senior research fellow at the Institute for Advanced Studies (IAS), Central European University (CEU), Austria. As a postcolonial scholar, his research aims to decolonize art history through the Afrocentric revision of modern African art scholarship to contextualize African artistic expressions globally. He has published widely on African modernism, avant-gardism in twentieth-century Nigerian art, restitution and decoloniality, and the semantics of found objects in art. Among his books is *Nigerian Modernism 1900–1965: Anti-Europeanisation, Nationalism and Avant-garde Art*, published by the University of Calabar Press (2019).

Maria Nepomuceno uses traditional methods of rope weaving and straw braiding, as well as techniques of her own design, in her fluid forms that articulate space and sometimes invite tactile exploration. She explores the potentially endless permutations of this adaptable form in sculptures and installations that incorporate beads, playful ceramic forms, and found objects of varying sizes. In recent years collaboration has become a more overt factor in her work. She has worked with indigenous Huni Kuin people in the state of Acre in the north of Brazil to develop weaving techniques and has also formed links with community groups to realize projects for her exhibitions.

Ruby Hodgson works for the Victoria and Albert Museum (V&A), London, UK, as the Collections Move Team Manager, overseeing documentation and location control of 260,000 objects as they move to V&A East Storehouse. She has previously worked in the V&A Furniture, Textiles & Fashion department as an assistant curator and a collections management assistant. Her research centers on eighteenth- and early nineteenth-century British fashion history, with focus on early industrialization, the historic reuse of textiles, and the constructions of class and gender through fashion. She was a contributor to the V&A/Thames & Hudson book, *Silk: Fibre, Fabric and Fashion*, edited by Lesley Ellis Miller, Ana Cabrera Lafuente, and Claire Allen-Johnstone.

Carol Christiansen has been Curator and Community Museums Officer at Shetland Museum and Archives, Scotland, since 2006. She received her doctorate in archaeology with a specialism in textiles from the University of Manchester in 2003. Her research on Shetlandic, Scottish, and Nordic archaeological and historical textiles has been published widely. She is the author of *Taatit Rugs: The Pile Bedcovers of Shetland* (2015) and *Shetland Fine Lace Knitting: Recreating Patterns from the Past (2024)*.

LOkesh Ghai is an independent artist, researcher, and educator working with traditional craft practice. He is interested in cultural-making of craft and clothing. He has showcased his textile art at the Museum of Childhood, London, UK. As a designer and associate curator, he presented the "India Street" exhibition in Scotland; the show was a runner-up for the most sustainable design practice award. LOkesh co-founded the *Katab* project, is a member of the design faculty at the University of Petroleum and Energy Studies, Dehradun, and has been a founding faculty member at Somaiya Kala Vidya, Kutch, India's premier design institute for traditional craft communities. In 2022–23, he was a recipient of the Karun Thakar Fund, awarded by the V&A Museum, London, UK.

Venny Mary Nakazibwe is Senior Lecturer of Textile Design at the Margaret Trowell School of Industrial and Fine Art, Makerere University, Uganda. She holds a Ph.D. in art history (Middlesex University, UK), a Master of Fine Art majoring in textile design, a postgraduate Diploma in Education and a BA (Fine Art) degree from Makerere University. She has carried out extensive research in the visual arts and other intangible cultural heritage of Uganda, focusing on revitalizing indigenous knowledge as well as fostering innovative approaches in art and design using the local material culture of bark cloth.

Denise Jones completed her practice as research doctorate in textiles at the University for the Creative Arts (UCA), UK, in 2020. Her thesis was entitled *Embroidering and the Body Under Threat: Suffragette Embroidered Cloths Worked in Holloway Prison, 1911–1912*. Denise holds a degree in embroidered textiles (Middlesex University, UK), an MA in textiles (UCA), a PGCE (West London Institute, UK) and a degree in economic and social history (University of Nottingham, UK). She was a teacher specializing in the acquisition of language and literacy and has always had a practical interest in textiles.

Susan T. Avila is an artist and Professor of Design at University of California, Davis, USA. **Alicia Decker** is a fiber artist, textile designer, and the Adjunct Professor at Portland State University, Oregon, USA. They met at UC Davis, where Avila chaired Decker's Master of Fine Arts thesis committee. Decker's thesis on narrative-based textiles aligned well with Avila's interest in TEXT/iles and together they worked through many connections between cloth and community enhancing a mutual appreciation for textiles' unique ability to communicate. After Decker moderated a panel on social justice for Portland Textile Month in 2020, they decided to work together and co-author an expansion of this topic further exploring the role of textiles in building community.

Mary Stark has performed, screened films, and exhibited internationally. She was a finalist in the Arts Foundation Awards 2022 for experimental animation. She has a practice as research Ph.D. from the Manchester School of Art Research Centre (2020). In 2017 she won an inaugural Oram Award for innovation in sound and music. Her visual essay, *Film as Fabric: Signalling the Importance of Clothing in Expanded Cinema Performance* was published in *Studies in Costume and Performance* (2022). Her work is in publications: *Cinema Expanded: Avant-garde Film in the Age of Intermedia* (2021) and *The Crafty Animator* (2019). Since 2018, she has been co-director of Analogue Farm CIC, Rossendale.

Pippa Hetherington is a lens-based artist addressing postcolonial identity and fragments of separated histories. Working with photography, textiles, and rock pigment, she explores stories around loss, grief, and remembrance. By excavating collective and personal memory and working with fragmented recollection, Hetherington reflects on the pieces in history storytelling that are so often buried or erased purposefully, forcefully, or conveniently. Amplifying tiny slivers of history, she reveals what is deemed invisible, a metaphor of overlooked detail. Hetherington graduated with an MFA (distinction) from ICP-Bard, New York, USA, in 2019 and was shortlisted for the Contemporary African Photography prize in 2021 and 2022.

Celia Pym is an artist living and working in London, UK. She has been exploring damage and repair in textiles since 2007. Working with garments that belong to individuals as well as items in museum archives, she has extensive experience with the spectrum and stories of damage, from small moth holes to larger accidents with fire. She is an associate lecturer in Textiles at the Royal College of Art in London and has published her first book, *On Mending: Stories of Damage and Repair* (2022).

Becca Rose (Goldsmiths, University of London, UK), **Hannah Perner-Wilson** (KOBAKANT; Spiel und Objekt, University of Performing Arts Ernst Busch Berlin, Germany), **Irene Posch** (Crafting Futures Lab, Design and Technology, University of Art and Design Linz, Austria) and **Laura Devendorf** (ATLAS Institute and Department of Information Science, University of Colorado, Boulder, USA) are e-textile practitioners with diverse disciplinary backgrounds spanning art, design, computer science, and media. Their work connects through individual and collective artistic and research-oriented explorations. The things they craft and share have contributed to shaping the field of e-textiles since 2007.

Sonja Andrew is an associate professor in the School of Design, University of Leeds, UK. Crossing the disciplines of design, semiotics, and narratology, her research focuses on textile semantics, communication, and cultural memory, exploring the multimodality of cloth through its visual, tactile, and contextual representations. Her work on semiotics, mnemonics, and visual narrative was selected for an Arts and Humanities Research Council Image Gallery Award and publication in *Beyond the Trenches, Researching the First World War* (Arts and Humanities Research Council WW1 centennial publication, 2014). Sonja exhibits internationally, with commissioned work including pieces for the United Bristol Healthcare Trust and Wells Cathedral. Her recent work involves art–science collaborations across biophysics and paleontology.

Katharina Sand is currently Visiting Professor at the Akademie Mode & Design, Munich, Germany, after teaching at L'Université du Québec à Montréal, the Kunstuniversität Linz, HEAD- Genève, and Parsons Paris (The New School). Following her BA from Goldsmiths College (University of London) and her MA at Université de Paris 8, she is completing a Ph.D. in digital fashion at the Faculty of Communication, Culture and Society of USI (Università della Svizzera italiana). She co-curated the exhibition "Making FASHION Sense" at the House of Electronic Arts Basel (HEK), and the upcoming "Women Designers and Textile Design" at the Centre de Design in Montreal.

Carmen Hijosa, Founder and Chief Creative and Innovation Officer of Ananas Anam Ltd, developed Piñatex®—a natural plant-based material made from pineapple leaf fiber. She is an ethical entrepreneur with a vision for a more sustainable future, connecting people, ecology, and economics. Originally from Spain, Carmen's career has taken her around the world. The journey of Piñatex® began when she realized the toxic impact of mass leather production while consulting in the Philippines. Driven to find an alternative solution, Carmen undertook a Ph.D. at the Royal College of Art (UK) to develop Piñatex. As a result, she has spearheaded a vibrant new industry that is socially, environmentally, and economically responsible.

ACKNOWLEDGMENTS

This volume has given us the opportunity to work with long-standing colleagues and make new connections. We thank the authors for their contributions, which express the depth of their expertise and commitment to the field of textile discourse. They have been generous and patient.

We have had invaluable support from our institutions, University for the Creative Arts and Manchester School of Art, Manchester Metropolitan University. In particular, we would like to thank Gemma Potter for her extraordinary and meticulous assistance in the book's compilation.

Introduction

LESLEY MILLAR AND ALICE KETTLE

What is Made Now is Defined by What Has Been Made Before

Between March 2022 and January 2023 Tate Britain Gallery in London showed the artist Hew Locke's installation, *The Procession*. The work consists of 140 life-sized figures from different places and times carrying their historical and cultural narratives printed and stitched onto, and woven into, the very fabric of their clothes and banners. Figures included Mother Sally, wearing a dress with a capacious skirt printed with Locke's artwork depicting a share issued for the West India Improvement Company.

> Based in Jamaica, the Company was formed in 1889 in New York to acquire and develop the Jamaica Railway and large areas of land on the island. Locke decorated the certificate with a bunch of bananas and peeping out from behind it, the hands and head of the wooden figure of a bird-man spirit carved by the Taíno–Arawak people indigenous to the Caribbean.
>
> **TATE, 2022: online**

Visitors to the installation were invited to "reflect on the cycles of history, and the ebb and flow of cultures, people and finance and power" (Tate 2022: online) as communicated by the cloths. It was a timely reminder of the role of cloth in the materialization of human experience.

It is now over thirty years since Annette B. Weiner and Jane Schneider published their foundational book, *Cloth and Human Experience* (1989). In this book they wrote, "cloth represents the key dilemmas of social and political life: how to bring the past actively into the present. Ultimately, the opposing properties of cloth—its inalienability and its fragility—exemplify these universal needs and their contradictions" (1989: 26). Since Weiner and Schneider wrote this, much has happened in art practice, theoretical writing, and scientific exploration of the possibilities offered by this relationship between cloth and our sociopolitical and personal experiences. *Reading the Thread: Cloth and Communication* presents cloth as a record of experience within its social, historical, psychological, and cultural context.

In their article, "Her Eyes, My Body," Denham and Green write, "When a person weaves cloth using centuries-old techniques and tools passed down across generations, the cloth embodies identities that transcend time and materializes networks of social relations. This brings new possibilities to ethnographic research about processes of making. If we are what we make . . . then what are we when we make cloth?" (Miller 2020: 125). As makers of cloth we, the editors of *Reading the Thread*, interrogate this question from our own experience. We follow threads across the world, developing a "textually woven web" as we ask: What can the cloth tell about us, our history, our future?

Thread and Cloth—Thread as Way Finder

We start with cloth as a construct of woven threads that communicate the full multidimensional aspect of experience, mapping the line of history and the interweaving of its complex sensations. Ingold's (2007) theoretical model and taxonomy of lines describes threads and traces, of movement through the world and the enduring imprint that is left upon its surface. The line of the wayfarer is where life is experienced: "the traveler and his line are one and the same" (Ingold 2007: 76).

Cloth is the interrelationship of thread lines, each separately connecting to make a double-sided material, facing both back and front. Weiner and Schneider (1989) suggest that this cloth echoes life's ebb and flow and its contradictions within its material substance and composition. A fold has the quality of simultaneously having both an exterior and an interior. The surface serves as an interface, while the folded space conceals and protects. The fold as a figure demonstrates how to conceive in terms of "both–and" rather than "either/or."

As a membrane, cloth covers and separates, mediating in between spaces and people. Our quotidian experiences place cloth between ourselves and all our encounters, whether in the clothes we wear, the porous fabrics that we employ to clean, use to soften the light, to provide warmth and so much more. Michel Serres's concept of milieu is a useful analogy that allows us to connect cloth at the center of our experiences and to see how it projects and protects our human interactions. Serres says, "[m]ediators are not static betweennesses; rather, they are go-betweens, in

Figure 0.2 *The Procession (figure 86)*, 2022. © Hew Locke. All rights reserved, DACS 2023.

Figure 0.3 GROUND, 2018 (one of three works, Ground, Sea and Sky), Thread Bearing Witness project. © Alice Kettle with contributions from Pipka/Lesvos Solidarity, Ahmad Ali, Somaya Hossaini, Yakob and many other residents at Calais refugee camp working with Suzanne Partridge; Nahomie Bukasa, Sahira Khan and Ai Ling with Linda Leroy at the Helen Bamber Foundation; Nisrin Albyrouty, Khouloud Alkurd, Heba Almnini, Heidi Ambruster, Marwa Ammar, Amal Ayoubi, Stella Charman, Susan Colverson, Jenny Cuffe, Lama Hamami, Miriam Jones, Asmaa Kamar Aldin, Ruth le Mesurier, Vanessa Rolf, Samar Sobeih, Chaymae Yousfi and many children from English Chat Winchester; Farhia Ahmed Ali, Nawad Hersi Duale, Amran Mohamud Ismail with Refugee Action working with artists Jenny Eden and Richard Harris; Julie Firman, Victoria Hartley, Louise Jung, Susan Kamara, Saam. Stitch on printed canvas, 3m x 8m. Photographer: © Michael Pollard.

movement" (O'Connor, quoting Serres, 2005: 321). If we use this analogy of cloth as active, alive, and implicated in the expression of our encounters, we see the movement of pliable fabric as mediating and absorbing the interiority and outward expression of human experience. Hunt (2014) has written of the capacity of cloth to archive our intimate existence, and proposes that cloth has a "mnemonic energy" which, "in its everyday use as naturally recording and preserving human imprints, become[s] a form of memory itself" (2014: 208). Cloth simultaneously mediates commonality and difference, while thread connects and knots, as in Haraway's critique of mortal entanglements (1994). She uses the thread metaphor of the cat's cradle, a string game, as a method to analyze our complex and entangled interactions as individuals, communities, and societies and between technology and nature. "Seems to me that the cultural critic is faced by a world that is very much like tangled balls of yarn. And that one way to approach the situation is to pull on a thread and begin to untangle the ball of meanings. And begin to trace through one thread, and then another" (Magnan and Williams 1987: 01:22:00). This unraveling of meaning becomes patterned and structured as the threads interweave and loop back and forward and where cloth is an essential substrate and carrier of experience.

Kettle's *Thread Bearing Witness* project records the diverse personal narratives of refugees and asylum seekers on cloth, utilizing the non-linguistic capacity of thread, "the rhetorical possibilities of non-alphabetic composing" (Arellano 2022: 20). The work seeks to affirm experience, to conceptualize a common ground, and mediate the value of human dignity and the abject tragedy of conflict and terror. Making as a mode of intervention, therefore, is political, not consistently in the sense of activism and organized dissent, but in fostering autonomy using the building materials of everyday life, identity, and, of course, textiles. Grounded in the fabric itself, the work provided a physical site to present the multiple testimonies of those who contributed to its vast patterned landscape. The assemblage of imagery references distinctive textile cultural heritage, recording places that have been left behind. The cloth acts as an emancipatory medium and a safe space to express what has taken place through escaping, journeying, and way finding with "[m]aking's potential as a means of enacting embodied knowledge . . . and for enabling dissonant voices to be heard"

(Hackney et al. 2016: 58). Within the cloth, lived experience is secured as what would otherwise not be told. *Reading the Thread* author Pippa Hetherington has developed a methodology that includes collaborative dressmaking and embroidery in order to materialize "the complex relationship between female descendants of the Eastern Cape amaXhosa nation and those of the 1820 British settlers" (Hetherington, p.** of this volume). As the women worked together, today, they discovered "an articulation of the female voices that history (both oral and written) has ignored" (ibid.).

The deeply embedded relationship between cloth and human experience can be found in the earliest fabric: felt, an accidental outcome of experience. Sheepskin wrapped around the feet for protection when walking, the woolly interior subject to friction and sweat was slowly transformed into a form of felted cloth. This is a graphic and embodied example of cloth as an active recorder of experience. Once we know where to look and how to read the narrative, all around us there are examples of cloth holding the traces of who and what we were and are.

In 2016 archaeologists in Peru discovered a fragment of indigo-dyed cloth that was more than 6,000 years old (Splitstoser 2016). The cloth told of a sophisticated understanding of chemistry and botany. In the museum of the northern UK town, Bolton, sits a fragment of Egyptian textile over 7,000 years old, this time telling us of technical and material knowledge. Both examples are a record of passing, and now, through micro-examination of their threads, these cloths reveal information about the way they were made and the people who made them. It is a reading beyond intervention, which endures as long as the material itself, and such recording and revelation continues still. An example would be, again from Peru, in the most remote corners of the Andes, where ID documents are a rarity, and where textiles have provided the clues used to identify the exhumed human remains of the "disappeared." Cloth: witness, storyteller, connector, activator, and, in this case, tool for redemption. A relentless truth teller.

The "material vitality," or even matter as its antecedent, draws us into Deleuze and Guattari's idea of energy where matter has intrinsic substantial power (Deleuze and Guattari, quoted by Bennett, 2010: 54). Cloth is alive to experience, conductive, receptive to sensations, forces, and thoughts. This extension of human experience, which

Figure 0.4 *Cuttings* #2, 2019. © Pippa Hetherington and Keiskamma Art Project. Photographer: © Pippa Hetherington.

is drawn from and absorbed into the cloth, allows us to see the vitality in cloth as reverberations that are within its materiality. Writing through the lens of new materialism, Jane Bennett describes "the agentic contributions of nonhuman forces" (2010: xvii) and she sees aliveness in matter, which opens human experience to "impersonal affect" (2010: xiii) and to "following the scent of a nonhuman, thingly power" (2010: xiii). This distribution of agency and dialogue between cloth and humans is a way for authors to describe communication through, in, with, by cloth, and draw from its interiority, to soak up the experience of cloth into themselves and vice versa, not as separate but allied and strengthened by embodied, formal, and symbolic qualities.

The sensory, emotive, and affective encounters are embodied in the substance of cloth. Corso Esquivel (2019) draws upon affect theories to describe his own interpretation as being in a state of flux, where the transmission of experience is through and with the cloth itself. He describes how, "by departing from a highly symbolic vocabulary, fiber art and craft harness a unique proto-political role in an ontology of becoming" (2019: 8). In cloth, these sensations evolve, reconfigure, and are entwined. Cloth expresses and even encourages and deepens experience through accessing the intimacy of emotion.

Following the scent of the material power that Bennett (2010) describes, is a useful concept through which to consider Ariadne's thread—the archetypal mythological thread. Let us consider Ariadne's singular thread, which is a means to express desire and to effect her own and the subject of her desire's transformation. Theseus escaping the labyrinth through Ariadne's gift of thread offers rich metaphorical resonance. The labyrinth is a complex construct lurking with evil and can be only navigated through tracing convoluted pathways. The thread is thus a means to wayfare the emotional and physical self into the world as well as to retrace experience. Thread is a metaphor for thoughts leading into another world, and if we follow it, we are "forever transformed" (Harrison, quoting Sullivan Kruger 2008: 14). Thread operates as the lines of connection, of direction, and of movement, and in its

Figure 0.5 *Warp and Weft, Cloth and Memory* (2), 2013. © Katharina Hinsberg.

complex network of threads, cloth mediates the many layers of temporal happenings, provoking reaction and recording what has taken place.

Reading the Thread

In 2013, in an old mill in Yorkshire, UK, a young woman works alone in a large empty room; a very large room; in fact, when it was first built and opened in 1853 it was, at 168 meters, the longest room in Europe. Then it housed 120 huge industrial spinning machines, the space filled with overwhelming noise. Now, the machinery is gone, and the room is heavy with silence, paint peeling, pools of oil seeping up through the floor on the hot summer day. The young woman sits at her spinning wheel, the only noise the gentle, persistent clicking of the wheel as she presses her foot on the pedal, pulling out the fibers, allowing the wheel to twist them into a thread. It is a very special thread, communicating to us across the centuries. Along the walls of the spinning room are small alcoves in the wall where, at the end of their shift, the workers placed leftover fibers to be collected. However, some were missed and slipped into the wall cavities. Now, long years since the machinery had disappeared from the room, she, the artist Hannah Leighton-Boyce, has found the fibers in the wall. She has carded them and is spinning a thread of material connection—to a time, a place, and a community. From this historical thread she is constructing a living present. The thread holds the DNA of an artist working in 2013 and those who handled the fibers and worked the machines sometime between 1853 and 1986.

For Leighton-Boyce, the intent of the thread could only be learned through bodily experience. As Lucy Lippard has written, "The scale and pace of hand-work match those of the body . . . The rhythms of these gestures mark time, and the physical proximity of material, tools and body situates a person in space" (1995: 138). The subject of Leighton-Boyce's work is contained in, and communicated through, the thread. By her spinning, she is erasing the distance that separates subject and object, disrupting the norm of historical order. When all the fibers have been spun, she winds the thread into balls, which she places on a plinth. Her work is titled *If Walls Could Talk: The Last Yarn*, a thread

Figure 0.6 Video stills from *The Last Yarn, Cloth and Memory* (2), 2013. Performance: © Hannah Leighton-Boyce. Video: © Mary Stark.

Figure 0.7 *Haiku*, 1961. Anni Albers, © The Josef and Anni Albers Foundation/Artists Rights Society (ARS), New York and DACS, London 2023.

that will never be transitioned into cloth, spun together as a meditation on the relationship between art and politics, past and present, the public and the private.

Anni Albers, the iconic modernist weaver, uses her expertise to generate knowledge and to express prosaic human sensations. Albers describes how, if we listen to threads and draw in upon this experience, imaginative possibilities emerge through the making process, linking the past to the present, resolving thoughts that are in our heads and showing how material and content are folded together (1982: online). The method of making the cloth is central to its narrative. It may be that the making is a repetition of tradition, patterns holding stories, secret codes of community or otherness. It may be that the cloth draws on traditional practice, but the outcomes are placed within a wholly contemporary context. The historical thread, the cultural narrative, or the personal story will be embedded in the cloth, and the making sometimes becomes a "strategy for survival" (Bhabha 1994: 247). It is a method of communication without words, leaving space for interpretation and the interleaving of other stories. Such an embedding and strategy for survival is interrogated by Denise Jones in her chapter for this book, "Small Acts of Refusal." She writes of the suffragette embroideries stitched in Holloway Prison between 1911 and 1912. She "scrutinizes the embroideries for the explicit documentary evidence they record ... Moving beyond the discursive, the embroideries are examined for the implicit material evidence they communicate" (Jones, p.** of this volume).

Cloth can be seen as a perfect example of mutual exchange. It emphatically surrounds us with its communicative agency, as part of commonplace experience; we are wrapped in its form and responsive to the resonance of its texture and its very particular symbolism, and its denoted meaning. Cloth acquires value, absorbs tradition, becomes overwritten, and actually changes through its centrality to the everyday occurrences. This relationship with the social world, mediating the moments of human encounter and interaction, shows cloth as an agential medium, actively conversant in a network of happenings. Latour describes this complexity of reality where human and nonhuman elements are in dialogue, actors and actants, conjoined in the constant flow of connections ([1990] 1996) as happens between the maker and their material. As Latour says, "[a]n actant can literally be anything provided it is granted to be the source of an action" ([1990] 1996: 373). It is a mutual exchange where, as Dormor states when writing of thread and stitching, the "needle and thread and cloth [that] pass through each other in the forming of the seam or join, engage in a tactical creation" (2018: 304). Such a flow of connection is referenced by the Canadian organization The Public Studio when describing Sarit Cantour's work, *A Cloth Called Witness*: "Creating this quilt was a practice of listening, remembering, and of acknowledging intelligence other than our own. It was an effort of co-creation and collaborative relationship" (The Public Studio, n.d.: online).

Communication requires participation, making common what has been isolated and singular; and the conveyance of meaning gives body and definiteness to the experience of the one who utters as well as to those who listen. Dewey, in his *Art as Experience* (2009), extols the power of aesthetic experiences, where art communicates ways to feel, think vicariously, and to discover a sense of the mystery and potential that surrounds us. Through communication, we talk with, "not to" each other, and how the ensuing dialogue involves both the transmission and reception of meaning even if transformed or lost in translation. Communication involves exchange and engagement as social beings. Sennett argues that communicative relationships can be formed through listening while handling material and observing the vernaculars of making: "the craft of making physical things provides insight into the techniques of experience that can shape our dealings with others" (2009: 289). In this book we explore the shared language of making, mutual dialogue, and meeting in cloth as one that transcends culture and language, as a means to communicate meaning and be in relationships with each other.

This dynamic and communicative role of cloth in collaborative practice is discussed here by Susan T. Avila and Alicia Decker in their chapter "Stitching Justice: Textiles as a Means for Contemporary Social Justice" (p.** of this volume). They take a radical look at social media and its impact on participatory textile making. They describe how "[t]he communicative properties of textiles in particular, while possibly the antithesis of digital technology, thrive in the cyber environment, increasing viewership and participation" (p.** of this volume). Small acts, associated with intimate lives such as stitching or knitting in the home, when brought together can, as Bennett has written, "make big things happen" (2010: 94). Resulting projects have spread beyond national borders, for example in the knitted pink hats of the Pussyhat Project 2017. A sea of pink hats

Figure 0.8 *The Plants That Hold Us*, 2021. © Sarit Cantour. Photographer: © Sarit Cantour.

were worn in collective action in 600 cities worldwide against the forthcoming Donald Trump administration in the United States as a global symbol of female solidarity. More recently, in the protests over Black Lives Matter, textiles were used to veil contested statues and ropes, where utilized, to pull them down.

David Gauntlett, in *Making is Connecting* (2011), suggests that all making involves the connecting of materials, people, and ideas. Gauntlett posits that acts of creativity have an inherently social dimension, as making and sharing things increases makers' engagements with their "social and physical environments" (2011: 2). In 1999 the artist Maja Bajevic, a Bosnian non-Muslim woman, invited five Muslim women from the region around Srebrenica, who were living as refugees in Sarajevo, to join her in a remarkable project. All five of the women had each lost a male member of their family during the Bosnian war and whose body had never been found. According to Muslim tradition, no ritual mourning can take place until the body is found. Taking part in the project, the five women climbed scaffolding covering the façade of the Museum of Art. They then sat and each silently wove a tapestry, thread by slow thread, as a public act of mourning. When their tapestry was completed, the maker cut it off and left. In her lecture of 2005, the art historian and curator Bojana Pejic said, "[b]y inviting these women to work with her on the façade, Maja Bajevic made their invisible mourning socially perceptible and provided it with a due dignity. This performance, then, could be recognized as a labor of mourning being performed within the institutionalized framework of art" (Pejic 2005). Most importantly, cloth/textile was the medium of choice. Cloth with its relationship to the body absent and present, cloth with its role in ritual. Cloth communicating the narrative without words.

The Book

In this book we interrogate ideas associated with cloth as record and its ongoing role in the reading of the sustainability of a culture, of a way of living. The book explores and develops the following themes as expressed through art, design, anthropology, ethnography, politics, and performance. These threads are:

- Cloth as a record of the everyday, past, present, and future.
- Cloth and its role in rituals.
- Cloth and the processes of making.
- Cloth as a record of identity, personal and political histories, and memories.
- Cloth as a record of patterns, symbols, associated colors, and emblems of culture.
- Cloth as a record of passage and geographical interaction with the world.
- Cloth as a witness to a moment: of celebration or of distress or sorrow.
- Cloth and its role as past and future material and cultural sustainability.

We are presenting a variety of viewpoints that interrogate cloth as a record of experience within its social, historical, psychological, and cultural context. The book is divided into four sections, each developing ideas around cloth as a record with contributions firstly confirming this notion. The second section challenges the orthodox reading of cloth; the third evidences the role of cloth in transition; and the fourth looks to its future role as recorder. The areas defined for investigation concern the recognized human encounters with cloth where the processes of production and the actions of making are integral to the record. The agency of cloth allows for the exploration of identity and biography and represents passage, exchange, life, and death.

Communicating narratives through cloth has a direct and specific resonance for artists using textiles as their medium of choice. Threaded through the book are interviews with two such artists for whom the exchange of stories with others through the agency of cloth is central. Alice Kettle is in discussion with Brazilian artist Maria Nepomuceno, who describes how she uses traditional methods of rope weaving and straw braiding, often working in collaboration with indigenous Huni Kuin people in the north of Brazil to make vast conceptual sculptures and installations, which connect the past with the present. Lesley Millar is in discussion with British artist Celia Pym, who is known for her visible repairs to, mainly knitted, garments that hold stories for their owners. In this way we hope to call the reader back to the importance of tacit knowledge in the reading of the threads.

PART 1
READING THE RECORD

Cloth carries the imprint of cultural identity and nationhood. In its production, pattern, and use, it affirms the associative beliefs and customs of belonging to a place or people. Cloth and thread record the rituals and traditions that bear witness to life stories and the practices of societies and institutions. The imprint in cloth records the historical timeline, it commemorates and memorializes the past as a form of remembering. Cloth symbolizes and embodies the familial and cultural bonds that remind us of our personal and collective sustainable inheritance that situates us in the world.

PART 2
FOLLOWING THE THREAD

Cloth records the processes of change in human experience, of life's movement and of rites of passage. The absorbency of cloth soaks up the continuous flux of life events, of decay, degeneration, and regeneration. We revive traditions and transform experiences and the past to create new constructs and meanings, all of which have a contemporary relevance. Everyday events are encountered through cloth, which marks changes of time and un-fixes established approaches, acknowledging received wisdoms and shifting predetermined attitudes. Cloth is used to map the emerging and alternative versions of these encounters, which reimagine our relationships to physical and nonphysical ways of being.

PART 3
CHALLENGING THE READING

Challenging the orthodox reading of cloth gives us the opportunity to subvert the structures around us. Cloth is used as an agent for social and political change and as a dynamic membrane that is implicated in how we adapt and transform the institutions we are part of. Cloth as a site for resistance materializes the body under threat, engages with notions of justice, repression, and the legacy and problematic histories of political projects and of trade and labor.

PART 4
DRAFTING THE FUTURE

Through e-textiles technology, coding, and issues of material and cultural sustainability, cloth changes its relationship with the body and being in the world. Human experience, and its relationship with cloth, is presented as a site for constant reinvention. The fundamental contemporary challenges of how textiles are produced, consumed, and discarded are seen alongside the preservation of knowledge. The sustainability of practices and future means of production are critically interwoven. In this section, cloth itself may never materialize, since through e-textiles and technology the physical sensation of cloth becomes represented through abstract and conceptual form. Questions concerning finite resources call for constant translation and interpretation. The physical and material form of cloth and the processes of production are seen to create new versions of human experience.

Through shared material understandings and interaction between the small-scale individual and the large-scale collaborations, we recognize the human encounters with cloth where the processes of production and the actions of making are integral to the record. The agency of cloth in the exploration of identity and biography, and as record of passage, exchange, life, and death, and ultimately the sustainability of material practices has been taken for granted for millennia. These are the threads of connection throughout the book that signpost how textiles can engage with, communicate, and reflect upon the critical contemporary challenges of a world in flux.

References

Albers, A. (1982) *Material as Metaphor*, https://www.albersfoundation.org/alberses/teaching/anni-albers/material-as-metaphor (accessed April 23, 2023).

Figure 0.9 *Rice Dreams*, 2013. © Yoriko Yoneyama.

Arellano, S. C. (2022) *Quilting as a Qualitative, Feminist Research Method: Expanding Understandings of Migrant Deaths*, Rhetoric Review, 41:1, 17–30, DOI:10.1080/07350198.2021.2002058

Bennett, J. (2010) *Vibrant Matter: A Political Ecology of Things*, Durham NC: Duke University Press, p. 94.

Bhabha, H. K. (1994) *The Location of Culture*, New York: Routledge, p. 247.

Corso Esquivel, J. (2019) *Feminist Subjectivities in Fiber Art and Craft: Shadows of Affect*, New York: Routledge.

Dewey, J. (2009) *Art as Experience*, New York: Perigree Books.

Deleuze, G. and Guattari, F. (1987) *A Thousand Plateaus; Capitalism and Schizophrenia*, trans. Massumi B. Minneapolis: University of Minnesota Press.

Denham, A. and Green, D. N. (2020) "Her Eyes, My Body: Negotiating Embodiment Through Maya Backstrap Weaving." *Journal of Fashion, Style, & Popular Culture*, 7(1), 125–41. DOI:https://doi.org/10.1386/fspc_00008_1

Dormor, C. (2018) *The Event of a Stitch: The Seamstress, the Traveler, and the Storyteller*, Textile DOI: 10.1080/14759756.2018.1432144 pp.3–10.

Gauntlett, D. (2011) *Making is Connecting: The Social Meaning of Creativity*, Cambridge, Polity Press p2

Hackney, F. Maughan, H. and Desmarais, S. (2016) *The Power of Quiet: Re-making Affective Amateur and Professional Textiles Agencies*, Journal of Textile Design Research and Practice, 4:1, 33–62, DOI: 10.1080/20511787.2016.1256139

Haraway, D. J. (1994). *A Game of Cat's Cradle*: Science Studies, Feminist Theory, Cultural Studies. *Configurations* 2(1), 59–71. doi:10.1353/con.1994.0009.

Harrison, A. (2008) *The Fabric of Myth*, Compton Verney catalogue.

Hunt, C. (2014) *Worn clothes and textiles as archives of memory* Critical Studies in Fashion & Beauty, Volume 5 Number 2, Intellect Ltd Article. doi: 10.1386/csfb.5.2.207_1

Ingold, T. (2007) *Lines: A Brief History*. Cambridge, MA and London: Harvard University Press.

Latour, B. ([1990]/1996). *On Actor Network Theory: A few clarifications plus more than a few complications*. Soziale Welt, Vol. 47 (1996), pp. 369–81.

Lippard, L. (1995) *Overlay: Contemporary Art and the Art of Prehistory*, New York, New Press, p.138.

Magnan, N. and Williams, S. (1987) video Donna Haraway Reads the National Geographic on Primates Directed by New York, Paper Tiger Television, https://archive.org/details/donnaharawaynationalgeographic (accessed April 23, 2023)

Millar, L. (2012), *Cloth and Memory*, Salts Mill (exhibition catalogue).

O'Connor, S. (2005) "Michel Serres Five Senses." In Howes, David (ed.) *Empire of the Senses the Sensual Culture Reader*. London: Berg, p. 321.

Pejic, B. (2005) "Ambiguous Space: Views of materials and materiality" [Lecture], University College for the Creative Arts at Farnham. 11 November. http://transitionandinfluenceprojects.com/2121Vision/Pejic_paper.html (accessed April 28, 2023)

Sennett, R. (2009) *The Craftsman*. London, Penguin Books, p.289.

Splitstoser J.C (2016) *Early pre-Hispanic use of indigo blue in Peru* in Science Advances Vol 2 No 9. https://www.science.org/doi/10.1126/sciadv.1501623 (accessed January 7, 2023).

Tate online Hew Locke https://www.tate.org.uk/whats-on/tate-britain/hew-locke/hew-locke-the-procession (accessed January 2, 2023)

The Public Studio: *A Cloth called Witness*, https://thepublicstudio.ca/gallery/a-cloth-called-witness (accessed April 23, 2023)

Weiner, A. B. and Schneider, J. (1989) Cloth and Human Experience. United Kingdom: Smithsonian.

PART ONE

Reading the Record

In this section the authors speak of cloth carrying the imprint of lineage, cultural identity, and nationhood. In the topologies of its production, pattern, and use, it affirms the beliefs, customs, and commemorative moments, which are markers of attachment to family, place, or people. The unique material and symbolic qualities of cloth act to sustain indigenism and kinship and to record the rituals and traditions that bear witness to those important life stories and the practices of societies and institutions. Thus, cloth affirms and records what happens in daily life, and it adapts through the challenges of geopolitics, economies of trade, and in the face of "extreme global interculturalism" (Akpang, p.** of this volume).

The handwoven cloth of the Alurung in Indonesia denotes the social roles and ancestral clan affiliation of patrilineage. Linda McIntosh chronicles how cloth acts as a means to solemnize and celebrate belief and allegiance through generations and as a present-day record of enduring customs and ceremonial rituals. For the Alurung, this is a kind of myth making, where the foundational symbolic forms of textiles evolve and accumulate new meanings linking the familial past to the present.

The human imprint in cloth records the historical timeline; it commemorates and memorializes the past. The "stuff" of memory structures our sense of family and identity, of personal and collective expression, whether it is Robert Burton's retelling of his hereditary history of mill workers in northern England or as a form of cultural identification for the ethnic groups of the Niger Delta, Yoruba, and Hausa in Nigeria. In both cases, cloth carries emblematic and semiotic resonance with regional and community affiliations corresponding to the deep ties with culture. Indeed, the distinctive African cloths are described by Clement Emeka Akpang as "transforming for those who wear them into allegorical cultural and social subjects of specific civilizations" (Akpang, p.** of this volume).

Identity is commemorated through cloth to record conflict. Carol Quarini describes two lace memorials of the First and Second World Wars that include iconography of the destructive social effects of war, with motifs drawn from local traditions of lacemaking. Cloth can be seen as powerfully emblematic of the histories, the communities and industry reliant on textile production, and of the resilience and determination to continue in its making. Cloth symbolizes and embodies the familial and cultural bonds that remind us of our personal and collective inheritance that situates and sustains us in the world.

"Cloth embodies the realm of women, the producers of cloth and the providers of their families in many parts of the world. Cloth provides warmth and most of all identity."

Linda S. McIntosh

1

Tenapi: Markers of Clan Identity of the Alurung, East Indonesia

LINDA S. MCINTOSH

Little has been published about the handwoven textile traditions of Alor Regency, East Indonesia. The author has attempted to fill this gap by co-writing articles about the textiles of the Alurung ethnic group of Uma Pura Village in the regency's Northwest Alor Subdistrict with Ms. Yulianti Peni, curator at the Museum 1000 Moko in Kalabahi or Alor Regency's capital (McIntosh and Peni 2021; Peni and McIntosh 2020). They also wrote an e-book introducing the textiles of Alor Regency's textile-producing groups for the museum in 2020 (McIntosh and Peni 2020). Earlier publications about Indonesian textiles suggest that the weavings found in the Alor Archipelago composing Alor Regency originated from other parts of Indonesia, such as Lembata and Adonara Islands in the neighboring Solor Archipelago (Marian Klamer 2011). Similarities exist between the textiles produced by the Alurung and the Lamaholot ethnic group living in the Solor Archipelago due to physical proximity, linguistic relations, and social, economic, and political ties. However, Alurung weavers have developed design-distinct formats for their handwoven cloth, especially textiles used to compose traditional attire signifying clan affiliation. These formats include different colored stripes and various-sized bands containing warp ikat patterning. These traits distinguish Alurung textiles from warp ikat-decorated textiles woven by the Lamaholot and other ethnic groups in East Indonesia.

The textiles of the Alurung are also distinct from the cloth made by five other ethnic groups that weave in the Alor Regency. The Alurung, the sole indigenous Austronesian culture of the archipelago, utilize warp ikat to decorate the cloth that they weave, while these other groups use other techniques, such as complementary warp and discontinuous supplementary weft, to create designs. The handwoven cloth of the Alurung serves various roles in society not only as clothing but as commercial goods to be sold within and outside their group, as ceremonial gifts, offerings, and markers of ethnic identity and patrilineal lineage affiliation. Design formats of some *tenapi* (tubular lower garment) worn by both men and women symbolize membership in one of the patrilineages composing Alurung society. The Alurung wear these patrilineal clan identity markers for important occasions.

The number and names of the patrilineages in former Alurung kingdoms varied. The names of some of the lineages are identical in more than one settlement, since males from the ruling clan of an older kingdom founded new ones by carrying the line over to rule another Alurung community. Thus, some types of tenapi were produced and consumed in several Alurung communities. Rulers also gifted tenapi representing membership in their patrilineage to respected visitors, including leaders of non-Alurung communities in the Alor Archipelago, since alliances were formed with these neighboring groups for sustenance and security.

The knowledge regarding the design formats of these tenapi and their use as patrilineal identity markers is disappearing. Modern transportation from the twentieth century until the present conveniently allows for the relocation of people to other parts of Indonesia and other countries, disconnecting them from their birthplace. Intermarriage with other ethnic groups sometimes leads to a lapse in upholding cultural customs, including wearing patrilineal clan identity markers for important occasions. The research is unfinished due to challenges in finding the few surviving elders who still possess this knowledge. The name of a tenapi serving as a clan identity marker is given, but no examples can be found, and the interviewees have so far been unable to describe its design format. For example, the Tenapi Lagareala is the patrilineal identity marker of the Uma Apukulung patrilineage of Alor Besar, but extant examples have not been discovered as of yet.

Different types of tenapi, both clan-specific ceremonial and clan-neutral daily attire, have become one of the ethnic identity markers of the Alurung. Weavers produce examples for commercial sale, and now tenapi are found worldwide.

Background

Alurung settlements are solely located in Alurung Regency. The ancestors of the Alurung settled along the southwest coast of the Bird's Head Peninsula of Alor Island or present-day Northwest Alor Subdistrict of Alor Regency, and these settlements are Alor Besar—formerly called Bungabali—Alor Kecil, and Dulolong (Emilie Wellfelt 2016). They also founded polities in coastal areas of Pantar Island or present-day West, Central, and North Pantar Subdistricts. The Alurung also inhabit the regency's smaller islands called Kangge, Marica (also spelled Marisa), Buaya, and Ternate (Emilie Wellfelt 2007).

Figure 1.1 Alurung women wearing various types of tenapi while attending the Al Quran Festival held in Alor Besar, Alor Regency, East Indonesia, in 2020. Photographer: © Yulianti Peni.

LANGUAGE

The Alurung language, also called Alorese or Malay Alor, belongs to the Central Malayo-Polynesian branch of the Austronesian ethnolinguistic family and is housed in the eastern subbranch of the Peripheral-Lamaholot group. Linguistic research has suggested that the ancestors of the Alurung migrated west from Lembata to Adonara and Solor (islands of the Solor Archipelago, which is due west of the Alor Archipelago), before traveling east to the Alor Archipelago or present-day Alor Regency (Hanna Fricke and Marian Klamer 2018). Alurung and Lamaholot are distinct languages and not dialects of one another with less than 60 percent commonality (Klamer 2011: 18–19). Alurung is the sole Austronesian language of the Alor Archipelago (present-day Alor Regency), while the majority of the regency's population speak non-Austronesian languages that belong to the Alor-Pantar group of the Trans-New Guinea ethnolinguistic family. This distinction creates a unique environment for the regency's citizens, since most of Indonesia's population speaks an Austronesian language, including the national language Indonesian.

HISTORY

Historic written records provide scant information about the people of the Alor Archipelago. The first written mention of Galiyao, which refers to Pantar, is found in the fourteenth-century text *Negarakertagama* from the East Javanese Majapahit kingdom (Robert Barnes 1982). "Mallua" referred specifically to Alor Island or the group of islands composing the Alor Archipelago, and a small polity centered in the mountains of Southwest Alor was the source for this name and was later replaced with Ombu or Ombai on maps from the same period (Hans Hägerdal 2010: 221).

Historians and linguists agree that the Alurung arrived in the Alor Archipelago by the beginning of the fourteenth century. The Alurung kingdoms of Pandai, Baranusa, and Bungabali were members of the Galiyao Watang Lema or "Galiyao alliance of five coastal domains" consisting of Baranusa, Pandai, Bungabali (Alor Besar), Blagar, and Kui (Syarifuddin Gomang 1993: 28–30). The Galiyao Watang Lema established ties, including marital, military, and economic, with the Solor Watang Lema, an alliance composed of five coastal Lamaholot kingdoms in the neighboring Solor Archipelago. The kingdoms in both alliances exchanged goods with one another and participated in regional maritime trade stretching from Timor Island to the islands of North Maluku and Sulawesi.

The Alurung kingdoms received foreign visitors from other areas of present-day Indonesia and the Eurasian continent. Regional trade occurred with merchants from South Sulawesi, North Maluku, and other parts of present-day Indonesia for the archipelago's natural resources found in the land and sea. Ships passed the Alor Archipelago to travel to and from Timor Island and into the northern waters of Australia and anchored there to collect food supplies for their onward journeys. A Dominican missionary text written around 1642 described both the islands of the archipelago (present-day Alor Regency) as "having plenty of foodstuffs including rice, maize, and other edible plants" (Hägerdal 2011: 224). The sailor merchants exchanged imported textiles and metal items including weapons, gongs, and kettledrums for foodstuffs, beeswax, and other goods in the ports of Alor and Pantar.

The Alor Archipelago was governed by the colonial Dutch administration by the end of the nineteenth century. The descendants of its former rulers lost their power to govern, but they are still respected and revered by the local community. They are responsible for carrying out rites based on indigenous beliefs and Islam.

CULTURAL TRAITS

Members of the Alurung ethnic group generally uphold Islam. Different accounts exist regarding the introduction of this religion to the Alurung. One describes five Muslim scholars from the Ternate Empire of North Maluku going to the five domains forming the Galiyao Watang Lema of Alor Regency with a Holy Qur'an and other gifts in the late sixteenth century, and one version of this story includes a knife for circumcision and a spinning wheel for preparing thread for weaving (Susan Rodemeier 2010: 28–33).

The primary occupation of Alurung men is fishing and trade, while women carry out small-scale farming and weaving. The amount of arable land available in the coastal areas of Alor Regency's islands was not sufficient for subsistence farming, much less cotton cultivation. The Alurung developed relationships with non-weaving groups living in the islands' interiors where foodstuffs were abundant. Coastal residents such as the Alurung exchanged fish, salt, and imported goods such as metal tools and prestige items, ceramics, and beads for food, raw cotton, dyestuffs, and ingredients for areca nut chewing. Textile production was costly due to the lack of raw materials available via cultivation or foraging. However, the Alurung communities produced cloth in the past that served as gifts, shrouds, and clothing that signified ethnic and clan identity as well as prestige. They also wove textiles for the non-textile-producing groups living in the islands' interior and continue to produce cloth for this purpose but are paid in currency instead of goods.

Patrilineages or *uma* play important roles in Alurung society (Gomang 1993: 50–1; Emilie Wellfelt 2014: 19). The eldest male of the ruling patrilineage is generally the sacred leader of a settlement, previously a kingdom. The eldest male of another clan is responsible for secular governance. Other patrilineages handles religious affairs while others oversaw the law. Other patrilineages are warriors who defended the settlement and go to battle when commanded. More than one clan composes a patrilineage, and all of its members recognize the same founding father. Foundation stories often describe a man arriving from afar by ship marrying a local woman, even a mythical entity such as a *hari* or an invisible person who lives under the sea.

Bungabali or present-day Alor Besar is the oldest Alurung kingdom on Alor Island. Its society is organized into three patrilineages: Uma Bungabali, Uma Apukulung, and Uma Lelang Kissu. The Alurung consider this royal seat to be the most sacred of the three kingdoms on Alor, and the king or raja of Bungabali continues to lead major religious festivals and other customs.

Alor Kecil was an active trade port on the Bird's Head Peninsula at the mouth of Mutiara Bay until the Dutch colonial administration founded the capital of Kalabahi inside the bay in the 1910s. Maritime traders from diverse backgrounds settled here and intermarried with the local population. Some of these unions led to the foundation of other patrilineal clans within these patrilineages.

Alor Kecil's five patrilineages are Uma Baorae, Uma Manglolong, Uma Lekaduli, Uma Gelae, and Uma Modilaung. The name of the ruling lineage, Uma Baorae, is derived from the name of the banyan tree that Alor Kecil's founder sat under while weaving a fishing net (Gomang 1993: 29). The founders of some clans composing the Uma Baorae were traders or religious teachers such as the founder of Uma Sina, who was a Chinese merchant who married one of the ruler's daughters. Another example is the Uma Baorae Watang founded by a trader from South Makassar. The ritual houses of both of these clans are located along the coast, while the other clan houses of Alor Kecil are on a hill overlooking the coastline. The founding ancestors of some clans, such as the Manglolong, are considered to be indigenous.

Dulolong is the youngest of the three Alurung kingdoms in the Northwest Alor Subdistrict. One oral account regarding the establishment of this domain states that the grandson of the founding father of Uma Baorae of Alor Kecil established Dulolong (Gomang 1993: 30). The founders of four of Dulolong's patrilineages were direct descendants of the founding father of Alor Kecil's ruling lineage Uma Baorae. These include the ruling lineage of Uma Kakang, Uma Tukang, Uma Kapitang, and Uma Dopu. Other patrilineages of Dulolong are Uma Lekaduli, Uma Lamaholo, and Uma Wolba. Uma Lekaduli of both Alor Kecil and Dulolong share the same founding ancestors who originated from the Munaseli kingdom centered on Pantar Island. The founding father of the Uma Lamaholo belongs to the Lamaholot ethnic group and was from Solor Island in the Solor Archipelago.

Textile Production

Women continue to be primarily responsible for hand weaving in Alurung culture. Cotton was cultivated, but the amount of raw cotton produced in one year was often insufficient to complete a single garment, since arable land along the coasts and on the small islands was scarce. Cotton was acquired from groups living inland on Alor and Pantar Islands. This raw material was also sourced from Lembata and Timor Islands. Chinese silk was desirable, and the supply of this luxurious imported item was limited. Some Alurung weavers created a silk-like fiber by spinning milkweed pod fibers with cotton, a distinct trait of Alurung weaving (Wellfelt 2014). Presently, cotton and synthetic threads are available to purchase in the markets, ceasing the inter-island trade of raw cotton.

Alurung weavers rely on the surrounding environment, both the land and sea, for dyestuffs. They use marine life such as sea cucumbers, sea hares, sea urchins, and sea sponges as well as plants, including indigo, turmeric, and morinda, to color threads (McIntosh and Peni 2021). They also purchase synthetic dyes and pre-dyed threads in the local markets presently.

Over the last century, textile production has been declining in some Alurung areas due to the availability of manufactured clothing and textiles. Most women in Alor Besar, except in Hula Commune, ceased weaving in the 1970s. Several nearby Alurung villages—i.e., Uma Pura on Ternate Island and the sole settlement on Buaya Island—continue to weave and specialize in producing textiles for sale to different ethnic groups in the regency, including to other Alurung, and in the region, such as to Kisar Island of Maluku Regency. These primary producers of cloth are the main source of handwoven, warp ikat-decorated textiles available in the regency today, and trade of Alurung weavings at the weekly markets is ongoing.

WEAVING

Women of the Alurung ethnic group utilize a backstrap loom similar to the looms found in other parts of Eastern Indonesia. The warp is circular, generally producing two panels of cloth with identical patterning. Warp ikat is the primary decorative technique besides warp stripes. Some Alurung weavers apply complementary and supplementary warp techniques or decorative methods used by other textile-producing groups of Alor Regency.

The tenapi is the traditional tubular garment worn by both Alurung men and women. Depending on the type of tenapi, a garment is composed of two or three panels of handwoven cloth. If a tenapi is composed of two panels the design format is identical on both generally. However, the design format of the two sides of some tenapi types differs slightly. For example, the tenapi belang consists of two white stripes on one half and a single white stripe on the other half for a total of three white stripes decorating a garment. Some tenapi consist of three panels of cloth with the outer sections identical. The middle section contains a different design format and patterning and is woven on a separate warp.

Several oral stories describe the origin of textile production and the introduction of the warp ikat technique. One tale explains that Eko Sari, a *hari* or invisible person from the sea who married the founding father of the Manglolong patrilineage of Alor Kecil, taught women how to create designs decorating the imported *patola* or double ikat-decorated textiles from Gujarat, India (Gomang 1993: 107–8; Wellfelt 2014: 8). The weavers of Uma Pura continue to pay respect to this mythical teacher in an annual ceremony, Fae Tuang. This rite takes place during the harvest festival that occurs in the spring and involves immersing threads decorated with warp ikat in the sea as offerings to the mythical people living underwater (Wellfelt 2014: 8).

Tenapi—Patrilineal Identity Markers

Specific design formats and warp ikat motifs distinguish tenapi serving as markers of membership in the patrilineal clans of the various Alurung settlements. Other types are considered neutral with no affiliation to a patrilineage. Regardless of ethnicity or patrilineage, men and women could wear neutral garments only decorated with warp stripes. They may also use tenapi with warp ikat patterning that does not designate a specific patrilineal clan.

Generally, the warp ikat designs are organized into bands that have a horizontal orientation when the textile is worn. An exception is when the warp ikat designs cover an entire panel of cloth, emulating the patterns decorating Indian trade textiles such as patola. When describing the design format of a tenapi, the primary band refers to the largest or main row of warp ikat, while the secondary band denotes the second-largest row of patterning. The term tertiary indicates the third-largest row. Primary, secondary, and tertiary do not infer importance. Several types of tenapi will be described below.

The tenapi that is called tenapi patola locally possesses the highest social value among the Alurung and other ethnic groups in Alor Regency. Its name is derived from the plural of the word for an Indian silk textile decorated with the double ikat technique (*patolu*, singular, or *patola*, plural). The pronunciation of the name patola varies depending on the Alurung dialect, and it may be called patola in Central Alurung, watola in East Alurung, or fatola in West Alurung. Foreign sea merchants gifted these imported textiles to local rulers to open or strengthen trade relations between the sixteenth and nineteenth centuries. Communities throughout Indonesia held these silk fabrics in high regard. These prestige items were the prerogative of local rulers including those of Alor Regency's kingdoms. Some examples are preserved as sacred heirlooms in clan houses in Alor Regency presently, but many were destroyed by the elements over time. Their numbers also declined, since one of their functions is as a shroud. An Indian patolu, the term for a single textile from India, would accompany its deceased owner to the grave (Rodemeier 2006).

The design format and patterning decorating the midsection of a locally woven tenapi patola are inspired by the designs adorning these imported textiles that became sacred heirlooms throughout Indonesia, including among communities in the Alor Archipelago. Previously, only the ruling elite had the right to own and wear the locally woven tenapi patola composed of warp ikat-decorated cotton cloth woven by Alurung women. The tenapi patola is the identity marker of the ruling patrilineages or the Uma Bungabali or Alor Besar, Uma Baorae of Alor Kecil, and Uma Kakang of Dulolong. Individuals who were given examples from members of this elite patrilineal clan could also use this prestigious garment. The community considers a person wearing a tenapi patola to be wealthy and a member of one of the ruling patrilineages. Its use is not restricted to the eldest male or leader and his immediate family members but to anyone who belongs to this patrilineal clan. Members of the culturally diverse population of Alor Regency continue to purchase and reserve examples to use as shrouds and not as clothing. Often, distant relatives are unaware of a relative's ownership of a tenapi patola until it is used in funerary rites.

DISTINGUISHING FEATURES OF A TENAPI PATOLA

A tenapi patola woven by an Alurung weaver consists of three panels of fabric. The two peripheral panels are identical in patterning and design format while the middle section differs. The ground color of the top and bottom parts is usually brownish-red traditionally created with a dye of morinda roots, but some examples have a blue ground formed with indigo or black ground produced with morinda red overdyed with indigo.

A recurring design decorating a tenapi patola's midsection is a lattice pattern derived from Indian trade textiles including various types of patolu. In Alurung, this motif is called *bao lolong sambung* (connecting banyan tree leaves). A banyan tree is always found in the center of a raised mound where the Alurung conducted rituals such as in front of the clan house of the ruling lineage of Alor Besar. A patrilineal clan of Alor Kecil is named after the banyan tree named Baorae that the founding father once sat under to weave a fishing net, according to legend. If a lattice of connecting banyan tree leaves decorates the central panel, a design in the shape of a triangle with spikes always occurs at its sides. This motif is called *ufe kotong* (head of the sea hare). Sea hares were an important trade item in the Alor Archipelago, and some Alurung weavers utilize it as a dyestuff.

Variations in the design adorning a tenapi patola's central panel do occur. The patterns include a single large diamond shape or rows of various motifs such as *ufe kotong* or *bao lolong* (banyan tree leaf) that are not linked to each other at their sides. The formats consisting of warp ikat patterning arranged in rows or a single diamond shape symbolizing a banyan tree lead may have been recently produced, since they are easier to create than the overall lattice design.

The design format of the peripheral sections of a tenapi patola can vary slightly regarding the number of secondary and tertiary rows decorating them. However, one primary band of warp ikat decorating each of these panels is generally located near a garment's top and bottom ends. The design filling these rows is generally the same as the primary motif of the central section, or connecting banyan tree leaves. Variations do occur, mainly in the tenapi patola of the ruling lineage of Alor Besar and Alor Kecil. The motifs replacing the lattice are inspired by patterns of dragons from imported Chinese ceramics, and the Alurung have incorporated the portrayal of these mythical beasts into their own iconography to represent the mythical snakes *ula naga* (snake Naga) that inhabit the lands. Their likenesses appear at the entrance to the ritual area of Alor Besar and the entrance to the ceremonial hall of the ruling lineage of Alor Kecil. Chinese traders settled in both Alor Besar and Alor Kecil, and some married the daughters of the rulers of these Alurung kingdoms, creating new patrilineal clans in the ruling patrilineages. One of these clans is the Uma Sina (Chinese house/patrilineal clan) of Alor Kecil.

Secondary and tertiary rows of warp ikat and different colored stripes also decorate these peripheral panels, and a weaver may select the designs to fill these bands. These patterns include *plinta* (bursting kapok), *malu gilu* (broken sirih fruit), *utam pei* (candle nut), *kago no eking* (intertwining snakes), and *nura* (boat). The items that the motifs represent are found in the Alurung people's immediate environment. Bursting kapok indicates the end of the dry season and the onset of the rainy season. Sirih fruits are an ingredient of chewing areca nuts (often referred to as betel nuts), and these items are given as gifts when visiting a household. Hosts also offer the essentials for chewing areca nuts. Traveling by sea continues to be a major mode of transportation for coastal groups such as the Alurung in Alor Regency. The founding fathers of the ruling lineage of Alor Besar arrived on Alor Island by boat. People from other patrilineages may wear textiles with any of the designs mentioned above, but their combination and organization in the design format, especially the number or color of the warp stripes, of a tenapi are essential for it to be a patrilineal clan identity marker.

DISTINGUISHING FEATURES OF A TENAPI MATANG KARING

The distinguishing design element of the tenapi matang karing (tenapi with the small eyes) motif is the presence of numerous narrow or quarternary bands decorated with warp ikat dashes. These dashes are called *malu gilu*. Two panels of cloth compose a tenapi matang karing, and there is one primary warp ikat band near the top and bottom ends. Six or more quarternary rows of dashes surrounded by a plain ground alternating with groupings of secondary and tertiary bands of warp ikat occur between the primary bands. Another distinctive characteristic of the tenapi matang karing is the presence of purple and pink stripes adjacent to the primary bands of warp ikat designs. This tenapi represents membership in the Uma Aring.

DISTINGUISHING FEATURES OF A TENAPI SONTO RAJA

The tenapi sonto raja consists of two identical panels of fabric with a blue or black ground traditionally produced with indigo dye. Three warp ikat bands of similar size decorate each end of the garment or a secondary row flanks each side of the primary one. The section in between the groupings of warp ikat bands contains green and blue stripes. Occasionally, other colors, such as red and white, join the green and blue stripes in some examples. Narrow tertiary bands of warp ikat dashes also decorate the midsection on some garments. The stripes in the middle section are the qualifying characteristic of a tenapi sonto raja, and this tenapi is the identity marker of the Uma Lelang Kissu patrilineage of Alor Besar.

Roles of Tenapi in Alurung Society

Tenapi garments are exchanged during marital rites, and some serve as payment to make amends for wrongdoing or to compensate persons who have helped to dig a grave or contributed items for funeral rites (Hägerdal 2011: 57–60). Due to the scarcity of handwoven cloth in Alurung society, the system of marital gift exchange of textiles is not as complex as the types or grades of garments woven by the neighboring Lamaholot (Ruth Barnes 1989). In Alor Regency, the groom's party does not gift elephant tusks but metal such as bronze kettledrums, another contrast with the Lamaholot (Andaya 2016). The bride's family may present a tenapi to the groom's mother. The tenapi may be a clan-neutral garment or a locally woven tenapi patola if the bride's family had the means to acquire one. As stated earlier, honored guests receive tenapi as presents.

Tenapi tubular garments serve various roles in Alurung society. As articles of dress, this tube skirt-like clothing protects the wearer from natural elements such as sunlight and cold temperatures if it is worn unfolded with the top end covering the head rather than folded over at the waist. Both Alurung men and women wear tenapi as lower garments. An Alurung man may also utilize an example as a hip wrapper placed horizontally at the waist covering the top portion of trousers or a lightweight sarong. This method of wearing a hip wrapper resembles how men from other ethnic groups living in coastal areas of present-day Indonesia such as Malay or Bugis, for example, wear traditional attire. The Alurung upheld Islam and were also involved in regional trade like these groups. Some historians apply the term *pasisir* (coastal) in Indonesian to these groups who differ in ethnicity but share other cultural traits (Robert H. Barnes 1995: 497). An Alurung man wearing international-style clothing of a button-down shirt with pants also has been observed draping a tenapi folded lengthwise over a shoulder during ceremonies. Both ways of wearing a tenapi reflect the wearer's other identity as either pasisir or modern, but the presence of the handwoven, warp ikat-decorated tenapi reasserts a man's ethnic identity and patrilineage membership. The tubular garment also contrasts with the traditional attire of males belonging to other ethnic groups in the Alor Regency. The traditional lower garment of men from other groups is a fringed textile wrapped around the hips instead of a tubular garment.

MARKERS OF PATRILINEAGE MEMBERSHIP

Specific types of tenapi garments have served as symbols of membership in one of the Alurung patrilineages. Both male and female members of these patrilineal clans reserve the use of these garments for important rituals rather than wearing them on a daily basis. Creating the warp ikat designs of these patrilineage-specific garments using natural dyes was time-consuming. As stated above, the amount of homegrown cotton produced in a year was scarce. Alurung weavers had to rely on other sources for this material via trade, and the output of their textile production was thus limited. Tenapi and other handwoven textiles have both social and economic value in Alurung society.

An Alurung person can identify which patrilineage other Alurung people belong to by the tenapi they wear during a major festival or rites such as a group circumcision or annual harvest festival. During these important occasions, some participants continue to revert to the traditional roles of their patrilineages. For example, the eldest male of the ruling lineage leads the ritual as the community's sacred leader. Men and women belonging to patrilineages who were formerly responsible for the defense of a settlement dance to eradicate harmful spirits purifying the site where a festival or ritual is held. Leaders of clans concerned with religion carry out their duties related to traditional beliefs or Islam. Members of the same clan wear

Figure 1.2 The Alurung man on the left has a patola draped over his shoulder to indicate his patrilineage, while the two other men wear tenapi in the traditional manner or as sarongs. Photographer: © Yulianti Peni.

the same type of tenapi, and the observer could recognize the design format of the tenapi with the patrilineage and link it with their role in an Alurung community.

Non-Alurung people are generally able to identify the tenapi signifying major Alurung patrilineages such as the ruling one. The tenapi patola is conspicuous with its design format and easily recognizable as the marker of the ruling lineage. The Alurung kingdoms had forged alliances with neighboring polities composed of the Adang and Pura ethnic groups, and citizens from all would join the major events. Some of the Adang and Pura peoples would have been exposed to the various kinds of tenapi witnessing the duties members of various Alurung patrilineages carried out.

CHANGES IN THE PRODUCTION AND USE OF TENAPI

Living in coastal areas with little arable land, Alurung women wove not only for personal use but for trade and presently commercial sale to other Alurung and people from non-weaving ethnic groups such as the Adang, who also live in Northwest Alor District. This is especially true for Alurung women living on the small islands of Buaya and Ternate. Factory-produced threads and synthetic dyes became readily available in Alor Regency beginning in the 1970s, allowing these weavers to increase production and expand sales to other parts of Alor Regency and beyond. They receive orders to produce textiles of other cultures, and fashion designers from West Indonesia introduce new patterns and formats. Since the 1980s, local government programs have supported the commercialization of textile production for the tourist market and for school and government staff uniforms. The weavers have developed new motifs inspired by marine life for the tourist market. People who use Alurung textiles for various uniforms demand low prices. The increase in other types of textiles has led to a decline in the production of tenapi, especially markers of patrilineage affiliation. Some weavers from Uma Pura

Village, the sole Alurung settlement on Ternate Island, are reluctant to take orders for these types of tenapi due to the amount of time to create complex warp ikat designs and a warp consisting of different colored warp stripes and warp ikat-decorated bands of varying sizes.

Textile production in more accessible Alurung settlements, such as in Alor Besar and Alor Kecil on Alor Island, ceased in the last forty to fifty years. Their inhabitants can purchase some types of handwoven textiles produced in Buaya and Ternate Islands in the local markets, and Alurung weavers from Ternate Island have relocated to Alor Island north of Alor Besar to access the market. The Alurung weavers from these smaller settlements, however, do not know some types of tenapi originating from Alor Besar or Alor Kecil. Since knowledge about weaving is passed down orally intergenerationally, much has been lost. Some women from the community from which a tenapi is derived can remember its name but cannot describe it. A few women stated they were reluctant to document the different types of Alurung textiles since they are afraid other groups will copy the designs.

Members of the Alurung group also have different identities presently. They have been Muslims for several centuries and have adopted different clothing and accessories to reflect this identity. Alurung men wear lightweight sarongs and kufi skullcaps similar to the styles worn by Muslim men throughout Indonesia, and Alurung women have adopted hijabs. Their occupations have diversified from fishing, trading, farming, and weaving to include teachers, business owners, tour guides, etc.

However, the Alurung may wear both traditional handwoven tenapi and Muslim attire for rituals concerning traditional beliefs or Islam. Both men and women continue to wear tenapi for traditional rites such as the annual harvest festivals for corn and rice, and Muslim women wear headscarves composed of handwoven cloth instead of factory-made hijabs that they wear daily. A combination of styles has been observed for modern festivals including those related to Islam. In the first Ancient Qur'an Festival of Alor Regency held in 2021, participants wore traditional clothing composed of handwoven textiles including tenapi representing their patrilineage on the first day. In subsequent days, some men changed to Muslim attire or wore a combination of both styles. A kufi is worn with tenapi, for example. Many Alurung women, regardless of age, wore hijabs in place of handwoven headscarves during the first Ancient Qu'ran Festival.

The ongoing commercialization of textile production including patrilineage-specific tenapi allows anyone, regardless of ethnicity or nationality, to purchase any of these items. Tourists and textile collectors purchase old and new weavings when visiting Alor Regency. Individuals from other ethnic groups continue to purchase tenapi patola to use as shrouds or coffin covers since they also give this garment high status in their own culture. Previously, they had access to patrilineage-neutral tenapi, and only wealthy individuals could acquire high-status garments such as tenapi patola. Presently, anyone regardless of ethnicity or nationality can buy these garments once reserved for members belonging to the ruling patrilineage. Members of various Alurung communities may continue to wear patrilineage-specific tenapi with changes in their design format, such as a reduction in the decoration whether warp stripes or ikat design, while other types of tenapi are lost altogether. Weavers are minimizing the design structure of a tenapi and a reduction in the complexity of warp ikat patterning has also occurred. Only a few Alurung weavers continue to produce tenapi resembling those made by their mothers and grandmothers presently.

Changes in society, such as diversification of occupations and increased mobility, are reflected in the loss of traditional knowledge, not only of the textiles but of the roles the various patrilineages once held in a community. Many Alurung people have relocated to other parts of Alor Regency, Indonesia, and even moved to other countries, leading to a loss of traditional knowledge and customs. However, some Alurung diaspora do return to Alor Regency for major events, especially occasions when the participation of the Alurung patrilineages is mandatory, and the traditional roles of some clans are revived for these occasions. Members of patrilineages responsible for ceremonies and religion continue to carry out functions when required, and men from the warrior clans perform ritual dances before a religious rite, whether indigenous or Muslim, begins.

In the Alurung communities where handwoven textile production still occurs such as Uma Pura Village, there is growing interest among some weavers to revive the production of patrilineage-specific tenapi of their own and other Alurung settlements. It is unclear whether the intricacy of the older design formats and warp ikat designs can be recreated or if new versions of these garments emerge to replace the older formats. Time is money, and many weavers prefer a quick return on a sale of a textile rather than taking time to create an intricately decorated garment. Hopefully, the consumers of tenapi, whether Alurung or not, will demand high-quality weaving, leading to the preservation of tenapi that represent the patrilineages of the Alurung.

References

Andaya, L. (2016). "The Social Value of Elephant Tusks and Bronze Drums among Certain Societies in Eastern Indonesia", *Bijdragen tot de Taal-, Land- en Volkenkunde*, 172: 66–89.

Barnes, R. H. (1982), "The Majapahit dependency Galiyao", *Journal of the Humanities and Social Sciences of Southeast Asia*, 138 (4): 407–12.

Barnes, R. H. (1995), "Lamakera, Solor. Ethnohistory of a Muslim Whaling Village of East Indonesia", *Anthropos*, 90 (4/6): 497–509.

Barnes, R. (1989). *The Ikat Textiles of Lamalera: A Study of an Eastern Indonesian Weaving Tradition*, Leiden: Brill.

Fricke, H. and M. Klamer. (2018), "Reconstructing Linguistic and Social Histories of the Lamaholot Region", 7th East Nusantara Conference, Kupang, 14–15 May 2018.

Gomang, S. R. (1993), "The People of Alor and their Alliances in Eastern Indonesia: a study of Political Sociology", MA diss., Department of Sociology, Wollongong University, Australia.

Hägerdal, H. (2010), "Cannibals and Peddlers", *Indonesia and the Malay World*, 38 (111): 217–46.

Hägerdal, H. (2011) "Van Galen's memorandum on the Alor Islands in 1946. An annotated translation with an introduction. Part 2", *HumaNetten*, 27: 53–96.

Klamer, M. (2011), *A Short Grammar of Alorese (Austronesian)*, Munich: Lincom Europa.

Klamer, M. (2012), "Papuan–Austronesian language contact: Alorese from an Areal Perspective", in N. Evans and M. Klamer (eds), *Melanesian languages on the edge of Asia: Challenges for the 21st century. Language Documentation & Conservation Special Publication* 5, 72–108, Honolulu: University of Hawai'i Press.

McIntosh, L. S. and Y. Peni. (2020), *Textiles of Alor*, Kalabahi, Alor Regency, Indonesia: Museum 1000 Moko.

McIntosh, L. S. and Y. Peni. (2021), "Alorese Textiles, specifically Tenapi, and Their Production of Ternate Island, Alor Regency, NTT, Indonesia", *Archipel*, 102: 209–39.

Peni, Y. and L. S. McIntosh. (2020), "Rarely-Documented Textiles: *Tenapi* of Umapura Village, Ternate Isle, Alor Regency, Indonesia", *Textiles Asia* 12 (1): 6–14.

Rodemeier, S. (2006), "*Tutu kadire in Pandai—Munaseli. Erzählen und Erinnern auf der vergessenen Insel Pantar (Ostindonesien)*", Berlin: Lit-Verlagm.

Rodemeier, S. (2010), "Islam in the Protestant Environment of Alor and Pantar Islands", *Indonesia and the Malay World*, 38 (110): 27–42.

Wellfelt, E. (2007), "Diversity and Shared Identity: A case study of interreligious relations in Alor, Indonesia", MA diss., University of Gothenburg, Sweden.

Wellfelt, E. (2014). "The Secrets of Alorese 'Silk' yarn: Kolon susu, triangle trade and underwater women in Eastern Indonesia", in *Textile Society of America 14th Biennial Symposium Proceedings: New Directions: Examining the Past, Creating New Futures*, Los Angeles, September 10–14, 2014.

Wellfelt, E. (2016), "Historyscapes in Alor: Approaching indigenous history in Eastern Indonesia", unpublished Ph.D. thesis, Linnaeus University, Sweden.

"Cloth frames our lives in stories that tell of beginnings and endings, of lives lived and myths endured. Cloth touches each part of our being in a space of becoming bringing together the sensual and haptic in aesthetic narrative. Cloth language speaks of lives and histories."

Robert Burton

2

The *Powerful Whispers* Project: A Reimagined Story of Mills, Menders, and Archived Family Memories

ROBERT BURTON

Introduction

The *Powerful Whispers* project brought together intimate stories in the memory texts of photographs and as traces of the intimate and the familiar, reimagined them in their temporality and the temporality of the lives that they captured in the fragility of textile and the creation of translucent surface. The works not only examined images within the memory texts but the textile artworks themselves exist to remake familiar myths. The technical explorations that successfully bound together thread, starch, and dye sublimation digital printed image reveal the material processes behind the communication of the fragile, the delicate, and a floating sense of memory in fibers and imagery. The fragility of the structures and the explorations of technique reach for a visual and haptic form of the immanent and temporal: new techniques innovated with analog and digital processes to capture the fragile moment. In this way, this project explored the potential for crossing the polarities between the intimacy of the personal and a narrative intertextuality of fiber. The sensuality and materiality of cloth within the contested spaces of haptic "art textiles" exposes the subjective narratives that make textiles as art a potent vehicle of cultural and artistic expression. In the creation of fragile fibers that become in their bonded quality narrative threads there arises an expression of the trace, the immanent, the temporal in the objectified texture of memory. The works speak in layers of the temporal and impermanent through metaphors and memories captured within the printed surface.

> My mother's parents lived in Bramley, a suburb of Leeds in West Yorkshire, England, at the beginning of the twentieth century. A working-class family of the time, my grandmother was a fine worsted mender at Airedale Mills in Rodley, next to the Leeds and Liverpool canal where we, as small children, would go fishing for "tiddlers"; the small fish we would hook out of the canal. My grandfather was a tanner at the Turner Tanning Company in Bramley. The back-to-back working-class terrace they lived in had a cold stone basement cellar used as a cool store pantry before the invention or affordability of refrigerators and also acted alternatively as a bomb shelter during the Second World War. There was a small living room and kitchen on the ground floor and two small rooms upstairs. In my memory, the house had an inside toilet although the older outside toilet buildings are still there today. They are now used as outhouses, spaced between every two houses, with a gate and yard to each double toilet block. The early to mid-twentieth century appears to me now a life of ritual and routine with Saturday rugby football at the Old Boys Club and Monday was washing day; the whole street filled with sheets and clothes like quotidian bunting for a weekly coronation. All very discreet though, with no "smalls" hanging on the line. Each house had an attic and, I seem to recall, my mother told of how the attics were all connected at one time and you could walk from one to another. The attic, a space of mystery, held forgotten stories and secrets as in children's books and faery tales; a monster under the bed or strange lands through hidden doors, magical routes to other worlds. A large wardrobe full of clothes once worn but now forgotten, handmade dresses created by skills now lost, thrifted, and remade during the war, those no longer fitting, shaped as memories of former times and other people, stood forlorn now in the corner. As Stallybrass states, the wardrobe in memory and reality is an archive of ghosts waiting to step out to "appall us, haunt us, perhaps even console us".
>
> **STALLYBRASS 2015: 72**

> These clothes told stories of presence and intimacy recalling past lives lived through sight, touch, and smell (Crewe 2017: 125). The attic was filled with a large bed with quilted, crafted, and crocheted covers, and the dressing table was filled with memory objects, forgotten objects, mythical objects, objects with stories; old hairbrushes, hand mirrors, shoes, and inlaid boxes. These scenes are now preserved in the fading memories of my childhood where oneiric myths bring about subconscious remembrance through an appropriated play of analogies that embrace a synaesthesia of evocative forms; floating images as liquid memories dissolved in the fluid of the past.
>
> **BACHELARD 2012: 59; SVANKMAJER 2009: 39; LEHMANN 2007: 30**

In the attic was a garment box from the department store Schofields; a large retail store that traded from 1901 to 1996, regarded, for much of the twentieth century, as the pinnacle of shopping in Leeds. This Schofields's garment box, originally holding a newly purchased wedding dress, contained a wealth of family photographs and memorabilia such as postcards and letters going back to the early days of image making when the practice of taking a photograph was an event in which each member of the family would dress in their "Sunday best" on one special day and visit the town centre to solemnly stand next to arrangements of antique pillars in poses that they had practised for days in front of the mirror.

SEABROOK 2000: 179–80

Remaking and Remembering Through Images of the Past

From these family photographs I can see that the ladies in their big hats would head out for their promenades on a Sunday with the men equally suited in large top hats. There are records of the mill buildings and a large house with an extensive lawn and one particular image of two men holding up the oars of a rowing boat on a boating lake. It seemed an ideal life in Victorian England for the Brown family. The family myth tells of great-great-grandpa Brown, who had several wives including Agar, who had a face as stern as her name, and the mill that he bought with the wealth that he amassed from his investments in the American railroad. The mill with its extensive grounds and boating lake, or mill pond as it would have been known, and the pastoral Sundays on the pond, which the photographs record, are true frozen moments of certain salad days in the sun. The 1891 census records John Brown and his wife Mary Brown as residents in Elmfield House, the mill house belonging to Elmfield Mill of Back Lane in Bramley, Leeds, where they lived with their five sons and daughters Sarah, Benjamin, Hannah, George, and the youngest Mary.

The *Powerful Whispers* project began with a collection of images found in a box of photographs from the 1850s to the 1980s, which is now a closed archive since my grandmother's death in 2002. The pictures appear as distant fading memories of the mythic times they capture in their sepia and waning grays. This collection has become a form of material culture linking the familial past to the present only through a post-memory relating to metaphors and narratives of a past that now structures our sense of family and identity; a fantasy that is both social and romantic, that conceals and reveals a politics of the social and the everyday (Holland 2000: 14). The box of family photographs as an archive for reflection, creative investigation, and re-evaluation through expressive imagination became a site of discourse where the archive images of family myth began to suggest the potential for narrative textile forms. These were the intimate images of my familiar past that once were the sites of family remembering now to become the image texts of narrative textiles. The material archive and the collecting of images in society, community, and culture are embedded in everyday practices that contribute to the formation and, later, the loss of a person, family, community, and society. Maddock suggests that "archives are places where we might find answers, extend or question our knowledge"; opening the cherished container of photographs is "another form of undressing" that creates sites of longing and desire (2018: 33). In the same way, this collection existed as the "stuff" of memory that recalls the "traces left by the person in the social matrix" (Miller 2016: 136). The intimacy of clothing and textile, figures and setting in photographic emulsion and paper became the cadavers and echoes of past experiences and forgotten memories that began to form new narratives through fiber and digital reimaging. The reimagined fibers and imagery forming narratives of biographies, autobiographies, genealogies, and memories possessing a material link to the lives that look out from the nostalgia of a foreign country revisited (Barthes 2000: 99–100; Healy 2015: 94; Prain and Ow 2014: 103).

The images in the archive take the form of post-memory experiences, stilled moments captured, telling stories of landscapes and peoples that are now mere family myths (Lowenthal 2015). In the translation into narrative textile and cloth, these images represent the human desire to still the movement of time like a time traveler's journey back to earlier lives and loves known, or those that we only acquaint with, through the image itself (Warner 2012: 198–202). The ladies in big hats and the men in blazers become visionary beings forming a mythic narrative. Myth simplifies the complexity of human acts establishing a world without contradictions through an absence of depth. Myth purifies signs and fills them with new meanings that correspond to the culture and communities from which the myths arise. In the text of *Camera Lucida* Barthes (2000) examines themes of presence and absence in photography and investigates the nature of photographs using his own reflections on an image of the Winter Garden Photograph of his mother. The photograph is always a "what has been," with photography offering an immediate presence to the world that is both of a political and a metaphysical order. Barthes proposes that this intense "defeat of Time" is visibly legible in historical photographs in evidencing the authenticity and essence of a beloved person. It testifies to an object that has existed and has been where I see it (Barthes 2000: 115). It is this quality of the *punctum* of the archive of photos that captured my attention as I started to remythologize a heritage through fiber and image. The stories are told through the family images as myths brought to life by those that had walked the promenades at the seaside and boated in the mill pond in their big hats. I was struck by the familiar faces with a striking youthful aliveness; their whole lives before them captured in a frozen moment (Barthes 2000: 96).

Mythmaking: Post-Mythology in Cloth and Narrative Thread

The visual arts and visual culture express ideas and concepts through symbolic mythic forms which form mythic narrative threads. These symbolic threads are not only the semiotic meaning of signs and symbols inherent in the structures of modern visual and cultural theory but also the psychological symbolic forms of the cultural myths that are the foundations of our society. They evolve in their telling and retelling throughout different, new generations and as we retell them in new ways. These symbolic forms are our collective and societal "mythic imagination . . . facts of the mind made manifest in a fiction of matter" (Campbell 1973: 10). Joseph Campbell cites Carl Jung in his analysis of cultural myth, who states that, when correctly read, myths talk to us in a visual language of the human soul, mind, and spirit, and show the capacity to act in a particular way, thereby reflecting the "wisdom of the species by which man has weathered the millenniums" (Campbell 1973: 13). Throughout Campbell's work, he returns to the importance of myth and mythic symbolic forms put forth by the unconscious mind and recognized by the conscious in continuous interactions as being the significant collective consciousness within a healthy culture, society, and community. The archaic myths that can be found in world mythologies are structured in similar ways across the world and are often interpreted as narratives and metaphors of society, its morals, and its rites of passage and reflect our human needs. The same kind of symbolic forms and narrative structures are found in the faery tales that became the vernacular oral stories of the world, with similar narratives arising throughout different regions with the same underlying story and structure. Myth becomes a way of ordering the world around us and, although mythical stories often appear meaningless and absurd, they are formed from the basic need for the human mind to create order (Lévi-Strauss 1989: 11).

French philosophers Michel Serres and Bruno Latour (2014) expand the discussion of the mythic and metaphorical significance of the object in their discursive essay, *Where Things Enter into Collective Society*, in which they suggest that the social sciences are infatuated with only subjects whereas there is a need to introduce the object into the relationship and that such a relationship should be through myths. In this way my innovations with cloth and narrative image as objects form a mythic metaphor in tactile fiber and layered image. Serres proposes the apple from the biblical myth of the Garden of Eden as the first referent, a metaphor of love, rebellion, knowledge, chance, and peril, and of mad prophecy, "cause and thing," the first object (Serres and Latour 2014: 37). Serres goes on to state that nothing is spoken of if we do not talk about something, therefore suggesting that mythic ordering and metaphors as visual and haptic signs are part of a natural discourse in human relations, society, and culture. In the previous modern era of ideas, what Serres terms an "archaic" era, relations formed and produced objects in a linear trajectory from idea to production and that, in contemporary culture, the opposite is true, with object as narrative forms directly creating relations. The haptic, sensual, and tactile in the form of textile, cloth, and clothing have become powerful semiotic signs full of symbolic meaning that effectively engage with history, heritage, memory, culture, identity, belonging, politics, and society. Leder, calling on the phenomenology of Merleau-Ponty, suggests that the world is filled with meaning through man's sensory powers as individual subjects that experience the perceptual world as being one of appearances (Leder 1990: 5).

Textile arts and our shared cultural narratives in cloth also possess elements of this symbolic language, the "picture language of powers of the psyche," in the methods in which they communicate through symbols that provoke responses and emotive feelings, formed through a unified collective consciousness. As Moore states in her commentary on the texts of twentieth-century French hermeneutic phenomenologist philosopher Paul Ricoeur, "we cannot help but tell stories about ourselves" (Moore 1992: 118).

In her essay, *Textiles, Text and Techne*, Victoria Mitchell examines the relationship between text and textile and correlates the similarities between language and the sensual, the sensory and haptic in cloth, clothing, and textile forms. There are similarities in the derivation of words used around the world for text, textual, and textile. All have their foundation in the same root. The word "language" etymologically comes from the tongue that makes the sound and, in weaving, the point at which the yarn emerges is called the orifice. Texere in Latin, to weave, shares an association with text, which, Mitchell argues, is a correspondence between making and speaking. A system of communications exists in an intertextual language of textiles, cloth, and fabric. This intertextual system of communication directly expresses itself through physical forms, bodies, things, spaces, and places within a particular time and place (Mitchell 2015).

Remythologizing Memory and Post-Memory: Fictions and Alternative Worlds

The material culture of memory and post-memory includes all the ephemera of contemporary life with evocative

Figure 2.1 *Doris Hainsworth née Wilson*, 2017. Materials: cotton yarn, found object, starch glue, dye sublimation print construction, 42 × 40 cm. © Robert Burton. Photographer: © Robert Burton.

objects of reflection and contemplation by way of memory and post-memory, not only cloth and clothing but those images that record the wearing of the garment. These narrative threads set the garment within a past that is often another world; familiar but oddly strange (Lowenthal 2015). In reflection, it appears that the reimaging of photos into sensual and tactile threads and cloth is a weaving together of times and spaces in an ever-folding and unfolding. In taking the images from the box and onto cloth, they fold together and unfold in their ability to reveal new stories and questions and expose more beneath their surfaces. As a visual artist working in textile surfaces and imagery on fiber, creating fabric forms and innovations with materials and materiality, my work forms new intimate myths within the passages of time and history as cited by Deleuze in his study of Leibuiz and the Baroque, where the fold is not only the billowing and flaring of clothing and cloth but the folding and unfolding of time and space hiding some aspects of the world and revealing others at different times (Deleuze 2011: 206–59). Maddock (2018) refuses to cut into cloth and fabric bought many years ago, used, and loved, as if cutting into them was a "cutting our shared past, editing my own history" (Maddock 2018: 32). My work involves transforming the images, textiles, and cloth of the past in a remaking of stories in cloth (Figure 2.1). As the mill workers that both my paternal and maternal grandmothers were, I perceive myself as a fine mender in fabric; both the image and textile yarn working with the faults in the fabric of myth. In the same way, that fabric has a softness and fragility; the images I create and recreate as a new re-formation of the archive recall the fading of memory. Formed from cotton and silk shantung natural fibers bound together with starch, they appear as a fine web through which one touches the past. In responding to the fibers and dye sublimation prints and then further looking at the archival images printed on them, questions have arisen, such as "who are these people?", "what's the story?", and "can you tell me about them?" This invites new stories and metanarratives through making, creative practice, and the archival stories of ancestors and stories told at family gatherings over many years; myths of belonging that bind together the community and our societal relations. Samuel (2012) analyses the pleasure arising from viewing evocative images in old photographs, and the same can be argued for these evocative layers of printed threads, as, on the one hand, a "narcissistic ego-identification" and also, an alternative reading as a "hallucinatory oneness with the past," creating a sense of belonging and home but also an otherness and dreamscape that is strangely familiar. They possess a valedictory role with the thread and image as a eulogy for the dead. Everyday idealized images and decisive moments that create the family's identity disappear into myth as each moment folds in on the other, each thread sits translucently on the next, and the surface translucently hides the faults and folds of the conflicts and contradictions of the past (Spence 1986: 203–4). Barnett (2015) in her analysis of *Cloth, Memory, and Loss* talks of mending and repair as a similarly repetitive performative act and in so doing quotes artist Zoe Leonard:

> This mending cannot possibly mend any real wounds, but it provided something for me. Maybe just time, or the rhythm of sewing. I haven't been able to change anything in the past, or bring back any of the people I love who have died, but I've been able to experience my love and loss in a measured and continuous way; to remember.
>
> HARRIS et al. 2015: 30

Our feelings of belonging and social relations are constructed, collectively, with the mistiness of these ghostly forms and shades through which we are shaped by their loss. Deleuze talks of this sense of recalling lost time in his study of Proust's *In Search of Lost Time*, as the "revelation to see again those familiar to us, for their faces no longer a habit, bear in a pure state the signs and effects of time, which has modified this feature, elongated, blurred, or crushed that. Time, to become visible, seeks bodies and everywhere encounters them, seizes them to cast its magic lantern upon them" (Deleuze 2008: 13). In this space, the textile I make becomes spectral; haunted by that which is excluded. To Derrida this haunting is "a trace always referring to another whose eyes cannot be met; a ghostly presence, oppressed by the ever-expanding weight of the past" (Coverley 2020: 86).

In remaking myths in the narrative thread of silk and cotton that capture the fragility of the past a metanarrative arises through imagination and the representation of memory text within a fragile cloth that begins to frame the "uncanny," which, as Freud stated in his essay of 1919, is that which is familiar, but where something lies beyond it that cannot be reconciled with the familiar or the homely;

the conjoining of two things or more that are familiar but which do not belong together (Freud 2003; Fisher 2016). This is the "other" place of the installation exhibited in the Artifex gallery in Vilnius in 2019, where soundscapes of whispering textile machinery surrounded the ghostly large-scale printed fiber artworks (Figure 2.2). The narrative cloth installation utilized historic sounds gathered from Bradford Industrial Museum's collection of textile machinery and synthesized these to create a presence in absence of human noise behind the echoes of the past. Utilizing interactive sensors and contemporary technologies, four speakers worked alongside digitally printed narrative thread works to create a visual, haptic, and aural experience that recalled a social and relational culture of the past in the present. The worsted and woollen mills where my ancestors worked melded with the voices of the past calling ambiently in *Power Whispers* around them.

Kuhn speaks of the imagery and objects of post-memory as evocative and emotive objects of memory that speak of "silence, absence, and contradiction" as much as authenticity. In the "performative nature of remembering" the stories revealed by my narrative textiles reimagine the past, healing past hurts, and may also be transformative in informing how we as individuals and communities live in and relate to the present and the future (Kuhn 2002: 158).

Memory weaves its narrative as a collective imagination in a mediation of memory through creation, iteration, reworking, and recontextualization. Memory embodies both union and fragmentation and is involved as much in forgetting as "re-membering." This is the fragmentation, not only of fibers and threads but of the printed images upon them. As memories come together in clusters, they mediate shared meanings and conceptions of what is ours and belongs to us. Evocative archives and evocative images become phantasmagorias building tensions between the familiar and the other, the real and the imagined, the emotive and sensed in everyday life. In his lecture presented at the Freud Museum on June 5, 1994, Jacques Derrida

Figure 2.2 *Powerful Whispers*, 2018. Materials: Silk shantung fiber, glues, dye sublimation print with embedded electronics, 4 × 70 × 140 cm. © Robert Burton. Photographer: © Robert Burton.

proposed the term "archive fever" in which the archive—due to the tension between the subjective and the objective—generates an "undecidability" whereby the archive employing the knowledge brought to it augments itself at a point where "at the same stroke it loses the absolute and 'meta-textual' authority it might have claim to" (Derrida 2017: 68).

In the archive, memories are collated for future re-enactment although it is unclear whether it is we who recall the past through memory, or whether it is us who have been recalled by the summons of those we remember. Post-memory as defined by Gibbons is the inheritance of past events or experiences that are still being worked through. In this, she agrees with Hirsch in post-memories construction as secondary memory formed by progressive generations (Gibbons 2013: 73). Gibbons (2013) argues that post-memory is a form of social memory that often discloses what has been inhibited by previous generations. In this way, Hirsch also states that the power of photographic images and their creative representation and exploration through material culture lies not in their "evocation of memory" but in their "prescience of history we cannot assimilate" (Hirsch 2016: 41).

In evoking post-memory, the fragility of fibers in the artworks captures the worn and fraying temporality of the photographic image, suggesting at each moment that the past will disappear in another fold of time and each grain of light and shade on the photographic paper being as transient and temporary but as meaningful as the textile that becomes worn into the shape of the human body and becomes one with the identity, body, being, and belonging of the wearer. My artworks take on the concept of what Griselda Pollock sees as "a visible tactility that touches the internal organization of the drive through materiality and structure rather than representation" in a "borderspace" through a liminality of production and representation (Barnett 2015: 78). As Lévi-Strauss (1989) correlates, music and mythology are two sisters born by language, "who had drawn apart, each going in a different direction." The textile as narrative device formed in haptic metaphor performs the same relationship through remythologizing the familial past in thread and dye. In the *Powerful Whispers* project, the trace of lives passed and stories told softly appear upon the surface of fibers and constructed fabric substrates; traces of the fading frozen moment blown up to a now lifeless but interactive and expressive mythic fragile fiber shroud.

The family archive of images and objects found in the attic, the source material for the *Powerful Whispers* project, will continually repeat itself in its remaking in thread and fragile cloth printed with representations of a past–present that continually responds to difference and otherness as well as familiarity and belonging. The narrative threads form cloth that repeatedly reduces the lives it proclaims to objectify through itself. In the emotive sensual textile forming a narrative thread as memory image-object, there is the paradox between the real and imagined, the familiar and the other.

References

Bachelard, G. (2012) *House and Universe//1958* in Farr, Ian. *Memory: [Marina Abramovic; Eija-Liisa Ahtila; Kutlug Ataman . . .]*. London [u.a.]: Whitechapel Gallery [u.a.].

Barthes, R. (2000) *Camera Lucida* London: Vintage

Barnett, P. (2015) *The Alchemists Workshop//1997* in Lange-Berndt, Petra. *Materiality*. London: Whitechapel.

Campbell, J. (1973) *Myths to Live by*. New York: Bantam Books.

Coverley, M. (2020) *Hauntology* Harpenden: Oldcastle Books Ltd.

Crewe, L. (2017) *The Geographies of Fashion: Consumption, Space, and Value*. London, UK: Bloomsbury Academic, an imprint of Bloomsbury Publishing Plc.

Deleuze, G. (2011) *The Fold: Leibniz and the Baroque*. Repr. ed. London [u.a.]: Continuum.

Deleuze, G. (2008) *Proust and Signs*. London: Continuum.

Derrida, J. (2017) *Archive Fever: A Freudian Impression*. N.p.: University of Chicago Press.

Fisher, M. (2016) *The Weird and the Eerie* London: Repeater Books

Freud, S. (2003) *The Uncanny*. London: Penguin.

Gibbons, J. (2013) *Contemporary Art and Memory: Images of Recollection and Remembrance*. London: I.B. Tauris.

Healy, R. (2015) *The Parody of the Motley Cadaver* in Hemmings, Jessica. (ed.) *The Textile Reader*. Reprinted ed. London: Bloomsbury Academic, an imprint of Bloomsbury Publishing Plc.

Holland, P. (2000) *History, Memory and the Family Album* in Spence, Jo (ed.). & Holland, Patricia (ed.) *Family Snaps: The Meaning of Domestic Photography*. N.p.: Virago Press.

Hirsch, M. (2016) *Family Frames: Photography Narrative and Postmemory*. Reissued. ed. Cambridge, Mass.: Harvard University Press.

Harris, J., Barnett, P., Bryan-Wilson, J., & George, A. (2015) *Art textiles*: [exhibition the Whitworth, Manchester, October 10, 2015–January 31, 2016]. Manchester: Whitworth.

Kuhn, A. (2002) *Family Secrets: Acts of Memory and Imagination*. New edition. ed. London: Verso.

Leder, D. (1990) *The Absent Body*. Chicago: University of Chicago Press.

Lehmann, U. (2007) *The Uncommon Object: Surrealist Concepts and Categories for the Material World* in Wood, Ghislaine. (ed.) *Surreal Things: Surrealism and Design*. London: V&A Publications.

Lévi-Strauss, C. (1989) *Myth and Meaning*. London: Routledge.

Lowenthal, D. (2015) *The Past Is a Foreign Country—Revisited*. Cambridge: Cambridge University Press.

Maddock, A. (2018) *Folds, Scissors, and Cleavage in Giocanni Battista Moroni's Il Tagliapanni* in Millar, L. (ed.), and Kettle, A. (ed.) *The Erotic Cloth: Seduction and Fetishism in Textiles*. London: Bloomsbury Academic, an imprint of Bloomsbury Publishing Plc.

Miller, D. (2016) *Stuff*. Cambridge: Polity Press.

Mitchell, V. (2015) *Textiles, Text and Techne* in Hemmings, Jessica. (ed.) *The Textile Reader*. Reprinted ed. London: Bloomsbury Academic, an imprint of Bloomsbury Publishing Plc.

Moore, H. (1992) *Paul Ricoeur: Action, Meaning and Text* in Tilley, Christopher. (ed.) *Reading Material Culture: Structuralism, Hermeneutics and Post structuralism*. Oxford: Blackwell.

Prain, L. and Ow, J. (2014) *Strange Material: Storytelling through Textiles*. Vancouver: Arsenal.

Samuel, R. (2012) *Theatres of Memory: Past and Present in Contemporary Culture*. Rev. pbk. ed. London: Verso.

Seabrook, J. (2000) *My Life is in that Box* in Spence, Jo (ed.). & Holland, Patricia (ed.) *Family Snaps: The Meaning of Domestic Photography*. N.p.: Virago Press.

Serres, M. and Latour, B. (2014) *Where Things Enter into Collective Society, 1995* in Hudek, Antony, and Blazwick, Iwona. The Object. London: Whitechapel.

Spence, J. (1986) *Putting Myself in the Picture: A Political, Personal, and Photographic Autobiography*. London, England: Camden Press.

Stallybrass, P. (2015) *Worn Worlds* in Hemmings, Jessica. (ed.) *The Textile Reader*. Reprinted ed. London: Bloomsbury Academic, an imprint of Bloomsbury Publishing Plc.

Svankmajer, J. (2009) *The Magic of Objects* in Phosphor issue Number 2 Autumn Beamreach Printing West Yorkshire

Warner, M. (2012) *Phantasmagoria: Spirit Visions, Metaphors, and Media into the Twenty-first Century*. Reprinted. ed. Oxford: Oxford University Press.

"Cloth signifies comfort, security and domesticity encapsulating multiple layers of meaning and memory. Domestic fabrics are forensic records of the home, absorbing fluids, odors, atmosphere, whispers, and sighs within their folds, but, like the commemorative cloths I describe in these pages, they can also bear witness to world events and record collective memories."

Carol Quarini

3

Drapery and Napery: Lace War Memorials

CAROL QUARINI

Lace and war seem an unlikely combination, but this chapter considers two commemorative lace artifacts—a large curtain panel and a tablecloth—that, although separated by time, place, and function, entwine the personal and the political to record memories of war. The machine-made Battle of Britain commemorative lace panel was produced in Nottingham after the Second World War, while the Belgian tablecloth was worked in needlelace at the convent lace school in Erembodeghem, which was part of the lace cooperative formed to provide famine relief in Belgium during the First World War. Having carried out research into the Battle of Britain lace panel (Quarini 2020), then encountering the tablecloth at an exhibition in Bruges, the parallels between the two artifacts were manifestly apparent. This chapter considers the social history, design, and manufacture of both pieces of lace and surmises why lace was considered a suitable medium for these war memorials.

Drapery and Napery

The two pieces of lace are ostensibly a curtain and a tablecloth, but both represent far more than their domestic origins would suggest. Both are works of art rather than functional items and were made to commemorate world wars. However, their origins in domesticity are significant because they embody quotidian responses to war. The curtain panel was made by factory workers usually employed in producing items for the home and the tablecloth was made by women making piecework lace between their daily chores.

The Battle of Britain curtain lace panel is 180 inches long and 65 inches wide (450 × 163 cm) and was made by the Nottingham machine lace company Dobson and Browne in 1946 in a limited edition and presented to organizations and people associated with the battle (Figure 3.1). The number produced is a matter of debate, but the best estimate is thirty-six (Quarini 2020). They are held in various museums, airforce headquarters, and private collections (Farr 2015). One example is on permanent display at Bentley Priory, London, which was the headquarters of fighter command during the Second World War and is now a museum. Ostensibly, the panel celebrates the pivotal air battle that is considered to be the turning point

Figure 3.1 Battle of Britain commemorative lace panel made by Dobson and Browne of Nottingham, 1946. Photographer: © Carol Quarini.

of the war, as it convinced Hitler that an invasion of Britain was impossible. However, in its size and design, with five small outer panels on each side, flanking a central larger image, the panel also references prize-winning nineteenth-century machine lace exhibition pieces. This use of layout, by recalling more prosperous times, was also a subtle attempt to revitalize the drapery and napery sector of the British machine lace industry, which dealt with curtains and tablecloths.

Figure 3.2 Queen Elisabeth's needlelace tablecloth completed in 1919 as part of the Belgian war lace initiative (Royal Museum of Art and History, Brussels: accession number D.4432). Photographer: © Carol Quarini.

The tablecloth, in contrast, is a unique piece, made entirely by hand in needlelace (Figure 3.2). It was made during the First World War in Belgium and presented to Queen Elisabeth in 1919 on her return from exile by the Brussels Lace Committee, part of the Belgian Relief Fund. It measures 88.5 by 62 inches (225 × 158 cm) and is held in the Royal Museum of Art and History, Brussels (accession number D.4432). This piece also has a dual function. While it was a gift to a beloved queen from her grateful subjects and a reminder of Belgian resilience during the war, it was also a showcase for the talent of Belgian lacemakers and an attempt to revitalize their handmade lace industry.

Lace in the Twentieth Century

The two main types of handmade lace are bobbin and needlelace and both techniques had been used throughout Europe since the sixteenth century. The tablecloth is made of needlelace, which comprises a series of buttonhole stitches worked to form patterns made up of areas of dense and open work. Regions of Belgium had been celebrated for exquisite handmade lace since the 1500s, but the development of machine-made lace throughout the nineteenth century had led to severe competition. By the early twentieth century, handmade lace was in decline as a result of poor designs, lack of standards, the time-consuming nature of the work, and changes in fashion, which favored machine-made lace. The art of handmade lace was dying and Belgian lacemakers were struggling to earn a living. In an effort to preserve the lacemaking industry, many well-to-do ladies instituted lace groups that aimed to improve the quality and designs of the lace and ameliorate the working conditions of the lacemakers (Bruggeman 2018: 87). One of these groups was *Les Amies de la Dentelle*, which, in 1911, came under the patronage of Queen Elisabeth (Kellogg 1917: 70).

The machine-made lace that caused the decline of the handmade lace industry had its origin in nineteenth-century Britain, where the first lace machines had been invented. There are a variety of machine-made laces, produced using different techniques and machines. The lace panel was made on the Nottingham lace curtain machine, which produces a firm lace based on a square net, which sounds limiting, but in skilled hands is amenable to shading and subtle effects. At the start of the First World War, machine-made lace was fashionable for garments and furnishings and trade was buoyant with total UK lace exports valued at over £4 million (Mason 2010: 146). This figure rose to over £8.5 million after the war. However, by the start of the Second World War in 1939, the export trade had declined to about £1.25 million (Mason 2010: 146). Despite an increase in export sales after the war to values of £6.5 million, changes in fashion and a minimalist approach to interior design resulted in the use of less net and lace for curtaining and sales fell in the 1960s (Mason 2010: 146).

Design of the Lace Memorials

The two lace pieces were made to celebrate victories, but neither is jingoistic; both reference the destruction of war and the resilience of those who experience it rather than triumphalism. The two pieces show many similarities, for example they both incorporate inspiring messages from national leaders as well as symbolic floral iconography. The Nottingham panel includes images of London landmarks bombed in the Blitz and the Belgian cloth records Belgian towns where battles took place by depicting their municipal insignia as well as the country's patron saints. Unusually, both include the names of the designer, as well as the sponsor in the case of the tablecloth, and the draftsmen and lace company in the case of the panel, probably because they were considered works of art rather than functional items. At different times both pieces were linked to charitable functions.

TEXT

The inspirational words spoken by King Albert on August 4, 1914, the day German troops invaded Belgium, form the centerpiece of the tablecloth, surrounded by a rectangular border. As he left the Parliament Chamber, sword in hand, his defiant message was "J'ai foi dans nos destinées! Un pays qui se défend s'impose au respect de tous, ce pays ne périt pas!" (I have faith in our destinies! A country that defends itself imposes itself on the respect of all, this country does not perish!) (Wardle 1989: 87).

The Battle of Britain panel also includes rousing words from a parliamentary speech, in this case Winston Churchill's address in 1942 when he praised the valor of the airmen involved in the Battle of Britain, saying, "never in the field of human conflict was so much owed by so many to so few," which has been abbreviated on the panel to read, "never was so much owed by so many to so few." In the panel these words are depicted above an image of St. Paul's Cathedral wreathed in smoke but unharmed by bomb damage, an iconic image of the time that came to represent the resilience of London and Londoners.

PLACES

The image of St. Paul's on the Battle of Britain panel was based on an official government photograph, as were the other images of London bomb damage depicted on the two outer borders. They show the damage and destruction of some well-known London landmarks following the bombing raids of the Blitz, including collapsing buildings in Queen Victoria Street, City Temple Holborn, the Old Bailey, Buckingham Palace, Bow Church, St. Clement Danes, the Guildhall, and the House of Commons. The center panel also includes a cottage and castle showing that rich and poor alike were involved in the war. Instead of images of places, the Belgian tablecloth includes the coats of arms of sixteen Belgian cities where the war was fiercely fought.

FIGURES

The Battle of Britain panel contains few figures. There is one large image of an airman ready for action, and smaller figures of men with parachutes baling out of planes and others manning guns or clearing rubble from bombsites. In contrast, four saints feature prominently in the center of the Belgian tablecloth enwreathed with olive branches. St. Elisabeth of Hungary and St. George, depicted in round medallions, represent the Belgian king and queen, while the patron saints of Brussels, Gudula and Michael, appear in oval medallions (Wardle 1989: 86). St. Gudula, representing resilience, is shown with the devil, who tried unsuccessfully to blow out her lamp, which miraculously relit every time.

St. Elisabeth appears above a symbol of the Red Cross, referencing Queen Elisabeth's nursing work in the war. A crowned initial E appears below and the saint is surrounded by eight lozenges, including the text of an extended version of the Seven Works of Mercy: "Encourager les déspérés, Loger les réfugiés, Nourir les affamés, Vêtir les pauvres, Guérir les blessés, Délivrer les captifs, Consoler les affligés, Honorer les morts" (Wardle 1989: 87). These entreaties to comfort the doubtful, pray for the dead, feed the hungry, clothe the poor, and free the imprisoned refer directly to suffering during the war. St. George represents King Albert and below him is the Belgian decoration for bravery and a crowned initial A, wreathed with oak leaves and acorns symbolizing strength. Surrounding him are eight lozenges including the names of the battles that took place before 1916 in which he participated (Wardle 1989: 87).

FLORAL BORDERS

The tablecloth includes three decorative borders incorporating ferns, wildflowers, and seaweed, emblematic of the forests, fields, and waters of Belgium (Kellogg 1920: 193). A thin border of stylized lily-of-the-valley flowers surrounds the central images of the saints, symbolizing the return of happiness (Kellogg 1920: 193). It is encircled by a wider border including the coats of arms of the sixteen Belgian cities where the war was most fiercely fought amongst a background of stylized seaweed (Wardle 1989: 87). The seaweed references the Allied stand at the river Yser in 1914 when the dikes were breached, flooding the land and halting the German advance (Wardle 1989: 79). The outer, wide, scalloped border comprises alternating ferns and oval medallions each surmounted by an eel, referencing the Yser victory. The medallions include toadstools and sprigs of plants drawn from the local flora, such as ivy, grass, mistletoe, hawthorn, sloe, wood anemones, celandine, marguerites, violets, campion, snowdrops, wood sorrel, anemones, honeysuckle, and Solomon's seal (Wardle 1989: 87). The choices are symbolic, for example mushrooms and ferns symbolize rebirth following war as they grow out of rotting leaves toward the light (Cooreman 2018: 308). The hawthorn references St. Joseph of Arimathea who buried Jesus and was considered an important protector of war sufferers. Violets represent humility. Mistletoe, being evergreen, represents immortality. The entire tablecloth is edged with small ivy leaves, the symbol of endurance.

The Battle of Britain panel also incorporates floral iconography. The scalloped outer border is composed of ripening ears of corn, representing the season during which the battle took place. The central area at the base of the panel includes the floral emblems of the four countries of the United Kingdom: the English rose, the Scottish thistle, the Welsh daffodil, and the Northern Irish shamrock. The rose, thistle, and shamrock are also included in the two narrow borders that flank the images of bombed London landmarks on each side of the panel. At the top of the panel appear the floral emblems of other Allied countries, the airmen of which took part in the battle. These depict wattle for Australia, protea for South Africa, a fern leaf for New Zealand, and a maple leaf for Canada. Like the tablecloth, the panel also includes oak leaves representing strength and endurance.

Origins of the Lace Memorials

The needlelace tablecloth was commissioned as part of the war relief effort in Belgium during the First World War. It was designed as an official gift for the queen on her return to Belgium as a token of regard and to showcase the skills of the lacemakers. It also provided continued work, and therefore remuneration, for the lacemakers after the end of the war and was a special gift that highlighted the volunteer work of those who had managed the Lace Committee. In a similar way, the Nottingham lace panels were presented to airforce associations as patriotic tokens of regard for the part they had played in the Battle of Britain during the Second World War. They were commissioned by the manufacturer rather than an official body and were a showcase for the machine lace industry.

BELGIAN RELIEF FUND

The German army invaded and occupied Belgium in August 1914 and the British responded with a naval blockade to cut German supply routes. This resulted in a shortage of food and a subsequent threat of famine in Belgium. It was in these circumstances that the Commission for the Relief of Belgium (CRB) was established under the chairmanship of Herbert Hoover (US President from 1929 to 1933), who had recently organized the repatriation of 120,000 Americans trapped in Europe at the start of the war (McMillan 2018: 5). Alleviating the Belgian famine required keen negotiating skills, as Hoover had to reassure the Allies that the food would only be given to the civilian population and obtain assurances from the Germans that the food would not be requisitioned. The CRB organized the importation of food aid from many countries and, with the help of thousands of volunteers, enough food was imported to provide a basic meal of soup and bread for over 9 million people every day for four years (McMillan 2018: 6).

A contemporaneous account of how the relief was distributed and delivered is given by Charlotte Kellogg, an American writer and social activist, who was permitted to enter Belgium in July 1916 as the only female American member of the CRB (Kellogg 1917). She also returned in 1919 to report on the postwar condition of the civilian population (Kellogg 1920). When she visited in summer 1916, $250 million had already been raised and spent on relief, including securing ships to convey food to Rotterdam (Kellogg 1917: 4). She estimates that one ship docked with supplies every weekday and that 200 canal boats were constantly in use ferrying the supplies down the canals to the CRB warehouses throughout Belgium (Kellogg 1917: 28).

However, food and clothing were not the only means of relief. Before the war, Belgium had an international lace industry and at the outbreak of war approximately 50,000 women were supporting themselves, to some extent, through lace work (Kellogg 1917: 70). Most lace schools closed at the start of the war but local lace committees were set up in some areas, such as Bruges, to provide work for lacemakers and to buy their work for sale in Britain (Bruggeman 2018: 88). Other charitable groups such as the English Ambulance Service in Flanders and Flemish exiles in Britain also established lacemaking initiatives to raise funds (Bruggeman 2018: 89). Unfortunately, their efforts were hampered by the British naval blockade that not only hindered the importation of thread from Ireland and Britain, which was vital to the Belgian lace industry, but also the export of the finished lace.

Early in 1915, the Vicomtesse de Beughem, an American married to a Belgian, approached Hoover to explain the plight of the lacemakers and he agreed to help. He negotiated an amendment to the CRB agreement by which Britain agreed that a weighed amount of thread could be imported into Belgium and the corresponding weight of lace could be exported for sale in France, Britain, and the United States. The CRB guaranteed that no lace would be sold in the open market or in occupied territories, although permission was given for some lace to be sold in October and November 1915 at exhibitions in some Belgian cities (Kellogg 1917: 71). Lace that was not sold had to be held in the neutral city of Rotterdam (Kellogg 1917: 71). Orders for the war laces were managed through the CRB offices in London and most of the lace was sold through agents, shops, and department stores in London, Paris, New York, and other US cities (McMillan 2018: 6).

The organization that dealt with the lace and lacemakers was the Brussels Lace Committee, which oversaw the lace schools and regional lace committees, improved designs, and ensured that the lacemakers were paid fairly (McMillan 2018: 6). Thought was given to the designs and type of articles that would sell well in the target export countries (Kellogg 1917: 71). Different areas of Belgium specialized in specific types of lace and the regional committees were responsible for distributing the thread and transporting the resulting lace to the central depot in Brussels. Every piece of lace arriving in Brussels was carefully examined and any substandard work was rejected. The committee had been set up by members of *Les Amies de la Dentelle* with Ella Whitlock, the wife of the US Ambassador, as the honorary president (Wardle 1989: 79). It was eventually run, with the support of the CRB, by the Comtesse Elisabeth d'Oultremont, who was a lady-in-waiting to Queen Elisabeth, the Vicomtesse de Beughem, Madame Josse Allard, and the lace specialist Madame Kefer-Mali (Wardle 1989: 79; McMillan 2018: 6). They were supported by Ella Whitlock and Lou Herbert Hoover (McMillan 2018: 6). Their aim was not only to provide work for the lacemakers but also to ensure that a strengthened lace industry survived the war.

Approximately 45,000 lacemakers were employed by the Lace Committee and of these, 25,000 were considered skilled workers, 10,000 were of average ability, and 10,000 were beginners (Kellogg 1917: 72). In order to help as many women as possible there was a cap on the amount of lace that each person could make; no one could work more than thirty hours a week or receive more than 3 francs in wages (Kellogg 1917: 72). When Kellogg visited the Lace Committee in November 1916 it had already dispensed 6 million francs in wages and on average employed each lacemaker for two weeks every month (1917: 72).

This resumption of lacemaking and the export of Belgian lace not only gave the workers a source of income but also hope and pride that they were working for the war effort. The committee also assured Kellogg that when the war ended, they would return the queen's chosen industry to her three years ahead of where she left it, with improved standards and with Belgium re-established as the lacemaker of the world (Kellogg 1917: 73).

BATTLE OF BRITAIN

The Battle of Britain was a pivotal moment in the Second World War, not only strategically but also as a huge morale boost for Britain and therefore was an obvious choice for a commemorative panel (Quarini 2020). The German air offensive began in July 1940 when airfields were bombed, in an attempt to destroy the British air defenses, as a prelude to invading Britain. Toward the end of August some areas of London were bombed, followed by attacks on other cities, after which the sustained aerial bombardment of London began in the Blitz. The crisis of the battle occurred on September 15 when the Germans sent two waves of 500 aircraft across the English Channel, resulting in the greatest defeat they had experienced; it became known as the Battle of Britain. Two days later Hitler canceled his invasion plans, although the Blitz continued until May 1941.

In Britain, during the Second World War, machine lacemaking was strictly controlled and plain net machines and some curtain machines were repurposed to make mosquito, sandfly, and camouflage nets for the war effort. Lace could still be made for export, but thread and a labor force were in short supply; therefore little was made, although the manufacturers maintained the lace machines in the hope of renewing the industry after the war. It was in this atmosphere that the idea for the Battle of Britain panel was conceived. From the nineteenth century onwards lace manufacturers had made large lace panels to commemorate events and people, mainly as showpieces for their stands at international exhibitions. It was while admiring one of these old panels in 1942 that the managing director of Dobson and Browne decided that the company should produce a lace panel commemorating the Battle of Britain (Quarini 2020). The Battle of Britain panel therefore was commissioned almost on a whim as a patriotic project to thank those who had turned the tide of the war and saved the country.

Design and Manufacture

THE DESIGNERS

Both commemorative lace pieces were designed professionally, the tablecloth by Isidore de Rudder, a well-known Belgian artist, and the panel by Harry Cross, a machine lace designer. Both had studied flowers and plants during their artistic training and accurate depictions of flora feature prominently in both pieces of lace.

The Brussels Lace Committee was keen to obtain high-quality designs for the war laces and Isidore de Rudder was one of the designers they approached. He came from an artistic family and although influenced by the Pre-Raphaelites he worked in many styles and many branches of the applied arts and was well known for a series of embroideries he produced in collaboration with his wife in 1890 (Wardle 1989: 74). The original designs of the tablecloth and other war laces are housed in the Royal Museum of Art and History, Brussels.

The designer chosen for the Battle of Britain panel was Harry Cross, who had been head designer at Dobson and Browne before his retirement. He was an alumnus of the Nottingham Art School and had spent his working life in the drapery and napery section of the lace trade, designing curtains, tablecloths, and bedspreads. He based his design of the panel on the layout used for previous commemorative panels with a central large design, flanked by columns of vignettes, interspersed with floral iconography on either side.

Most of the designs for the Battle of Britain panel no longer exist but the family of Harry Cross have some tracings of parts of the original design. These working tracings are interesting because they reveal alterations made during the designing process, showing for example how he altered the way the famous words from Churchill's speech were incorporated into the panel. Although only a few of these tracings remain, Harry Cross decided, when he was 92 years old, to paint a life-sized color copy of the entire panel. He achieved this by painting each section separately and these beautiful paintings have recently been loaned to the Lace Archive at Nottingham Trent University thanks to Harry Cross's family (Quarini 2020).

MANUFACTURE

Those who made the two lace artifacts could not be more different. The tablecloth was made in a convent by women working by hand using a needle and thread and the panel was made by men operating a lace machine in a textile factory. However, what they both have in common is that they were made in difficult wartime conditions by skilled textile workers with great expertise in using their chosen materials. In both cases those who made the lace required the highest standards of technique and interpretation to fulfill the ideas of the designers—a fact acknowledged by Harry Cross when he included in the panel the names of the two draftsmen who were responsible for interpreting his design into the instructions for the lace machine.

The needlelace tablecloth, like many other handmade laces, was made in separate parts that were subsequently joined together. Kellogg describes seeing 220 of the pieces of lace that were to form the queen's tablecloth ready for assembly when she visited the convent at Erembodeghem in 1919 (1920: 190). At the time of Kellogg's visit, the convent was freezing cold and in disrepair and had been requisitioned in turn by the German, Italian, and French armies. The French still occupied four classrooms; despite this, there was enough coal for a small fire in the lace room where girls aged about ten were working at their lace (Kellogg 1920: 193). However, the tablecloth would have been worked by some of the older students, local lacemakers and the nuns, all chosen for the expertise of their lacemaking.

Reviving the Lace Industries

In the long term, neither piece of commemorative lace succeeded in reviving its industry. Although Belgian lace was bought during the war for charitable reasons, after 1918 less lace was used in fashion and furnishing and certainly less handmade lace, which was too expensive to compete with machine-made lace. The fashion historian James Laver notes that in the early twentieth century there was "a passion for lace in every part of the gown," but by 1910 fashions had become simpler and remained so through the war and in its aftermath (1972: 216). The displays of original and artistic machine lace at the 1910 Brussels International Exhibition raised its prestige in comparison with handmade lace, resulting in the latter being no longer commercially viable. The lace historian Pat Earnshaw notes that by 1926 only three specialist "lacemen" remained in London, supplying lace for weddings and baptisms but no longer for fashion (Earnshaw 1985: 106).

The demise of handmade lace finally ended the "large-scale production of high-quality pieces by the Belgian lace industry" (Wardle 1989: 88). Although a lacemakers' union was established in 1919 as a "cooperative sales syndicate," it was disbanded in 1924 (Bruggeman 2018: 97). However, Earnshaw suggests that the industry should not be mourned; she notes that most lacemakers worked extremely long hours for little pay, and in many cases ruined their eyesight merely to inflate the visible importance of those who wore lace and did not appreciate the skill involved in its production (Earnshaw 1985: 108).

Although machine lace appeared to benefit from the demise of handmade lace, its own survival was in question. Although beautiful machine lace was produced throughout the 1930s for evening wear, the heyday of lace as a fashion fabric was over. When the Second World War ended in 1945, machine lace dress fabric was briefly popular in Britain because, unlike other material, no clothing coupons were required to buy it (Earnshaw 1985: 111). There was also a brief increase in the demand for curtain lace as people rebuilt their homes and lives; however, the British machine lace industry never recovered to previous levels. In 1935 the machine lace workforce in Nottingham and the East Midlands numbered 14,310 but by 1945 it had reduced to 6,630 (Mason 2010: 109). In the early twenty-first century only two machine lacemaking companies survive in the UK, one making drapery and napery and the other producing specialist fashion laces.

During her visit to Belgium after the war, Kellogg found many lacemakers were grateful to the Lace Committee for helping them and even raising wages during the war. Many sought assurances that the committee would continue their work and she found it frustrating that she could not reassure them (Kellogg 1920: 102). She was cautiously optimistic, however, and when she met some trainee lace teachers in Bruges, she noted that although their future was uncertain they should have "no difficulty in securing places" (1920: 164). Kellogg was also heartened to meet Dr. Rubbens, who had recently established the Zele "Trade Union Lace School" for bobbin lace and was planning another for needlelace, but she notes that the designs the lacemakers are using are not as "light" as the popular French ones (Kellogg 1920: 267).

Kellogg's concern about designs is a valid one. When she visited Herzele, the lacemakers emphasized the importance of good design by explaining that before the war the lace dealer had distributed his own copyright patterns and during the war they had received many beautiful designs from the Lace Committee, but whenever that source was cut off "they realized their helplessness"
(Kellogg 1920: 242). Their solution was that some of them should be trained in designing so they could devise their own patterns (Kellogg 1920: 242).

It seems, however, that even professional designers were not the solution. Although de Rudder had designed many of the Belgian war laces, when the tablecloth was exhibited in the Belgian pavilion at the 1925 Paris Exhibition his "solemn, static" cloth was not as popular as the "light-hearted figurative designs" of the Czechoslovakian lace on display, which "stole the show" (Wardle 1989: 87). The UK machine lace industry, despite having access to a wealth of professionally trained lace designers, focused on cutting costs and in many cases was not interested in new designs, preferring to reproduce period styles. Many others sought designers who could "reproduce another company's design, retaining the style of the original, but with sufficient adaptations to make it appear to be a fresh new design" (Coles et al. 2019: 22). This lack of design input in lace fabrics probably contributed to the decline of the machine lace industry.

Commercial Success

Undoubtedly the CRB and the associated work of the Lace Committee was successful; it saved Belgium from starvation and was instrumental in persuading the United States to join the Allies' military efforts to liberate Europe. Allied propaganda often used the image of a Belgian lacemaker bent over her lace pillow in a war-torn landscape to represent the suffering in Belgium (Bruggeman 2018: 88) and this figure obviously resonated with the public and increased fundraising efforts. The Lace Committee also provided women with employment and an income, allowing them to help feed their families, and enabled many orphans and children to attend the convent lace schools where they received food and protection. Many lacemakers came together to make lace communally and this probably provided them with comfort and companionship. The act of sitting and absorbing themselves in their lacemaking may have provided a short respite from the concerns of the war and the knowledge that they were contributing to the war effort also raised morale. However, after the First World War, the London office of the CRB contained 4 million francs worth of extremely high-quality handmade lace, suggesting that although the Lace Committee had helped the lacemakers, it had failed to sell enough of their lace (Wardle 1989: 88). Wardle notes that the Belgian war lace project, although "worthy and well intentioned," was not a commercial success because "philanthropic energy failed to be combined with business acumen" (1989: 87).

At the end of the Second World War, the Battle of Britain panel engendered much interest, but this was not converted into sales of lace. It was exhibited at the 1947 and 1949 British Industries Fairs in London and Birmingham as well as in Australia and New Zealand (Farr 2015). However, it was seen as a feat of manufacturing, and a patriotic endeavor that resonated with the mood of the time in celebrating the victory and the ties that bound the Commonwealth rather than an example of furnishing fabric. The manufacturers did not attempt to commercialize the panel by reproducing sections of it for sale or even producing smaller commemorative panels for consumers to purchase.

The panel was also linked to charitable causes, not during its manufacture but after the war, when it was used in fundraising efforts for the Royal Air Force (RAF). One of the London churches severely damaged by the German bombing was St. Clement Danes and after the war it was decided to rebuild it and dedicate it as the central church of the RAF. The money for the rebuilding was raised by general subscription and as part of the fundraising effort one of the Battle of Britain panels underwent a twenty-month tour of the country in 1947. The panel was displayed in department stores and was very popular—one estimate suggesting that in Newcastle alone 250,000 people came to see it (Quarini 2020: 33).

Conclusion

Lace seems an unlikely material for a war memorial; however, as a medium for commemorating world wars that involved civilians to such a great extent, it appears more apt. Images of war on lace curtains and tablecloths speak of domesticity subverted. These laces entwine the personal and the political and embody quotidian responses to war. The nature of lace as a twisting of threads also epitomizes the war spirit of people coming together and overcoming threats by their joint enterprise. Even the designs of the lace, in small separate pieces or panels, suggests that small increments, like battles won, combine gradually to achieve the whole. However, it seems that those commissioning these memorials chose lace not because it was the ideal medium, but because they wanted to commemorate the war in the only way they could and highlight the small part their industries had played in it, both socially and materially.

Both of these lace initiatives harked back to more prosperous times to raise morale, retain employment and, crucially, to revive their respective industries following a period of decline. They were both initiated just before their respective wars ended when their designers and commissioners obviously thought the war was nearly won. Harry Cross began designing the lace panel in 1944 (Quarini 2020: 27) and Kellogg comments that the women who made the tablecloth had worked on the pieces "during the darkest days of the war" (Kellogg 1920: 193). This suggests they were begun as initiatives to raise morale and in a spirit of optimism to encourage the lacemakers.

Both pieces provide a double memorialization, ostensibly to two world wars but also to two lace industries that had flourished and competed in the nineteenth century but were eventually swept away by the changing way of life engendered by the wars. Interestingly, neither piece is celebratory and both highlight the destruction and symbolism of war, perhaps prefiguring the demise of their own industries.

These two commemorative memorials of war, recorded in lace, thirty-seven years apart, highlight the social effects of war, both in their manufacture and themes, and the role played by hand and machine lacemakers in that process. Both raised morale and provided employment for those who made them. Though neither led to the revival of their industry, both displayed exacting workmanship and both remain memorials to the ravages of war and the resilience of those who experience it. Although separated by time, place, and function, they stand as memorials not only to two world wars but also to the lace industries they represent.

References

Bruggeman, M. (2018), *Lace in Flanders: History and Contemporary Art*, Tielt: Lannoo Publishers.

Coles, R., Briggs-Goode, A., Baxter, G. (2019), "Principles and Pilfering: Nottingham Lace Design Pedagogy", *TEXTILE*, 18 (1): 12–23.

Cooreman, R. (2018), "Iconographic study of War Lace Masterpieces. A Case Study: D.4432", in: M. Bruggeman (ed),

Lace in Flanders: History and Contemporary Art, 308–9, Tielt: Lannoo Publishers.

Earnshaw, P. (1985), *Lace in Fashion*, Guildford: Gorse Publications.

Farr, B. (2015), *Battle of Britain Commemorative Lace Panels Illustrated*, published by the author.

Kellogg, C. (1920), *Bobbins of Belgium*, New York: Funk & Wagnalls Co.

Kellogg, C. (1917), *Women of Belgium: Turning Tragedy into Triumph*, Moscow: Dodo Press.

Laver, J. (1972 originally 1969), *A Concise History of Costume*, London: Thames and Hudson.

Mason, S. A. (2010), *Nottingham Lace 1760s-1950s. The Machine-made Lace Industry in Nottinghamshire, Derbyshire and Leicestershire*, Nottingham: Alan Sutton Publishing.

McMillan, E. (2018), "Gratitude in Lace. World War I, Famine Relief, and Belgian Lacemakers", *Lacemaking, The Newsletter of the Lace Society*, no. 222: 5–8.

Quarini, C. (2020), "Unravelling the Battle of Britain lace panel", *TEXTILE*, 18 (1): 24–38.

Wardle, P. (1989), "War and Peace. Lace Designs by the Belgian Sculptor Isidore de Rudder (1855–1943)", *Bulletin van het Rijksmuseum*, 37 (2): 73–90.

"Cloth, for me, is a puissant visual code for ethnic assignation and cultural promotion. Wearing certain cloth types bestows on us sociocultural importance contextual to the value systems of our respective societies."

Clement Emeka Akpang

4

Cloth, Nationalism, and Cultural Identity: The Symbolism of Traditional Attire in Defining Nigeria's Diverse Ethnic Indigenism

CLEMENT EMEKA AKPANG

Introduction

A complex relation to identity, style, and social stratification eclipses the functionality of cloth as a protective covering or portrayal of modesty. Today, the public perception of clothes and the specific cloth societies use in making them depends on how they convey style, personality, and certain ideologies implied by distinct customs. This sociological connection means that fabrics and their embellishment reflect a sense of self or collective expression and identification, thus allowing for the possibility of reading cloth from diverse perspectives—as articles of communication and identity or for expressing nationalism and indigenism. Alison Lurie, a specialist on dress iconography, observes that clothes communicate through nonverbal announcements codified in the material of specific fabrics and societal references to their symbolic designs (1991). Lurie's theory presents cloth as a powerful communicative device for constructing a person's persona and cultural identity based on nonverbal cues from which assumptions on first impressions derive. While clothes communicate through the symbolism of their constituent cloth, they also project unique identities on people and communities. In this sense, a piece of cloth constitutes a material reference that symbolizes individual, collective, or community assignation to a specific race as "an important part of the identity construction process" (Dorrance 2011: xi). This ability to construct identities and reference people's ethnic origins and sociological and political alignment means that cloth transcends the normativism of covering to become powerful semiotic devices. They draw visual boundaries between people, linking individuals with real social identities, thus, transforming those who wear them into allegorical cultural and social subjects of specific civilizations (Özdil 2021).

The Afro-Caribbean political philosopher Frantz Fanon refers to this transformative power of cloth in his theory that "the way people clothe themselves, together with the tradition of dress and finery that custom implies, constitutes the most distinctive form of a society's uniqueness. Significant areas of civilization and immense cultural regions can be grouped based on original, specific men's and women's dress" (2007: 19). In other words, cloth helps categorize community, ethnic, state, and national allegiances as symbols of power, fostering nationalism, culturalism, and indigenism. In corroborating Fanon's theory, Kiera Seidenberg argues that cloth represents a means of acknowledging indigenous history, customs, and specific philosophical persuasions (2018). Fanon and Seidenberg's theorization of cloth and clothes as a reference to indigenism best describes Africa's clothing cultures. In Africa, clothes indicate socially significant categories, with distinct cloth typologies representing and emphasizing ethnic groups and even national affiliation, as exemplified by the Ghana *Kente* cloth. Nigeria's diverse ethnicity, numbering over 370, makes the country a gallery of compelling garbs inspired by indigenous affiliated fabrics that symbolize different ethnic cosmologies. In this chapter, I explore the reflection of indigenism in Nigeria through ethnic-specific cloth associations. I begin by analyzing the precolonial[1] context of cloth and clothing and then reflect on colonialism's impact on Nigeria's clothing culture as the point of departure to establish the entangled origins and context of cloth in contemporary Nigeria. As the crux of the chapter, I emphasize cloth as a form of cultural identification and expression in the Niger Delta, Yoruba, and Hausa ethnic groups. The aim is to connect history, indigenous cosmologies, and religion to customized traditional clothes as related sociological constructs in Nigerian cultural experiences. Although the chapter does not focus on dressing as its main subject, it makes overarching reference to clothes simply as a mechanism to deconstruct the iconography of special cloth in each ethnic group.

The Context of Cloth in Premodern and Colonial Nigeria

Before trade contact with Europeans in the fifteenth century and imperialism in the nineteenth century, many ethnic groups that now comprise Nigeria had developed clothing traditions centered on particular cloth geographically suited to their terrains or iconographically reflective of their worldviews. The British explorer Captain Hugh Clapperton noted that the people of the black continent had long developed unique textiles in his expedition diary through the *Bight of Benin, Niger River, Kano, Katsina, Sokoto,* and *Zaria* (1823). Clapperton's reference to uniqueness regarding the dressing of Africans relates to a traditional sophistication in cotton processing, weaving, and fabric embellishment. As far back as the 1400s, weaving, tie-dye, and embroidery in the northern parts of the then Sokoto Caliphate, as well as advances in cotton/raffia weaving and explorations in bark cloth production in the Eastern, Central, and South-South regions, were already commonplace. Clapperton's submission—one of the earliest to record premodern African advances in clothes production—dispels the libel epithet of primitive-nude misrepresentation in Western narratives by colonialists to frame the barbaric and primitive Africa as the obverse of Europe's modernity to legitimize colonial subjugation.[2]

With developed clothing traditions, premodern inhabitants of present-day Nigeria clad themselves distinctly. Women predominantly wore locally produced wrappers embellished with symbols such as *Uli*, Insibidi, and other ornaments. In the Niger Delta region, some women wore wrappers around their waist, crossed at diagonals around their chest, and anchored behind their necks to cover their breasts. In communities in the East, women fastened wrappers under their armpits. Men equally tied wrappers around their waists, complemented with indigenous caps to signify their age and social status. The same context applied to the northern part of Nigeria regarding men's and women's clothes that would only change significantly with influences from Sudan and the Islamic religion. Traditional cotton wrappers used by Nigerians were thick and neatly woven, but their iconography exceeded their materiality. Although wrappers made from raffia and cotton were large rectangular pieces of cloth, more significantly, they were items of social stratification. Those who occupied the upper echelon of society appeared in cotton wrappers as their identitarian cloth. At the same time, those at the lower spectrum of the societal scale predominantly wore commonplace raffia wrappers. As traditional cloth, wrappers also differentiated age grades in the Northern, Central, Southern, and Eastern regions. Amongst the Itshekiris, Urhobos, Kalabaris, Nupes, Ijebus, and other tribes, young girls anchored their wrappers behind their necks while advanced women tied them under their armpits. As the dominant precolonial cloth typology, wrappers constituted material modalities of identification and the hierarchizing of Nigerian communities.

The advent of colonialism altered clothing and the symbolism of cloth in Nigeria, particularly in the Southern, Eastern, and Western parts of the country, where wrappers lost their position as the dominant cloth. With the flooding of European materials into the country as part of the imperial process, a new clothing culture emerged that hybridized indigenism with Westernization throughout colonial Nigeria. *Thingification*—the destruction of the material culture of the colonized *Other* by pretending to rid them of fanatical behavior (Césaire 1955; Fanon 2004)—inspired widespread cultural cleansing.[3] The imperialist notion of modernity tied to the abandonment of antiquity, including art, dressing, ethnic cloth, and music, led to attacks on the material cultures of the colonized as primitive and barbaric; this coloniality logic legitimated cultural imperialism and the eradication of indigenous customs (Olaitan 2021). In colonial Nigeria, colonialist-imposed modernity in the model of Western thoughts created an inferiority complex permeating different artistic expressions and material culture, including the colonized attire. The colonizers also developed a concept of corporateness tied to European clothing conventions, just as they intensified the condemnation of traditional African clothes as primitive. Another factor was the rise of Nigerian colonial elites with Western-style education who imbibed the colonial logic of anti-traditionalism as the hallmark of modernity. Keen to demonstrate their modern advancement, these emergent elites adopted the attire of civilization projected to them in the typologies of European cloth and fashion (Ekeh 1975).

Consequently, handwoven wrappers gave way to Western cashmere and silk as part of the imperial cultural imposition to contain and civilize the natives. Therefore, silk and cashmere became a tool for subjugation and control during colonialism, further facilitated by church missions that promulgated the philosophy of modernizing Africans tied to the concept of modesty as morality.[4] The French philosopher Gilles Lipovetsky succinctly articulates this imposition of European clothing on the colonized as a form of control: "it [fashion] has become an exceptional institution, a sociohistorical reality characteristic of the west and modernity itself. From this standpoint, fashion is a way out of the world of tradition, negating the age-old power of the traditional past" (1994: 4). Lipovetsky's observation reveals the philosophical intersection of Western clothes, fashion, modernity, coloniality, and imperialism, thus highlighting the implications of European cultural imperialism through the imposition of Western-centric garments and fabrics in the guise of civilization.

By the late 1920s, dress paraphernalia and cloth divided Nigeria into two publics. Elite men and women who adopted Western-style clothes to demonstrate their education and employment portfolio appeared in European machine-weaved silk and cashmere. Furthermore, the colonialists enforced these cloth typologies and European appearance as official dress codes in offices and schools to enculturate the colonized into Western civility and modernity. A second public also existed in Nigeria, which comprised influential natives without Western education. They adopted a creole form of dressing to project their new status outwardly. It hybridized the traditional and Western so that while most men appeared with traditionally woven wrappers or thick cotton trousers, they combined them with Western silk or cashmere shirts. Women juxtaposed wrappers in silk, cashmere, or cotton with European-style blouses. For this group, such creole adaptation represented a conscious hybridism as a visual projection of empowerment by the colonized to seize the apparatus of Western modernity (cashmere and silk cloth) and localize them to maintain their identity during imperialism, articulated by Homi Bhabha in *The Location of Culture* (2012). This conscious hybridism explains why, for example, silk or cashmere shirts and European-style hats became juxtaposed with traditional cotton wrappers among men of the *Kalabari* ethnic group of southern Nigeria.

At the apotheosis of imperialism in Nigeria, cashmere and silk were the symbolic agentic modalities for conforming to Western canons of dressing to obtain employment, education, missionary salvation, and civilization. In other words, silk and cashmere constituted the symbol of modernity and the mark of subjugation simultaneously as the material force of cultural imperialism. This context of clothes in colonial Nigeria changed during the independence decade. The rise of Pan-Africanism and the promulgation of cultural revival as a mechanism for decolonization revived mild interest in indigenous clothing and cloth association. Diverse assortments of indigenous cloth became central visual frameworks for Pan-African resistance to colonialism. Nigerian nationalist politicians advocated the return to traditional roots as a visual protest. Thus, they began appearing in reinvented traditional attires invoking the indigenous sentiments associated with ethnic-specific cloths to express their indigenous identities as a form of empowerment. Pioneer politicians such as Chief Obafemi Awolowo, Tafawa Balewa, and Chief Nnamdi Azikiwe adorned traditionally inspired clothing made from locally handwoven cotton or adaptations of European fabrics as an expression of resistance to cultural imperialism and to foster decolonization advocacies. Their cultural revivalist efforts galvanized a sense of traditionalism in Nigerian clothing, which extends to this contemporary age. Although Nigerian official spaces continue to vilify traditional attires, different cloth types unique to specific groups still abound, promoting ethnic assignation.

Cloth as Symbolic Expression and Cultural Identity

In Nigeria, each ethnic extraction has developed or adopted a unique cloth significant to its history and way of life as symbolic cultural expression. In this chapter, I have chosen to discuss three types associated with the Hausas, Yorubas, and Niger Deltans to attempt a sociological theory of cloth in Nigeria.

LACE AS EXPRESSION OF OPULENCE IN THE NIGER DELTA

The Niger Delta region covers a large geographical expanse with many ethnic groups, including the *Urhobos, Itsekiris, Isokos, Ijaws, Kalabaris, Okrikas, Ikweres, Ibibios, Efiks*, and numerous others. However, a dress style of elaborate and flamboyant garbs, particularly the dominance of lace cloth, bounds this vast area. Occasions in the Niger Delta are a carnival of vibrancy, displaying opulence through expensive fabrics such as damask and laces as the pageantry of wealth. Among the men, one distinct clothing style is prominent. They wear a free-flowing knee-length, long-sleeved lace top with cufflinks over a brightly colored lace wrapper tied around their waist. Their shoes are locally fashioned, made with velvet material, and bearing the wearer's initials in stylish embroidery. The full glare of the glamour of Niger Deltans' traditional attire reflects in the appearance of women, who are often excessively clad. Throughout the region, women wear fitted puff-shoulder blouses stoned with beads and tie two wrappers of expensive lace measuring three yards (2.74 m) each.

While this attire is prominent amongst *Urhobo, Itsekiri, Isoko, Ijaw, Okrika*, and *Ikwere* women, for those of the

Kalabari, *Ibibio*, and *Efik* extractions, the *Onyonyo* provides a variant of the region's identity. The *Onyonyo* is a free-flowing adaptation of a Victorian-style gown richly embellished with coral beads and culturally localized for the projection of sophisticated womanhood in the region. It is made with lace fabric produced in Lustenau, Vorarlberg, southwestern Austria, but decorated and sewn to traditional fitting in *Efik* style. With Calabar recognized as the hub of Scottish missionary activities, Mary Slessor popularized this dress amongst the natives of *Efik* land, which they have since adopted as their indigenous identity.

As the prevalent cloth typology, lace holds an extensive symbolism of the region's experience, indicating a sociological connection between the people of the Niger Delta and their clothing tradition. The opulence displayed by both men and women through a localized Western material (lace) is a visual reference to their cosmologies, history, and pride, especially viewed through the context of women's clothing. Although foreign, lace is culturally symbolic in helping the region materialize its canonization of women as extraordinary beings. The reason is that Niger Deltans celebrate women for their cardinal role as progenitors of the human race and moral arbiters of society. More so, women are considered the visual symbolization of a man's wealth. In other words, society judges a man's financial and social status through his wife's glamour (Williams 2015). The *Onyonyo*—an overflowing layering of expensive laces—best symbolizes this extreme celebration of womanhood. According to Louisa Onuoha, the former director of the Nigerian National Museum, "both the Lace and *Onyonyo* speak opulence, radiating beauty, elegance, and glamour. They are both symbols of prestige and convey supreme elegance and value" (2017: 5). Through *Onyonyo*, the Efiks and Ibibios deploy lace to radiate royalty and establish the wearer as the center of attraction in all gatherings. In it, women of the region assume queenly status as they glide in opulent glamour for the admiration of others. Lace, therefore, constitutes the material codification of adulation for women culturally materialized into bogus attire in the region. In this sense, it represents their glamour, royalty, beauty, and feminine grace. By implication, as a traditional symbol, lace holds a cosmological value coding of femininity that defines ideal indigenous womanhood, thus exemplifying a unique case of the adaptation and recontextualization of a Western material brought to Nigeria through the agency of imperialism into a prestigious ethnic symbol.

Figure 4.1 Onyonyo dress of the Efiks. © Mary Enembe Edet.

Secondly, lace also acts as a symbol of pride for the region's precolonial advancement. It serves as the material affirmation of the region as the first to make contact with Europeans. Thus, the region's love for lace cloth is a materialization of its precolonial intercontinental entanglement, proving recorded advancement before colonialism (Williams 1995). Lace further speaks to the region's influence during colonialism as a major producer and exporter of palm oil: the British Oil Rivers Protectorate. It references its wealth in natural resources. Abundant crude oil endows the Niger Delta region, which is why it is recognized globally as the petroleum-rich region of West Africa—the engine of Nigeria's wealth and economy (Balouga 2009). In this sense, the flamboyant padding of shimmering lace in men's and women's clothing invokes a materialistic sense of riches as the owners of Africa's most extensive oil-producing lands. Particularly for women, the cloth is a transformative device that transposes mundanity to sophisticated glamour (Oduah and Bohn 2014). That is,

Figure 4.2 Onyonyo dress as worn by a cultural dance troupe, Yenago, Nigeria. Photography: © PIUS UTOMI EKPEI/AFP via Getty Images.

lace animates their social stratifications in an instance of a dashing appearance. Thus, through them, opulence has become the identity of Niger Deltans globally. To speak of the region's dress is to invoke the vibrancy of colors and the display of expensive laces, which connects historical and modern advancement to the richness of the oil wetlands of the South-South area of Nigeria. Lace fabric, therefore, represents a cultural symbol of wealth, opulence, the adulation of women, and a reference to Niger Delta precolonial trade interactions with Europe now immortalized through a unique fabric in contemporary society.

YORUBA ASO-OKE AND ADIRE AS SYMBOLS OF ETHNIC SOPHISTICATION

From prehistory, the Yorubas of southwestern Nigeria have developed unique dress codes in line with their philosophies of life. *Aso Ibile*, *Ibante*, *Kijipa*, *Buba* (for women), *Buba*, *Esiki*, *Sapara*, *Dandogo*, *Agbada*, *Gbariye*, *Sulia*, *Oyala*, and *Ewu Awoleke* (for men) are traditional clothes popular with the indigenes of *Oyo*, *Ile Ife*, *Ilesha*, *Ibadan*, *Ilorin*, and *Ijebu-Ode*. This plethora of clothing owes much to their weaving tradition and ethnic philosophy of sophisticated appearance as a cultural identity. *Aso-Oke* constitutes the defining feature of their clothing culture. It is a famous traditional cloth worn by the ordinary, noble, and royal for all occasions in Yorubaland, including weddings, coronations, and rites of passage. Used for women's wrapper/wrapper skirts (*Iro*), blouses (*Buba*), and shawls (*Pele*), or men's shirts (*Buba*), bogus trousers (*Shokoto*), and tunic coveralls (*Agbada*), *Aso-Oke* is the material transposition of Yoruba philosophies of sophistication into visual form. Through it, one can deconstruct Yoruba cosmologies and philosophies.

The Yorubas believe in hierarchical public life, and cloth is vital in defining their social stratification (Clarke 1976). According to Bukola Oyeniyi, since the Yorubas conceive of clothes as an assemblage of modifications that

Reading the Thread 56

supplements the human body, "to be a Yorùbá man or woman is, therefore, to dress well and to dress well is to be a Yorùbá man or woman—Yorùbáness, therefore, is impossible without Yorùbá dress and Yorùbá dress is impossible without Yorùbáness" (2012: 2). Elaborate dressing to augment one's visage, to build social stratification and public perception of elegance is the core concept of Yorubaness. It (Yorubaness) translates as the overarching display of material affluence. The agentic modality to expressing such Yorubaness is the *Aso-Oke* and their stylishly embellished fabric called *Adire*. *Aso-Oke* is a densely woven cloth that displays an abundance of cotton. It encapsulates the material codification of Yoruba's traditional philosophy of sophisticated dressing as a reflection of a charismatic personality. Yoruba cosmology holds that clothes convey one's personality and social status (Onyinye 2022b). *Aso-Oke* symbolizes that sophistication among men and women. It represents a timeless material culture with which the Yorubas negotiate and explicate their socioeconomic space; it is an epitome of their pageantry in dress and a signifying identification of their ethnic extraction. It also represents the Yoruba advancement in cotton production. The southwest is the largest cotton producer—a significant crop of great importance to Nigeria's economy (Kriger 2005). The abundance of this crop and the people's ability to harness its qualities as early as the fifteenth century led to the advancement in textile production that they pride themselves on. *Aso-Oke*, therefore, is also a symbol of agricultural advancement reflected in cotton's abundance and textile exploitation, especially as it (*Aso-Oke*) translates as cloth from the hinterland's material wealth.

Yoruba clothes also provide perspectives on the region's sociological orientation. The Yorubas are gregarious, often appearing in traditional uniforms known as *Aso-Ebi* to mark cultural festivities and authenticate family ties. Their materialistic social sense of solidarity demonstrated by *Aso-Ebi* "reflects a model where families relate in a web of links that offers support and patronage to social group members who are celebrants in events" (Oladejo 2022: 1). Today, any mention of *Aso-Ebi* throughout Nigeria is tantamount to merriments due to its southwestern cultural affiliation. *Aso-Ebi* is also crucial in symbolizing the people's pride in their region's well-developed premodern kingdoms. Yorubaland was the most urbanized in precolonial Africa; the Yorubas formed numerous kingdoms, each centered on a capital city ruled by a hereditary king or *Oba*. Elaborate festivals, highlighted by the display of sophisticated traditional attires, marked the celebration of their kingdoms, and still do so. While the rich density of *Aso-Oke* implicitly and explicitly expresses this symbolism, *Adire*, one of the fabrics used for the production of *Aso-Ebi*, holds more ethnic cosmological associations in Yorubaland. *Adire* is another iconic traditional cloth; its uniqueness lies in rich surface embellishments, characterized by the population of indigenous symbols composed into motifs and expertly distributed on the fabric surface using the wax resist method (batik). The ideographs on *Adire* are the direct transposition of traditional ideologies in graphic systems onto the fabric so that the wearer becomes a mobile conveyor of indigenous Yoruba beliefs. *Adire* thus symbolizes cultural promotion in the face of extreme globalization and a material link between premodern and contemporary Yorubas.

According to Seun Adeyemi, *Adire* is a symbol of Yoruba cultural heritage that conveys ethnic ideas through distinct patterns defined by indigenous idiosyncrasies (2019). Popular symbols on *Adire* include zoomorphic and floral forms such as *Adaba*, *Agbufon Opeere*, *Pepeye*, and *Tolotolo*. Others include *Ejo*, arthropods, annelids, mollusca, pisces, and amphibians. Plants are also prominent symbols, including *Ewe Ege*, *Ogede Agbagba*, *Koko*, *Odan*, and *Fulawa Koro Owu*. Stylizations of kings and queens also feature as standard motifs. There are other dominant celestiomorphic ideographs, such as *Irawo* and *Osupa*. Skewmorphic ideographs (adaptations of manufactured objects) such as *Yeti*, *Ileke Bebe*, *Amuga*, *Sekere*, *Akete*, *Aago Owo*, crown, staff, cowries, and *Ilu Gangan* are commonplace.

Each category holds iconological connections to the Yorubaland, thus conveying the people's cultural norms in design forms. For example, cowries represent money; cassava leaves represent the flourishing of life. Talking drums are symbolic of the constellation of Yoruba sounds and music. They also convey specific messages and accentuate traditional festivals. Earrings project the customary injunction for all sons and daughters of the land to hear only good news. Mirrors represent reflection in two dimensions: personal meditation and the reflection of others in one's life as a guide to interpersonal relations. Guinea corn projects a cultural adage that the hand that feeds (gives) never lacks. With this rich constellation of ideographs,

Adire cloth conveys deep traditional philosophies that define Yoruba ethnicity, codified into distinct ideographs for fabric embellishment. In this sense, *Adire* does more than cover the body. It is a statement of traditional belief systems and a modality to visually staking one's claim to ethnic assignation. This symbolism explains why Pa Johnson Olubokola posits that "in wearing *Adire*, the wearer propagates indigenous wisdom so that they become the conduit for edifying society through their mobiliary display" (2022). The iconography of *Aso-Oke* and *Adire* as a visual articulation of ethnic identity and class structure is practiced globally by the Yorubas (Ijimakinwa 2020). The southwest region shares clothing sensibilities with *Hausa* and *Nupe* ethnic groups from the northern part of Nigeria; however, what sets them apart is the Hausa's affinity for brocade fabrics (Oladejo 2022).

BROCADE BABBAR RIGA AS HAUSA EXPRESSION OF BIGNESS

Hausas and Fulanis are unique ethnic groups in Northern Nigeria with a clothing sense rooted in strict religious and societal norms. They are populated in *Kano, Katsina, Bauchi, Lafia, Kebbi, Sokoto*, and *Yobe* and are famous for weaving and tie-dying traditions. Amongst the Hausas, men dress in bright colors of simple flowing gowns and trousers in monochromatic shades of white, sky, or indigo blue. This dress code is a standard form for ordinary citizens; a more flamboyant clothing typology abounds amongst the wealthy and affluent—*Babbar Riga* (King of Clothes). The *Babbar Riga* is an elaborate outer robe with dense embroidery designs around the neck and chest. It covers a *Caftan* and a trouser worn inside, often in complementary or contrasting colors. Compared to men, Hausa women are more colorful due to their skills in manipulating *Atampa* or *Ankara* fabrics in making wrappers and fitted blouses called *Zani*. Another clothing variant among young women is a long ankle-length wrapping skirt called *Dan Kwali*.

Hausa clothing represents a sophisticated intersection of religion, societal belief systems, and geographical adaptation with physical appearance. The agency of conveying this sociological connection is the brocade. For many reasons, it is a specific cloth synonymous with the Hausas, Fulanis, and Nupes. Firstly, the simplified design patterns foster the projection and propagation of modesty and respect for the human visage as a beautiful creation in the Islamic religion. This religious inclination accounts for the choice of brocade for the overarching covering of the body in Northern Nigeria,[5] explaining why Ryan Mutuku submits that Islam has significantly impacted the North by devising strict dress codes throughout its communities (2020). This strictness extends beyond the demands for outright covering to dictating the typology of cloth for different demographics. Being commonplace and coming in predominant colors of white, indigo, and sky-blue brocade depicts a modest appearance—one that does not draw unnecessary attention. This simplistic characterization of brocade cloth chimes with the Islamic dictate of followers of Islam not dressing to draw attention, since its simplistic quality does not constitute visual design noise.

Besides religious strictness, brocades serve unique topographical functions in Hausa clothing. The Northern states of *Kano, Katsina, Bauchi, Lafia, Kebbi, Sokoto*, and *Adamawa* are amongst the hottest regions in West Africa, with temperatures rising to 45 degrees during the dry season. Therefore, brocades' loose weave and shimmering surface that deflects sunlight used in making *Caftan* and *Jalaba* constitute adaptations to deal with such extreme heat. The Hausas also use brocade colors to address this problem; their choice of light blue and white as their preferred colors, especially for men, is a conscious clothing adaptation that explores colors and atmospheric temperature in fashion design. Bright colors reflect sunlight, helping the body stay cool, while dark colors absorb sunlight, consequently heating the body. Hausas have been dubbed the "Blue Men" due to their sophisticated understanding and application of white and blue brocade as a dominant fashion coping mechanism to their geographical challenges.

Sociologically, brocades also visually hierarchize Fulani, Hausa, and Nupe societies through the iconic *Babbar Riga*. The density of the layering of shimmering brocade to produce the men's outer garment represents power and the projection of charisma by *Alhajis*. In this context, brocade transposes from displaying modesty to conveying prestige, pride, and bigness. The designs and superfluous layering of brocade in the making of *Babbar Riga* outwardly project a personality force and reinforce the self in expressing such charismatic power (Last 1988; Douny 2011). It symbolizes prestige, leadership, and identity through grandeur (Sofaer 2007). Amongst men of status, therefore, brocade represents self-empowerment, success, and a visual affirmation of societal affluence in Northern Nigeria. It creates a sense of sophistication and superiority in the wearer that announces his societal importance and stratification (Rowlands 1994). Nigeria's political class from the Northern regions adopt this cloth as their official attire even though the government has outlawed traditional clothes in official spaces. The rationale is that there is no better way to express a sense of bigness or charisma in Nigeria than masquerading in swats of multilayered brocades (*Babbar Riga)*, with its material grandeur that culturally symbolizes wealth, prestige, and affluence. With this iconographical representation of religious, societal, and geographical idiosyncrasies, it is easy to construct the identities of all Hausas, Fulanis, and Nupes at first glance throughout Africa from brocade fabrics.

Conclusion

I have attempted to plot an iconographical interpretation of Niger Delta, Hausa, and Yoruba regions through lace, *Aso-Oke*, and brocade as symbolic references to ethnic nationalism, cosmologies, and beliefs. I submit that lace cloth in the Niger Delta region reflects cultural adulation for women, natural resource wealth, and pride. The material expression of cotton abundance and the cosmology of sophisticated visual appearance as social stratification in the clothing traditions of the Yorubas through the symbolic *Aso-Oke* constitute another theoretical submission. While in Northern Nigeria, religious sentiments, geographical adaptation, and the projection of charisma and bigness through brocade form the conceptual basis for reading their clothing culture. The aforementioned demonstrates that cloth constitutes a symbolic form of identification, ethnic nationalism, indigenous assignation codified in fabrics, and the symbolism of their history in a specific culture. In this context, Fanon's implied customary identification and expression theory reflect on the iconic *Onyonyo*, *Agbada*, and *Babbar Riga* in Nigerian clothing culture. While Western influences continue to dominate corporate identity in official workspaces, true *Nigerianness* appears in the full glare of dress traditionalism that affiliates individuals and groups to specific ethnicities. It suffices to submit that although institutions and attitudes have become extremely Westernized to date, various ethnic-specific cloth remains the primary article for the visual identification of Nigerians. Through cloth, Nigerians invoke their origins and promote indigenous worldviews so that the materialism of such unique fabrics and symbolic embellishment sustains their cultural norms and precolonial intercontinental advances in the current face of extreme global interculturalism. Such precolonial intercontinental entanglement is crucial for further exploration to interrogate the adaptation and adoption of Western materials that constitute part of the imperial process into indigenous cultural identities that continue to represent many ethnic groups in Nigeria to date. Since this is beyond the purview of this chapter, I recommend it for further research.

Notes

1. I acknowledge that the term precolonial has sometimes been used to debase Africa's diverse histories. Yet, I employ it not to conform to Eurocentric notions but to denote the era preceding European colonization of Africa.
2. Jama debunks the myth of primitive-nudes as a subjugating stereotype invented for imperial gains, writing that "most white scholars claim Africans moved around half-naked, with minimal clothing which only covered their private parts. This largely fictitious depiction of Africans as savage, uncivilized and animal like beings was particularly sold to black slaves in the Americas and is now misconstrued as historical fact by Africans themselves. In Western films, Africans are portrayed as such, with black men exposing their buttocks and women their breasts. While there were and continue to be some isolated and often nomadic groups in Africa that dressed this way, it is inaccurate and not objective to paint all of the ancient Africans as such. The perverted minds of whites' feast with excitement on the partial nudity found among the Swazi, Namu and Khoi among other groups. However, in Zimbabwe between 700 CE and 1300 CE, most people have been wholly covered even long before the coming of whites" (Jama 2020: 1).
3. Europe's quest to replicate its model of modernity was responsible for the colonial onslaught on the cultural mores of developing countries which it misconstrued and branded barbaric. According to Rabah Omer, "Europe created the concept of savageness and barbarism as an antithesis to its modernity and civilization; hence Europe was to represent the modern model, and the rest was to represent the antiquity or traditional" (Omer 2018: 16).
4. Clothing and the imposition of Western-style clothes on the colonized was a tool of colonial domination and control.

Temilade Olaitan succinctly writes that, "it afforded European imperialist control over the dressing of their subjects and the mission to clothe 'the natives' was enforced by the missionaries as a tactic to convert their subjects to Christianity. This tactic was mostly successful. For instance, the Samoans accepted to cover up their bodies by producing ponchos made of bark cloth, Melanesians created a dress that incorporated European floral designs and embroidery, and the *Herero* dress was created in southern Africa and is accepted as the national dress" (Olaitan 2021: 2).

5 The religious inclination of Hausa clothing can best be deciphered from Christine Dodge's paper titled "Islamic Clothing Requirements." She submits that, "Islam's standards of modesty call for a woman to cover her body, particularly her chest. Most Muslims interpret this to require head coverings for women, although some Muslim women cover the entire body, with a full body *chador*. For men the minimum amount to be covered on the body is between the navel and the knee. Islam also guides that clothing must be loose enough so as not to outline or distinguish the shape of the body. When in public, some women wear a light cloak over their personal clothing as a convenient way to hide the curves of the body. In many predominantly Muslim countries, men's traditional dress is somewhat like a loose robe, covering the body from the neck to the ankles. Islam encourages people to be proud of who they are. Muslims should look like Muslims and not like mere imitations of people of other faiths around them. For this reason, Muslim men are forbidden from wearing gold or silk, as these are considered feminine accessories. Clothing worn by Muslims should be clean and decent, neither excessively fancy nor ragged. One should not dress in a manner intended to gain the admiration or sympathy of others" (2019: 1).

References

Adeyemi, S. (2019), "Adire Motifs and Their Meanings," *MEDIUM, February 28*. [Online] Available at: https://seunandez.medium.com/adire-motifs-and-their-meanings-bac7c58873aa (accessed August 3, 2022).

Balouga, J. (2009), "The Niger Delta: Defusing the Time Bomb," *First Quarter*, 8–11.

Bhabha, H. K. (2012), *The Location of Culture*. London: Routledge.

Césaire, A. (1955), *2000 Discourse on Colonialism*. Trans. Joan Pinkham. New York: Monthly Review Press.

Clapperton, H., Denham, D., & Oudney, W. (1823). *Narrative of Travels and Discoveries in Northern and Central Africa: In the years 1822, 1823, and 1824*. Cambridge: Cummings, Hilliard & Company.

Clarke, W. H. (1976), "Travels and Explorations in Yorubaland 1854–1858," *Bulletin d'Information et de Liaison. CARDAN*, 9(2).

Dodge, C. H. (2019), 'Islamic Clothing Requirements,' *Learn Religions* June 25: [Online] Available at: https://www.learnreligions.com/islamic-clothing-requirements-2004252 (accessed April 26, 2022).

Dorrance, E. A. (2011), *The Language of Clothes: Nonverbal Communication Intention and Misinterpretation* (Doctoral Dissertation, College of Charleston).

Douny, L. (2011), "Silk-embroidered Garments as Transformative Processes: Layering, Inscribing, and Displaying Hausa Material Identities," *Journal of Material Culture*, 16(4): 40115.

Ekeh, P. P. (1975), "Colonialism and the Two Publics in Africa: A Theoretical Statement," *Comparative Studies in Society and History*, 17(1): 91–112.

Fanon, F. (2004). "Algeria Unveiled." In *Decolonization*. London: Routledge, pp.60–73.

Fanon, F. (2007), *The Wretched of the Earth*. United States: Grove/Atlantic, Inc.

Ijimakinwa, F. (2020), "Turn Up in Your *Aso-ebi*': The Dynamics of Identity Construction and Homeland Connection Among the Yoruba in Canada," *Routed Issue 11, August 15*. [Online] https://www.routedmagazine.com/aso-ebi-yoruba-canada (accessed April 17, 2022).

Jama, S. (2020), "Clothing in Precolonial Africa: Insight into Nudity Claims," *The Patriot*. [Online] Available at: https://www.thepatriot.co.zw/old_posts/clothing-in-pre-colonial-africainsight-into-nudity-claims/ (accessed August 29, 2022).

Kriger, C. E. (2005), "Mapping the History of Cotton Textile Production in Pre-colonial West Africa," *African Economic History*, (33): 87–116.

Last, M. (1988), "Charisma and Medicine in Northern Nigeria," In Cruise O'Brien, D. B, Coulon, C. (eds) *Charisma and Brotherhood in African Islam*. Oxford: Clarendon Press, 183–204.

Lipovetsky, G., Porter, C., and Sennett, R. (1994). *The Empire of Fashion: Dressing Modern Democracy*. Princeton, NJ: Princeton University Press.

Lurie, A. (1991), "The Language of Clothes," *Human Ecology Forum*, 19: 32–4.

Mutuku, R. (2020), "Hausa: History, Culture, Traditions, Dressing, Food," *YEN Interesting Facts, October 12*. [Online] Available at: https://yen.com.gh/171329-hausa-history-culture-traditions-dressing-food-interesting-facts.html (accessed April 26, 2022).

Oduah, C. and Bohn, L. (2014), "In the Niger Delta, Fashion Helps Women Leave the Fighting Behind," *GlobalPost December 11*. [Online] Available at: https://theworld.org/stories/2014-12-11/niger-delta-fashion-helps-women-leave-fighting-behind (accessed May 2, 2022).

Oladejo, M. T. (2022), *A History of Textiles and Fashion in the Twentieth Century Yoruba World*. Newcastle: Cambridge Scholars Publishing.

Olaitan, T. (2021), "Modernising the 'Primitive African': The Influence of Colonialism on African Dressing," Decolonizing Thought. [Online] Available at: https://www.decolonialthoughts.

com/post/modernising-the-primitive-african-the-influence-of-colonialism-on-african-dressing (accessed April 23, 2022).

Olubokola, J. (2022). "The Meaning of *Adire*," Interviewed by Clement Akpang. [Zoom], April 15.

Omer, R. (2018), "The Modern and the Traditional African Women and Colonial Morality," *International Journal of Culture and History*, 5: 30.

Onyinye, A. (2022a), "The Popular Hausa Mode of Dressing Styles," *AFRINIK*. [Online] Available at: https://afrinik.com/the-popular-hausa-mode-of-dressing-styles/ (accessed April 26, 2022).

Onyinye, A. (2022b), "What Yoruba Traditional Clothing Styles and Accessories Look Like," AFRINIK. [Online] Available at: https://afrinik.com/what-yoruba-traditional-clothing-styles-and-accessories-look-like/ (accessed April 25, 2022).

Oyeniyi, B. A. (2012), *Dress and Identity in Yorubaland, 1880–1980* (Doctoral Dissertation, Leiden University).

Özdil, M. A. (2021), "The Effect of Clothing as a Marker on Identity," *Motif Akademi Halkbilimi Dergisi*, 14(33): 117–30.

Rowlands, M. (1994), "The Material Culture of Success: Ideals and Life Cycles in Cameroon," *Consumption and Identity*: 147–66.

Seidenberg, K. (2018), "Wearing Our Identity," *The McGill Tribune*, November 20. [Online] Available at: https://www.mcgilltribune.com/a-e/wearing-our-identity-article-20112018/ (accessed April 22, 2022).

Sofaer, J. (ed.) (2007) *Material Identities*. Oxford: Blackwell Publishers.

Williams, O. (1995). "Cultures in the Southern Protectorate." *Calabar Journal of Arts, CAJOLIS* 4(2), pp.76–87.

Williams, O. (2015). "The Niger Delta Region and Culture," Calabar Journal of Liberal Studies, CAJOLIS, 6 (2): 89.

Williams, P. (2015), "Niger Delta Festival Clothing," *Journal of Fashion Research*, 3 (5): 79.

Artist Maria Nepomuceno in conversation with Alice Kettle

Part 1

ALICE KETTLE

AK: As a Brazilian artist can you tell us how that is reflected in the impetus and use of textiles in your work?

MN: My first experience with textiles was when I was twelve years old. I went to my father's house and my stepmother taught me how to make a braid out of crochet. It became a rope and I sewed it in a spiral with another needle. So, since I was very young, I became obsessed with spirals. At this time, I liked to paint and to make experiences with many materials. I started to do other sewn things, a patchwork with a lot of small pieces and then painting over it. I discovered that I liked to sew. When I was around fourteen, I joined a painting course at the School of Visual Arts at Parque Lage, this was just the first of many other courses. Then I went to the School of Industrial Design at university where I worked with different machines, different techniques, and different materials. At this moment, although I didn't realize it until later, the handmade process became important for my work. From the beginning, I was more interested in the many different ways of making and using materials as a kind of expression of painting.

AK: What is special about using textiles? What does it communicate and how?

MN: It is the idea of the touch, it's a different touch. With painting you usually use a brush and with textiles you touch the material. It's different, this touchable relationship with the material. Also, time is very counted in the fabric itself. It's a way of counting time. It's almost like holding the time with your hands.

Figure MN1 *Untitled*, 2010, ropes and beads, 440 × 170 × 1230 cm, 173 1/4 × 66 7/8 × 484 1/4 in. © Maria Nepomuceno, courtesy the artist and Victoria Miro.

AK: That's a lovely phrase.

MN: Yes, it is a metaphorical idea of holding time with your hands. I always have a fascination with still work where you can note that the piece has taken a long time to be done. We can see that in all craft and in Brazil we have a very strong tradition of craft. I link with craft through braiding and in particular the use of braided straw.

AK: You draw from a traditional practice, is this lineage of craft held within the metaphor of time and in your hands?

MN: The kind of braided straw I use is typical of the northeast of Brazil, from Ceará. The leaves of the big and beautiful palm Carnaúba give us wax and the straw. It is common to see hats made of Carnaúba straw in the northeast of Brazil. Part of my family came from there. In 2007, I started to be interested in this material. I went there to find out more about my family and about braided straw practice. I went to some very small villages in Ceará, where women especially do the braiding. They usually do it in groups. They sit in a circle and they start to talk and sing during the work. It's beautiful. So I asked if they could make different forms and grow the scale. It was an amazing challenge for them and we started a partnership to make completely different shapes and develop special techniques.

We have a strong ancestral tradition of textiles and handmade work in Brazil. I always saw my work primarily as sculpture but after I started to work with groups and communities, I understood my work also as textile and recognized the importance of being connected to this tradition.

AK: Are you sharing knowledge between yourself and the groups? Is your work representative of a new hybrid form of making?

MN: The exchange made these group of artisans of Sobral think differently. When they saw my first drawings with some ideas of braided sculptures, they thought, "she's completely crazy" because of the complexity. Now they can undertake an incredible vocabulary of complex shapes and they have developed a different consciousness of their work and their practice.

AK: So this circularity in the rope, the spiral, is also about recovering and reclaiming ancestral practices and making work that returns to itself. You use the straw and it becomes part of the place that it has emerged from in the way you describe time as generative.

MN: Yes, I use many different materials but always with this intention of evoking vital energy and regenerating organisms.

PART TWO

Following the Thread

Woven cloth consists of vertical, warp threads cut to a predetermined length, intersected by horizontal wefts threads whose length is determined only by the length of the warp. Space and time. When the Japanese artist Chiyoko Tanaka was asked to describe what she was weaving, her answer was, "I am weaving time . . . transforming the weft into accumulated space, replacing the vanished time" (Uchiyama, Millar & Tanaka 2002: 29–31). In this section of the book, vanished or vanishing time is traced through the cloth, linking embedded cultural identity to the narrative of the cloth itself.

Both LOkesh Ghai and Venny Mary Nakazibwe describe and analyze the central role of traditional cloth within their communities, holding the stories of a vanishing time, either though the materials used, the manner of making or of wearing. Often this narrative can be read through the traces of use and reuse, from love or necessity, as Ruby Hodgson discovered as she follows the history of eighteenth-century silk through "examining both the silk and the (re)construction of the garments" (Hodgson: p.** of this volume). In so doing she reveals both the domestic and the sociohistorical lives contained within the fabric.

Thread and cloth are often central to the myths and tales of enchantment that are the ways we have tried to make sense of who we are, sometimes to the extent that they become a part of daily life, incorporated into domestic habit. The Shetland Taatit Rugs, as described by Carol Christiansen, with their folkloric motifs, served to remind the owners of the myths, and to protect and remove unwanted influences—often the rugs were marriage gifts and comfort coverings after childbirth.

References

Takeo Uchiyama, Lesley Millar and Chiyoko Tanaka (2002), *Portfolio collection*, Winchester: Telos.

"Cloth—and particularly clothing—connects us to the past in such a tangible way. It is an expression of both self and society that we wear directly against the body and that we all have experience of. I grew up in my mother's vintage clothing shop, early obsessed with the eras of fashion, the cycle of trends, and the traces of the lives left behind in the fabric."

Ruby Hodgson

5

Robe à la Grand'mère—the Reuse of Eighteenth-Century Silks in Romantic-Era Fashion

RUBY HODGSON

Introduction

Museum collections in Europe and North America hold dozens of evening dresses from the 1820s to the 1840s constructed from eighteenth-century silks. While this recycling could be interpreted as thrift—the material being the most expensive element of any garment—these antique silks could in fact imbue the dress with personal, emotional connections and even enhance the social standing of the wearer. The reasons for this are manifold. Using case studies from the Victoria and Albert Museum (V&A), London, this chapter will look at two examples of remade dresses and identify reasons for their creation and survival.

The primary methodology of this study will be first-hand examination of several of the dresses in question. By examining both the silk and the (re)construction of the garments, it is possible to establish the dates of original formation and the final alteration, as well as track traces of previous iterations of the dress's form.

This will be supplemented by archival records that were created as the objects entered the V&A, fashion plates and magazines from the eighteenth and nineteenth centuries, final wills and personal inventories from the families thought to own the dresses through points of their history, and family legends suggesting possible routes of inheritance. It will use theories of psychology and philosophy to propose the reasons for survival, reuse, and acquisition of the garments through their long history, from weaving to museum artifact, and why this sort of reuse may have been particularly prevalent during the Romantic period.

The chapter will start with an overview of the silk production process, identifying key points in the decline of the Spitalfields silk weaving industry and how this will have impacted the quality of silk available during the Romantic period.[1] It will then investigate the Romantic period itself, the dates and defining characteristics of what is considered Romantic, and the changes to the fashionable silhouette during this era. There will then be two case studies for interpreting the fashion, drawn from examples in the V&A collection. The first of these will look at the external standing garnered by wearing antique silk and the value of inherited luxury during the early industrial revolution. The second will take a more inward look, using theories from the field of consumer psychology to find links between the Gothic Romantic mood of the era, high mortality rates, and the personal comfort found by consuming and wearing "vintage" clothing.

The Silk

The quality of European silk production peaked in the eighteenth century, with weaving capitals in Lyon in France and the Spitalfields region of London, England, setting the standard and fashion throughout Europe and North America (Farrell 2014: 19–22). Weavers produced silks on hand-operated draw looms, which required two people to operate—a weaver controlling the weft (the threads that run across the width of the silk), and an assistant draw-boy or -girl working in perfect synchronicity to lift and lower the warp threads (those that run the length of the silk) (Miller, Cabrera Lafuente, and Allen-Johnstone 2021: 109).

Mastery of the most complex weaving processes took years of training—a master weaver had to apprentice for seven years—and the process itself was laborious. Depending on the complexity of the pattern, translating a brocade silk design sketch onto squared-up paper could take up to two weeks (2021: 109), this would be transferred onto the loom, and threading the machine over three to six weeks (2021: 111). The weaving itself could then proceed, at a pace of 2–5 cm per day (2021: 113). The time this took, the cost of the silk fiber itself, and the lengths of silk required to make a garment meant that the fabric was by far the most expensive element of any item of clothing (Spilker et al. 2010: 73).

Technological advancements were made throughout the century, incrementally replacing hand labor with mechanical. Silk threads could be carded and spun by machine, but faster speeds with less direct oversight led to blemishes in the thread that would be visible in the final fabric (Jones 1987: 83).

Through the 1820s, factory systems were being established around the country, employing operational weavers to produce lower grades of silk (Warner 1921: 75). Demand for silk products increased with the developing purchasing power of the emerging middle class, with European imports competing with local production and pressuring factory owners to reduce costs. Decline of British production that started in the 1780s culminated in a Spitalfields recession in 1826 (Brown and Rothstein 1996: 8). At the same time, the jacquard loom attachment, invented in 1801 and gaining popularity in British factories in the 1820s, replaced the role of the draw-boy, allowing complex designs to be woven by a single operator (Bell 1895: 27).

In the eighteenth century, once woven, a length of silk would be sold through a mercer to the consumer, who would take this to her mantua maker to be constructed into her preferred style. The shape this took could be a collaboration between the purchaser and her maker, picking and choosing from fashion dolls and, later, fashion plates displaying the latest styles (Dyer 2021). The construction was fast and cheap compared to the weaving process; fabric was pleated on the body, pinned in place during fittings and sewn together with minimal cutting away of excess fabric. Seams hand stitched, the petticoats would use whole widths of silk and the selvedge—woven more tightly to prevent fraying—were used as a built-in seam allowance and finishing.

Given the initial expense of purchasing silk, it was common for the fabric to be reused once a silhouette fell out of fashion. A wealthy lady could take her mantua back to a mantua maker and have it remade over several decades, or pass it down to a favored maid, who could rework the gown herself or pawn the fabric. Remaking and wear over decades would lead even the most luxurious of fabrics to be cut down to the smaller and smaller surviving parts, sold and resold, made into children's clothing, patched, and decreasing in value along the way (Lemire 2005: 29–48; Dove 2021).

This is certainly one journey that silk could take, and accounts for the rarity of survival in museum collections worldwide. However, if the mantua survived the decade or two it might take for the fabric design itself to fall out of fashion, perhaps packed away and forgotten, subject to benign neglect, it might have been rediscovered at precisely the right time for the Romantic revival, where, this chapter theorizes, the age adds to the fabric's value rather than takes away.

The Romantic Era

Periods in history are often bookended by definitive events: the coronation to death of a monarch, the declaration to ceasefire of a war. Others are defined by revolutions or movements, and these can have more fluid edges. The Romantic era is one of the latter, with claims for its emergence ranging from the 1740s (Blanning 2011: 3–5) to the 1810s (where artists and authors started to self-identify as Romantics) (Blanning 2011: 5–6), and most accounts drawing it to a close around the 1850s. Professor Tim Blanning defines Romanticism as a collective feeling or mood, as intangible and wistful as the poetry it inspired (2011: 6). Romantics—poets, authors, and artists—are identified by the weight they place on the importance of emotion over reason, rather than a unifying look or style. Indeed, Blanning explains that it was explicitly *not* a style: "Romanesque, Gothic, Renaissance, Mannerism, Baroque and Rococo all had stylistic concepts, but romanticism never developed anything similar. Especially in architecture almost every conceivable style was tried—neo-Gothic, neo-classical, neo-Renaissance, neo-Egyptian, neo-baroque, neo-everything" (2011: 6).

There are common themes of nostalgia, the yearning for mythologized past, and a leaning toward nature and the natural world, rejecting the Enlightenment ideals of logic, science, and reason. In her book, *Gothic to Goth: Romantic Era Fashion and its Legacy*, Lynne Z. Bassett explains, "The fantasy of history and natural beauty offered by Romantic-era fine art, decorative art, landscape design, literature, music—and costume—acted as a screen from the harsh realities of sooty factory smoke, departed loved ones, and financial turbulence" (2016: 17).

Romantic fashion is therefore not defined by a single silhouette or defining characteristic. The period from 1810 to 1850 (which this chapter will take as the prevailing agreement for the Romantic era) suffered frequent changes in the fashionable style for women. Following on from the Regency neoclassical style, sleeves started to puff at the shoulder around 1816 over a tight sleeve, becoming more exaggerated in the early 1820s. A gigot (or leg of mutton) sleeve was introduced to day dresses about 1824 and remained popular until about 1836. Around 1829–31 the shoulder puffed sleeves reached their widest, with Nancy Bradfield recording full widths of the shoulder at 29 inches (73.6 cm). At the same time, the location of the fullness started to slope off the shoulder, and a long-sleeved dress may find the widest point just above the elbow and gather into a tight cuff. These oversized sleeves fell out of favor around 1836, replaced by a tight cap sleeve or a long sleeve made tight with rouching or pleating along the upper arm and an isolated puff at the elbow (Bradfield 2009: 107–82; Tarrant 1983: 3–33).

In concert with this, the waistline slowly dropped from the Regency underbust of the turn of the century, to midway down the ribcage and slightly pointed by 1825, to hitting the small of the waist and deep point by the 1840s (Tarrant 1983: 3–5). The skirt filled out, from the straight, clinging style to a full bell, with multiple layers of petticoats required to support the look (Bradfield 2009: 107–82). Romantic fashion introduced additional historical influences, borrowing elements anachronistically from Roman, Medieval, Tudor, Stuart, and Georgian fashion, architecture, and art.

Examples in the V&A Museum

The V&A holds approximately 120 dresses in the collection of Textiles & Fashion that date from 1820 to 1849. Of these, eleven have been identified as being constructed of silk woven in the eighteenth century. Other examples are held throughout the Western world, with notable examples in the Metropolitan Museum in New York and the Burrell Collection in Glasgow. They are also not confined to womenswear. Both the Metropolitan Museum and the V&A hold Romantic-era menswear made from eighteenth-century silks; these trend toward indoor wear: dressing gowns, or banyans.

The rest of this chapter will look at just two of these examples from the V&A collection as stand-ins for the broader trend.

CASE STUDY 1: EXTERNAL STANDING

The first dress (Figure 5.1), museum number T.854-1974, came into the V&A collection via sisters Jean Shaw and Anne Crothers, with a potential family lineage. The silk dates from the 1770s or 1780s and was made into its current form in the 1840s.

The dress is crisp and lightweight, the cream ground divided by alternating blocks of pink and white to form thin stripes. Between these are floating sprigs of flowers in pinks and purples, and, more subtly, figured silk leaves. It has a scooped neckline and a long bodice formed into a point that some contemporary ladies' journals would have described as à l'antique.[2] The fullness of the skirt is held by organ pleats, also serving to accentuate the dramatic shape of the waistline. Although in overall good condition, the cap sleeves are evidently pieced together—an additional triangle of fabric required on each side. There is a double waving line of pin pricks across one sleeve, where the former trimming has been unpicked. Similar lines of delicate holes can be found across the gown. One hip appears to have had an oval of additional fabric patched in, possibly to make up for a shortfall of fabric, or to repair damage.

Mrs. Shaw wrote a letter to the museum at the time of donation, outlining her investigations into the family legend behind the dress:

> We think that the material for this dress probably belonged to Sarah Stratton, who married an ancestor of mine, Arthur Forbes of Culloden, in 1779. She was an heiress, and her father came from Ripley in Surrey. Sarah was very likely to have bought expensive material in England to take to Scotland at that time.
>
> Sarah's daughter, Sarah Louise Forbes, married Hugh Duff of Muirtown, near Inverness, and had a family which included a daughter, Emilia [sometimes spelled Emelia or Emily] Mary, who married my great-grandfather, Alexander Warrand, and they went to India. On the journey home, Alexander Warrand died at sea and Emily arrived back with his coffin and three children, a son and two daughters. They went back to live at Muirtown, where the estate was now run by trustees and Emily was very short of money. We have letters to show this and therefore it is most likely that Emily used the material, or dress, which had belonged to her rich grandmother, Sarah Stratton, to be made, or re-made, for her two daughters, Louisa and Catherine. They would have needed a dress at this time as they would have been coming out about 1840.
>
> **SHAW, 1975, Letter to Dr. Strong, V&A Museum**

Shaw goes on to explain that the dress was passed down to her aunt Emily Catherine Warrand, the niece of Louisa and Catherine, who in turn passed it down to her and her sister. The line of inheritance matches with the dates estimated for the silk and the dress construction, but the story is still unverifiable. The matrilineal inheritance path means that documentation is scarce; investigation has thus far only turned up a will for Louisa, in which she leaves varying the skirt or the underarms of the bodice. They have perhaps benefited from being descendants of extravagant mantuas, which used copious amounts of fabric; other remade dresses in the V&A collection have had to be more economical in their use of fabric, heavily patchworking together panels for the bodice and sleeves, and supplementing the skirt with additional materials (search T.187-1970 on V&A Explore the Collections for one such example), which may indicate that the garment has been remade several times before surviving in its current form. That traces remain visible may lend authenticity to the romance of the garment, an additional signifier of age and history, or it may detract, showing an insufficiency that ought to be hidden away.

Conclusion

The period from 1820 to 1849 saw a fashion for constructing dresses from eighteenth-century silks. These silks were particularly well made, having been woven during the pinnacle of British silk manufacture, which had subsequently fallen victim to mechanization and competition from printed cottons. The renewed interest is often attributed to the lightweight, crisp silks holding the shape of the new dress styles well, but may have also provided a cultural shorthand for ancestral wealth at a time of the rising middle class and provided the wearer comfort when mortality rates were high.

The prohibitive cost associated with purchasing luxurious silk brocades in the eighteenth century meant that they had always been candidates for reworking, reuse, handing down, and selling on. This chapter has looked at the developments in silk manufacture toward the late eighteenth century that prioritized output, the moving of silk weaving from home working to factory settings, and mechanization that drove down the quality of production.

After a period of reduced interest in intricately woven brocade silks during the Regency period, the Romantic era saw a revival for the patterns "à la grand'mère," printed newly on cotton, woven at great expense, or, if possible, reclaimed from attics and pawnshops. The reveling in nostalgia combined with anachronistic jumbling of historic styles created a perfect opportunity for the silks to gain new life through the reworking into a fashion that was distinctly its own.

The first case study gave an example of a dress with a direct, albeit unconfirmed, ancestral lineage. The family legend of its journey from eighteenth-century Spitalfields until its donation to the V&A in the 1970s provides an illustration of what Stobart and Rothery described as the "patina of age," a cultural capital that could not be bought. Meanwhile the ladies' journals provide descriptions of the fancy dress costumes inherited from the ballgowns worn by their grandmothers and create a fantasy of what the dresses had seen in their lifetime. This indicates that the silks could be kept within the family and reused, that spectators could recognize the quality of silk, and that there was a romanticism associated with the history of the garment.

The second case study introduces the concept of meaning threat—an awareness of one's own mortality—and the comfort that can be found in situating oneself within a longer historical time period as a means of mitigating this threat. The chapter posits that meaning threat was experienced broadly during the Romantic era as migration and mortality rates kept death and farewells at the forefront of the public's minds, reinforced by the gothic art and literature that swept through society. The second dress, by virtue of its antique silk and the faint evidence of remaking, serves as a meaning threat mitigator for the wearer.

To conclude, the chapter conceives that the reuse of eighteenth-century silk was not merely a product of thrift and necessity, rather that the choice was loaded with deeper meaning to the individual and within the wearers' social circle, on a conscious and subconscious level. The wearing of the imperfect garment, with the shadows of its former life softly unhidden, encapsulates the Romantic idyll as well as any of the great paintings or poems of the time.

Notes

1   While not all the examples have been constructed from Spitalfields, or even British, silk, these would have likely been the most readily available for consumers in Britain in the eighteenth century and thus most likely to have been handed down over the proceeding generations.

2   The *Lady's Magazine* had a Paris-based fashion correspondent whose column, written in the form of personal letters, described the general changes in fashion as well as the exact outfits worn at important balls. She regularly describes trends using the French turn of phrase, including a "corsage [at this time, a bodice, rather than a small bouquet of flowers] à l'Antique, which you know means with a point" (*Paris Chitchat &c.* July 1833: 168).

References

Bassett, L. Z. (2016), *Gothic to Goth: Romantic Era Fashion & Its Legacy*, Norway: Wadsworth Atheneum Museum of Art.

Bell, T. F. (1895), *Jacquard Weaving and Designing*, London; New York: Longmans, Green.

Blanning, T. (2011), *The Romantic Revolution*, Illustrated Reprint Edition, London: Orion Publishing Group, Limited.

Bradfield, N. (2009), *Costume in Detail, Women's Dress 1730–1930*, 8th edn. England: Eric Dobby Publishing.

Brown, C., and N. Rothstein (1996), *Silk Designs of the Eighteenth Century from the Victoria and Albert Museum*, 2nd ed. London. New York: Thames and Hudson.

Burman, B. and A Fennetaux (2020), *The Pocket: A Hidden History of Women's Lives, 1660–1900*, United Kingdom, Yale University Press.

Davenport R. J. (2020), "Urbanization and Mortality in Britain, c. 1800–50", *Economic History Review*, 73 (2): 455–85.

Dove, D. (2021) "'Cast-off skins' and Second Selves: Garment Stories in Second-Hand Clothes Markets", paper presented at Garment Stories and Sustainability: Past, Present and Future, University of York, UK, June 4.

Dyer, S. (2021), Material Lives, Women Makers and Consumer Culture in the Eighteenth Century, New York; London: Bloomsbury Visual Arts.

Farrell, W. (2014), "Silk and Globalisation in Eighteenth-Century London: Commodities, People and Connections c. 1720–1800", unpublished Ph.D. thesis, Birkbeck, University of London.

Gülen, S. A., K. D. Vohs, R. Hamilton and A. Ulquinaku (2017), "Stitching Time: Vintage Consumption Connects the Past, Present, and Future." *Journal of Consumer Psychology* 27(2): 182–94.

Jones, S. R. H. (1987), "Technology, Transaction Costs, and the Transition to Factory Production in the British Silk Industry, 1700–1870." *The Journal of Economic History*, 47 (1): 71–96.

Lemire, B. (2005), "Shifting Currency: The Culture and Economy of the Second Hand Trade in England, c. 1600–1850", in Palmer, A. and H. Clark (eds) *Old Clothes, New Looks: Second Hand Fashion*, New York: Berg Publishers, pp. 29–48.

Miller, L. E., A. Cabrera Lafuente and C. Allen-Johnstone (eds) (2021), *Silk: Fiber, Fabric, and Fashion*, United Kingdom: Thames & Hudson.

"Paris Chitchat &c.". (July 1833) *The Lady's Magazine and Museum of the Belles Lettres, Music, Fine Arts, Drama, Fashions, &c.*, 3 (1), London: Published by J. Page.

"Paris Chitchat &c.". (July 1836) *The Lady's Magazine and Museum of the Belles Lettres, Music, Fine Arts, Drama, Fashions, &c.*, 9 (1), London: Published by J. Page.

Shaw, J. (1975), *Letter to Dr. Strong, director of V&A Museum*, 17 February. [Letter] Held at: Victoria and Albert Museum, ref RP 1974/2316.

Spilker, K. D., K. Chrisman-Campbell, N. LaBouff, S. S. Takeda, C. M. Esguerra (2010), *Fashioning Fashion: European Dress in Detail, 1700–1915*. Germany: Los Angeles County Museum of Art.

Stobart, J., and M. Rothery (2014), "Fashion, Heritance and Family: New and Old in the Georgian Country House." *Cultural and Social History*, 11 (3): 385–406.

Tarrant, N. E. A. (1983), *The Rise and Fall of the Sleeve 1825–1840: A Catalogue of the Costume and Accessories in the Charles Stewart and Royal Scottish Museum Collections*, United Kingdom: Royal Scottish Museum.

Warner, F. (1921), *The Silk Industry of the United Kingdom. Its Origin and Development*, United Kingdom, Dalcassian Publishing Company.

Will of Louisa Sarah Georgiana Forbes (1897). National Records of Scotland: Inverness Sheriff Court. Reference SC29/44/30.

"Cloth represents human ingenuity and creativity through the manipulation of fiber. Even the simplest cloth is a complex structure. It is made more complex by what it may represent through design, the messages it conveys, whether that be comfort and love or more challenging and confrontational ideas."

Carol Christiansen

6

Layers of Comfort: Shetland Taatit Rugs

CAROL CHRISTIANSEN

Introduction

The surviving corpus of Shetland folklore is dominated by trow (troll) stories. A recurring theme is the interference of trows in human life. It is used to explain the disturbance or theft of household goods, the disappearance of humans for long periods of time, and the replacement of healthy humans or livestock for helpless or dead changelings (Edmondston and Saxby 1888; Nicolson 1937; Spence 1999; Stewart 1892).

Events in trow stories take place in darkness, at night when humans are sleeping, or during Yule, the time of year with the least amount of daylight. The setting of nighttime or darkness is not always expressed in the narrative, but is implied by the understanding that trows were nocturnal and had to remain hidden during daylight or they were turned to stone or left motionless until darkness returned (Saxby 1932: 150; Nicolson 1937: 4). The complete blackness of the premodern night required a different approach to living to which humans adjusted themselves, their animals, and property each day.

Similarly, another paranormal being, the Mara, was believed to visit some humans as they slept, sitting or "riding" on their chest and making it difficult to breathe. The affliction is now known as sleep paralysis, but the experience of sufferers has long been a sinister theme in European folklore (Koski 2020: 67–8; Davies 2003: 182–4). In Nordic folklore the Mara also visited cattle or horses at night, causing the animal to sweat and become disturbed (Asker 1967: 14).

Humans were not completely powerless, however. They had the ability to sain, a form of magic using devices to deter, trick, or lessen the impact of the harmful night visitor (Edmondston and Saxby 1888: 136, 141–3, 207, 211). Objects or materials were formed in the shape of a circle, balanced cross, or multipart object. In so doing, the forms became powerful devices imbued with magic. They were strategically placed near where the trow or Mara would present itself: at thresholds to the house, on or within the bedclothes, and above barn doors and byre stalls (Saxby 1932; Asker 1967: 26–7; Raudvere 2020: 54, 57).

It is within the beliefs in paranormal dangers of the dark and saining strategies that a traditional type of pile bedcover is considered. As a group of over eighty textiles dating from 1760, they offer an opportunity to investigate their common forms of design and embellishment. The bedcovers are decorated with motifs of the same symbolic forms used in saining rituals against trows and the Mara in Shetlandic and Nordic folklore. Many of the bedcovers were marriage rugs and carried added significance in the belief that the trow threat to humans increased during the life-changing events of marriage and childbirth. It is argued that the bedcovers had a dual purpose: to provide warmth for physical comfort, and as saining devices easing psychological worry and distress during sleep, childbirth, and illness. Their design forms and motif placement may be interpreted as thresholds to the bed and protection for the individuals who lie within.

Taatit and Rya Rug Construction

Shetland's pile bedcovers, known as taatit rugs, are part of a long tradition of pile fabrics in northern Europe. They were in widespread use within Shetland until the end of the nineteenth century and continued to be used in rural areas into the mid-twentieth century. About 100 survive in museum and private collections, mainly in Shetland (Christiansen 2015).

Taatit rugs were made in Shetland by and for Shetlanders and unlike knitwear and tweed, were not an export product. Many rugs are recorded as marriage rugs or have designs such as hearts and initials, which indicate they were for a betrothed couple (Christiansen 2015: 18–19). In the late eighteenth century, a rug was considered as essential as a cow or spade before marriage should take place (Dishington 1978: 22). Anecdotal evidence suggests the two halves of marriage rugs were embroidered separately by each of the couple's families. Research indicates, however, that rugs also were made by the future bride or groom, or members of only one of the families. Besides grooms, fathers or other male relatives of the couple made rugs, since as they were fishermen or sailors they had skills in sewing and working cloth. A few rug makers, mainly women, worked professionally.

Like Scandinavian rya rugs, taatit rugs were composed of a woven ground fabric into which thick threads were inserted and fixed to form a pile on one side, or two sides in the case of some Finnish ryijys. Both rug cultures applied the pile on a single long length of ground fabric, which was cut in half and the two halves sewn together to

Figure 6.1 Taatit rug with center circle, border, and central field all containing crosses. Some areas of the central field have cross-like forms which join to form checkerboards, delineated by color. TEX 1992.25. Reproduced with the permission of © Shetland Museum and Archives.

Figure 6.2 The non-pile side of a marriage rug, laid as it was in use. The hearts, divided circle, crosses, and checkerboards were visible from outside the bed. TEX 8637. Reproduced with the permission of © Shetland Museum and Archives.

form a rectangular bed cover. On the pile side, rya and taatit rugs look similar, but their differences in construction are evident in the way the pile threads were applied and visibly apparent on the smooth side of the rugs.

Rya rugs were woven usually in a twill fabric, whereas taatit rugs had a plain weave ground. The pile threads used in rya rugs were applied by knotting them around two warp threads as weaving progressed, with several weft rows between the knot row. Shetland taatit rugs were made using a finished woven backing cloth, which was embroidered once off the loom. Two double-stranded thick threads were sewn with a large needle twice around two weft threads, allowing one of the passes of the needle to form a loop on one side. The loops were later cut, forming the pile.

The knotting method of Scandinavia required the rug to remain on the loom for a longer period than the weaving of the simple tabby taatit ground. The extended time required for the Scandinavian knotting method may have been a disadvantage in the small, two-room Shetland houses, where a floor loom required a separate outbuilding. Warp-weighted looms were in use until the very early nineteenth century, but a taatit rug dating from *c*. 1780 with a starting border, evidence that it was woven on a vertical loom, was completed using the embroidery method.

Knotting during weaving made the design more challenging to execute accurately and evenly, since each half was woven successively on the single length of ground fabric but the two halves were designed as mirror images of each other once sewn together. Therefore, the design had to be knotted in reverse horizontally to achieve this. Some Nordic and Shetland bedcovers have a bold center motif that had to be aligned and joined. This was easier to accomplish with the embroidery method, since the fabric was off the loom and the two halves could be physically compared next to one another.

On the smooth side, the knots were not visible in rya rugs, whereas on the back of a taatit rug, the embroidered taats appear as dots of color against the woven tabby ground. The twill ground of rya rugs was often warped in colored stripes to make it more visually interesting. This was important, because the pile side was laid down against the sleeper, with the smooth side most visible. This is apparent in that hems are turned toward the pile side on both rya and taatit rugs and local memory of taatit rug use confirms the warm, soft pile was next to the sleeper. Such placement made the rug warmer, possibly less heavy, and may have had significance in the motifs being foremost next to the body.

Once the pile was completed, whether knotted and woven or embroidered, the two sides were sewn together to form a rectangular covering. When the rug was to be laundered, the center seam was cut and the two halves separated to make it easier to wash and dry the heavy, wet fabric.

Taatit and Rya Rug Design

Despite differences in construction, taatit rugs are similar in design to local traditions of rya rugs in Norway, Sweden, and Finland (Englestad 1942; Kjellmo 1996; Sylwan 1934; Sirelius 1926; Vahter and Linnove 1955; Pylkkänen 1974). In both traditions, rugs have borders, central fields, and a varied repertoire of motifs, making each rug unique but with similar design elements and placement. Some of the similarities between Shetland and Scandinavian rugs are striking, especially Swedish rugs from the Uppland region north of Stockholm, from western Norway, and parishes in southwestern and central Finland. There is, as yet, no historical explanation for the similarity in design, other than Shetlanders often crewed on trading ships, with Norway and the eastern Baltic common destinations. However, most of the Scandinavian rugs similar to taatit rugs predate them by at least a century, leaving the ways in which similarities in design resemblance came about an open question.

The focus of this discussion is the three most common design elements found in taatit rugs: the balanced cross, the circle, and squares, either placed consecutively checkerboard fashion, evenly spaced, or scattered. The majority of rugs dating from the last 150 years usually incorporate more than one of the three main symbols in their design.

Scandinavian rya have been catalogued and their motifs described and compared according to design principles, age, and geographical origins. There has been little reference to context, to cultural function. In her study of Norwegian *åkle* (woven, non-pile bed, wall and floor covers), Wang argues that design form as created by the weaver had a cognitive function and is the most important aspect for understanding these textiles (Wang 1983: 27). Like rya and taatit rugs, *åkle* were woven with similar motifs, especially balanced crosses. It is within this context of heavily motif-laden design that taatit rugs must be understood. As the most colorful furnishing in the house, the design was time-consuming and costly to achieve through dyeing and the large amount of wool required for the three dimensional pile effect. Furthermore, they were considered an essential household furnishing for those who could afford them and had added significance for their use with the most intimate of furniture, the bed. The nature of the three most common motifs and their typical placement on taatit rugs suggest that motifs had specific purposes in use.

Balanced crosses are placed predominantly in the border, usually spaced evenly around the border's four sides. Crosses also appear in the central field, often in each of the four corners, or spaced throughout. They are used in combination with the circle, appearing in the segments of the divided circle placed in the middle of the central field. Crosses are made of five squares, four arms and a center. Some rugs have additional squares around the five-part cross, creating a large, double or compound cross.

Squares appear as regular, evenly spaced motifs around a border or throughout a central field, as scatters of different sized squares dotted throughout the design, or close together, as a checkerboard. Small checkerboards often appear in the corners of the border or the center of the central field. In some cases, checkerboards are placed within the central field *en masse*, but with a clever use of color in each square, it is possible to see balanced crosses embedded and merged with the checkerboard design, making the two motifs compete for recognition.

Circles appear singly as a large, bold motif in the middle of the central field. They are nearly always divided and then only in even-numbered segments, from two to twelve. In some rugs, each of the divisions also contains a cross or one or more squares. All three main design elements in taatit rugs are found in ryas, with crosses and squares predominating.

Most studies of rya rugs and other decorative Scandinavian textiles record design elements but have only taken tentative steps to consider their possible cultural meanings. It would seem imperative to relate bedcovers to their intended use: to warm and cover the body, primarily at night during sleep or when ill or infirm. Going to bed meant placing the body in a prone position, getting rest, and probable sleep. During sleep one entered a different level of consciousness, temporarily divorced from the active world. Humans were less alert and more vulnerable. Nightly rituals of preparing for bed may have involved latching or locking doors and gates, tidying living spaces, preparing children and animals for the night, and regulating the household hearth. These activities assured a level of safety during the night, adding peace of mind for tired householders, aware of their vulnerability in the state of sleep.

In cultures where the belief in nocturnal paranormal beings was significant, added stress was placed on the household. Additional measures were required to guard against unwanted visitations, destruction of property, and the harming of family members. To understand the cultural significance of taatit rugs, it is important to investigate commonly held beliefs in nocturnal paranormal activity and the responses taken by people as they negotiated the unpredictability of this side of life.

Paranormal Activity in Shetland Folklore

The folklore, placenames and historical material culture of Shetland reflect its heritage as a Norwegian territory between the late ninth and mid-fifteenth centuries, and as a Nordic cultural outlier until the mid-nineteenth century. By then Shetland's Nordic language, folklore, and folk beliefs mainly had failed to survive several centuries of Scottishization and encroaching modernism. The fervent missions of Protestant ministers from the British mainland by the early nineteenth century were a constant presence and had a detrimental effect on the continuation of indigenous beliefs in enchantment, the paranormal, and the use of magic. Folk beliefs were further compromised by the understanding that retelling one's encounter with paranormal beings would compromise one's own magical powers or bring bad luck. Most evidence was not recorded until the late nineteenth century, albeit from sources recounting knowledge from one or more previous generations. Furthermore, the evidence was recorded in English rather than the Norn language of pre-Scottish Shetland. Although words in the Norn language describing references to magic, foreboding, and paranormal creatures and events have been recorded in Norn dictionaries, they are rarely included in the published collections of folk tales. Nevertheless, the folk stories are variations of Norwegian migratory legends but recognizably set within the Shetland landscape and culture (Christiansen 1992).

Comparatively, Shetland's placename evidence has been retained and well recorded. It is overwhelmingly Old Norse in origin and historical sources identify many places associated with trolls, giants, elves, and fairies (Jakobsen 1993: 61, 102, 138–9). Placenames related to paranormal beings appear on modern and historical maps and in folk memory. In the main they are associated with trows. They identify trow settlements (Trollshouses, Trollagerts [trow farm]) or where trow activity took place (the loch of Trollawater), even if the story of the event has not survived. Most of the places are some distance from human settlement along the coastal fringe, as established by the Norse in the tenth century. Some folktales make reference to prehistoric structures being trow-haunted, as are some very early Christian chapel sites, which themselves may have been located on prehistoric ritual sites (Saxby 1932: 14–17, 27, 34). The placename evidence for specific trow dwelling and activity areas indicates that trows figured greatly in Shetlandic belief traditions and complement surviving stories where specific trow localities are identified.

Difficult Neighbors

Trows in Shetland folklore are not the troll giants of Norwegian folk culture, but are similar to *huldufólk* (hidden people) or *álfar* (fairies) in Icelandic and Faroese folklore. They are described as small, human-like beings who lived in the earth, in remote, hilly or rocky areas where humans rarely traveled (Nicolson 1937: 3). Their lifestyle paralleled that of human culture: they had partners and children, grew old, needed food, washed clothes, were partial to collecting silver, adept at composing music and playing the fiddle, enjoyed dancing, and hosted parties. Trows regularly dressed in gray clothes, thereby providing a level of camouflage during their nocturnal activities. They were quick to anger and displayed passive-aggressive tendencies and vindictive behavior. Humans feared and attempted to placate them.

The human-like aspects of trow life naturally fostered a one-sided dependence in which trows came to humans to use or take what trows themselves did not have. They were mischievous and insulting trespassers, who arrived unannounced at night once the family were in bed, whereupon they spoiled, damaged, or stole property.

Trow behavior was manifested most disturbingly in the belief they took away humans. Stories involving human kidnap usually take place during transitional periods for the community or in the lives of the human victims. Some centered on the twenty-four days of Yule, the shortest and darkest days of the year when trows were able to roam for more hours and longer distances. Other periods of danger were during the night when the household was asleep, the days leading up to a marriage, and during labor, birth, and the days following. In the past, Shetlanders celebrated Christmas on January 6 and marriages usually were held in the days around December 25. During these events, everyday life was suspended. Humans were distracted, sometimes made more so by merry-making and alcohol consumption. Trows were aware of human vulnerabilities and posed a greater threat to human life and property during these periods, aided by the lack of daylight during winter.

Accomplished fiddlers were taken to play at a trow event, sometimes returning home years after their family had passed away. Midwives were taken to assist at a trow birth. When kidnapped by trows, the human experience was not altogether harmful, but could last a year or decades without the victim being aware of time passing. Some humans were saved or released from trow enchantment and returned home. Others were never seen again.

Most alarmingly, human mothers and children were believed taken by trows to replace deceased equivalent members of a trow family. In their place were vacant and dependent changelings, some surviving only for a few days. The reasons for changelings appearing in the days following a birth or when young children were taken during Yule were blamed on adults who failed to invoke protective measures.

Protection and Saining

Shetland's trow stories record generally held beliefs centering on magic and enchantment practiced by both humans and supernatural beings in their encounters with one other. Humans were not wholly passive victims. When armed with an understanding of paranormal behavior, they could avoid or overcome intentions of harm using magic and supernatural powers. The power of trow enchantment could be avoided by using ploys to escape their attention, or by knowing their methods of trickery. For example, humans would be forever under the spell of trows if they ate food offered by them. Trows went so far as to mark butter with a cross to trick a human into thinking it was safe to eat, but recognizing the ploy meant the intended victim avoided being duped (Saxby 1932: 163).

Storylines indicate premeditative human agency was key to protecting life and property through the use of objects symbolic in their form to thwart the path of threatening behavior. Employing a method of protection meant humans did not have to keep constant vigil over livestock, property, and vulnerable adults and children. It was the responsibility of parents to sain their children regularly before being left unattended or throughout Yule (Saxby 1932: 82–3, 86, 147, 164–5). Magical devices were made or mimed, becoming barriers beyond which trows would not pass. Such methods of saining were ritualized by forming a cross or a circle from one or more objects. It was recommended to lay stones in the grass near the front door in a circle formation, with spokes as in a wheel to keep away evildoers (Saxby 1932: 35). The Reverend Mill records that when his wife went into labor with their second child in 1756, the local midwife took "a table knife, and made crosses over the bed after the childbirth, according to her superstitious custom" (Mill 1889: 23). Saining devices of a special character also were left for the Mara in Norwegian folklore.

There remained an alliance in the minds and actions of Shetlanders between folk belief and Christianity. Both beliefs remained concurrent and do not appear to conflict but worked in tandem to offset the powers of supernatural agency. Thus, one could sain with a pair of iron shears or an open bible, their powers were equivalent. Overwhelming forces of Christianity had the power to put an end to trow culture altogether, ironically reported by a trow woman, who explained to a local man why she was now alone. Her community in North Yell had been forced to emigrate to Faroe due to the fervent prayers of the local Church of Scotland minister, but she being too old could not travel with them.[1] In this late story from the early nineteenth century, Christianity may have had an increasingly prominent role, as ministers and missionaries from a number of Protestant denominations were actively engaged in securing believers and putting an end to beliefs of Norse origin throughout the islands.

Thresholds

The significance of thresholds figure prominently in Norse culture (Eriksen 2013; Rohrbach 2017). They are seen as a demarcation between inside and outside, center and periphery, enclosed protected space versus open vulnerable space. Homes had levels of public and private spaces within which thresholds played an important role in defining movement between public and private, communal and intimate. Thresholds also acted as points of transition between one space and another, the liminal space one inhabits during this transition. As such, thresholds were vulnerable barriers and special measures were used to ensure they remained secure when necessary.

In Shetland folklore, humans populated both inside and outside spaces during daylight when paranormal beings were not present. When darkness fell each day, the situation changed dramatically and thresholds became part of the ritualization in keeping paranormal beings separate from humans and livestock. Thresholds were important locations for the placement of saining devices, thereby strengthening the threshold and limiting its use as a transitory space.

Objects used for saining had to be visible to the paranormal being, in a location that would halt the intended behavior before it could be carried out. The area before the outer door of a house, the door itself, and common pathways within the dwelling were all used as points of saining. Gates and styles to outdoor spaces where grain was kept were also sained with a cross formed of straws during Yule (Saxby 1932: 80).

Beds and Bedclothes as Thresholds

The vernacular house of early modern Shetland was a simple, two-room stone structure with a single door and a hole in the roof to let out smoke. A main room (*but*) contained a central hearth, where cooking and other tasks took place owing to the presence of light from the fire. The room had benches around the walls, used for seating during the day and as sleeping spaces at night for some family members and any servants. For rural households, this room was also home to pets and temporarily to dependent livestock. The trespassing of trows into the central room at night to eat food, fetch water, and use the heat of the fire while the household slept is a recurring convention in Shetlandic folklore.

The second room (*ben*) held a few chairs and stools, chests and boxes for storage, and a bed for the household couple. It did not usually have a hearth but served as the "best" room for visiting guests.

These two rooms typify the division between public and private, of communal and intimate spaces. The ben room was the more private, except when it was used to host important guests. It was separated by a doorway, sometimes delineated only by a suspended cloth drape, but which served as a threshold into the inner reach and more private space of the house.

Box beds were introduced in the late eighteenth century and with their sliding doors, provided a barrier to the nighttime world and another level of privacy (Fenton 1978: 192). Their tightly enclosed space and small opening made it difficult to gain access or have light to attend a birthing mother or ill patient (Taylor 1948: 94). The folklore of Shetland originates before this time and it must be considered that beds for the head of household, including the birthing space, were likely bench constructions, probably within the communal space with no obvious threshold other than the outer door to the room.

In this scenario we may consider bedclothes as thresholds, the last protective barrier before the ill or slumbering body. This is made clear in the detailed account in *Sturlunga* saga, when a woman protects herself and a young girl from marauders by going to a long bench, tucking the girl next to her, positioning themselves close against the beams, and covering themselves with a blanket (Rohrbach 2017: 361). Here the blanket becomes a protective barrier in an otherwise exposed position.

Pillows feature in Shetlandic folklore when describing the need to protect against the taking of mother and newborn by trows and replacing them with changelings. It was the duty of the midwife to ensure trows did not come near the childbed. When attending a birth, they brought with them saining tools. A country doctor practicing in northern Shetland in the last decade of the nineteenth century reported that midwives opened scissors to form a cross and placed steel razors under the pillows of mothers to ward off trows (Taylor 1948: 93). Failure by the midwife to place crossed straws at the threshold or lay a circle of pins on the pillow led to a mother and newborn taken by trows and replaced with changelings (Saxby 1932: 144).

Design in Use and Meaning

It must be considered that the design layout of taatit and rya rugs had purpose in use. The border formed the rug's edge and ran along the sides of the bed, at the slumberers' necks and shoulders, and feet. It was nearest the heads and exposed limbs of sleeping bodies, where gaps in the bedclothes caused by the movement of bodies were most likely to occur. The placement of rows of crosses around the border formed a barrier of saining symbols along the edges of the bed and around its inhabitants. In this way, the motifs in taatit rugs may be considered visual messages to paranormal visitors, not humans.

The majority of cross forms used in Norwegian material culture has been noted as not the cruciform type, but the "Greek" or balanced cross (Tin 2007: 74). This form predates the Christian period and is considered a symbol of the conjoin of two parts: heaven and earth, the north–south/east–west axis of the earth, man and woman (Kostveit 1997: 36). In Norway, it was used as a protection symbol in many areas of life: crosses were carved on the doors of food stores; lambs and calves were tarred with crosses to keep them safe; butter molds and containers were incised with crosses to signify it was not troll butter (Kostveit 1997: 41–2). "Crossing" an infant ensured it would not become a changeling (Asbjørnsen and Moe 2012).

Sylwan considered the balanced cross to be a protective symbol in Swedish material culture, comparing its use in rya rugs by the weaver with the farmer who carves crosses into barns and byres to guard against evil on the farm (Sylwan 1934: 86).

Circles in taatit rug design are usually placed directly in the center of the rug, with each rug half comprising one half of the circle. The circles are large and dominate the center field. In use, they are positioned on the lower torso of the sleeper, over the abdomen and vital organs. The remaining central field covered most of the body from the upper chest to ankles. The use of crosses, checkerboards, and the compound nature of these motifs throughout many central fields appear to have a sense of density and urgency in motif placement.

Checkerboards and the Mara

The affliction of sleep paralysis affects people around the world and therefore the folklore addressing the symptoms of the affliction appear in most cultures. Sleep paralysis causes sufferers to feel motionless while being wide awake, and to have a feeling of chest compression and difficulty breathing. Some experience the sound of footsteps approaching or a presence near the bed prior to the feeling of chest compression.

In folklore, the symptoms have been described as a creature or a woman "riding" the chest of the sufferer. The Mara also is believed to disturb horses and cattle, leaving them sweaty and agitated, sometimes with a tangled mane.

In Norwegian folklore it was believed the Mara could only count to three, so that placing an object with more than three parts above the bed or over the byre stall would frustrate and drive the Mara away. Pine branches and dead birds were nailed to byre walls where animals were stalled. A checkerboard pattern was carved onto food store boxes, chests, and byre beams (Asker 1967; Landsverk 1989: 30). The checkerboard formation of squares on woven textiles for the Norwegian home are considered Mara barriers (*muruspjeld*), similar to those found in rya bedcovers (Haugstoga 1967: 37–8).

Checkerboards appear on taatit rugs as a large central motif, thereby placed over the chest of the sufferer. They also occur in corners of the border or central field. Repetitive squares, although they are not joined, may be considered a Mara barrier, according to Norwegian folklore, as would the scatter of squares seen on so many rugs.

Conclusion

The significance of taatit rugs to the families that made and used them is inherent in their functionality and design. They served as the householder's main bedcover from at least the time of marriage and were expected to last a lifetime. Rugs covered the family bed, where consummation, birth, illness, and death took place. Many have been handed down as heirlooms.

Their design similarities to rya rugs of Scandinavia is striking. Many of the same motifs are used and the design form of rugs is often similar, although construction techniques are quite different between the Scandinavian and Shetland types. The repetitive use of certain forms in rug design requires consideration of the use of rugs as nightly bedcovers when humans are more vulnerable. The motifs applied to rya and taatit rugs are the same symbols reported in folklore and used ritually in folk practice to ward off nocturnal, harmful paranormal beings. Darkness in the European north becomes an essential element in understanding human agency in creating barriers to perceived danger. Everyday materials fashioned into magical devices by the form they are given provide tools for premeditative action. In so doing, the uncontrollable world of daily darkness becomes a more manageable environment.

Protecting the interior of the home was vital and the use of saining devices at thresholds to provide an extra level of protection was commonplace. The designs of taatit and rya rugs can be seen in this context as providing saining mechanisms through the weaving and embroidery of symbols used in similar ways as other devices used throughout the household and property. Bedcovers were an ideal vehicle for saining motifs, covering the family during sleep and vulnerable periods of illness and childbirth. The rugs enable an understanding of the meaning of symbols and their significance in space and time, providing multilayered, physical, and mental comfort.

The belief in trows is no longer practiced in Shetland, although it remains in parts of Iceland and other areas of Scandinavia. Modern medicine provides cause for the death of mothers and infants in childbirth. Yet one motif, the balanced cross, endures in modern life throughout the world as a symbol of help, protection, and health. It is used by the Red Cross and military units during war and disaster relief. It is a common sight in European cities for the location of a pharmacy and is used to indicate the location of hospitals on maps. This ancient, pre-Christian symbol is still used to provide a universal visual message of protection and safety.

Notes

1. The Rev. Dr. James Ingram (1776–1879) was Church of Scotland minister in the parish of North Yell and Fetlar from 1803 to 1822, and of Unst Parish from 1821.

References

Asbjørnsen, P. C. and J. Moe (2012), "En Signekjerring", *Norske Folkeeventyr*. Available online: http://runeberg.org/folkeven/038.html (accessed March 23, 2022).

Asker, R. (1967), "Noen karvestkurdskister med muruspjeld", *Årbok Drammens Museum 1965–66*: 9–36.

Christiansen, C. (2015), *Taatit Rugs, the pile bedcovers of Shetland*, Lerwick: Shetland Heritage Publications.

Christiansen, R. Th. (1992), *The Migratory Legends*, Helsinki: Academia Scientiarum Fennica.

Davies, O. (2003), "The Nightmare experience, sleep paralysis, and witchcraft accusations", *Folklore*, 114 (2): 181–203.

Dishington, Rev. A. (1978), "United Parishes of Mid and South Yell", in D. J. Withrington and I. R. Grant (eds), *Statistical Account of Scotland*, XIX, Wakefield: E. P. Publishing.

Edmondston, Rev. B. and J. M. E. Saxby (1888), *The Home of a Naturalist*, London: James Nisbet.

Engelstad, H. (1942), *Norske Ryer: teknikk, form og bruk*, Oslo: Cammermeyer.

Eriksen, M. H. (2013), "Doors to the Dead: The Power of Doorways and Thresholds in Viking Age Scandinavia", *Archaeological Dialogues* 20 (2): 187–214.

Fenton, A. (1978), *The Northern Isles: Orkney and Shetland*, Edinburgh: John Donald.

Haugstoga, S. (1967), "Muruspjeld-former i vev", *Årbok Drammens Museum 1965–66*: 36–8.

Jakobsen, J. (1993), *The Place-Names of Shetland*, Kirkwall: Orcadian.

Kjellmo, E. (1996), *Båtrya, i gammel og ny tid*, Stamsund: Orkana.

Koski, K. (2020), "Nightmares—from demonic attacks to self-knowledge", *Tidskriften Sömn och hälsa*, 4: 64–75.

Kostveit, Å. Ø. (1997), *Kors I Kake, Skurd I Tre*, Oslo: Landbruksforlaget.

Landsverk, H. (1989), "Murutusten og muruspjeldet", *Årsskrift Notodden Historielag*, 30–1.

Mill, Rev. J. (1889), *The Diary of the Reverend John Mill, Minister of the Parishes of Dunrossness, Sandwick and Cunningsburgh in Shetland, 1740–1803*, Edinburgh: Scottish History Society.

Nicolson, J. (1937), *Restin' Chair Yarns*, Lerwick: Johnson and Grieg.

Pylkkänen, R. (1974), *The Use and Traditions of Mediaeval Rugs and Coverlets in Finland*, Helsinki: Suomen muinaismuistoyhdistys.

Raudvere, C. (2020), "Maror och mardrömmar i bondesamhället", *Tidskriften Sömn och hälsa*, 4: 49–63.

Rohrbach, L. (2017), "The Chronotopes of Íslendinga saga: Narrativizations in Thirteenth-Century Iceland", *Scandinavian Studies*, 89 (3): 351–74.

Saxby, J. M. E. (1932), *Shetland Traditional Lore*, Edinburgh: Grant & Murray.

Sirelius, U. T. (1926), *The Ryijy Rugs of Finland, a historical study*, Helsinki, Otava.

Spence, J. (1999), *Shetland Folk-Lore*, Felinfach: Llanerch Press.

Stewart, G. (1892), *Shetland Fireside Tales*, 2nd edn, Lerwick: T. & J. Manson.

Sylwan, V. (1934), *Svenska Ryor*, Stockholm: Bokförlaget Natur och Kultur.

Taylor, H. P. (1948), *A Shetland Parish Doctor*, Lerwick: T. & J. Manson.

Tin, M. B. (2007), *De Første Formene*, Oslo: Novus Forlag.

Vahter, T. and A. N. Linnove (1955), *Vanhoja, Kauniita, Käsitöitä*, Porvoo: Werner Söderström Osakeyhtiö.

Wang, M. (1983), *Ruteåklær: bidrag til en karakteristikk, ordning og plassering*, Bergen: Universitetsforlaget.

"Readings of transforming cloth into clothing represents the knowledge, awareness, and concerns of the maker and the wearer. These attributes manifest through the cultural-making; the conscious act of cutting and stitching the shifting identity of a society at a given time in place."

LOkesh Ghai

7

Making of Kediyun: A Conscious Approach to Cloth

LOKESH GHAI

Background

The Indian subcontinent has a rich heritage of the flat rectangular cloths such as the saree or the dhoti which are woven in different structure, weights, width, lengths, and designs, draped around the body depending on the region and community. Saree is both a cloth and a piece of clothing and in the colloquial language, cloth and clothes are one. Parallel to the uncut cloth there is also a rich heritage of ways to cut cloth to make clothing. While the making of the off-loom and the uncut cloth has attracted several studies over the decades (Baker 1999; Chishti and Singhi 2010; Shamanna 2020), there are very few publications on the transformation through cutting and stitching of the cloth into stitched clothes.

Textbooks used in an Indian context and general publications on using fabric to construct clothes, such as *Metric Pattern Cutting* (Aldrich 2013), *Pattern Making for Fashion* (Pearson and Armstrong 2013), are either American- or Europe-centric. This chapter is an attempt to decolonize how the regional cloth and the making of a regional garment, the kediyun, is understood. Cutting and stitching the cloth in the making of the kediyun is explored from a cultural context. Apprenticeship of this cutting and stitching as a methodology was followed by me, the author.

Introduction

The kediyun (pl. kediya) is a regional upper garment worn by men in most pastoral communities in Kutch (Jain 1980). Historically, Kutch was part of the Indian Valley Civilization with evidence of cotton cultivation and handwoven cotton, dating to 500 BCE. As a living heritage, the semi-desert of Kutch had been home to various communities who migrated from as far as Central Asia to the north of India. The men of the various communities such as the Ahir, Rabari, and Patel and until a few decades ago, even Vankar, the weaver community, wore the kediyun. The garment with variations is a community-identity signifier. This is not one single feature, but a combination of elements in making that denote the specific community and even its subgroups. These elements include its length, detailing features such as gathering and tucking, techniques of stitching, and of joining parts of the garment. The cloth used for making the kediyun, until some four generations ago, was handspun and handwoven *desi* cotton. The cotton is grown locally in Vagad, Kutch district and Surendranagar district. As a daily worn cloth, the kediyun was typically plain white but for special occasions, the kediyun was embroidered with styles unique to each community. Thereafter, handloom plain weave locally known as "doubling" became popular and since the 1980s, the twill weave cotton mill fabric became popular due to affordability and strength. Around the same time there were a few instances of Rabari men traveling to Saudi countries as contract laborers. Mercerized and other varieties of cotton were brought back as souvenirs for making kediyun.

Until recently, most Rabari communities kept camels, sheep, or goats; annual migration was undertaken to find green pasture for the cattle. Now, there are only a handful of families who still make this migration. Fresh milk from camels and goats was readily available for daily consumption and bartered for other commodities, such as flour, pulses, oil, spices carried for cooking. Wool was handspun by the Rabaris and given to the weavers for weaving; the spinner could recognize the yarn spun by them and could identify if the cloth was woven from their yarn. Men of Patels and Ahirs communities cultivated desi cotton besides food grains. The women of Ahir community were particularly known for hand spinning of cotton, which they provided to the weavers. The weaver received grains and other commodities for weaving by the community yet as a consequence of being on the move with the cattle, the semi-nomadic lifestyle meant self-sustenance. Temporary *chula*, the earthen gas fire, is used for cooking; the cattle are parked for grazing for a few days until a new pasture is required. Cattle dung provides manure to the farms, in return for which the caravan is compensated in kind or cash (Edwards 2010). While at home or during periods of travel, and in between all the domestic activities, time is taken out by the women to repair, stitch, and embroider the regional clothing. Primarily the kediyun was made by women only for the same community as those who wore it. While almost all women could stitch the kediyun in earlier times, only four in a hundred knew about the cutting of the cloth. Currently, it is rare to find even one woman out of a population of 10,000 practicing the techniques.

Making of Kediyun as a Traditional Folk-Craft Practice

Should the kediyun be described as a craft object? The World Craft Council (WCC 2020: online) defines handicrafts as objects produced partly or completely by hand or with help of tools, where the "manual contribution of the maker remains the most substantial component of the finished product." The raw materials used in handicrafts are ecologically sourced. In the case of the kediyun in the traditional context, the cotton was grown, handspun, and handwoven locally. Kutch being a dry region grew the desi cotton variety, as the farming did not need much water—one period of rainfall was enough to sustain cotton growing and no chemicals were used to promote production. Since cotton dyeing was not a heritage among the weavers or spinners, the fabric was always off-white, the original color of cotton.

"Handicrafts are a major element of folklore developed in India. These are objects made by the skill of the hand and depict the ingenuity of the creator and cultural heritage evolved over centuries. Created primarily to serve the ritual and personal needs of the community, these handicraft objects have entered the market for commercial trade" (Kutty 2002: 20). Traditionally, Indian folk craft is not rooted in commercial exchange and the kediyun may thus be categorized as folk craft. The folk aspect of the garment is an important consideration while studying the making process. The symbolic value and the maker's direct involvement is critical.

Units of Measuring the Cloth

India had its own indigenous system of measurement depending on the region. The Indian Weights and Measures Act passed in 1870 introduced the British imperial system. In 1956, almost a decade post-independence, the Indian Parliament implemented the metric system of measurement. However, most village artisans continued using their body for measurement. When a traditional house, such as a *bhunga*, was built, the height was calculated according to the height of the inhabitants. The weavers handwove the fabric according to their body parts such as their handspan. For measuring the cloth, the maker's body was used which includes the variations of size. Cloths were thus measured according to each woman's individual body for making the kediyun. The same method is even used today by the last few makers. The smallest unit to measure cloth is "unglee," the width of the finger; "tasu" refers to one handspan and "vaar" the distance from shoulder to thumb with outstretched arms.

To measure the body, the cloth is held against the body and markings are taken. The measuring of cloth against the body is fundamentally different to the use of a tape measure since when the cloth is measured directly against the body, the drape and the fall of the cloth are also accounted for.

Changes Adapted in Measure in the Units

Almost fifty years ago, the introduction of mill-made cloth gained popularity in Kutch. However, the women who earlier purchased cloth from the weaver or the *pheriwala* (cloth seller who moves from one village to another) according to "vaar" were confused about the new measure in meters. Soon the locals devised the method of measuring the meter as per the body. A meter length is derived by stretching of the fabric from the nose to the thumb. The incorporation of meters measured according to the body as a tool shows how adaptive the locals have been and how tradition evolves (Ghai 2014).

The Body as a Creative Tool to Stitch the Cloth

The making of the kediyun was like a performance in a domestic environment since the makers incorporated their body into the technique of making the garment. The skill of making the kediyun is tacit knowledge, passed on from one generation of women to another. It is not just the making process that was was specific to each garment due to the varying finger widths, handspans and arm lengths that were employed. The makers also developed a personal approach to measuring and working with their own bodies. The hand was used for the purpose of stitching but also as a measure for the cloth and wearer and the foot was employed to hold the fabric, with the big toe and the thigh

Figure 7.1 The incorporated character of making the kediyun is seen here in Jamnaben's use of her big toe, legs, and hands in stitching of the cloth. Photography: © LOkesh Ghai.

used to secure the thread and cloth. The palms of the hands then performed the twisting of the thread to make a double-ply. Thus, each kediyun had a direct, personal relationship to the individual body of the maker.

Cutting of the Cloth

Garments that predated the invention of mechanical looms relied on short fabric widths for cutting. Hence, the width of the fabric is important in guiding the cut of garments (Burman 1973). For stitched clothing over the last few decades, wider-width mill cloth replaced handlooms. Besides the width of the fabric, the structure of the weave and how tightly or loosely it is woven matters for both stitching and breathability. The weavers' community in Kutch, which earlier handwove fabric for kediyun, have now completely shifted to weaving new products such as sarees, stoles, and dupattas for tourists or urban markets. According to Jamnaben Ahir, one of the last makers of kediyun, when the current generation of weavers weave cloth on the handloom for local clothing style, it is very tight and not as smooth for the needle to handstitch. Additionally, handspun yarn used in the warp and weft of the cloth was softer than the mill-spun.

Zero Cloth Wastage in Making

The calculations involved in making the kediyun can be described as a method that is shared socially. Yet the method is quite flexible, as there is no one strict way of cutting the pattern—it can be adapted according to the maker's experience. Part of the maker's intelligence is that the pattern will be cut in a way that wastes almost no fabric. It can also be adapted according to the selvedge and width of the fabric. The cloth is cut in blocks, the smallest block, or from fabric that comes out through the cut of the necklines; this is where strings are made from. Nothing is wasted. For "chaar," the largest part of the kediyun, which drops from the waist across the body, the fabric is cut against the off grain (i.e., it is cut in horizontal grain instead of vertical grain). Wherever the selvedge reaches the side or bottom hem of the garment, it is left unstitched, making most of the finished edges of the cloth.

Chaar of the Kediyun

"Chaar" refers to the panel attached to the waist of the kediyun, which is where the maximum amount of cloth is consumed. The chaar gives a distinct and dramatic character to the garment. According to the makers, the chaar is the most important part of the kediyun. The length of the chaar and how it is stitched signifies what subgroup the wearer belongs to.

In the case of Dhebaria Rabari (as practiced by Bhaddiben and Puriben), the cloth for chaar is gathered, stitched to the edge of the bodice with a running stitch, leaving a six-finger space unstitched as an open space to insert a pocket. In another case of Dhebaria Rabari (Jivaben), the cloth is carefully pleated, each pleat is nail-pressed, and the finely pleated cloth is held by a backstitch. These could possibly have been different fashions of making the chaar and may have evolved with different kinds of fabric use. In the case of Machhoya Ahir (Jamnaben), the cloth is tucked and held by a fly stitch.

Stitching the Cloth

The cloth is cut as blocks and joined step-by-step, starting with the back and the two fronts that overlap. Where required, the fabric basting is made by long running stitches that are cut later, once the final stitching is made. The cloth is secured by a variety of hand stitches depending on the part of the kediyun. The side seams are made using running stitches, the collar is slip hemmed, the yoke is always attached with a back stitch providing strength at the double-layered cloth. The gusset is attached by a variety of fishbone stitches, depending on the community the maker belongs to.

The craft of stitching the cloth to make the kediyun on the one hand binds a particular subgroup together and on the other, establishes and communicates the differing identities of various regional subgroups. For example, according to Jamnaben Ahir from the subgroup of Machhoya of the Ahir caste, the sewing needle is uniquely positioned in a diagonal direction during the process of *cheen-bandhan*, which is the feather stitch that links the chaar to the bodice.

The stitching of the cloth to construct the kediyun can also be read as a form of personal expression because hand stitching has its own recognizable and idiosyncratic form. Indeed Millar (2012) describes hand stitching as a form of handwriting. Frater (1995) describes the hand embroidery of various subgroups of women in Kutch as dialects of a language. Since the measurements depend on the size of the maker's features, this too adds to the unique identity of the kediyun. Together, hand measurements and stitching make each kediyun a distinct part of an individual's creativity.

Cultural-Making in Stitching the Cloth

The "processes" of stitching the cloth for adornment and making into "clothes" to fit the body serves as deity of a community—emotionally, religiously, and spiritually unique to the maker's group.

According to belief, it is important to have good thoughts while stitching the cloth, as thoughts too get hand stitched into the seam (Ghai 2013).[1] The stitching of clothes is a domestic and private activity for the women, like offering prayers to gods in the morning, milking a cow, or cooking. On the surface it may appear that a dish may not taste good if made in a hurry or when in a bad mood; similarly, the cloth may appear not stitched well; on a deeper level it is about the spiritual aspect of the maker. While the memory of a not so well-made dish may be forgotten, a stitched cloth lasts longer and represents the person. Although now coming to an end, there was a cultural practice within the Kacchi Rabari community of introducing the first cousin to the community through the kediyun hand stitched by her for her brother as a groom, worn by him during one of the marriage ceremonies.

No weaving of cloth, stitching of cloth or any activity where a knot may be formed is avoided on particular days to honor Shitala Mata. Shitala in Sanskrit refers to smallpox and mata means mother. Freed and Freed (1962: 265) state that she is "the most feared of the goddesses of sickness" in India. She is described as the oldest of deities associated with smallpox and measles, possibly dating back as long as 2,000 to 3,000 years. She is believed to cause and clean the germs of the disease and to have the power to cool the patients. It is believed that the Shitala Mata could get stuck in the knot while weaving or stitching the cloth, thus causing the virus to pass to the child in the house. Shital means cool, the opposite of hot. Even fire is not lit on the day, and cooking avoided, food prepared on the previous day is eaten; it is a day to slow down, rest, in honor of the protective goddess.

Folk songs and how the cloth is cut or hand stitched gave expression to the women, enabling them to find their voice within the community and the region at large. Due to the semi-nomadic lifestyle, most of the pastoral community relied on visual and verbal communication over text. Literacy among the communities is a recent phenomenon; even today, the majority of the pastoral community above the age of fifty do not know how to read or write and the rate is higher amongst the women. It is in the stitching of cloth where the women have found their expression over the generations: through the embroidery of the kediyun and other regional clothing or through the cloth itself as an additional adornment, and through stitching used to construct the clothing.

Kutchi is a distinct language from Gujarati; however it does not have a script, so folk songs became an important expression for commutation passed on from generations.

The following is a translation of an Ahir song related to stitching of the cloth:

> One by one with the needle I stitched the mirror on the kediyun; in the mirror I saw the reflection of Lord Krishna's face. I hemmed the chaar of the kediyun, stitched the shoulder, and attached the tie-ups. For the "cheen" I used red and yellow colored thread. With a diagonal movement of the needle I stitched the kediyun.[2]

Through the stitching of the cloth, the song romanticizes the relationship of the disciple who is the maker of the kediyun. It details, in the maker's voice, how she has constructed the kediyun. It is notable that these details of kediyun making are specific to the Machhoya Ahir subgroup. Although Jamnaben has a sewing machine, she believes that a good and true Machoiya Ahir's kediyun is only possible by hand stitching. Hand stitching is considered a personal act of dedication or identity, which is lost according to her with machine stitching. Additionally, it may be noted that certain stitches such as fly stitching or variation of a fishbone stitch may not be possible with a sewing machine. Even if the stitches were possible with a sewing machine in future, it would still not be the same. A machine follows an algorithm, where personalization is not the same as something that is hand stitched.

The following is a translation of a song sung by the Rabari women related to stitching of the cloth:

> O Ram let me worship you . . . Let me wear the kediyun where the cloth is stitched with a backstitch.[3]

The song lists emotions and desires that a disciple wishes to do as part of dedicating to God. Stitching of the cloth for making the kediyun and wearing of kediyun is part of these.

Conclusion

The making of kediyun exemplifies addressing cloth with a conscious approach. Many lessons can be learned which I reflect upon here. Climate change, land, air, and water pollution are all related to consumption patterns. The fashion and textile industry, with cloth as its staple, is one of the largest industries contributing to the damage. What if the same sensibility of having good thoughts while stitching the cloth is exercised as with the kediyun? These foundational good thoughts equate to the Sustainable Development Goals (SDGs),[4] or any such manifesto that encourages wellness in the act of making and consuming.

The construction of the kediyun exemplifies circular making. The fiber used for the cloth in the traditional context is from locally grown desi cotton, it is handspun and woven using local skills, supporting local makers, and no electricity is used in any of the making stages. Cotton yarn/cloth is not dyed, avoiding water and land pollution.

Worn-out kediyun are mended. Three to four kediyun suffices the wearer: two to three as a daily wear, in plain white cotton, and a special one for festive occasions with embroidery detailing. The embroidered kediyun is occasionally worn and often passed from one generation to another. The making of the kediyun is also about slowing down, pursuing quality over quantity. On certain days, the women in honor of the goddess need to take a break from domestic chores, including stitching of cloth.

The making of the kediyun is also unique to the hot climate of the region. The maker literally sits on the cloth laid on the ground, body parts are used efficiently to hold, press, shape, and stitch the cloth. The maker's body is usually quite athletic, working in this fashion. Further research is required in this subject area. However, it could be suggested that there is a muscle memory involved in using the cloth with the involvement of different parts of the body. For making the kediyun, no fabric is wasted while cutting the cloth. It is remarkable that zero waste is adapted to different widths of fabric. Acquiring knowledge from the heritage of cutting the cloth with zero waste could be an approach that is popularized in design education.

Translating cloth to clothes is an approach that draws upon the cultural-making and the traditional concepts of economy and no waste. The process of making, from the cloth to clothes, is deeply rooted in the specific cultural approach to making but can have wider resonance and application. The folk songs from the region point to the importance and use of "emotional design," and where the maker is known to the wearer. In this way the cloth holds emotional value in the care taken to make each handmade kediyun.

Fashion and textile design students and established designers across the globe often take "visual" inspiration from culture-specific cloth and clothing such as the

Figure 7.2 Jamnaben Karna Hungla Ahir, with her husband wearing a kediyun made by the author. Photography: © LOkesh Ghai.

Making of Kediyun: A Conscious Approach to Cloth

kediyun. However, they fail to address the concept, the knowledge, the ideas embedded in the making process—that is, the journey of cloth to become clothes. This cycle of production acknowledges the importance of sustainability: traditional sustainable practices that can inform slow fashion. The kediyun reminds us of the ethics around making, where there is inclusivity at each stage of production as an interlocking chain of people and making. The kediyun also signposts the emotional value of design, where those involved are connected; of the importance of well-made objects; of skill and meaning in making through the process of construction. The making of kediyun has lessons that relate to modern design processes and future responsible garment making.

Notes

1. The term "stitching" implies all kind of stitching, such as hemming, seam construction, as well as embroidery. Hence, to single out "seam" would limit the proudness of the phrase, implying to care in thoughts while only making seams and not other hand stitching processes of the cloth.
2. "Ahir song" sung by women of the Ahir community (of Kutch), recorded in person, May 2012 in Kutch, Gujarat. I recorded this song in the Kutchi language, sung by Jamnaben Ahir and her daughter Champuben Ahir, together. A tentative translation with help of Dayalal Atmaram Vankar is presented in English.
3. "Rabari song" sung by women of the Rabari community (of Kutch), recorded in person, May 2012 in Kutch, Gujarat. I recorded this song in the Kutchi language, sung by Hasuben Mohan Rabari and Bhaddiben Rabari, separately. A tentative translation with help of Lakhabhai Rabari is presented in English.
4. The United Nation's Sustainable Development Goals (2015) "are an urgent call for action by all countries—developed and developing—in a global partnership. They recognize that ending poverty and other deprivations must go hand-in-hand with strategies that improve health and education, reduce inequality, and spur economic growth—all while tackling climate change and working to preserve our oceans and forests" https://sdgs.un.org/goals (accessed April 30, 2023).

Acknowledgments

Manchester Metropolitan University for research grant.
Kediyun makers: Jamnaben Karna Hungla Ahir, Jivaben Rabari, Bhaddiben Soma Rabari and Puriben Meghabhai Rabari.
Alison Welsh, Amanda Ravetz and Judy Frater for their guidance during the research.

References

Aldrich, W. (2013). *Fabrics and pattern cutting*. John Wiley & Sons.
Baker, T. D. (1999) *Uncut cloth: Saris, shawls and sashes*.
Burman, D. (1973). *Cut my cote*, Toronto: Royal Ontario Museum.
Chishti, R. K., Singh, M. and Kelkar, R. (2010). *Saris of India: Tradition and beyond*.
Edwards, E. (2010). "Textile and dress among the Rabari of Kutch", In Simpson, E and Kapadia, A., *The idea of Gujarat history, ethnography and text*, New Delhi: Orient Blackswan Pvt. Ltd, pp. 199–202.
Frater, J. (1995). *Threads of identity*, Ahmedabad India: Mapin.
Freed, S. And Freed A. (1962), "Two Mother Goddess Ceremonies of Delhi State in the Great and Little Traditions". *Southwestern Journal of Anthropology*, 18 (3): 246–77 [Online] http://www.jstor.org/stable/3628878 (accessed July 1, 2022).
Ghai, L. (2014). "Don't cry over spilt milk: apprenticing with the last makers of the 'Milkman's dress'", unpublished Masters Dissertation, Manchester Metropolitan University.
Jain, J. (1980). Folk Art and Culture of Gujarat, Ahmedabad: Shreyas Prakashan.
Kutty (2002). *National Experiences with the protection of expressions of Folklore/Traditional Culture Expressions: India, Indonesia and the Philippines* (Vol. 912). World Intellectual Property Organization.
Miller, M. (2012). "Embroidery and the F-word" In McKeating, J and Kettle, *Hand Stitch, Perspectives*, UK, Bloomsbury. pp. 116–32.
Pearson and Armstrong (2013). *Patternmaking for Fashion* |Fifth Edition| Pearson Education India.
Shamanna, S. (2020). *Tana Bana: The World of Sarees*. Notion Press.
United Nation's Sustainable Development Goals (2015) [Online] https://sdgs.un.org/goals (accessed July 1, 2022).
WCC [Online] http://wccapr.org (accessed May 18, 2021).
WIPO [Online] http://www.wipo.int/tk/en/tk/ (accessed May 18, 2021).

"From my African perspective, cloth is a sum-total of the culture of a given society. It reveals and yet conceals the underlying traditions and values of a people at any given time across the social, economic, and political continuum. Cloth is a powerful medium of communication and agency. It encodes and radiates the identity and political histories of humanity, thus making the sartorial past a valid reference for the contemporary and future creative generations."

Venny Mary Nakazibwe

8

Transformations in the Making and Meaning of Bark Cloth in Uganda

VENNY MARY NAKAZIBWE

Introduction

Throughout history, cloth has been central to the social, cultural, and political organization of societies in Africa. Amongst the historical textile traditions known in Africa is the indigenous technology of bark cloth making, which involves careful extraction of the bark of selected plant species and beating it with specially grooved wooden mallets until it turns into a soft pliable material suitable for clothing and upholstery purposes. The mutuba, *ficus natalensis*, is the most commonly known source of bark cloth in East Africa, particularly in the central and southern Uganda kingdom of Buganda, which is believed to have been in existence from around the twelfth or thirteenth century. The *mutuba* (pl. *mituba*) belongs to the phylum *spermatophyte*, class *angiospermae*, family *moraceae*, and genus *ficus* (Ipulet 1993: 1). It is also commonly referred to as the bark cloth tree.

The bark cloth, *olubugo* as it is referred to in Luganda, language of the Baganda, is historically and culturally imbued with meaning. It served most of the essential functions, ranging from clothing, bedding, partitioning of space, securing valuable cultural items, covering the living and the dead as marker of social hierarchies, and as a signifier of royalty in the dominant kingdoms of Buganda, Bunyoro, Toro, and Busoga in Central, Western, and Eastern Uganda respectively (Nakazibwe 2005: 85). With many of its functions currently replaced by industrial products, the technology of bark cloth making has subsided. However, the Uganda bark cloth has conversely gained new functions and new meaning since it was declared by UNESCO in 2005 as a masterpiece of oral and intangible heritage of humanity. Pockets of bark cloth making activities are still visible in the districts of Masaka, Bukomansimbi, Kalungu, and Rakai, all located in Buddu, in Southern Uganda, which is the historical hub of bark cloth making in the precolonial Buganda kingdom. Within the banana and coffee plantations, the Baganda planted *emituba* (sing. *omutuba*) for the production of bark cloth.

Historical Cultural Importance of Bark Cloth in Precolonial Buganda

The popularization of bark cloth can be traced back to around the last quarter of the eighteenth century, a period when Ssekabaka Ssemakokiro (1779–94) passed a decree for all his subjects to propagate bark cloth trees in their gardens.[1] Prior to this, the technology of bark cloth making was kept secret between the members of the *Ngonge* (otter) clan, one of the original clans that joined four others to form the kingdom of Buganda. A member of this clan is believed to have made this artistic discovery and introduced it to the king. Ssekabaka Ssemakiro is revered by the Baganda for having revolutionized the bark cloth industry when he made bark cloth making a mandatory activity. Every Muganda male of adult age was required by royal decree to plant *emituba* and process enough bark cloth for the needs of their family. Thenceforth, bark cloth became a significant material culture in all the cultural rituals of the Baganda. Bark cloth symbolizes continuity of the ethnic lineage that runs through the royal blood, as in the case of the Buganda kingship, and also through the clan and family structure, as in the case of the ordinary people.

As will be noted later in this chapter, the transformative power of bark cloth has continually manifested through various cultural ceremonies as well as in contemporary fashion and dress, thereby articulating the historical and contemporary cultural exchanges in Uganda and on the global stage. Historically, bark cloth was central in all ceremonies that marked the life cycle of the Baganda, including child initiation ceremonies, twin initiation ceremonies, pre-marriage introduction ceremonies, and marriage ceremonies. Historically, bark cloth was a garb of royalty, exclusively worn by Kabaka, the king of Buganda, members of the royal family, and some great chiefs. The king dressed in two pieces of bark cloth: one knotted on the right shoulder and another on the left, over which he swathed a leopard skin. The *bakembuga* (royal women) dressed in two layers of bark cloth wrapped in form of a skirt, over which they draped a third piece from below the armpits swathing down to the ankles. They secured the draping bark cloth from the waistline with *olwebagyo*, a sash of a lighter hue. The sartorial code for the chiefs, however, consisted of one bark cloth (dressed in toga style) covered with a well-dressed cowhide in apron style that was secured tightly with a bark cloth sash. The exceptional categories of people outside the royal domain that were privy to wearing of bark cloth included diviners, chiefs, court musicians and court dancers, contingent on the special duties they performed at the royal palace.

Bark cloth making also became a major economic industry for the Baganda. Bark cloth was in great demand by the aristocratic class in Karagwe (in the current northwestern region of Tanzania), Bunyoro, Nkore, Tooro, and as far as Rwanda, who obtained the fabric through the market centers that were operational in the region. The Kiganda sartorial style in bark cloth was eventually noted among royals in the kingdoms of Bunyoro, Tooro in Western Uganda, and Busoga in Eastern Uganda (Lugira 1970). The transformative power of bark cloth is continually manifested through dress and costume during cultural ceremonies as well as in contemporary fashion and visual artistic expressions and cultural exchanges in Uganda and on the global stage.

Cloth is a powerful means of communication; it identifies and secludes, and it is a clear marker of social hierarchies based on politics and gender roles in a given community. Bark cloth therefore was associated with royalty, and only members of a specific clan who were believed to have exceptional skill in bark cloth making were assigned a special duty to provide high-quality bark cloth for the king and other members of the royal domain. Bark cloth replaced animal hides and skins, the earliest forms of dress by the royals in many precolonial indigenous communities, in the region that was later mapped by the colonial establishment to create the present-day Uganda.

From the cultural perspective of "tradition," the dress code of the various members of the royal domain evidently was a sign of prestige and a psychological interpretation of proximity to the royal center, the powerhouse. From a scholarly perspective in the context of this chapter, the bark cloth dress code at that time was imbued with visual narratives associated with power, dominance, and separation of gender roles that are deeply embedded in indigenous societies not only in Africa but all over the world. Through cloth, one can unravel historical layers of information in order to articulate the early anthropological perspectives on dress, power, and gender roles across different segments of society. Moreover, Susan B. Kaiser (1997), a social psychologist and specialist in the psychology of dress, clearly observes the polysemy of cloth. As she states, clothes rarely convey single meanings; more often, their messages may be described as consisting of *layers of meaning*, with some layers more applicable than others in a specific context.

By the time the Swahili-Arab traders arrived in the interior of East Africa around the 1840s, they found a lucrative bark cloth industry in Buganda. The notion of dress in bark cloth by the Baganda communicated their values and level of civilization, which were documented by the Western missionaries, anthropologists, and colonial officers who arrived in Buganda during the last quarter of the nineteenth century. Meanwhile, the palace remained the main consumer of bark cloth, which was used for different functions. As a material for interior decoration, it was used to line the walls of the palace and royal burial shrines. One such royal shrine of key importance to date is the Kasubi Tombs, a burial ground for the past four kings of Buganda. According to the architectural design of the *masiro*, a large piece of bark cloth was used to partition the building into two parts in order to seclude the royal tombs from public gaze.

Most importantly, bark cloth was used to preserve the umbilical cord of every newborn child in the family. According to customs of the Baganda, the legitimacy of membership to a family lineage and clan was proved, based on presentation of the child's umbilical cord, by mothers during the *okwalula abaana* (child initiation ceremony).

In addition, as a shroud, bark cloth made a visible impact on generating identity narratives that connect the Ganda kingship to the afterworld. Until recently, bark cloth served as an important connecting thread between the past and present generations in several indigenous societies. It served as a marker of social hierarchies and a measure of value. The kings, chiefs, and clan leaders were buried in as many as , one hundred, or even more bark cloths, signifying their status in the earthly world from which they are transiting to the afterworld. In most indigenous societies in Africa, it is assumed that the king does not die, but instead recedes into a spiritual realm. Therefore, he recedes with all the accolades and power, which are exemplified through dress. Again, the prince, and heir to the king, is presented with a bark cloth to carry out a ritual of *okubikka akabugo*, meaning to cover the body of the king—a symbol that marks the end of reign of the receded king, and the transfer of authority. From thenceforth, he becomes a king in waiting, and is heavily guarded.

Amongst the ordinary people, upon the death of a family member, neighbors and other people associated with the family of the deceased, either by blood relation or marriage, contributed bark cloth for the burial ceremony, for it was a matter of necessity for the Baganda to bury their deceased in enough bark cloth to protect the skeleton of the deceased from disintegration as they transcend to another world in a dignified manner. It is also a tradition for the heir to the deceased to be dressed in bark cloth at the installation ceremony. According to the customs of the Baganda, the ritual of dressing the heir in bark cloth symbolizes continuity of the ethnic lineage that runs through the clan and family structure in the case of the ordinary Baganda, and through the royal blood in the case of the Buganda kingship. This ceremony marks the end of the mourning period. Thus, whenever presented, irrespective of whether as part of a dowry at a pre-marriage ceremony or at the burial ceremony, bark cloth extended and bridged social relations amongst members of the broader family lineage and other members of the community.

Arguably, the liberalization of the technology of bark cloth making in Uganda revolutionized the sartorial options that were available to the indigenous societies in the country. Similarly, as Lou Taylor (2012) has observed, the late seventeenth and early eighteenth centuries were significant periods that were characterized by major shifts in the usage of fabrics around the world. As rightly noted, the social change of fashion fabrics was no longer so controlled by the sumptuary laws of court and church, but had become subject to new forces—those of market economies that created a whole new set of economic and cultural pressures. In East Africa, the Baganda sharpened their skills and turned bark cloth into a lucrative industry and significant form of trade with the neighboring kingdoms and chiefdoms in and beyond the boundaries of the present-day sovereign state of Uganda. The intra-regional and inter-regional trade not only facilitated exchange of goods and ideas, but also provided space for exchange of historical and contemporary narratives about these cultural artifacts in relation to identity, power, gender, and other social phenomena.

Figure 8.1 Coronation of Kabaka Muwenda Mutebi II. Photographer: © Pascal Le Segretain/Sygma via Getty Images.

Ojuku (1986) mentions that in the south and southeast of Uganda, the Konjo and Amba people wore bark cloth as loin cloths, which were tied around the waist and in between the legs, while the Tusi and Hima women of Western Uganda adopted a style covering the head and body using bark cloth. Yet in the Central, Western and Eastern regions, among the Baganda, Banyoro, Basoga, men wore a strip of bark cloth tied toga-wise and hung over one shoulder. Further, in Eastern Uganda, the Gwere, Sebei, Jopadhola, Gishu, Gwe, Samia, and Teso at one time wore skin but later adopted bark cloth for clothing. However, as noted elsewhere (Nakazibwe 2005), whereas there has been a wide use of bark cloth amongst the East African societies, it is in Buddu County, the Southern region of Buganda, where the tradition of bark cloth making has persisted against all odds at a fairly significant scale into the twenty-first century.

Bark Cloth Processing in Brief

The process of bark cloth making is relatively well documented and shared by many elders in Buganda. Harvesting of bark cloth is carried out during the two rainy seasons from March to May and from September to December. The harvesting process begins by making an incision around the base of the trunk and another one at the area where the branches split out. The bark cloth maker then makes a slightly deep longitudinal incision into the bark (though not too deep to damage the stem) from the top to the base of the stem and cuts it open. Using a sharpened banana stalk, the bark is carefully separated from the trunk. The freshly harvested bark is rolled up and taken to the bark cloth production workshop, ready for processing. Immediately after extraction of the bark, the exposed trunk is carefully wrapped in a bandage of green banana leaves to protect it from damage that can be attributed to bacterial infection, wind, or tropical heat. The trunk is opened after three or four days to allow it to aerate and to precipitate the regeneration of a new bark.

Upon harvesting, the *mukomazi*, the bark cloth artisan undertakes additional treatment of the bark to make it ready for production into a high-quality fabric characterized by a soft feel and terracotta brown coloration. The most common preparatory method is by way of steaming the bark, which is parceled in layers of fresh banana leaves for about 25–30 minutes until steam begins to escape through the banana leaf seal. The bark is kept aside in a damp condition until the time for processing. During the beating process, the bark is continuously moistened with water in order to keep it soft and prevent the fibers from splitting, and on completion, the newly processed bark cloth is stretched flat in an open area *(ekyano)* to precipitate oxidation, which is a necessary factor in the coloration process and which can take several hours or days, depending on the weather conditions.

The process of bark cloth making is conducted in a well-set and well-aerated environment, usually in the shade of a banana plantation, not far from the homestead. A beam made out of hardwood measuring about 12 feet long (365.76 cm), 6–8 inches in width (15.24–20.32 cm), and about 12 inches (30.48 cm) in height, is firmly embedded in the ground. The top part is smoothened and rendered flat. A simple shelter is built to cover the workshop area. Three sides of the shelter are made out of grass or dry banana leaves, leaving the front elevation open to allow light and circulation of fresh air.

The mallets of varying sizes used in the production process are predominantly carved out of *enzo (teclea nobilis)* and *omusaali (mimusops ugandensis or garcinia buchananii)* in varying lengths, weight, and size of grooves, according to the required functions. Generally, the mallets used for bark processing in Buganda can be classified into three categories: *ensamo esaaka* (the biggest and heaviest mallet with deep grooves used in the initial process), *ensamo etenga* (the medium-sized mallet with shallower grooves), and *ensaamo enzituzo* (the smallest mallet with fine grooves, used for the final beating of bark cloth). All three sets of mallets perform a crucial function of intermeshing the fibers, thereby softening the bark and rendering it pliant and usable for upholstery and sartorial purposes.

Conversations Around the Bark Cloth Workshop

The bark cloth makers devised various methods of transmitting cultural information to the young ones through a conversational approach and using the apprenticeship method of learning by doing. It was a common practice for parents to teach their children the skill of bark cloth making from an early stage, when they were about four or five years of age, as a means of extending this cultural knowledge into posterity. Kyeyune (2003) emphasizes that such activities as bark cloth making were matters of cultural and social significance affecting the well-being of the whole community, of which the *mukomazi* (bark cloth maker) was an integral part. For that reason, whenever the *mukomazi* made the bark cloth, he was always conscious of his role in the perpetuation of this historical discovery and the relevance of this indigenous knowledge to the heritage of the Buganda kingdom. As such, through the conversations that prevailed at the bark cloth workshop, each apprentice meaningfully reflected on the values of their heritage as embodied in the symbolism of bark cloth. By the end of the last quarter of the nineteenth century, the mediators of a new form of education had arrived in Uganda and other global influences had taken root and disrupted the process and functions of bark cloth making in Uganda.

Global Influences on Bark Cloth: The Changing Meaning of Bark Cloth

At the time that Uganda had external contact with the rest of the world, the manufacture of bark cloth was still a lucrative activity in Buganda. In this section, we examine the extent to which global influences altered and negotiated the process and functions of bark cloth in Uganda. The Swahili-Arab trade interventions, Christianity, Western colonial influences through religion, education, and international tourism were some of the global influences that sparked transformations in the making and meaning of bark cloth in Uganda. Intra-regional and regional trade, and local politics are some of the other phenomena that influenced the redefinition of Uganda bark cloth manufacture in the past two centuries.

The mid-nineteenth century witnessed significant political, economic, and cultural transformations, which consequently impacted the making and meaning of bark cloth in Uganda. By the time there was external contact, initially by the Swahili-Arab traders, bark cloth manufacture was a lucrative industry. The pioneer coastal traders that were intent on reaching the interior of East Africa arrived in the 1840s during the reign of Ssekabaka Suuna II (1824–56) and traveled via the southern–northern route through Karagwe, in northwestern Tanzania, into Buddu (the southern county of the kingdom of Buganda). The Swahili-Arab traders, *abalungaana*, as they were referred to by the Baganda at that time, paved the way for significant changes that were later to be realized in the dress style of the Baganda and in a decline in the economic and cultural symbolic value of bark cloth. By establishing contact with Ssekabaka Suuna II, the Swahili-Arabs made formal commercial relations between the kingdom of Buganda and the Sultanate of Zanzibar, which not only resulted in formal trade between the two countries, but also culminated in the exchange of ideas and skills. In addition, this Swahili-Arab contact in Buganda engendered cross-cultural transfer of values and traditions between the two peoples.

A significant outcome of the Swahili-Arab contact with Buganda was the introduction of textiles (woven cloth). The fact that weaving technology was not known in Buganda at that time—bark cloth being by far the most highly developed fabric technology—the woven textiles appealed tremendously to the aesthetic sensibilities of Ssekabaka Suuna II. Other items included copper coils, salt, chinaware, beads, cowries (which were later to be used as form of currency), mirrors, musical instruments, and other exotic commodities. Initially presented as diplomatic gifts, *khila*, from the Sultan of Zanzibar to the Kabaka of Buganda, these were soon to become trade items between the two parties. Possession of imported goods from the coast became a royal privilege even though it took much longer for the king to adopt imported textiles for clothing purposes. However, he directly took charge of custody of his collection, including the bark cloth that was embellished in pattern and color, more or less like cloth. Ssekabaka Suuna II perceived his ownership of cloth and patterned bark cloth as a way of accentuating wealth, power, and privilege in much the same way that the leopard skin was a valuable royal insignia.

However, significant changes occurred during the reign of Ssekabaka Muteesa I (1856–84). By the last quarter of the nineteenth century, imported textiles had become a fully fledged symbol of royalty, authority, prosperity, and prestige. Kaggwa (1999) reports that a caravan headed by a rich and influential merchant from Tabora arrived at

Ssekabaka Muteesa I's palace at Nakawa, near Kampala, in 1867. Khamis ibn Abdullah, originally from Muscat, presented to Kabaka Muteesa I a significant quantity of exotic goods, including a variety of luxurious Arab textiles and garments that changed drastically the sartorial style of the Kabaka, giving him an "Arab look." Kabaka Muteesa I distributed some of the textiles to his wives, to the princesses, and to his favorite pages.

Muteesa I adopted a style of dress comprising a closely fitting coat that draped down nearly to his feet. It was dark blue trimmed with gold. He wore a turban and his general appearance was decidedly Arabic. From his waist was suspended a Turkish scimitar supported by a gold belt richly worked, said to be a present from the Sultan of Zanzibar. Muteesa I's decision to change the sartorial code of the Baganda chiefs and, later on, that of the rest of the Baganda had socioeconomic implications toward the sustainability of the bark cloth industry, which was patronized by the royal domain. In around 1875, Muteesa I lifted the ban on textiles and allowed his officials to begin wearing the white *qamis* (Swahili-Arab form of shirt) or *kanzu*, which, until the present, became known as the traditional cultural wear of several ethnicities in Uganda.

Impact of Western Missionaries

The European missionaries on their part introduced Western ideologies to the indigenous societies in Uganda, and their reactions toward the indigenous artifacts and cultural practices in Buganda affected the narrative about bark cloth. The first direct contact made with Europe that led to the arrival of Christian missionaries occurred in the year 1862, when J. H. Speke came searching for the source of the River Nile and thereby visited Kabaka Muteesa I's palace at Mengo. In 1875, Henry Morton Stanley, who had been on a Royal Geographical Society expedition and whose objective was to complete the unfinished work of Speke, also reached the Buganda royal capital. During his visit, Stanley introduced to Kabaka Muteesa I the subject of the Christian religion. The first two Church Missionary Society missionaries—Lieutenant Shergold Smith and Reverend C. T. Wilson—finally arrived in Buganda on June 30, 1877. Another Christian mission of the Roman Catholic faith comprised two French missionaries—Père Lourdel and Reverend Brother Amans—who arrived in Buganda in 1879. On arrival, the missionaries found the Baganda using bark cloth in all rituals pertaining to their day-to-day economic and social life. Historians have noted that burning ritual objects became a prerequisite for the Baganda to convert to Christianity, and later it followed that the most honored catechists and chiefs, royals, and the rest of the Baganda Christians were those who had the courage to burn cultural artifacts in their possession. Bark cloth was perceived as a "satanic" fabric, a connotation that has lingered on amongst some Christian teachings right up to the present day. The complacency by the church toward local artifacts propagated negative narratives about the materiality and usage of bark cloth in Uganda.

As religious struggles were taking place in Buganda, European colonial powers were, in the meantime, engaged in concluding treaties that culminated in the division of Africa into several portions of colonial interest, a political phenomenon that signified the closure of the nineteenth century and dawn of the twentieth century. The first quarter of the twentieth century was characterized by the transformation of the kingdom of Buganda from a state of self-governance to a British protectorate sealed by the signing of the Buganda Agreement in 1900. Bark cloth was amongst the most important tax products. Before then, in every household, several trees were reserved specifically for the manufacture of bark cloth for the royalty.

Arguably, the partitioning of Africa was politically motivated in order to serve the interests of the metropolitan economy. As a result of the technological achievements realized in the wake of the industrial revolution that allowed the manufacture of cheap products in Europe, and later North America, it became essential for the industrial West to find raw materials for its fast-growing industries. Equally important, the West had to look for new markets for its products, most especially textiles, which constituted one of the main items of manufacture in Europe during the nineteenth century. As textiles became a popular trade item at the royal palace, the royal patronage of bark cloth, upon which the bark cloth industry relied, continued to diminish. Cotton and coffee cultivation replaced bark cloth making as these became distinct sources of tax to the protectorate.

Restoration of Cultural Institutions in Uganda and Appropriation of Bark Cloth

The coronation of Muwenda Mutebi II as the 36th Kabaka of Buganda on July 31, 1993 was a historical event as it marked a new chapter in the application of bark cloth. On the day of Mutebi II's coronation, Nnaggalabi Hill, the cultural site where the Baganda kings are enthroned, was drowned in bark cloth. According to the customs of the Baganda, a royal carpet *(ekiwu)* comprising a cow skin, a lion skin, and a leopard skin was laid on a piece of bark cloth upon which was placed the *Nnamulondo* (royal stool). The king's regalia was predominantly of bark cloth that was carefully made by the royal bark cloth makers. Because of its cultural importance, Kabaka Mutebi II's coronation anniversary has become an annual event and, on each occasion, bark cloth has featured prominently across the spectrum amongst people of various social backgrounds. Bark cloth has once again become a prominent artifact in the visual-cultural discussions relating to ethnicity, self-identity, and the notion of *Gandaness*, albeit with redefined meaning.

Significant innovations in the use of bark cloth during the coronation anniversary events have been observed, especially among the ordinary Baganda, who have interpreted the coronation based on their own lived experiences. It is increasingly becoming a common practice to see ordinary Baganda people dressed in garments and fashion accessories made out of bark cloth at coronation events. These range from Western-styled jackets, wrappers, neckties, caps, sashes, to semblances of academic attire, namely gowns and mortarboards. However, a critical analysis of these garments and accessories highlights a complex set of meanings underpinning this act of dress, which contributes in significant modes to the notion of change and retention in the symbolic value of bark cloth. The change and retention are further exemplified by artists and designers living in and out of Uganda who are utilizing bark cloth in their quest for creative explorations and their intent to highlight the aesthetic value of bark cloth and its relevance in artistic practice and a connecting thread between people, place, and memory of past traditions.

However, this recent appropriation of bark cloth raises a highly charged and emotional debate amongst scholars and the Baganda themselves. On the one hand, the commodification of bark cloth, and the production of "tourist" objects, has been criticized by some informants because of its demeaning tendencies to the cultural value of bark cloth. On the other hand, it was noted that although some of the "tourist" objects do demystify the cultural value of bark cloth, the commodification process has in some respects helped to revive and highlight its aesthetic and historical importance to the local and international community.

New Perspectives of Bark Cloth in the Realm of Art, Fashion, and Sustainability

Two major factors have contributed to the reappropriation and reinterpretation of bark cloth in Uganda since the last quarter of the twentieth century. The restoration of cultural institutions, which paved way for the coronation of Kabaka Muwenda Mutebi II in 1993, aroused narratives of self-identity and ethnicity through the different cultural activities in Buganda that preceded the coronation ceremony. Several artists and designers refashioned bark cloth using a creative interplay of bark cloth materials in order to produce visual art objects that gave bark cloth a new meaning of cultural renaissance (Nakazibwe 2013: 134). At the Makerere Art School, tutors and students explored the materiality of bark cloth for artistic expression in painting, sculpture, fashion design, and jewelry design, and created art objects that served as threads of communication on both the local and the global stage.

Secondly, the listing of bark cloth of Uganda by UNESCO as a Masterpiece of the Oral and Intangible Heritage of Humanity in 2005 gave impetus to the artists and designers to appropriate the bark cloth in their creative practice. Some of the artists include Ssana Gateja, Samson Ssenkaaba, Yakuze Ivan, Venny Nakazibwe, Sarah Nakisanze, and Jose Hendo, who have redefined bark cloth in fashion and textile design; as well as Fred Mutebi, a printmaker who has dedicated his post-coronation creative activities toward revitalizing the planting of bark cloth trees in communities in Buganda, and reviving almost from ground-zero the bark cloth value chain in his home district of Bukomansimbi, in Buddu County. These artists, and many others, have used bark cloth as the canvas to express

Figure 8.2 *All Things Fashion: Fashionista Catwalk*—Runway, London Fashion Week, September 2022, Jose Hendo. Photographer: © Stuart Wilson/BFC/Getty Images.

their artistic freedom and determination to engage new narratives about culture of the Baganda, and also to explore its potential value to address global issues that affect all people in the world. Through their efforts, it has emerged that in the twenty-first century, bark cloth is no longer only associated with tradition and "ritual" in the strict sense of the word. The symbolic capital of bark cloth is in a continuous flux, dependent on the way people in Buganda are influenced by the historical, political, economic, sociocultural, and global transformations, and how they choose to respond to these transformations, using the materiality of bark cloth as a point of departure.

Conclusion

In this chapter, I have highlighted the signifying functions of bark cloth; in other words, how, as a cultural artifact, bark cloth serves in the language and meaning system of the Baganda, and how that meaning has constantly been negotiated by social economic, political, and cultural factors. As has been demonstrated, the role and meaning of bark cloth is in a continuous flux contingent on the above dynamics. In conclusion, the role and meaning of Uganda's bark cloth is no longer confined within the cultural boundaries; other factors have come into play and will thus contribute to the current discourse on cloth and threads of communication. Bark cloth, which was earlier confined within the cultural boundaries of Buganda, has gained international recognition as a medium of visual artistic expression and a sustainable fabric in the last decade of the twentieth century, to date. Whereas it is easy to conclude that due to the forces of modernity there has been a lineal change in the functions of the bark cloth of the Baganda, my research findings have proved otherwise. Amidst these transformations, there has also been continuity as well as revival in the role and meaning of bark cloth in various social traditions of the Baganda.

Notes

1 Kabaka is the titular head of the kingdom, whose authority determines all cultural aspects of the Baganda society. This is when the title Ssekabaka is given to a fallen monarch.

References

Ipulet, Perpetua. 1993. "Distribution and Local Use of Genus (Ficus L.) (Family Morracea) in the Central Region of Uganda", unpublished MSc. Dissertation, Makerere University.

Kaggwa, Apolo. 1999. *Ekitabo kye Mpisa za Baganda: The Customs of the Baganda*, Kampala: Crane Publishers Limited.

Kaiser, Susan B. (1997). *The Social Psychology of Clothing: Symbolic Appearances in Context*. Second edition revised. New York: Fairchild Publications.

Kyeyune, George William. 2003. "Art in Uganda in the 20th Century", unpublished Ph.D. thesis, School of Oriental and African Studies, University of London.

Lugira, Muzzanganda A. 1970. *Ganda Art: A Study of the Ganda Mentality with Respect to Possibilities of Acculturation in Christian Art*, Kampala: Osasa Publications.

Nakazibwe, Venny M. 2005. "Bark cloth of the Baganda People of Southern Uganda: A Record of Continuity and Change from the Late Eighteenth Century to the Early Twenty-first Century", unpublished Ph.D. thesis, Middlesex University, London.

Nakazibwe, Venny M. and Nannyonga-Tamusuza, Sylvia. 2010. "Uganda", in *Berg Encyclopedia of World Dress and Fashion, Vol. 1 Africa*, edited by Joanne B. Eicher and Doran H. Ross, New York: Berg, 454–60.

Nakazibwe, Venny M. 2013. "Bark-cloth Making in Uganda: The Renaissance of a Historical Tradition", in Colloque International: L'Anthropologie Africaine, En Hommage a Jomo Kenyata, Ahmadou Hampate Ba, Mouloud Mammeri et Cheikh Anta Diop, Deuxieme Festival Culturel Panafricain: Centre National de Recherches Prehistoriques Anthropologiques et Historiques (CNRPAH), Alger.

Nakisanze, Sarah, 2021. "Social Sustainability and the Uganda Haute Couture Visual Aesthetic: Articulating the Contemporary Value of Past Traditions", unpublished Ph.D. thesis, Makerere University, Kampala, Uganda.

Ojuku, Ricky Milton. 1986. "African Bark Cloth: An Account, especially related to Uganda of its Production, Role and Decorative Development", unpublished B.Sc. Dissertation, Huddersfield Polytechnic.

Robertson, Lesli. 2014. "Rethinking Material Culture: Ugandan Bark cloth", a paper presented at the 14th Textile Society Biennial Symposium, *New Directions: Examining the Past, Creating the Future*, Los Angeles, September, 10–14, 2014.

Taylor, Lou. 2012. "De-coding the Hierarchy of Fashion Textiles", in *Textile Reader*, ed. Jessica Hemmings, New York: Berg. 419–29.

Trowell, Margaret and Waschsmann, K. P. 1953. *Tribal Crafts of Uganda*, London, New York, Toronto: Oxford University Press.

Worden, Sarah. 2016. "Tradition and Transition: The Changing Fortunes of Bark Cloth in Uganda, *Textile Society of America 15th Biennale Symposium Proceedings*, Savannah Gainesville, 19 23, 2016. http://www.digitalcommons.unl.edu/tsaconf.1012 (accessed December 15, 2022).

Artist Maria Nepomuceno in conversation with Alice Kettle

Part 2

ALICE KETTLE

AK: The relationship of life and aliveness in the work is a constant theme; it is shown in seedpods and organisms.

MN: I want to make works that are alive and breathing. This desire comes by creating forms that are inspired by nature but growing in an imaginary ecosystem.

I will talk about the hammock.

I chose the shape of the hammock because it is a useful object and very present in our indigenous culture; it is like a pod and a home. When traveling, the indigenous people take their hammocks with them because they can be at home in any place of the world. The amazing shape of the hammock makes you think about women, it is womb-like, uterine, a shape that keeps and holds you inside. I think about the hammock as containing opposing forces and the idea of tension. It is suspended, so there is a tension and tautness to the ropes while at the same time it is about relaxation in a cocoon-like slumber with a gentle swinging movement. This rhythm is hypnotic, it affects you . . . it is about love. A place of maternal love. The indigenous women sometimes give birth in the hammock and in many traditions, when they die they are put inside their hammocks and buried.

AK: Does the work concern the female condition where pliable materials express these experiences?

MN: Beyond the fertility is aligned with creativity, where planting of fertile new thoughts is cyclical and connected to nature. Through the work, we are held within the cycle of life. My sculptures, made of beads and rope coils, evoke the movement through life, birth to death.

AK: Is creativity a fertile place, to express through textiles what it is to be human?

MN: Everything related to giving birth influences me and work. The story of my birth, the stories of my children['s]

Figure MN2 Installation view. © Maria Nepomuceno, Afetosyntesis at Kunsthuset Kabuso, Norway. Photographer: © Foto Pål Hoff, courtesy Kunsthuset Kabuso, Norway.

birth. I love when my mother reminds me that my umbilical cord was buried in a beautiful tree. These are stories of my family that always come into my imagination and into the work.

The work "Force," I decided to use only blue ropes, some of which are used ropes that I exchanged with sailors and people with boats. There were different colors of blue because some of them are well used and lighter blue. I made a big sea animal, a surrealist organism that comes from the sea, as though in this case, from a canoe in England. The organism is attached to a boat as though bringing it from the water to the land. The work includes beads and giant pearls like eggs produced by this fertile organism. Fertility is an enduring subject in my work, here it concerns life giving birth to itself, where orifices extrude and enter inside and outside of each other. There are tentacles, mouths, parts that open and extend from these organisms and turn back into themselves, which refer to reproduction and regeneration. The circle and the spirals build this idea of reproduction, infinity, and time.

AK: The scale of the work means that you read them through this relationship between the body and nature. The works become a living landscape.

MN: I play with this scale. There is a repetition in small and giant scale, at the same time, which are the microcosmos and the macro-cosmos. This relationship between different scales creates an intensity of experience of being in the world connected to the evolution of time and living in this universe. We are simultaneously and/or changing between being giants and other times we are so, so small.

AK: What you're saying is that the work generates itself, it gives birth to itself and generates its own process into the future. The circle has a dynamic that generates energy and forward movement.

They feel optimistic works. Does that reflect new life and an imaginary, future world?

MN: For sure there is an optimistic point of view. My work has a YES to life as intention. It's about creating a connection between past, present, and future.

PART THREE

Challenging the Reading

Does orthodoxy need to be challenged in order to develop, to remain alive? In this section there are examples of cloth challenging political attitudes through placing the traditional reading within a different/unexpected context. The domestic conventions surrounding cloth are used to subvert the expected narrative in order to tell a different, hidden, story—one of singular and collective action.

Using embroidery as their last resort against dehumanizing practices that attempted to silence their voices, the suffragettes in Holloway Prison practiced the overlooked female pursuit of stitching to communicate their strength and solidarity to each other and to the outside world. By so doing, Denise Jones argues, they positioned embroidery "as an embodied, autobiographical and situated process" (Jones, p.** of this volume).

Throughout the twentieth and twenty-first centuries we have seen the softness of textiles, the expectation of a domestic, bodily context, give added narrative weight and power to cloth employed as a tool of collective protest. In their chapter, Alicia Decker and Susan T. Avila describe various group case studies and how "social media impacts and amplifies the textile narrative" (Decker and Avila, p.** of this volume).

Mary Stark's "studio-based and performance practice examines relationships between textile practice and filmmaking, questioning how and why these seemingly separate disciplines are in fact deeply conjoined" (Stark, p.** of this volume). In this very real, hidden story of the work that women do, she highlights the unsung creative impact of women film editors—they were a majority in the industry at one time. She links their skill in the cutting room to their familiarity with cutting, stitching, and piecing cloth back together to form a unified whole.

South Africa is a country of many challenging, painful, and entangled narratives. Pippa Hetherington, a descendant of white British settlers, is engaged in a long-term project with the artists "Nozeti Makhubalo, Nomonde Mtandana, Nomfundo Makhubalo, and Nothandile Bopani: direct descendants of the Eastern Cape amaXhosa who fought the British in the Frontier Wars" (Hetherington, p.** of this volume). They are stitching, together, pieces of cloth to create narrative clothing. As is, traditional when women meet in groups to sew or knit, they tell their stories while they cut and stitch—a highly complex and continuing act of reparation.

"In cloth, I can feel the past, the present, and the future. I mysteriously know cloth and it knows me. We have an understanding."

Denise Jones

9

Small Acts of Refusal: Suffragette-Embroidered Cloths Worked in Holloway Prison

DENISE JONES

Introduction

In February 1912, Emmeline Pankhurst, one of the leaders of the militant Women's Social and Political Union (WSPU), wrote to her fellow suffragette Ethel Smyth that soon "there will be an unannounced affair, a sort of skirmish, in which some of our bad, bold ones will take part" (*Votes for Women* March 22, 1912: 373; Rosen [1974] 2013: 157).[1] Mrs. Pankhurst was referring to the orchestrated window-breaking campaign of the WSPU and, most markedly, the turn by suffragettes toward the destruction of property. Hundreds of suffragettes were arrested and imprisoned during the campaign. Denied political status, their bodies were humiliated and threatened, and some women experienced the hunger strike and forcible feeding. The suffragette Janie Terrero, imprisoned for four months and forcibly fed in Holloway in 1912, echoed Mrs. Pankhurst's words in embroidery, re-ordering the words "Mrs Pankhurst's Bold Bad Ones" on an embroidered panel. Terrero also embroidered the names of nineteen other women who were fed by force on her wing of the prison.

This chapter refers to six hand embroidered cloths worked by suffragettes in Holloway Prison between 1911 and 1912, including that of Janie Terrero. They are: the Terrero panel (1912) (Figure 9.1); The Women's Library (TWL) panel of seventy-nine suffragette signatures (n.d.) (Figure 9.2); a handkerchief of sixty-six suffragette signatures and two initials (March, 1912); an embroidered shield badge "ASC" (1912); a small fragment embroidered by Cissie Wilcox (1911); and an embroidered "Brush and Comb" bag (March, 1912).[2] It scrutinizes the embroideries for the explicit documentary evidence they record about suffragette prison experiences, and moving beyond the discursive, the embroideries are examined for the implicit material evidence they communicate.

Through reflecting on my own practice as an embroiderer and using a methodological framework associated with New Materialism (which gives the matter of the body its due), this chapter offers a new perspective about embroidery and the material process of embroidering, rather than concentrating on the product, a finished piece of embroidery. It augments Rozsika Parker's contention in her seminal work, *The Subversive Stitch: Embroidery and the Making of the Feminine* ([1984] 2010), that embroidery is subversive. Parker writes:

"Limited to practising art with a needle and thread, women have nevertheless sewn a subversive stitch—managed to make meanings of their own in the very medium intended to inculcate self-effacement" ([1984] 2010: 215).

I argue that when imprisoned suffragettes embroidered through cloth they were making small acts of "Refusal." The sociologist Dick Hebdige writes of objects of "Refusal" with reference to the imprisonment of the homosexual Jean Genet and his jar of "dirty, wretched" Vaseline. The Vaseline becomes "a symbol of his triumph," a gesture of defiance or contempt, that expresses both "impotence and a kind of power—the power to disfigure," like graffiti (Hebdige 1979: 1–3). As with the Vaseline, I claim that the small, intimately scaled embroidered cloths worked by suffragettes in prison are also objects where tensions and power were played out. Through their making they became disobedient objects, where the act of embroidering challenged the disciplinary mechanisms of the prison system *par excellence*.

I also claim that the suffragette embroideries materially signal the presence of the corporeal and psychical "cloth–skin–body," danger, and transgression. Embroidering is therefore positioned as an embodied, autobiographical, and situated practice.

The chapter leans on Michel Foucault's seminal text on the modern prison, *Discipline and Punish: The Birth of the Prison* (1977), the psychoanalytical writings of Didier Anzieu with reference to the skin, the body, and the psyche, and the writings of the anthropologist Mary Douglas regarding theories of purity and danger and the leakage of excreta from the body.

Becoming Dangerous: The Context of the Embroideries

In February 1912 at a dinner for the released "stone throwers" of 1911, Emmeline Pankhurst announced that "The argument of the broken window pane is the most valuable argument in modern politics" (Pankhurst [1931] 2010: 372). Sylvia Pankhurst declared, "Since we must go to prison to obtain the vote, let it be the windows of the Government, not the bodies of women, which shall be broken," as window breaking ensured a speedy and less painful arrest ([1931] 2010: 309).

By 1912, suffragettes were vilified in the press and popular culture and were manhandled by the police at demonstrations and meetings. The reference by Sylvia Pankhurst to "broken bodies," however, harked back to a specific deputation to Parliament in November 1910, later

Figure 9.1 *Embroidered panel*, 1912. Janie Terrero. © Museum of London.

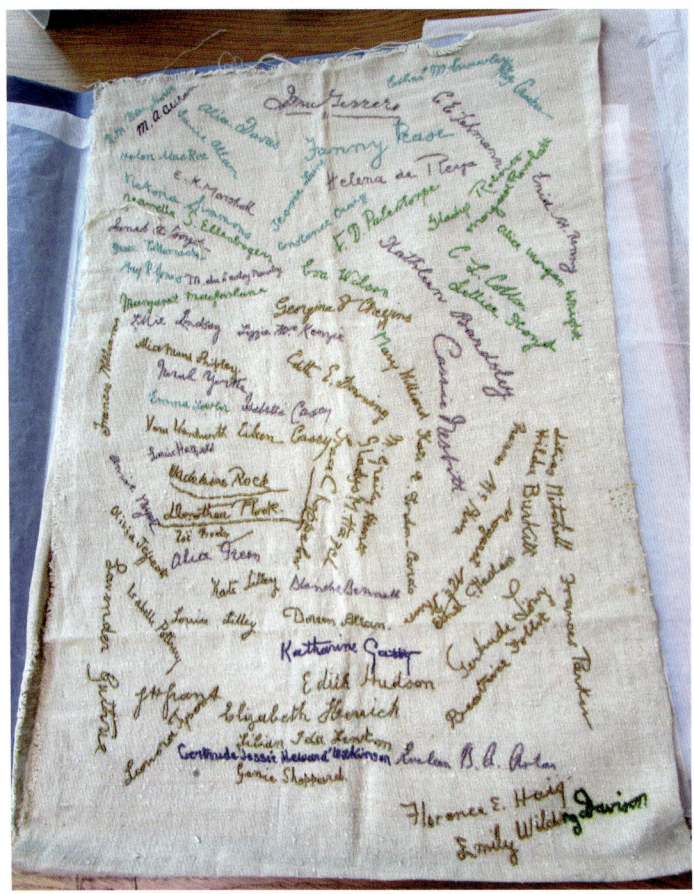

Figure 9.2 *Suffragette signatures*, embroidered panel, undated. © The Women's Library.

known as "Black Friday," when many suffragettes were violently beaten and sexually assaulted by the police in Parliament Square. In the aftermath of "Black Friday," the women re-emphasized their need to be more actively engaged in the fight for the vote (Morrell 1981; *Votes for Women* December 15, 1911: 179).

Militant activism was at the heart of WSPU policy, and consequently the suffragette corporeal body became both a political site and a political tool in the push for female enfranchisement. By early March 1912 smashing windows had dramatically escalated in scale. Janie Terrero took part in the raids beginning on Friday March 1, 1912, when windows were broken in the West End of London, causing thousands of pounds' worth of damage. Terrero was arrested for breaking the windows of an engineering firm Stedhalls on Oxford Street, valued at £150 (*Votes for Women* March 13, 1912: 382). The raid continued on March 4 in Knightsbridge and Sylvia Pankhurst stated that 9,000 policemen were stationed in anticipation in Trafalgar Square ([1931] 2010: 373–4).

Window breaking set a bold and dangerous precedent, a turning point in the struggle, as it extended suffragette action toward private property in general. The suffragette Katie Gliddon wrote from Holloway Prison in March 1912, "But you must choose a language understood by the enemy and the enemy has made property its God so we must attack property" (Gliddon 1912).[3] In fact more darkly, suffragette attacks on property intensified until the outbreak of war in 1914 and included arson, bombing, and the destruction of sporting facilities, churches, schools, and works of art. Between 1905 and 1914 over 1,000 women went to prison for women's suffrage and thousands more were arrested (Purvis 1995: 103).

In Holloway Prison

During March 1912 suffragettes were imprisoned *en masse* in Holloway and it became overcrowded with women.[4] In prison, the women faced brutish, dehumanizing conditions, lack of privacy, and small regulatory procedures. Following the writings of Michel Foucault, modern prisons such as Holloway were constructed to keep prisoners segregated and under constant surveillance. Incarceration was used to separate, divide, and discipline the prisoner's body. It ordered space and spatially arranged prisoners within it. According to Foucault, the enforcement of solitude was "the primary condition of total submission," the silence of isolation "providing an intimate exchange between the convict and the power that is exercised over him [or her]" (1977: 237). Solitude and silence in prison were thus meant to be corrective, allowing the prisoners time to reflect on their transgression. Foucault asserts that this helped to render the prisoner docile.

During March 1912 the women spent most of their time in the cell as the prison authorities were concerned about the influx of women and mutinous behavior.[5] Gliddon wrote home to her mother that she would not get involved in "the rows" in Holloway because she feared the consequences (Gliddon 1912).[6]

Foucault writes that the modern prison model was designed to reduce contact and dangerous communication between prisoners (1977: 200–1). The women were initially denied communication with the outside world as visitors and letter-writing facilities were refused (Gliddon 1912).[7] They were also not allowed to go to chapel or to exercise until the fear of the "mutiny" was over.[8] In early March, seven prisoners including the "ring leader," Catherine Marshall, were transferred to Aylesbury prison because of the fomenting trouble over the withdrawal of privileges and the lack of political status.[9] The Governor of Holloway wrote in a letter that "some of them have threatened another combined disturbance for Sunday (tomorrow) the 10th instant."[10]

According to Foucault, the modern prison model extended the power of surveillance beyond what was actually seen and into the mind of the prisoner so the inmate would never know when or if she was being looked at. Consequently, discipline would become internalized. Crucially for Foucault, prison is therefore more than a building. It is a system, a mechanism of power and control. It trains and corrects bodies. It is a "pure architectural and optical system" (Foucault 1977: 205). It fixes, distributes, arranges, and locates bodies in its geometry, and relies on isolation, visibility, and the gaze.

The suffragette historian June Purvis writes that from admission, prison procedures also stripped away the identity of prisoners. Prison dress and utensils were marked with the broad arrow, signifying that they were the property of the government (Ash 2010: 22–3). Although by 1912 the women had achieved the right to wear their own clothes and were not searched or bathed on admission, they remained acutely aware that these privileges could be rescinded. Inmates had to wear a yellow felt badge printed with the prisoner's cell and block number and each prisoner was allocated a prison number (Purvis 1994: 171). Prison numbers classified, homogenized, and dehumanized the women.

Following Foucault, prisoners were disciplined to become useful (1977: 137). Discipline would impose a "political anatomy of detail," a "new micro-physics of the body where small bodies, small movements, small actions would be controlled" (1977: 139). Small regulatory procedures such as inspections and petty punishments would keep the deviant in line and enforce hierarchical, vertical power relations. There was an emphasis on cleaning and correction (Purvis 1994: 171).

Foucault describes how work would form an important role as correction. It would train, reform, shape, and rehabilitate the prisoner as "it bends bodies to regular movements" and it is "a remedy against the wanderings of his [her] imagination" (1977: 242). It would establish rhythms and the division of time (1977: 149–51). Work time thus "penetrates the body" and would enable an "instrumental coding of the body" as it broke down gestures into usefulness (Foucault 1977: 153). For Foucault, enforced work, penal labor, would turn prisoners into compliant workers (1977: 242–3). It helped to "normalize" dangerous deviancy and delinquent persons such as suffragettes could be made "normal" through work.

For the imprisoned women, "hard labour" took the form of "corrective" needlework, or more specifically, utilitarian sewing and knitting (and not embroidery) (Purvis 1995: 109). Enforced needlework was expected to order and control messiness, wildness, nomadic and dangerous collective leanings, and it would nurture obedience and utility. It was enforced labor for the women, whereas their own embroidering was a voluntary activity that gave them a sense of freedom. The imposition of prison needlework also helps to explain how the embroiderers had access to tools such as needles and scissors.

Suffragette accounts of life in prison emphasize the assault on the senses of the women. The cells were constricting, cramped, and claustrophobic and the women complained of lack of air and not being able to breathe (Purvis 1995: 109). They were aware of disturbing noise: the slamming of prison doors, the rattle of feeding tins, women screaming and crying, and banging on walls to communicate. They ate poor food. The smell of prison was also referred to, and the lack of hygiene. In a petition to the Governor, Leonora Tyson complained about the indecency of the lavatories and the lack of privacy they afforded.[11] The women would have been sick in their cells after forcible feeding, and their slops were kept inside the cell. The feeding apparatus was often used from one woman to the next without being cleaned (Purvis 1994: 178). The women would also be aware of the harmful physicality of touch by the warders and prison doctor during forcible feeding. Gliddon wrote, "Being here is just like not existing" (Gliddon 1912).[12]

According to the historian Kevin Grant, two hundred and forty women went on hunger strike in British and Irish prisons prior to the war (Grant 2011: 137). The political theorist Amanda Machin writes that the hunger strike places embodiment at the heart of politics as it involves a "peculiar form of violence, a violence that is seized by the state by an individual who then wields this violence on themselves" (2016: 175). It is a "self-directed violence" (Feldman 1991, cited in Machin 2016: 175). The body can be used as a weapon and because of this it has a highly affective value. It deftly interiorizes the violence of the opponent within the body of the protestor (Machin 2016: 157). Through the hunger strike the corporeal body becomes cogent and not a docile subject. Thus, for Machin the corporeal body could serve as a political actor as well as a political text. Machin claims that the body becomes an important form of political resistance "for those who lack[ed] vote, voice and status" such as imprisoned suffragettes (2016: 159–61).

In September 1909, the government instituted the forcible feeding of suffragettes on hunger strike in order to curtail their early release.[13] So distressing and painful was the procedure that it has been likened to oral rape and torture and a punitive rather than a restorative measure (Purvis 1995: 123; Vicinus 1985: 271). It was a shocking and intensely felt act of intrusion into the suffragette body and the procedure had not been used on sane women in British prisons before. It was an act that blurred medical, ethical, and political boundaries (Miller 2013: 230).

Embroidering: The Discursive and the Material

Janie Terrero embroidered on her panel that she was "Arrested on March 1st 1912" and that she was "Sentenced by Judge Lawrie on Wednesday March 27th to four months." At the top center of her panel she embroidered, "W.S.P.U motto Deeds not Words," and at the center "Worked in Holloway Prison by Janie Terrero."

As mentioned, she also embroidered the signatures of nineteen women who went on hunger strike and were forcibly fed on DX wing of Holloway Prison between April 13 and April 19, 1912. She calls this the first hunger strike, as there was a second hunger strike in June 1912. Janie records this below a demarcating line on the panel, as "Second Hunger strike June 19th All released," possibly because by then her health had severely deteriorated and she was released on medical grounds before her sentence (and the embroidery) was completed (Terrero 1912).[14]

Terrero embroidered sixteen broad arrows, four hammers, the grid of a prison window, and a grille similar to that of the Ladies' Gallery in the House of Commons. She edged the panel in a tri-colored ribbon in suffragette colors.[15] In the center she embroidered a wreath of spreading violets of purple, white, and green tied with a purple ribbon. In the language of flowers, they symbolize faithfulness and loyalty (and they spread prolifically in March through seeds and as rhizomes). At the base of the panel there is a postcard of Emmeline and Christabel Pankhurst.

This panel has been the subject of previous research particularly because of the explicit documentary evidence it contains. It is a powerful record of the experiences of relatively unknown suffragettes. It is a textual and figurative historical record and it is a straightforward discursive "read." Roszika Parker first mentions the panel in *The Subversive Stitch* and writes that the "Embroidered signatures were gestures of solidarity and protest" combining "the political tradition of petition with the social tradition of embroidered signatures as mementoes to mark special occasions" ([1984] 2010: 192–3, 200).[16] Parker focuses on what can be read and seen rather than on the tactile and material process of making the panel.

Terrero understood that the women were making history and that through deliberately embroidering a discursive record of the women's prison experiences, their narrative might endure and be retold. She wrote to the disabled suffragette May Billinghurst, who was forcibly fed in 1913, that her "name would go down in history" (Terrero 1913).[17]

The suffragette Mary Ellen (Nellie) Taylor, the embroiderer of a white brush and comb bag worked in Holloway in 1912, also wrote home to her children about making "fancy work" in "memory of this fight" (Taylor 1912).[18] Taylor embroidered "March 1912" and "Holloway 15503 2/15" (her prison number) on the front of her bag, autobiographically situating herself in time and place. The embroiderer of a badge shaped like a small shield with the letters "ASC," and an embroidered handkerchief of suffragette signatures were also embroidered with the year 1912. The handkerchief reads "Votes for Women Holloway Prison March 1912." A small fragment worked by the suffragette Cissie Wilcox reads "WorKeD in HoLLoWAy," is dated "Dec 1911," and continues "CiSSie WiLcox NewcAsTLe DX2.11" along with five broad arrows.

While the textual record is important in explicitly locating the women and their embroideries in time and place, there is more nuanced material evidence to be had from examining the materials used and the process of embroidering. The philosopher Karen Barad writes of "intra-actions" where "material articulations of the world are seen to create and give form to the discursive and *vice-versa*." Thus, material processes and matter, including the matter of the corporeal body, are seen to be vital and possess agency. For Barad, boundaries (and we can include here the boundary of cloth and skin) are regarded as complex, porous, and interactive (Barad in Witzgill and Stakemeier 2017: 14–15).

There are more ambiguous "clues" in these embroideries that materially communicate defiance and "Refusal," community, commemoration, courage, danger, and transgression, and the presence of the corporeal and psychical body.

Following Foucault's model of the disciplinary prison we can deduce that acts that increase community and reduce isolation, avoid homogenization of the individual through "normalization" and conformity, avert hegemonic structures, deceive the gaze, diminish the utility of work, and insert the presence and agency of the corporeal body can be configured as acts of "Refusal."

All the embroideries referenced in this chapter were worked through even-weave cloth of linen, cotton, silk, or wool. The TWL panel was worked on an irregular piece of crude fraying linen, the Cissie Wilcox fragment was on a scrap of frayed silk, and the small embroidered badge shaped like a shield was made from a scrap of dirty, stained prison blanket. The embroideries do not materially fit with the stereotypical view of embroidery as decorative or domestic. With the exception of Nellie Taylor's bag worked in cotton and the badge worked in tapestry wool, the embroideries were worked in silk thread, an unruly thread that is lively, easily tangles, and becomes shredded and distressed when worked.

The shield badge defiantly claims that the woman had a name rather than a number as it was embroidered with the initials "ASC," and it may have been made in response to having to wear the official prison badge. It was worked horizontally in the hand, making use of the needle, a small tool, with small lengths of thread. Through embroidering this small badge, the maker was materially reacting to being systemized. Foucault writes of small regulatory acts that keep the body in line (1977: 238, 294, 300). Through her small repetitive act(s) of embroidering her initials, the embroiderer refused to be dehumanized.

The fact that the needle passed through the regular (and disciplined) grid of cloth, and it inserts more threads across the surfaces and into the structure of cloth, can also be juxtaposed alongside Foucault's concept of normalization and conformity. The needle and thread nearly always passed between the warp and weft and into the small, constricted spaces between the woven threads, disrupting the order and structure of the cloth grid. The embroidering threads added weight and dimension to the binary threads of cloth, like "third threads" adding other "voices."

Embroidering through the cloth would also have involved the continuous push and pull of the needle and thread. The needle and thread would have rubbed against the warp and weft structure, creating friction and resistance. The amount of tension required to work the embroidery would also have needed to be controlled to prevent the cloth from puckering. In fact, hand embroidering as a material practice is quietly and primarily concerned with managing the tension of the embroidering thread.

The TWL panel (Figure 9.2) records seventy-nine signatures and the embroidered handkerchief holds sixty-six signatures and two initials. The two embroideries indicate that the women gathered together to sign the cloths and that they communicated with each other. They show that they refused to be segregated and isolated. Some of the signatures of sisters, mothers and daughters, and friends are in close proximity, for example, the Rock sisters Dorothea and Madeleine, and their friends Zoe Proctor and Grace Chappelow. The spatial arrangement of the signatures reveals real relationships between the women. The lists of signatures on both cloths were not recorded formally as with the official lists of prisoners in Holloway. They travel around the edges of the handkerchief and along the sides of the TWL panel in a disorganized and disorderly fashion. Unlike a paper document of signatures, these cloths would have been squeezed in the hand, turned over, and flipped from front to back. The collection of the signatures and the embroidering of them thus communicate touch and being touched. The TWL panel has been embroidered by one hand and each name has been couched over an inner thread core. These inner threads have been tightly "bound," as with the binding cause of the women. The back of the panel reveals the ends of these concealed threads, as well as a network of threads that cross over, carry, and connect.

The handkerchief of embroidered signatures confirms that it was worked in March 1912 and the TWL panel is undated. However, sixty of the same signatures are present on both cloths, making it highly likely that the latter was also worked in Holloway in 1912. The signatures of the women who were sent to other prisons are not included on either embroidery, suggesting that the cloths were signed and worked after March 27, when the women were transferred. The cloths could have been embroidered at this time because their community was under threat following the transfers. The embroidered cloths are thus affirmations of the comradeship of the women, of their "combination," solidarity, and common purpose. They materialize support, affinity, and an aggregated defiance. Likewise, Terrero also refers to the togetherness of the women and the women's "rub" with power. Terrero was notably the spokesperson for her wing in Holloway and tried to avert the second hunger strike (Terrero 1912).[19] She negotiated with power as well as negotiating through cloth, back and forth with small gestures, mediating between the cloth surfaces and its structure.

Terrero also suggests commemoration in her use of lustrous silk thread and satin ribbon. The satin ribbon almost demands to be touched, while the content of the panel touches our sensibilities and elicits empathy.

Boundary Crossing: "Cloth–skin–body"

It is possible to dig deeper into the material meanings of the suffragette embroideries if we adopt a methodological approach that recognizes the agency of the thinking-feeling human (skin) body and one which theorizes about the power of material processes (Witzgill and Stakemeier 2017).

The corporeal body, which figured so largely in the WSPU campaign, seems to be absent in these embroidered cloths if we think of them as documents to be "read," but it is materially ever present. The psychologist Lisa Blackman calls for acknowledgment of the disavowed "absent present" corporeal body (2008: 6). She asserts that bodies are embodied, in that we interactively think and feel. Our skin is touched by the world and we are touched affectively (2008).

Through a close reading of literature, art, philosophy, and anatomical writings and drawings, Claudia Benthien refers to the significance of skin as the cultural border between the self and the world (Benthien 2002). She discusses the semantic and psychic aspects of touching, thinking, and feeling and draws attention to the encoding of flayed skin as an extreme inscription of power, which can be understood as an allegory of self-liberation and change (2002: 14). Benthien writes of flayed skin as "the textile, hairless garment of skin" and that it can be draped and hung, and can resemble a "loose cloth" (2002: 78, 79). Both cloth and skin can be imagined as "self edges." They can be seen to be malleable, flexible, permeable membranes, boundaries with faces, or *sur*faces that wear or bear the marks and traces of lived experience. Cloth and clothing, so proximate to the lived body, have also been referred to as "second skin."[20]

In the field of psychoanalysis, Didier Anzieu breaks from abstract language-centered theories and offers a concrete body-centered approach to contemporary psychoanalysis, Anzieu's theories emphasize the connection between the somatic and psychic lived experiences of skin. He connects somatic exteriority with psychic interiority and he contends that "the unconscious is the body" (Anzieu in Lafrance 2013: 21, 22).

Anzieu claims that the helpless infant acquires a skin ego, which enables it to make sense of primary processes (space/time, insides/outsides, subject/object, and self/other), and that the skin ego precedes the acquisition of language and thought. For Anzieu, the skin ego is an imaginary projected surface where deep-seated feelings associated with the psyche are recorded (Lafrance 2013: 22, 23).

Marc Lafrance writes that, according to Anzieu, the acquisition of the skin ego involves a traumatic rending or flaying from the imagined shared common skin with the (m)other, and this recognition does not come about without resistance and pain and an awareness of potential harms (Lafrance 2013: 24, 25). He writes that it is at this point that "these cutaneous phantasies . . . *clothe* that which is most profound in us, our surface" [my italics] (Anzieu 1989: 60; Lafrance 2013: 24, 25).

Drawing us further toward the psychoanalytical connections between the body, skin, and textile culture, Anzieu writes of the skin ego as having the fundamental functions of containment, protection, and inscription. Anzieu also adds the functions of individuation, intersensoriality, recharging, sexualization, and maintenance. The idea of holding and handling becomes important to help the infant to hold together, feel safe, and realize that the body is a *sac*-like container that inhabits a unique skin. The skin ego also enables the inscription and organization of the stimuli and somatic traces that surround the infant. The skin ego is thus "the original parchment," which preserves "the erased, scratched-out, written-over" first outlines of "preverbal writing made up of traces upon the skin" (Anzieu in Lafrance 2013: 29).

The idea of the psyche being projected onto an imagined surface is crucial to the connection between psychoanalysis and cloth and the potential for thinking about and proposing the concept of a "cloth ego." In his writings, Anzieu makes multiple analogies between cloth and the skin ego (1989, 2016). He describes the skin ego as a "backcloth" (2016: 238, 251, 253), "bag," and "tunic" (2016: 235, 234) and writes of inter-sensorial "psychic envelopes" or "psychical wrappings" (Segal in Anzieu 2016: xvii; Anzieu 2016: 216).

Following Anzieu, textile academic Stella North has developed the idea of the "clothing-ego" as a projected skin ego, being both in and on the lived clothed body (North 2013). She writes of clothing as "an external envelope made up of messages" (North 2013: 78). She argues that clothing takes on the functions of the skin ego, as in our daily lives we are rarely unclothed. Originally North posited the idea of a cloth ego, which emphasized the materiality of cloth and skin, but she preferred to foreground clothing as a finished product (2013: 86). What is important in the discussion about the "clothing-ego" and the potential of a "cloth ego" is the proximity of cloth to the body, and the idea that the skin-body can be projected onto cloth.

Building on North's proposal, I argue that through the constant micro-handling of cloth and thread associated with embroidering, and through the surfacing and resurfacing of thread and the needle, there is an expansive interfacing between the body, skin, and cloth, an interaction with the "cloth ego," where deep-seated somatic, preverbal, material, and psychical feelings can be articulated and recorded.

By applying Anzieu's theories to the suffragette embroideries, we can argue that embroidering through cloth can materially signal boundary crossing, and the crossing of the cloth–skin boundary. We can also posit that the embroideries were not only written on cloth but were materially wrought through cloth, and in doing so they communicate more than with a written or figurative paper document. Thus, Terrero's embroidered panel summons something more than a written account on the surface of paper. I suggest that her embroidering through cloth summons the skin ego, the protective, secure and supportive, imagined skin, which we know has been breached, and this is why we find her embroidery so emotionally charged.

The disavowed body is also present in other ways in these embroideries. The fact that the needle passes through the cloth boundary has potent implications when we consider that traces of the excreta of the body—blood, spittle, dead skin, and DNA from the embroiderer—are likely to be embedded in the cloth. This pervasive and hidden engagement with the body is quietly tied up with what the anthropologist Mary Douglas calls "dirt" and is deemed culturally disgusting, and raises pollution fears ([1966] 2002). According to Douglas, the presence of dirt signals danger as it communicates the crossing of a forbidden boundary, as well as ill-defined and interstitial positions (as with the enfranchisement of women). Douglas writes, "To have been in the margins, is to have been in contact with danger, to have been at a source of power" ([1966] 2002: 120). It also signals a site of renewal, of new statuses and new configurations, and thus dirt and boundary crossing can become formative ([1966] 2002: 200, 202).

We can imagine that the embroidered shield badge worked on a scrap of dirty prison blanket could also contain traces of vomit and tears. Terrero's fine embroidery and that of the signature handkerchief, worked in silk threads and through a tightly woven cloth, would have been embroidered with a fine, sharp needle that would prick the fingers. The end of each thread would most probably have been put to the lips and flattened with spittle in order to facilitate the threading of the needle.

What we can deduce from this material evidence is that embroidering is an autobiographical and embodied practice. In fact, Katie Gliddon inadvertently transcribed the word embroidery to read as "embrodiary" in a letter to her mother from Holloway in March 1912. She wrote "You might send me some easy embrodiary [sic]. Not traced so that I can invent the pattern myself" (Gliddon, 1912).[21]

Conclusion

In the Foreword to *The Subversive Stitch* ([1984] 2010), Roszika Parker quotes from *From Man to Man* (1926) by the writer Olive Schreiner (1855–1920). Schreiner asks, "Has the pen or pencil dipped so deep in the blood of the human race as the needle?" ([1984] 2010: ix). Parker replies, "The answer is, quite simply, no. The art of embroidery has been the means of educating women into the feminine ideal, and of proving that they have attained it, but it has also provided a weapon of resistance to the constraints of femininity" ([1984] 2010: ix).

The suffragette embroiderers of this study were well versed in the material practice of embroidering. They tacitly and implicitly knew about the feel of the materials they used, the tightness of the weave, and the qualities of the thread. Embroidery was, as Gliddon unwittingly transcribed in her correspondence, "embrodiary." It autobiographically expressed what the women thought and how they felt. They embroidered script and imagery knowing that embroidery could historically and textually document their experiences and that they were defiantly creating tangible and discursive records that might endure for posterity.

More than that, however, their embroidering transcended their deliberate and discursive messages. As a material and embodied "language," embroidering allowed the women to unconsciously articulate their feelings, their networks, their fears and tensions, and their opposition to the discipline of the prison as small, embodied acts of "Refusal." Embroidering for suffragettes became an embodied act of resistance as well as a symbol of defiance.

Embroidering, so often downplayed, dismissed, and denigrated as domestic and superficial, thus becomes radically reconfigured in this study. Reconsidered through the material process of embroidering and from the perspective of the material and the discursive, the suffragette embroideries worked *in extremis*, reveal rich, nuanced, and overlooked information that supplements Parker's original contention.

In the suffragette embroideries, cloth and thread quietly conjure the absent present physical and psychical body that was so crucial to the women's suffrage campaign. Silently, unobtrusively hidden within their surfaces and structure, the embroideries still contain the embedded matter of suffragette DNA, in spittle, hair, dead skin, sweat, and blood. Although not materially followed through by Parker's argument in *The Subversive Stitch* ([1984] 2010), Olive Schreiner's words regarding the needle and "the blood of the human race" were and are profoundly applicable.

Notes

1 The *Daily Mail* coined the term "suffragette" in January 1906 to distinguish members of the WSPU from the more constitutional "suffragists" (*Daily Mail*, January 10, 1906: 3).

2 The references are: the Terrero panel, the Suffragette Fellowship Collection (hereafter SFC), Museum of London (hereafter MoL), 50.82/1496; the Women's Library panel (hereafter TWL), 2012.24; the suffragette handkerchief, The Sussex Archaeological Society, The Priest House Museum, East Sussex; the shield badge, MoL.50.82/1213; the Wilcox fragment, MoL.50.82/1231; and the brush and comb bag, Taylor Papers TWL.7MET.

3 TWL.7KGG/1/1.

4 The National Archives (hereafter TNA), Prison Commission files (hereafter Pri/Com). 8/228.

5 TNA, Home Office files (hereafter HO). 220.196/20.

6 TWL.7KGG/2/1.

7 Ibid.

8 TNA, HO.220.196/474.

9 More suffragettes were removed to prisons in Aylesbury, Birmingham, and Maidstone between March 26 and 27. TNA, Pri /Com.8/228.

10 TNA, HO.220.196/20.

11 TNA, HO.220.196/104.
12 TWL.7KGG/1/6.
13 In 1913 the Prisoners' Temporary Discharge for Ill Health Act was introduced whereby suffragettes weakened by the hunger strike were released on license. They were rearrested once their health improved (Purvis 1994: 169).
14 SFC, MoL.50.87/67.
15 The WSPU colors were white for purity, green for hope, and purple for freedom and dignity (Tickner 1987: 93).
16 See Goggin (2009) and Wheeler (2012).
17 TWL.ALC.9/29/50.
18 TWL.ALC.9/26/002.
19 SFC, MoL.57.116/39.
20 See Pajaczkowska (2016); and *Textile: The Journal of Cloth and Culture* (2008) 6 (3), where cloth is discussed as "second skin."
21 TWL.7/KGG/2/1.

References

Anzieu, D. (1989), *The Skin Ego*, trans. C. Turner, New Haven: Yale University Press.

Anzieu, D. (2016), *The Skin Ego*, trans. N. Segal, London: Karnac.

Ash, J. (2010), *Dress Behind Bars: Prison Clothing as Criminality*, London: I.B. Tauris.

Benthien, C. (2002), *Skin: on the cultural border between self and the world*, trans. T. Dunlap, New York: Columbia University.

Blackman, L. (2008), *The Body: The Key Concepts*, Oxford: Berg.

Daily Mail, January 1906.

Douglas, M. ([1966], 2002), *Purity and Danger: An Analysis of Concepts of Pollution and Taboo*, London: Routledge.

Foucault, M. (1977), *Discipline and Punish: The Birth of the Prison*, trans. A. Lane, London: Penguin.

Gliddon Papers, TWL, (LSE).

Goggin, M.D. (2009), "Fabricating Identity: Janie Terrero's 1912 Embroidered English Suffrage Signature Cloth," in M. D. Goggin and B. F. Tobin (eds) (2009) *Women and Things 1750–1950: Gendered Material Strategies*, 17–42, Farnham: Ashgate.

Grant (2011), "British Suffragettes and the Russian Method of Hunger Strike," *Comparative Studies in Society and History*, 53 (1): 113–43.

Hebdige, D. (1979), *Subculture: The Meaning of Style*, London: Methuen.

Lafrance, M. (2013), "From the Skin Ego to the Psychic Envelope: An Introduction to the Work of Didier Anzieu," in S. Cavanagh, A. Failler, and R. Alpha Johnston Hurst (eds) *Skin, Culture and Psychoanalysis*, 16–44, Hampshire: Macmillan.

Machin, A. (2016) "Hunger Power: The embodied protest of the hunger strike," *Interface: A Journal for and about Social Movements*, 8 (1): 157–80.

Miller, I. (2013) "'A Prostitution of the Profession?' Forcible Feeding, Prison Doctors, Suffrage and the British State, 1909–1914," *Social History of Medicine*, 26 (2): 225–45.

Morrell, C. (1981), *"Black Friday": Violence Against Women in the Suffragette Movement*, London: WRRC Publications Collective.

North, S. (2013), "The Surfacing of the Self: The Clothing-Ego," in S. Cavanagh, A. Failler, and R. Alpha Johnston Hurst (eds) *Skin, Culture and Psychoanalysis*, 64–89, Hampshire: Macmillan.

Pankhurst, E.S. ([1931] 2010), *The Suffragette Movement: An Intimate Account of Persons and Ideals*, Milton Keynes: Lightning Source.

Parker, R. ([1984] 2010), *The Subversive Stitch: Embroidery and the Making of the Feminine*, London: The Women's Press, I.B. Tauris.

Pajaczkowska, C. (2016), "Making Known: The Textiles Toolbox—Psychoanalysis of Nine Types of Textile Thinking," in J. Jeffries, D. Wood Conroy, and H. Clark (eds) *The Handbook of Textile Culture*, 79–94, London: Bloomsbury.

Purvis, J. (1994), "Doing Feminist Women's History: Researching the Lives of Women in the Suffragette Movement in Edwardian England," in M. Maynard and J. Purvis (eds) *Doing Feminist Women's History: Researching the Lives of Women in the Suffragette Movement in Edwardian England*, 166–89, London: Taylor and Francis.

Purvis, J. (1995), "The Prison Experiences of the Suffragette in Edwardian Britain," *Women's History Review* 4 (1): 103–33.

Rosen A. ([1974] 2013), *Rise Up Women: The Militant Campaign of the Women's Social and Political Union 1903–1914*, London: Routledge and Kegan Paul.

Schreiner, O. ([1926] 1982), *From Man to Man or Perhaps Only –*, London: Virago Modern Classics.

Tererro Letters, ALC, TWL, LSE.

Terrero Papers, SFC, MoL.

Textile: The Journal of Cloth and Culture (2008) 6 (3).

Tickner, L (1987), *The Spectacle of Women: Imagery of the Suffrage Campaign, 1907–14*, London: Chatto & Windus.

The National Archives, HO. and Pri/Com. papers, 1912.

Vicinus, M. (1985), *Independent Women: Work and Community for Single Women, 1850–1920*, London: Virago Press.

Votes for Women 1910–1912.

Wheeler, E. (2012), "The Political Stitch: Voicing Resistance in a Suffrage Textile," Available online: https://www.digitalcommons.unl.edu.TEXTILESOC.TSAsymposium>758 (accessed June 8, 2023).

Witzgill, S. and Stakemeier, K. (eds) (2017), *Power of Material/Politics of Materiality*, Munich: Diaphanes.

"Cloth is simultaneously personal and public, loud and quiet. It provides both a means to hide and to be seen, to rebel and to assimilate, and to speak or hold one's tongue. Cloth is in every fiber of our being."

Alicia Decker

10

Stitching Justice: Textiles as a Means for Contemporary Social Justice

ALICIA DECKER AND SUSAN T. AVILA

Introduction

This chapter examines the prominence and importance of collective textile-based making as a means for communicating about contemporary social justice issues. We present our case studies within the theoretical and historical frameworks of protest aesthetics, visual communication, material culture, and community building, and discuss how social media impacts and amplifies the textile narrative. The invention of the internet and social media has transformed visual culture into something for constant and active engagement as well as an educational tool for creating change.

Social engagement through collaborative and participatory textile-making creates space for expressive dialogue, safe disagreement, reflection, active listening, critical thinking, and is a platform for tenacious resistance (Hackney et al. 2016: 34). A participatory approach to this type of textile-making can increase one's self-awareness and confidence to take action and make change through the support of a like-minded community (Crooke 2007: 3). Through social media's keen ability to strengthen voices through shared visual information, the quiet craft of stitching on cloth emboldens a sense of agency for both groups and individual makers. Communicative properties of textiles in particular, while possibly the antithesis of digital technology, thrive in the cyber environment, increasing viewership and participation. The contemporary participatory textile-making projects presented here—*25 Million Stitches, Tiny Pricks Project, Social Justice Sewing Academy,* and *Protest Banner Lending Library*—are exemplary of the power of textiles to provoke expression, communication, and solidarity; they additionally incite critical resistance, utilizing the power of social media to expand and encourage the collective voice through collaborative textile-making.

Textiles have long provided a powerful means for personal agency and communication, especially for women otherwise silenced in patriarchal societies (Kruger 2011: 21–3). As recorded by Aristotle, Sophocles coined the striking phrase, "the voice of the shuttle" in a now-lost play. Ovid's *Metamorphoses* uses this phrase to describe Philomela's deployment of weaving to communicate her gruesome rape by King Tereus, who cut out her tongue to prevent discovery of the violation (Gordon 2014: 209). In the nineteenth century, quilts were a socially acceptable outlet for women's creativity and within that realm provided a means for expressing their thoughts and feelings about anything from the personal to the political within their designs (Dewhurst et al. 1979: 53).

The activity of quilt making has a long history of community building and inspiring a sense of collective voice, as quilting bees allowed women to stitch together while discussing their views on the world around them. Participatory textile-making brings people together, stitch by stitch, inspiring a sense of collective agency that builds a stronger and louder coalition on behalf of a social or political issue. In the 1930s, as a response to the expanded opportunities for African Americans under the New Deal, Ruth Clement Bond designed quilts as activist art and brought together the wives of the Tennessee Valley Authority (TVA) construction workers to sew them as statements supporting African American culture (Smucker 2022: 24–8). One of these quilts included the now iconic Black Power Fist, which has become a resonant symbol of revolution and solidarity in US culture. In the 1980s the Boise Peace Quilt Project (BPQP) created quilts to protest the Cold War; the project began when two friends, Ann Hausrath and Diane Jones, set out to make a friendship quilt for the Soviet Union to convey their shared humanity—their first quilt *Of Idaho and Peace* was gifted to the Soviet Women's Peace Committee and displayed in Lithuania (Blain 1994: 27). The BPQP initially enlisted friends and community members to create quilts in support of peace; they expanded their network through phone calls and letter-writing campaigns and depended on support from traditional print and television news media to help convey their message. One of their most significant projects was the *Joint Soviet–American Peace Quilt*, which was collaboratively made with women in the Soviet Union and documented in the 1987 Oscar-nominated film *A Stitch For Time*. In Judy Elsley's monograph on the semiotics of quilting she states, "Although the Boise quilters produce beautiful quilts, their needlework is essentially a medium through which they empower themselves and communicate with others" (1996: 207).

Quilts carry a built-in narrative of warmth and comfort, which, coupled with a decorative façade, have been relied on by female makers like the BPQP to soften transgressive messages while still maintaining a powerful sense of agency. The non-threatening demeanor of quilts and most textiles can thus transmit messages that are often hidden in plain sight. For example, Hmong story cloths powerfully depict the displacement and political oppression of the Hmong people in China, Vietnam, and Laos through techniques such as sewing, embroidery, and appliqué. During the 1970s and 1980s in Chile, underground networks of women called *arpilleristas* made clandestine textiles on burlap grain sacks, which were appliquéd to produce scenes of human rights atrocities and extreme poverty under the Pinochet regime. The inconspicuous nature of these cloths allowed their subversive cries of resistance to be smuggled across the Chilean border to request help from international communities (Bryan-Wilson 2017: 148–9).

The universal familiarity of textiles enhances accessibility for creating common languages by communities whose members can all recognize the symbolic significance of what they are creating. For example, the white headscarves worn by the mothers of Plaza de Mayo in Buenos Aires, Argentina, were designed to look like diapers where mothers of the disappeared embroidered their child's name as a reminder of their birth and existence (Meade 2010: 157–8). The portable and foldable qualities of textiles lend themselves for use as banners and other forms of signage during protests. *The Ribbon International*, created in 1982, encompassed 18 miles of joined fabric panels stretched across the United States Capitol to protest nuclear war. Panels were sewn or painted by volunteer home crafters, displaying and proclaiming what they most wanted to protect by abolishing nuclear weapons (Macafee 2015).

One of the most well-known (and arguably the largest) communal textile project is the *NAMES Project*, colloquially known as the *AIDS Quilt*. While not a quilt in the true definition of three layers stitched together, it takes on the appearance of a quilt and brings together blocks (designs) to convey messages of loss and memorial (Bryan-Wilson 2017: 196–7). As a whole, it represents a strong visual statement about the AIDS crisis; however, each individual panel expresses grief and loss through personal, subjective narratives.

These early projects were made and created when the internet was just beginning and grew slowly and gradually without the advent of social media platforms such as Instagram, Facebook, and X (formerly Twitter) that propel participatory social justice textile projects today. Many of these projects took years to build momentum and were dependent on word of mouth—grassroots organizing, letter-writing campaigns, physical travel, and teaching workshops. Jennifer Marsh's *World Reclamation Art Project (WRAP)* in 2007/2008 as part of her International Fiber Collective (IFC) was one of the first collaborative textile projects to take advantage of email and a project website, yet she still depended on travel, teaching workshops to school children, and publicity through traditional analog media. She collected over 3,000 handmade textile panels from twenty-seven states and sixteen countries to fully cover an abandoned garage as an environmental statement against petroleum reliance (Marsh 2008: 34–7). While this was an incredible and important project, its fame was short-lived, and the project is relatively unknown today. In contrast, social media provides broad dissemination of craft activism. Additionally, as seen in the case studies below, social media often forms a connecting thread interweaving the slow creation of textiles with the rapid diffusion of information.

Viral social media engagement transformed the *Pussyhat Project* from a single act of stitched resistance into a global movement almost overnight. The *Pussyhat Project* began with free, downloadable instructions to knit a pink rectangle that when folded and sewed at the sides formed a hat with the appearance of cat ears. This was intended as a pun in response to President Trump's *Access Hollywood* comment, "Grab 'em by the pussy," in which he referred to women in a derogatory and obscene manner. The *Pussyhat Project* facilitators, Jayna Zweiman and Krista Suh, along with Kat Coyle, who created the original pattern, posted the instructions on the popular knitting forum, Ravelry (with over 7 million users), along with a call to wear one and participate in the women's march on January 21, 2017. Ravelry users tapped into additional social media networks and the result was an international phenomenon (Bruder 2019: 111–19); the pink "pussy hat" is now a recognized global icon of resistance and solidarity (Black 2017: 696–710).

In this chapter, we discuss four contemporary case studies that utilize the power of social media and reveal how textiles enable individuals to become part of larger communities promoting social justice. Jennifer Kim Sohn's *25 Million Stitches* and Diana Weymar's *Tiny Pricks Project* utilize small visual statements of embroidery to collectively form powerful messages of solidarity and community. With the Social Justice Sewing Academy, Sara Trail empowers youth to become agents of social change through textile art. Aram Han Sifuentes literally helps voice dissent with hand-sewn protest banners. Our discussion is based on interviews with the artists in spring 2022 and unless otherwise noted, all quotes are from the artists being discussed.

25 Million Stitches

The global human displacement crisis has continued to escalate year after year; the United Nations reported that over 90 million people were forcibly displaced as a result of persecution, conflict, violence, and human rights violations by the end of 2020. This number includes refugees and asylum seekers as well as over 50 million people displaced inside their borders by conflict (UNHCR 2022). The *25 Million Stitches* project was created by artist and activist Jennifer Kim Sohn in 2019, as a response to the Syrian refugee crisis. Sohn felt a personal connection to the refugees, recalling how her own Korean ancestors fled the Japanese, ending up in China. Sohn herself emigrated from South Korea to the United States as a teen; her artwork frequently reflects her own immigrant experience while bringing awareness to various social and environmental justice concerns. Grappling with the great emotional distress of remembering her own family's displacement and comparing it to the current Syrian crisis, Sohn decided to document the number of displaced people around the world with embroidery as a way to visually process her feelings; she pledged to continue until she reached 25 million stitches, one for every refugee displaced worldwide. Sohn believed she could not only communicate more viscerally through the naturally resonant medium of textiles, but that the process of stitching provided a physical action she could take toward a seemingly hopeless situation.

Sohn quickly realized the scale of her project was too much for one person, so for the first time in her artistic career, she reached out for help and transitioned from a sole author into the role of directing a collaborative effort. Sohn first relied on her friends and word of mouth; however, after launching the *25 Million Stitches* Facebook group with a public call to action, thousands of people worldwide soon asked to participate. Stitchers came from all walks of life, some of whom were refugees or displaced people themselves. Upon request, Sohn would send a uniform piece of sturdy cotton fabric to participants, who would then mail back their stitched reflections on the refugee crisis. Sohn in turn posted images of these embroideries on Facebook and Instagram, which inspired and motivated new participants. Most strikingly, Sohn noticed how each newly posted response influenced future designs: "The initial changes in the panel designs were small and discrete: tiny designs were added among the running stitch lines or straight lines became wavelike. Then the wavy lines took the shapes of pathways, mountains, and rivers" (interview April 4, 2022).

Social media helped spur a proliferation of ideas and designs encouraging the innate and unfettered connection humans have with cloth that transcends cultural barriers and political differences. As a pensive and reflective act, embroidery provided Sohn and participants with a physical and visual methodology for communicating about the refugee crisis and counteracting feelings of powerlessness in a dire situation. Additionally, the global, public presence of the social media posts moved the project from a visual testimony about the scale of the crisis to a deeply moving persuasion of why we should care about the refugees and their plight. In January 2020, when Sohn had collected just two million stitches, a flood of panels arrived from a Lithuanian community who were once displaced from the former USSR and over the next three months, Sohn received an additional 23 million stitches, allowing her to reach her goal.

While politics often dominate concurrent and conflicting narratives on the toll and causes of human displacement, Sohn's project asks people to choose empathy over politics in considering the grave humanity of the situation and the lived experiences of refugees. Although most of the project's stitchers have no lived experience as refugees themselves, each panel provides an opportunity to visually communicate their compassion through stitch-based pictorial and textual shows of support. The familiarity and accessibility of textiles coupled with the advent of social media provided a means for moving the project beyond the personal and into the collaborative public sphere. Viewing the accumulated stitched panels in a physical space evokes a dramatic effect that directly reflects the scale and intensity of the crisis. Upon visiting the traveling exhibition, patrons feel the compassion and energy of each stitch and experience the richness, diversity, and uniqueness of the laboriously created panels.

25 Million Stitches uses the simple and quiet actions of embroidery to bring the refugee crisis into the public eye through dissemination in both digital and physical space. With the help of social media, the project incites collective agency, sending a powerful message of support to refugees that transcends borders. Based on feedback from the public, the impact of this project is profoundly felt by both participants and viewers, as well as the refugee community itself. Sohn hopes that through the universal medium of cloth, *25 Million Stitches* will create dialogue amongst viewers and participants alike to bring about greater awareness, increase empathy that encourages a more welcoming community, and elicit political pressure for action.

Tiny Pricks Project

Diana Weymar studied English and creative writing at Princeton University, so it is not surprising that she approaches textiles as a substrate for embroidering words on cloth. The vintage textiles she inherited from her grandparents motivated her foray into sewing and embroidery, inspiring her to build on their rich histories and embedded narratives that she could enhance with photographs, family mementoes, and meaningful words. Weymar then moved this format of cultural memorial into the public realm by organizing a series of community-based projects that encouraged individuals to share their own memories of time and place through the creation of embroidered pages that she compiled into a textile document. Her first public project, *Interwoven Stories*, traveled extensively but centered primarily on building local communities through collective storytelling. Working on these collaborative projects eased the isolation of working alone in her remote British Columbia studio.

When Donald Trump was elected president of the United States in 2016, Weymar knew she had to do something in reaction to this shocking reversal of political ideology combined with a bizarrely unconventional form of presidential communication through the social media platform Twitter. She started embroidering Trump's tweets with the initial idea of creating one piece per week to generate a material record of his presidency. Her first piece proclaimed "I'm a Very Stable Genius" embroidered in yellow thread on one of her grandmother's needlepoints. This embroidered tweet was then posted as an image on Twitter and retweeted, creating a relationship between the textile thread and social media. Rather than quickly typed words shared onto a live feed, the image of embroidered text, with its nostalgic, antique style, demonstrated a thoughtful labored process, unlike other Twitter content. Viewers engaged with Weymar's Instagram posts, often tweeting images that recontextualized the absurdity of a fleeting sound bite through labor-intensive handwork. It also became apparent that Weymar could not keep up with the volume of language spewing from the White House to meet her goal of responding to all of Trump's tweets. Many followers were asking how they could contribute, so Weymar tapped into her previous community-building experience and started accepting embroidered donations through the mail from participants across the United States and posting them on the *Tiny Pricks Project* Instagram site. The project gave participants—both makers and viewers—an outlet for digesting a litany of tragically absurd commentary. The stitched pieces were a means of reflection and when shared, provided a moment of connection.

Embroidery requires puncturing the cloth with a needle prick, which also can serve as a metaphorical jab—a fitting response to the anger and frustration many felt during the Trump presidency. Weymar is not concerned with the quality and technical expertise of the stitching but appreciates the aspect of slowing down the rapid digital commentary and creating a physical object with more longevity than a single tweet.

While the embroidered objects form a permanent material archive that documents a tumultuous time in history, it is the relationship with social media that, as Weymar acknowledges, provided "a kind of magical element" that accelerated the project's growth. When the objects are exhibited in gallery shows, such as the Lingua Franca storefront in New York City, there is limited space to display the work. In contrast, the Instagram gallery has included almost 5,000 posts and has over 90,000 followers. Additionally, Instagram perpetuates the feeling of community because *Tiny Pricks* makers can see their objects displayed and feel pride and the satisfaction of being part of a larger political movement. Viewers who follow the site enhance the impact of the community through sheer volume, but also by posting comments that add not only dimension and scope to the images but also create a sense of camaraderie.

Figure 10.1 *I want Great Climate.* © Diana Weymar, Tiny Pricks Project.

Weymar sees the activity of making as a practice; the *Tiny Pricks* community becomes a safe space to express dissent through stitching. Embroidery is traditionally seen as something delicate and beautiful, but in this sense, it provides a decorative buffer for expressing a reaction or protest. This, in turn, opens up the project for makers who may not have previously felt comfortable expressing political ideas in their work.

Under the cover of community, there is strength in numbers and mutual appreciation for the work. Through stitching and posting, Weymar has learned to trust the creative impulse and understand that even when geographically isolated, there are others who will relate to the pieces and feel inspired to create their own remonstrative objects. In a reciprocal relationship, this mode of shared expression expands the community that would not exist without the public realm. Pieces submitted by individuals become part of a collective whole and it is this collaborative result that forms the crux of the project. Makers take pleasure in their embroideries being shared as part of the *Tiny Pricks* community and are excited and fulfilled seeing the responsive textiles of other makers. These textiles are shared as images on Instagram and "liked" by people who will probably never meet each other; the community's existence depends on these social media followers as well as the individual makers. Weymar believes that the project has given participants a way to stay engaged and aware without succumbing to an abyss of despair. She notes that for many, the project has helped them navigate a difficult period; they will hear something on the news and wonder . . . how soon before someone stitches that?

As the curator of *Tiny Pricks*, Weymar thoughtfully considers what to post and how to post in a way that keeps the community safe and growing without losing the gratifying, positive aspects that the stitched textiles bring to the work. While the project officially ended with Trump's 2020 presidential defeat, *Tiny Pricks* continues to post embroidered commentary that is sometimes acerbic, sometimes heartbreaking, and occasionally heartwarming.

Social Justice Sewing Academy

The home page of the Social Justice Sewing Academy (SJSA) proclaims: "Art. Empowerment. Advocacy." While these pillars of the organization guide many of the various activities of SJSA, they amply describe the ongoing youth workshops that teach young people to visually translate and convey conceptual ideas about social justice onto cloth. SJSA is the brainchild of Sara Trail, a young African American woman from Antioch, California, who learned how to sew when she was four. Trail's remarkable childhood included teaching children to sew; creating her own line of Simplicity sewing patterns; developing a line of textile prints; and publishing the book, *Sew with Sara*, as well as producing a nationally distributed DVD, *Cool Stuff to Sew with Sara* (2011). She was also the youngest member of her local quilt guild.

It was during a quilting class in 2012 that Trail, then seventeen and a freshman at University of California Berkeley, had an epiphany about the ideological divide between herself and her peers and mentors in the quilt world. Trail recalls entering her quilting class after the death of Trayvon Martin and trying to engage her classmates, mostly older white women "who were like grandmas to me," in a discussion about the horrific racially motivated murder. Instead of reacting to this news, they wanted to continue discussing grandchildren and other pleasant topics. It was at that moment that Trail shifted her attention from traditional quilting and began to create art quilts designed to promote social justice. Her first conceptual message quilt was in memory of Trayvon Martin (which she later gifted to his mother).

Upon graduation in 2016, Trail applied for and received the prestigious Judith Lee Stronach Baccalaureate Prize, which supports projects by UC Berkeley graduates designed to promote social consciousness and contribute to the public good. Trail's idea was to teach low-income and primarily black and brown youth sewing and design skills through projects relevant to social justice. She knew that sewing, no longer taught in most public schools, might be considered a luxury for many families who could not afford sewing machines, private class fees, required materials, or transportation to classes.

The first SJSA workshop was eight weeks long and combined education in critical race theory and social consciousness with sewing skills. Students learned how to develop a visual language using cloth that could express their feelings about social justice issues. Working on topics that were meaningful to them in turn motivated students to create and learn. The final project was a collaborative art quilt and students were excited to exhibit their work. That fall, Trail entered Harvard Graduate School of Education challenged to continue the momentum and enthusiasm generated by the workshop. She approached local schools in Cambridge, Massachusetts, and realized there was a high demand; there was also insufficient time to teach all the sewing skills necessary to create a quilt. Trail figured out how to streamline the workshop by placing less emphasis on sewing and more on design. Students could focus on developing the concept, choosing and cutting out the fabric, and laying out the quilt block by gluing the fabric into place. Trail could then complete the sewing. After quickly realizing that she did not have the time to complete the student blocks herself, she reached out to her California quilt guild for help with embroidery and sewing. Thus began an intergenerational collaboration with volunteers who had the luxury of time to offer their sewing expertise and the mostly teenage student designers who took the SJSA workshops. Students created the blocks and included any specific instructions (such as a request for additional embroidered text) as well as written statements about their design's significance and meaning. These were sent to volunteer embroiderers, who secured the appliquéd shapes with embroidery stitches and often added their own flourishes after interpreting the students' requests. The finished blocks were returned to Trail, who then sent them out to volunteer quilters to compile into a finished quilt. This formula proved successful and soon new workshop facilitators were trained. Instagram provided an outlet for displaying and discussing student work. It also became a powerful platform for initiating conversations that brought greater awareness of the issues featured in the students' work. These evocative posts helped recruit new volunteers and donors as awareness of SJSA spread throughout social media.

In an interesting and dynamic offshoot of this process, volunteers also became more aware of social justice issues through this exchange as young teenagers educated their sewing mentors about critical social justice issues. Trail recalls one example where an embroidery volunteer from Idaho received a block about mass incarceration and because of the eighth grader's statement, opted to watch Ava Duvernay's documentary *13th* to educate herself about how US prisons are disproportionately populated with African Americans.

As SJSA's social media following grew, Trail began receiving invitations to teach workshops across the country. SJSA workshops have been taught throughout the United States in various geographic and demographic venues, including schools, art centers, and jails. Trail considers her workshop leader role as a facilitator of dialogue. She tries to teach by example and allow each student to meet her at their own point of readiness, ideally creating "not just a safe space but a brave space." Even with the same prompt, "what social justice issue matters to you?" Trail observed that in wealthier, predominantly white areas students might choose topics such as income equality, climate change, or animal abuse, while in low-income neighborhoods students generally created blocks directly relevant to their own lives such as a jailed parent, community gun violence, or people who looked like them being killed by police. She notes that there is no hierarchy of social justice issues and that all of these issues are important.

Challenges to the SJSA process mostly came from attempts to disseminate the work in traditional quilting venues where strict rules denied the participation of community-made projects or where the quilt community felt that the social justice messages were too controversial for public exhibition. Another ongoing challenge is funding and support. When the initial UC Berkeley grant ended, Trail and her family became the primary funders of the organization. In 2017 it became a legal non-profit and Lauren Black, another young African American woman, joined SJSA as the executive director. The organization relies on a network of sponsors as well as monetary and in-kind donations in addition to the community of embroidery and quilting volunteers.

The Social Justice Sewing Academy provides young people with the tools to tell their own stories through textile art. Working with fabrics and learning basic design skills empowers youth to promote social justice and enhances self-esteem when the resulting art quilts are exhibited and receive public recognition. The familiarity of textiles creates an ease of access for students who might be intimidated by a lack of art skills. Additionally, SJSA primarily uses donated textiles adding a sustainability component, as the fabrics might otherwise end up in landfill. At workshops, students engage with their peers in the social justice dialogue before creating their cloth squares and then help perpetuate an intergenerational education cycle with embroidery and quilting volunteers. The finished quilts then educate spectators who not only admire and appreciate the handwork but also read the artist statements and achieve a greater understanding of the social justice concern.

Protest Banner Lending Library

Aram Han Sifuentes's community-engaged art projects confront social and racial injustice through multiethnic and intergenerational sewing circles that become places for empowerment, subversion, and protest, sharing skills as a point of connection. Sifuentes learned to sew as a child shortly after emigrating to the United States from South Korea in 1992. Her seamstress mother taught her this skill as a practicality to help in the family dry cleaning business in Manteca, California. Daily encounters with textiles and sewing became an integral part of Sifuentes' life and combined with her personal immigration story became the roots of her powerful political work. She utilizes textiles to investigate identity, immigration, immigrant labor, possession and dispossession, dissent and protest, and race politics in the United States.

Sifuentes' project, *Protest Banner Lending Library* serendipitously began in 2016 as a response to the US presidential election. Devastated by the election results, she started making protest banners in her apartment before organically creating a community of like-minded banner makers. As a non-citizen and a new mother, going to protests at the time was very difficult for Sifuentes, although she felt strongly compelled to act. Creating banners became a way for her to safely speak out and amplify her voice of resistance against what was happening in the United States.

Protest Banner Lending Library consists of two main components. A series of free workshops teach people how to create their own textile-based protest banners. The workshops evolved from the realization that many people feel compelled to participate, resist, and speak out about social and political injustice but often have barriers to protesting publicly such as fear of deportation, tenuous health, disability, or lack of childcare. Protesting rhetoric in the United States implies that it is a safe, accessible, and legal right for everyone. However, as Sifuentes points out, this is not always the case; many vulnerable communities cannot protest without high risks to their safety and status. The protest banner workshops facilitate a sense of solidarity through making and participants come to share a philosophy that making is, in and of itself, a form of resistance.

Sifuentes initially offered sewing ateliers in her own home, but as they grew, she accepted invitations from public and private arts organizations in the United States and internationally to facilitate protest banner workshops, resulting in the creation of over 3,000 banners. Workshops typically run 2–3 hours and might involve as few as ten or as many as one hundred participants. Sifuentes consciously makes the workshops unintimidating for those without sewing skills; she demonstrates the technique of adhering fabrics with fusible webbing requiring only scissors and an iron. Banners utilize standard fabric widths which are usually 42 inches (106.68 cm) and most fabric is donated. Participants determine their own narrative as Sifuentes connects them with the materials and process for taking action and speaking through cloth. Workshop participants are as diverse as the lending library banners, including a fetish community at the Leather Archives in Chicago, formerly incarcerated young adults met through the University of Massachusetts, and a refugee community in Hamburg, Germany.

The second component of the project, an actual lending library, began organically from the workshops. As Sifuentes made more and more banners, she started posting photos on Instagram. Friends and strangers quickly commented on her posts, asking to borrow the banners for upcoming protests. With the help of social media, the project took off as activists and artists alike, coping with the political unrest at the time, shared the project amongst their communities. Ten libraries in the United States, and two international, exist today and are all volunteer-run and collectively house over 1,000 banners. Each library contains a diverse collection of donated banners for anyone to check out, use for an indeterminate amount of time, and easily return. Additionally, banners with certain phrases have been requested through the library and created in time for specific protests. The collection continues to grow through banner donations from ongoing workshops and individual banner commissions.

The circulation from protester to protester has given life to these material objects, each banner carrying the history of the hands who made and held it in all the places it has traveled. Although Western society emphasizes identity and art creation through individualism, in many cultures,

Figure 10.2 Installation view of Protest Banner Lending Library. © University Galleries at Illinois State University, 2019. Photographer: © Jessica Bingham.

and in most non-Western cultures, communities often coalesce around creative practice through collective making. Sifuentes believes there is great significance and power in working collaboratively: building a shared identity through solidarity.

There is a long history of using fabric for protest banners. On a practical level, fabric is sturdier and reusable compared to commonly used cardboard signs, providing longevity that allows fabric banners to be borrowed time and time again. Fabric banners can also serve double duty as blankets and seating. Most importantly, fabric banners fold easily and can be carried inconspicuously if the protest climate gets heated. Throughout the project, Sifuentes has worked closely with HANA Center, a Chicago-based immigrants' rights organization, which she has supplied with banners for rallies and marches all over the country. Sifuentes has received feedback from this group that the banners are eye-catching in crowds; they get photographed by many people and are quick to grab media attention. The compelling visual impact of the banners seen while scrolling Instagram has positioned *Protest Banner Lending Library* in the center of online craftivist communities, helping to fortify a social network of activism and makers.

Sifuentes claims her biggest takeaway from doing this project over the years is that although unquantifiable, art plays an extremely important role in the fight for social, racial, and economic justice. *Protest Banner Lending Library* is an example of how collaboration and creating community through art making has a strong impact. The library creates a space for working together and sharing resources through the act of making, providing support, and strengthening the collective voice needed for meaningful change.

Conclusion

Betsey Greer popularized the term Craftivism as "a way of looking at life where voicing opinions through creativity makes your voice stronger, your compassion deeper & your quest for justice more infinite" (2014: 3–5). Presented here is historical and contemporary evidence to support Greer's sentiment and the interdependent communicative relationship between textiles and social justice. As seen through the contemporary case studies above, stitched resistance continues to empower and join people in powerful unison against some of today's most pressing issues. While textiles are the creative medium in all these projects, it is the community participation and shared access that brings them to life. David Gauntlett describes the benefits of this type of collaborative process in his book, *Making is Connecting*, and notes that through this creative engagement, people not only feel more connected ("becoming heard and recognized") but more empowered to make a difference (2016: 232–3). In the post-digital age, social media creates worldwide communities of activists and makers. Ironically, while the immediacy of social media propels rapid action toward social justice, it is the slow making of textiles that draws attention to the humanity of the issue.

In each of the contemporary case studies presented, social media played a significant role in either announcing the project, encouraging participation, and/or disseminating the cause, propelling the project's reach faster and further than earlier projects without this access. Additionally, unlike ever before, social media provides a robust and readily available digital archive of each project, making them available to viewers and future craft activists for years to come. It is interesting to note, however, that hands-on workshops, especially in the case of SJSA and *Protest Banner Lending Library*, are an integral component of each project, and that process and content are valued equally or more than the end product. Most of the textile finesse and craftsmanship in these projects comes from anonymous volunteers. Individuals may take pride in their unique contributions but release their ownership in deference to the greater community; this collective sharing magnifies the textile voice and amplifies the social justice message.

References

Black, S. (2017) "Knit + Resist: Placing the Pussyhat Project in the Context of Craft Activism", 696–710. *Gender, Place and Culture: a Journal of Feminist Geography* 24, no. 5: https://doi.org/10.1080/0966369x.2017.1335292.

Blain, A. K. (1994) *Tactical Textiles. A Genealogy of the Boise Peace Quilt Project: 1981–1988*, 27. Dubuque, Iowa: Kendall/Hunt Publishing Company.

Bruder, A. (2019) "Stitching Dissent. From the Suffragists to Pussyhat Politics" in Hinda Mandell, ed. *Crafting Dissent. Handicraft as Protest from the American Revolution to Pussyhats*, 111–19. London: Rowman & Littlefield.

Bryan-Wilson, J. (2017) *Fray: Art and Textile Politics*, 148–9. Chicago: University of Chicago Press.

Crooke, E. (2007) *Museums and Community: Ideas. London: Issues and Challenges*, 3. New York: Routledge.

Dewhurst, C. K. (1979), Betty MacDowell, and Marsha MacDowell. *Artists in Aprons: Folk Art by American Women*, 53. New York: Museum of American Folk Art.

Elsley, J. (1996) *Quilts as Text(Iles) the Semiotics of Quilting*, 72. New York: Lang.

Gauntlett, D. (2016) *Making Is Connecting: The Social Meaning of Creativity from DIY and Knitting to YouTube and Web 2.0*, 232–3. Cambridge, UK: Polity Press.

Gordon, B. (2014) *Textiles: The Whole Story: Uses, Meanings, Significance*, 209. New York: Thames & Hudson.

Greer, B. (2014) *Craftivism: The Art of Craft and Activism*, 3–5. Vancouver: Arsenal Pulp Press.

Hackney, F., Maughan, H. and Desmarais, S. (2016) The Power of Quiet: Re-making Affective Amateur and Professional Textiles Agencies, 34. *Journal of Textile Design Research and Practice*, 4 no. 1.

Kruger, K. S. (2011) Essay. In *Weaving the Word: The Metaphorics of Weaving and Female Textual Production*, 21–3. Susquehanna University Press.

Macafee, S. (2015) "History of the Ribbon" The Ribbon Project International. (accessed June 9, 2022). https://historyoftheribbon.blogspot.com/

Marsh, J. (2008) "Gas Station Cozy", 34–7. *Fiberarts*, 35 (3): EBSCOhost, https://search.ebscohost.com/login.aspx?direct=true&db=asu&AN=505352167&site=ehost-live.

Meade, T. A. (2010) *A History of Modern Latin America: 1800 to the Present*, 157–8. Hoboken, NJ: Wiley.

Smucker, J. (2022) "Quilts, Social Engineering, and Black Power in the Tennessee Valley." *Southern Cultures* 28, no. 1: 24–8. https://doi.org/10.1353/scu.2022.0002.

"UNHCR: A Record 100 Million People Forcibly Displaced Worldwide || UN News." United Nations. United Nations, May 23, 2022. https://news.un.org/en/story/2022/05/1118772.

"Clicking needles and counting stitches echo through my family history, many nimble fingers powered by tight budgets, creativity and love."

Mary Stark

11

Film as Fabric: Textile Practice as Feminist Critique in Expanded Cinema

MARY STARK

The American film editor Walter Murch describes the interior of a film editing room in the first quarter of the twentieth century as being "a quiet place, equipped only with a rewind bench, a pair of scissors, a magnifying glass, and the knowledge that the distance from the tip of one's nose to the fingers of the outstretched hand represented about three seconds" (2011: 75–6). He even makes an analogy with the tools and processes of cloth, and introduces movement and temporality, saying how, in "those manual, pre-mechanical days, the cutting room was a relatively tranquil tailor's shop in which time was cloth" (2011: 75–6). He describes what happens as the editors, who were mainly skilled women, viewed the film as still frames with a magnifying glass in the laboratory, memorizing the motion of the action and cutting the film in what they perceived as the correct place. Murch continues:

> Patiently and somewhat intuitively, she stitched the fabric of her film together, joining with paper clips the shots that were to be later cemented together by a technician down the hall. She then projected the assembly with the director and producer, took notes, and returned to her room to make further adjustments, shortening this and lengthening that, like a second fitting of a shirt. This new version was projected in turn, and the cycle was repeated over and over until the fit was as perfect as she could make it.
>
> 2011: 75–6

As this vivid description shows, the early filmmaking industry appropriated terminology, techniques, and apparatus from textile practice. But rather than being a way to recognize textile skills, associations with stitch have often been integral to devaluing women's contribution to cinema, distancing it from the work of celebrated male directors.

In this chapter, I will discuss how I came to engage textile practice as feminist critique in expanded cinema. My studio-based and performance practice examines relationships between textile practice and filmmaking, questioning how and why these seemingly separate disciplines are in fact deeply conjoined. The origin of my preoccupation with this area grew from the moment I first handled a reel of film in 2010. I immediately observed that the materiality of film offers a tangible visual equivalent to that of fabric. My initial hunch led to sustained historical analysis from a feminist perspective, which mapped a divergent narrative of shared materiality, terminology, and technology. A central goal of my practice became highlighting connections between the two fields through the creation of an expanded cinema performance involving hybrid objects, tools, and gestures.

There are three key connections between textile practice and filmmaking. The first is that terminology, techniques, and apparatus from textile practice were adopted by the early filmmaking industry in the late nineteenth and early twentieth centuries. The second is that many women worked in the cutting rooms of early cinema carrying out work seen as a menial task, similar to cutting and stitching cloth. The third is *Reel Time*, a seminal expanded cinema performance first performed in 1973 by the British artist Annabel Nicolson, in which a huge loop of film was punctured with the unthreaded sewing machine needle until it was so damaged it could no longer be projected. This chapter will take a closer look at these deep connections before examining how they informed the development of an expanded cinema performance, *Film as Fabric* (2013–17). I will also consider how links between textile practice and filmmaking have relevance to women's artistic practice. Connections between the fields prove that women played an important and mostly unrecognized role in a mainstream male-dominated creative industry. A potential direction for the future of contemporary textile practice is to further examine and highlight the interlinked histories of textile practice and filmmaking. More broadly, scholars need to interrogate male-dominated fields and their associated established histories to search for appropriation of terminology, techniques, and apparatus relating to denigrated domestic crafts and hidden female labor.

Common terms shared by textile practice and filmmaking relate to apparatus as well as actions, spool, reel, lace, and wind. These linguistic overlaps may originate in the relationship between the mechanisms of the sewing machine and the film projector. It is thought that the hand-crank film transport mechanism of the *Cinématographe*, a machine which is widely acknowledged as the first film projector, was based on the intermittent mechanism of the sewing machine (National Science and Media Museum 2009). Patented in 1851, this mechanism grips fabric, temporarily allowing the threaded needle to penetrate cloth. The *Cinématographe* had two pins, or "claws," which inserted into sprocket holes at each side of the film, moving it down and then retracting, leaving the film momentarily stationary for exposure and projection. Today, the mechanics of the film projector remain based on that of the sewing machine, albeit with the addition of electrical rather than hand-cranked power. The similar mechanisms of the sewing machine and the film projector were also fully synergized in the Singer Graflex 16mm film projector, which was manufactured by the sewing machine company until the late 1960s.

Further relationships between the technology, terminology, and tools of textile practice and filmmaking are clearly shown by three found hybrid objects. I have speculated on the exact reasons for their creation and use, but they all indicate how lack of access to conventional tools can lead to a sudden blurring of seemingly disparate disciplines. Two objects were found by British film archivist Brian Pritchard. The first consists of two fragments of 35mm film that have been hand stitched together with black thread. The second is a wooden cotton reel modified to substitute a purpose-made film core, which is a small cylinder of plastic specially designed for film to be wound onto. I came across the third object at an experimental film event in 2015: a 16mm film projector lens with a length of cotton thread wrapped around the ridges that allow the image to be focused. For the first object, it would appear that in absence of a traditional film splicer, two lengths of 35mm film were hand stitched together instead. With the second, a lack of film cores could have led to a wooden cotton reel being brought into use in its place. With the third object, the simple trick of wrapping thread around the ridges of the lens meant that it could be focused, despite this part of the film projector having broken. Whatever the reasons that led to these objects being formed, they show how a shortage of time, appropriate tools, or expertise can result in the generation of new interdisciplinary knowledge.

Splicing is an ancient method of joining fibers by twisting the ends together and wetting them with saliva. This work was carried out by ancient Egyptian women but is still practiced in some indigenous communities today (Gleba and Harris 2019: 2330). The verb "to splice" is thought to have originally been a word used by sailors, first used in the 1520s, from Middle Dutch, "splissen," ultimately from (s)plei, "to split, splice," meaning to join or connect (a rope or ropes) by interweaving the strands at the ends. "Splissen" was taken on by the French as "épisser."

The word was first used in filmmaking in 1912 to describe the practice of placing two pieces of film end to end, which are held in position by notches in the film splicer, and then joining them with film cement or splicing tape.

A photograph in a book, *Moving Pictures: How They Are Made and Worked* in the same year shows over sixty women working at the Pathé Frères film production studios in Paris. Many of them sit at edit benches next to large baskets of film, watched over by two men on the sidelines. The caption states: "Sorting, examining and joining the strips of film. The positives are prepared in varying lengths. The different sections of a subject have to be identified, trimmed and connected to form a continuous ribbon" (Talbot 1912: 156). The introduction of the term "splice" in France in 1912 and this captioned photograph of women working in cutting rooms in Paris the same year shows how deep connections between textile practice and filmmaking are evidence of undervalued female labor. Up to the late 1920s, women worked as "cutters" and "joiners" connecting thousands of feet of film by hand. Yet their work joining lengths of film into a "continuous ribbon" (1912: 156) was seen as menial because of its similarity to stitching cloth.

Furthermore, associations with stitch have been used to distance their work from male-dominated canons of film editing. Film historians have played down the importance of women's work in early cinema and distanced it from that of male directors. Brief descriptions allude to editing in early cinema being related to stitching cloth, sometimes without even mentioning that it was carried out by women. Shots were "strung together" (Dancyger 2011: 3) or "simply tacked on to each other" (Oldham 1992: 2). Stringing or tacking shots together implies a preparatory process requiring little skill. The acclaimed American film editor Walter Murch offers a description of a woman working in a cutting room in early cinema that builds on the portrayal of Svilova editing in *Man with a Movie Camera*.[1] Murch (2011) extends the metaphor of film as fabric and editing as stitching into film editing as creating a garment.

By the 1930s, editing was recognized as important in the film production process and was therefore a job for men. An archival film shows the different values given to the gendered practices of cutting and editing: "girl cutters work on the negative film but the actual cutting of the film is the job of the editors, masters of their craft who know exactly what to eliminate and what to keep in" (Kinolibrary 2018). Dominant historical narratives show advances in

SORTING, EXAMINING AND JOINING THE STRIPS OF FILM.   [*By courtesy of Pathé Frères.*]

The positives are prepared in varying lengths. The different sections of a subject have to be identified, trimmed, and connected together to form a continuous ribbon.

Figure 11.1 "Sorting, Examining and Joining the Strips of Film" (Talbot 1914: 156). The cutting room at the Pathé Frères Production Studios, 1912. Paris. Photographer: © F. A. Talbot. Not in copyright; openly available: https://archive.org/details/movingpictureshootalbgoog/page/n91/mode/2up (accessed March 1, 2022).

editing as following a similar pattern. Male directors are celebrated, such as Dziga Vertov, D. W. Griffith, and Jean-Luc Godard, but the women they worked with closely are often overlooked. Vertov's wife, Elizaveta Svilova, edited *Man with a Movie Camera*; Rose Smith edited eleven of Griffith's films including *Intolerance*; and Agnès Guillemot edited the majority of Godard's 1960s films (Wright 2009: 8). Margaret Booth started out as a "joiner" for D. W. Griffith and went on to be supervising editor at MGM until 1968. Anne Bauchens was employed as an editor for more than forty years and was the first woman to win an Oscar for Best Film Editing in 1941. Dorothy Spencer began working as an assistant editor in 1924 and by the 1960s had already worked on over sixty films. These women demonstrate how some cutters and joiners went on to have successful careers as editors. This highlights women's work in cinema and brings the hierarchy and clear distinctions between gendered roles into question.

Similarly, the widely celebrated film, *Man with a Movie Camera* shows how women's work in the cutting rooms of early cinema cannot be seen as separate from established historical narratives about editing. The aforementioned Svilova edited the film and also appears in the film editing, She was born in Russia in 1900 and began cutting film around 1914. By the 1920s, she worked closely with Vertov developing sophisticated montage editing techniques. *Man with a Movie Camera* features a sequence that intercuts Svilova working at the edit bench with a woman stitching cloth, first by hand and then on the sewing machine, before ending with a scene showing three women working in a textile factory. This sequence offers a powerful challenge to the idea that women's work in the cutting rooms of early cinema is of little importance. *Man with a Movie Camera* reinforces the idea that the practice of cutting and splicing film offers a tangible, material equivalent to stitching pieces of fabric, but it associates stitching with highly complex film editing, and shows Svilova gloriously working at the editing bench alone, in total control of her workspace and the construction of the film.

The lack of recognition given to women's contribution to the history of film editing has been discussed by the feminist film scholar Julia Wright, who states, "Female film editors undergo a 'double invisibility': already invisible to film history by virtue of their 'invisible art,' women are then edited out of books that intend to bring visibility to the editing profession" (Wright 2009: 8–9). Film editing remains a male-dominated profession, despite being an area of the cinema industry that continues to employ higher proportions of women.[2] I now argue that regardless of the level of sophistication or amount of creative responsibility cutters had (or did not have), their work needs to be acknowledged as having laid foundations that the filmmaking industry built upon. The previously discussed photograph of a room filled with women cutting film at Pathé Frères in 1912 is a case in point. This world-famous company was instrumental in the birth of the cinema industry and remains one of the largest production companies globally. But who knew their early films were assembled by teams of women working in cutting rooms concealed from public view, whose task was inherently hidden on screen in a seamless flow of moving images?

In contrast, the British artist Annabel Nicolson was strikingly visible when, in 1973, she sat at an unthreaded sewing machine while a film of her at the sewing machine was simultaneously projected, looping around the room, through the audience, then back to the sewing machine, where she used the needle to puncture and gradually destroy the filmstrip. Another unspooled projector cast her moving shadow. Members of the audience read from the sewing machine and film projector manuals, their voices layered with the mechanical noises. The filmstrip, gradually punctured by the needle of the sewing machine, reached breaking point and snapped, making a deafening sound. While the film was re-spliced and laced through the projector and sewing machine again, there was a quiet pause where voices reading out loud could more clearly be heard. This process was repeated until the film was so damaged it could no longer run in the projector.

Nicolson last performed *Reel Time* in 1975 and never worked with the sewing machine and the film projector again, moving into participatory performances involving light, shadow, and sound. *Reel Time* is repeatedly cited as a seminal work in the field of experimental and expanded cinema (Elcott 2008: 18; Rees 2011: 27–8; Webber 2016: 168–9) because of its concerns with the materiality of film, the theatricality of film projection, and the conceptual and physical relationships of the audience to the projected image. However, I agree with feminist critique by the filmmaker Lucy Reynolds, who argued in 2009 that existing contextualization of Nicolson's practice was too narrow (Reynolds 2009: 9). Reynold s's thesis, as well as research by Felicity Sparrow and Vicky Smith offer new insights into *Reel Time* that my research also aims to extend. Sparrow's analysis links Nicolson's performance with women's hidden labor, both in a domestic and an industrial context. She notes the political power of placing apparatus and practices that are usually concealed center stage (Sparrow 2005). Reynolds recognizes that stitching film makes its materiality more noticeable; "celluloid is stressed as a material fabric, rather than a translucent carrier of the film image"(Reynolds 2009: 96). Smith highlights the importance of Nicolson's body in *Reel Time* and argues that the significance of the artist's body has frequently been played down in the field of expanded cinema (Smith 2015: 4).

According to the artist Lis Rhodes, a reason why aspects of *Reel Time* such as craft, the artist's body, and personal meaning were not largely discussed may be due to "neat visions of experimental film having been written from narrow misplaced perspectives, which leave marginalised histories unacknowledged, and categorise works in terms of their similarities rather than their differences" (Rhodes 1979: 119). This position has been reiterated by other female experimental filmmakers (Blaetz 2007: 154; see also Hatfield 2006: 187; Reynolds 2009: 11, 2012: 52;). However, Nicolson asserts that *Reel Time* was not made with feminist intentions and was a personal response to the challenges of working with film. She describes *Reel Time* as coming about because her sewing machine, which had been her mother's, was a familiar object in her studio that she felt comfortable with (Curtis 2002: 1). However, a compelling reading by Sparrow recognizes *Reel Time* as "proto-feminist" (Sparrow 2005), because it connected textile practice, and its strong association with women's labor, with the male-dominated filmmaking industry.

Nicolson later co-founded Circles, a feminist film and video distribution network in the UK, which was born out of a desire to distribute and screen women's films on their own terms. The establishment of Circles came after an artistic protest motivated by the lack of female representation in the exhibition *Film as Film* at the Hayward Gallery in London in 1979, from which Nicolson was one of a number of female filmmakers who withheld their work. Instead, they used their space in the gallery to facilitate discussion, which led to publishing a chapter, "Women and the Formal Film," in the exhibition catalog. In the chapter, Lis Rhodes proposed that female filmmakers draw upon their own experiences as a way to reconstruct histories of experimental film and create contexts for their work: "Women have already realised the need to research and write their own histories; to describe themselves rather than accept descriptions, images and fragments of 'historical evidence'; and to reject a history that perpetuates a mythological female occasionally glimpsed but never heard" (Rhodes 1979: 119).

My expanded cinema performance, *Film as Fabric*, is a direct response to this feminist discussion and the historical connections between textile practice and filmmaking. Informed by the invisibility of women working in cutting rooms and the way that associations with stitch have been used to devalue their work, I now engage textile practice as feminist critique in expanded cinema performance to highlight and recognize women's labor, particularly their contribution to histories of editing. To clarify, I refer to the work of "cutters" or "women working in the cutting rooms of early cinema" because they were not called editors at the time, but I maintain the importance of their work within histories of editing.

Film as Fabric highlights existing relationships and forms new connections between textile practice and experimental filmmaking. The work developed through numerous iterations, which were devised, and often performed, in former cotton mills in Manchester. The performance shows analog film as fabric and stitching as editing. The dress I wear to perform highlights my personal history, as the fourth generation of needlewomen with many of my mother's family working in cotton mills close to Manchester. The sequence of actions in the performance are informed by the process of making a dress: 16mm film is cut with dressmaking scissors, stitched, spliced into loops, projected, measured, and worn on the body. My visible presence editing, stitching, and projecting film interrogates the hidden labor of women, with particular reference to their work in the cutting rooms of early cinema. I made a dress and a tabard to wear when performing, which matches the patterns in the film loops I project. I also wear a hand knitted cardigan made by my mother which represents the textile heritage in my family history.

Film as Fabric became a way to reveal and celebrate repressed analog filmmaking practices associated with women's work and hidden labor. One of the earliest film editing techniques, the substitution splice, is based upon the visibility of the join. These trick edits involved a sudden intense visual transformation enacted through a cut or a series of cuts to create appearance, disappearance, or substitution of something on screen—for example, a woman disappearing or transforming into a butterfly. They have been noted as offering "a way for seemingly distant ideas and images to be joined in easy association, if only for a moment. But this momentary instability and disruption offers the potential for new ideas to be formed and hidden meanings to be revealed" (Moen 2013: 965). *Film as Fabric* functions like a performed "substitution splice," as a live, visible, audible, tangible blurring of textile practice and expanded cinema.

Richard Sennett's idea of the domain shift describes "a tool initially used for one purpose being applied to another task, or the principle of one guiding practice applied to another activity" (2009: 123–9). Nicolson stitching film in *Reel Time* and the found objects discussed at the start of this chapter perfectly demonstrate Sennett's theory. The domain shift has been valuable in my own practice, underpinning the creation of hybrid tools, such as a clothes rail and paper clips becoming a rack on which to hang, organize, and display film. It also resulted in devising direct and camera-less techniques to transform machine stitch and patterned lace ribbons into moving images and optical sounds on 16mm film, which I call "stitched rhythms" and "pitched patterns."

The first technique involves puncturing clear, black or white film leader with the unthreaded sewing machine needle. This direct filmmaking method involves piercing holes at regular intervals in the soundtrack area of clear film leader with the unthreaded sewing machine needle, which is then spliced into a loop. The closeness of the holes dictates the tempo of the rhythm produced. The puncturing was tested every 24, 20, 16, 12, 8, 6, 4, 3, 2 and 1 frames , as well as the use of two "stitches" to a frame. The further apart the holes are, the slower the rhythm is

Figure 11.2 *Film as Fabric*, 2016. Expanded cinema performance at Radio Revolten International Festival of Radio Art. © Mary Stark.

created. When the holes become close enough, at two per frame, they become a continuous low pitch. A variety of pitches can also be created by adjusting the stitch length on the sewing machine and stitching clear film leader in the soundtrack area of the filmstrip with the threaded or unthreaded sewing machine needle. The longer the stitch length, the lower the tone, with the highest pitches resulting from stitches being as close together as possible before the filmstrip tears. Holes at intervals of 3–6 frames create pattering rhythmic sounds.

The second approach taken in the creation of optical sounds has involved creating black-and-white photograms[3] from over forty different patterned lace ribbons, tested for opacity, texture, and construction. To make a photogram in the dark room, I unwind a length of film and use scissors to cut a piece about the measurement of my forearm. I check which side is coated in emulsion by licking my lips and briefly kiss the filmstrip; the emulsion is on the side that sticks to my lips. I choose a lace ribbon and place it on the film before using a piece of clear glass to press the two materials down flat, which results in defined photograms and clear optical sounds. I expose small pieces of film, which have a duration of approximately 1.5 seconds, and splice them together into longer lengths to create sustained optical sounds.

As the photograms are being processed in photographic trays, I can see the image developing. It is a quick way to achieve results and to check the photographic chemistry before exposing and processing more film. There is a sense of magic each time I watch a photogram appear. As each lace ribbon is slightly different, there are variations in the depth of the blacks in the photograms of fabrics, but these inconsistencies emphasize the tactile process.

Making photograms from lace and fabric ribbons has shown how the material specificities of fabric translate into optical sound and moving images. When photograms of fabric are projected, the materiality of each fabric is magnified and animated. A humble everyday material is

Film as Fabric: Textile Practice as Feminist Critique in Expanded Cinema   149 elevated to the star of the screen. Dark-colored lace ribbon creates high-contrast graphic black-and-white images that produce defined sounds. Fabric made from fine threads with a regular grid-like construction produces clear tones. Cloth made with thicker course threads in irregular formations creates a rougher sonic quality.

The method of working with small pieces of ribbon and short lengths of film shows a linguistic meeting point between textile practice and film editing, because they can both be described as "trimmings." To "trim" a garment means to add decorative additions, usually to an edge or along a hem. But to "trim" also refers to the act of cutting material down to a required size or shape. Similarly, in analog film editing, a "trim" describes a small section of a shot that has been cut out (Collins Dictionary 2019).

Applying the embroidery practice of sampling to the production of moving images and optical sounds also creates new links between textile practice and experimental filmmaking. Sampling began as a way of copying and storing embroidery stitches in the sixteenth and early seventeenth centuries before imagery was available to copy from books. Early samplers were pieces of linen stitched with "a storehouse of motifs" and defined as an "exampler of a woman to work by" (Parker 2010a: 85). They took the form of a "spot" sampler, which involved stitching small test areas of patterns on a piece of fabric at random, or a "band" sampler, which featured strips of repeating patterns. The embroiderer then used their sampler to create embroidered designs.

My use of sampling in expanded cinema performance builds on a project called *Sampler-Culture Clash* by the British textile artist David Littler, which brought together embroidery and music production after identifying the technique as common in both fields. Sampling music involves selecting and looping a small section from an already existing recording to generate a new composition. Littler recognized that "spot" sampling in embroidery is similar to building up a library of samples to make music, while "band" samplers are visually similar to the appearance of multiple layers of soundtracks in sound editing software, with each band of stitched pattern relating to different elements in the music, such as the drumbeat, bass line, or vocals (Littler 2008). I extend these comparisons by examining optical sounds and moving images with recourse to fabric and stitch patterns to produce stitched rhythms of different speeds and a range of low, medium, and high-pitched patterns, which are edited and projected as film loops in expanded cinema performance.

In particular, producing sound from fabric and stitch has been informed by the long association of textile practice with both the oppression and subversive expression of women's voices. The seminal book, *The Subversive Stitch: Embroidery and the Making of the Feminine* by the art historian Roszika Parker examines how since the European Renaissance strict ideals of femininity have been fused with the act of stitching. Parker refers to a seventeenth-century poem, "In Praise of the Needle," which commends needlework as a way for women to "use their tongues less, and their needles more" (2010b: 86–7). As well as keeping women quiet, stitching also led to women being kept still, sitting with hands occupied, mouth firmly closed, "eyes lowered, head bent and shoulders hunched," exemplifying "utter submission to a domestic idyll" (Hurlstone 2012: 147). My active presence as a female artist loudly stitching in expanded cinema responds to this textile history, challenging links between stitch and the oppression of women's voices and bodies. While the live performance remains the richest way of engaging with my research, a website (Stark 2020) highlights the role of digital technology in documentation of performance. Performative process-based artwork often challenges the revered status of finished products, but also frequently uses film, video, photography, websites, and social media as documentation. Documents often subsequently become how the work is represented, remembered, and contextualized beyond the live event. While *Film as Fabric* follows this common model, I propose that performances that feature laborious textile practice increase the tension between live performance and documentation. In turn, the careful crafting of documentation highlights the labor and thought that may be dedicated to creating lasting records of performance.

Film as Fabric deliberately highlights and celebrates the materiality of photochemical film, but uses digital photography, video, and sound recording to document and reflect on performances. Repeated loops have been created between seemingly separate disciplines, live performance and documentation, digital and analog technologies. These interlocking cycles are grounded by my personal history and location in the north west of England, with its rich textile history. They formed a methodology I term crafting expanded cinema performance, which refers to the ongoing act of refining an expanded cinema performance through numerous iterations and the intention of engaging fabric and stitch as feminist critique.

This chapter builds on already established artistic traditions involving textile practice as feminist critique that highlights the value of women's work. I develop this by showing that textile practice offers a way to highlight women's contribution to histories of cinema. *Reel Time* is well known in the field of expanded and experimental cinema. The work has recently been highlighted for combining "the conceptual concerns of performance art with the demonstration of craft skill" (Husbands 2019: 53). My work is part of a new area of experimental cinema that builds on Nicolson's *Reel Time* and shows that combining textile practice and filmmaking offers myriad ways to generate new knowledge. Works by American artists include Jodie Mack's experimental animations or "fabri-flicker films," meticulously machine-stitched film quilts by Sabrina Geschwandtner, and Jennifer West's quilts made by working with film, her body, and sewing machine. In the UK, 16mm films by Jennifer Nightingale translate knitting patterns into film editing structures and Amy Dickson's live works present thermachromic cloth as central in para-cinema performance. But, apart from brief acknowledgment (Hemmings 2007: 58), *Reel Time* is barely known in the field of textile practice and the related boundaries of contemporary craft. This chapter positions *Reel Time* as significant to these fields, with the aim of driving future research into how textile practice might further integrate with performance art.

Notes

1. Svilova's contribution to film editing has been recognized more recently (Penfold, 2013; Pearlman, 2016).
2. The Celluloid Ceiling has tracked women's employment on top grossing films for the last twenty-one years. It is the longest-running and most comprehensive study of women's behind-the-scenes employment in film available. This annual study is sponsored by the Center for the Study of Women in Television and Film, San Diego State University. Women comprised 21 per cent of all editors working on the top 250 films of 2018. This represents an increase of 5 percentage points from 16 per cent in 2017, however it is below the 26 per cent achieved in 2015. Seventy-four per cent of the films had no female editors (Lauzen, 2019).
3. I work with Orwo PF2, a fine grain print stock with an ISO of 6, which is similar to photographic paper. It creates high-contrast black-and-white images and can be worked with under red light. I buy found footage for the purpose of making clear film leader. It is considerably cheaper than buying from a film supplier. I use fresh lengths for each performance, which are then recycled as leader for other films.

References

Blaetz, R. (2007), *Women's Experimental Cinema: Critical Frameworks*. London: Duke University Press.

Curtis, D. (2002), "'Annabel Nicolson Talking about Reel Time' Transcript."

Dancyger, K. (2011) The Technique of Film and Video Editing. 5th edn. Oxford: Elsevier.

Elcott, N. M. (2008), "Darkened Rooms: A Genealogy of Avant-Garde Filmstrips from Man Ray to the London Film-Makers' Co-Op and Back Again." *Grey Matter* Winter (30): 6–37.

Gleba, M, and Harris, S. (2019), "The First Plant Bast Fibre Technology: Identifying Splicing in Archaeological Textiles." *Archaeological and Anthropological Sciences* 11 (5): 2329–46.

Hatfield, J. (2006), "Imagining Future Gardens of History." *Camera Obscura*, 62 (21): 185–91.

Hemmings, Jessica (2007), "Reeling in the Years: Film, Video, Textile, Time." *Selvedge Magazine* (58–61).

Hurlstone, N. (2012) "Speaking up for Silence", in Kettle, A. and McKeating, J. (eds) *Machine Stitch Perspectives*. London: Bloomsbury, pp. 146–52.

Husbands, L. (2019) "Craft as Critique in Experimental Animation", in Ruddell, Caroline & Ward, P. (eds) The Crafty Animator. Cham, Switzerland: Palgrave Macmillan, pp. 45–74.

Kinolibrary. (2018), [Film] "1930s Film Studio, Film Processing and Editing, Cutting Room, 35mm." https://www.youtube.com/watch?v=AOHsGkonQwg (accessed July 9, 2020).

Moen, K. (2013) "Film and Fairy Tales: The Birth of the Modern Fantasy", in. London: I.B. Tauris.

Murch, W. (2011), *In the Blink of an Eye: A Perspective on Film Editing*. 5th ed. Los Angeles: Simon James Press.

National Science and Media Museum. (2009), "THE LUMIÈRE BROTHERS: PIONEERS OF CINEMA AND COLOUR PHOTOGRAPHY." https://blog.scienceandmediamuseum.org.uk/the-lumiere-brothers-pioneers-of-cinema-and-colour-photography/ (accessed October 9, 2018).

Oldham, G. (1992) First Cut: Conversations with Film Editors. London: University of California Press.

Parker, R. (2010a) "The Inculcation of Femininity", in The Subversive Stitch: Embroidery and the Making of the Feminine. London: I.B. Tauris, pp. 82–109.

Parker, R. (2010b) The Subversive Stitch: Embroidery and the Making of the Feminine. London: I.B. Tauris.

Pearlman, K. (2016) Woman with an Editing Bench. Australia. Available at: https://www.kanopy.com/product/woman-editing-bench (accessed July 17, 2018).

Penfold, C. (2013) Elizaveta Svilova and Soviet Documentary Film. University of Southampton.

Rees, A L. (2011), *Expanded Cinema: Art, Performance, Film.* London: Tate Publishing.

Reynolds, L. (2009), "British Avant-Garde Women Filmmakers and Expanded Cinema of the 1970s." University of East London.

Reynolds, L. (2012), "Hysteriography." *Sequence: New Artists' Film and Video* Winter: 52–7.

Rhodes, L. (1979), "Whose History?" In *Film as Film: Formal Experiment in Film, 1910–1975: (Catalogue of an Exhibition Held at the Hayward Gallery, South Bank, London SE1, 3 May–17 June 1979).*, London: Hayward Gallery.

Sennett, R. (2009), *The Craftsman.* London: Penguin.

Smith, V. (2015), "The Animator's Body in Expanded Cinema." *Animation: an interdisciplinary journal*: 1–16.

Sparrow, F. (2005), "Annabel Nicolson: The Art of Light and Shadow." http://www.luxonline.org.uk/aicolsoannabel_nicolson/essay(1).html (accessed February 28, 2013).

Stark, Mary (2020) "Film as Fabric: Connecting Textile Practice and Experimental Filmmaking through Expanded Cinema Performance", unpublished Ph.D. thesis, Manchester Metropolitan University, Manchester, viewed 12 November 2022. https://e-space.mmu.ac.uk/cgi/search/archive/advanced?contributors_name%2Fcorp_creators%2Fcreators_name%2Feditors_name—ary+stark

Talbot, F.A. (1912), *Moving Pictures: How They Are Made and Worked.* London: William Heinemann.

Webber, M. (2016), "Reel Time, 1973." In *Shoot Shoot Shoot: The First Decade of the London Film-Makers' Cooperative 1966–76*, London: LUX, 168–9.

Wright, J. (2009), "Making the Cut: Female Editors and Representation in the Film and Media Industry." In UC Los Angeles: UCLA Center for the Study of Women, 7–12.

Films

Film as Fabric is an expanded cinema performance (2013–2017) https://marystark.wixsite.com/filmasfabric/

Reel Time https://www.luxonline.org.uk/artists/annabel_nicolson/reel_time.html

Reel Time. Annabel Nicolson, 1973.

"*Wearing and feeling cloth often unlocks an unconscious and richly therapeutic revisiting and remaking of my identity. A bringing to light. A creative transfiguration. Through constant re-membering—making, unmaking, and remaking, over and over—I am reinventing and unburdening myself. In the overlaying of cloth in my practice, I reveal a self-portrait, a way of processing the weight of layers of memory, co-existing strata of joy and trauma laid down by my family history and childhood.*"

Pippa Hetherington

12
Cuttings 1820–2020

PIPPA HETHERINGTON

On September 12, 2019, what would have been my father's 82nd birthday, I embarked on a project with a group of women artists from the Eastern Cape who form part of the Keiskamma Art Project (KAP). Founded in 2000 by medical doctor, fine artist, and humanitarian, Dr. Carol Hofmeyr as a way of alleviating poverty and facilitating psychological healing through art making, KAP has grown into an enormously successful, empowering, and transformative community initiative. I have worked alongside many of the women for twenty years, built up deep bonds, and come to appreciate their significant, ongoing influence on my own artistic practice.

On that day in 2019, in the small rural village of Hamburg, Eastern Cape, I met with the artists Nozeti Makhubalo, Nomonde Mtandana, Nomfundo Makhubalo, and Nothandile Bopani—direct descendants of the Eastern Cape amaXhosa who fought the British in the Frontier Wars. The artists have been with Keiskamma for more than a decade, some since its inception. We began making inquiries into our heritage, retelling and sharing our stories, some passed down orally through the generations, told to us by parents and grandparents, others (typically from a white, male vantage point) documented in archives and history books. Then we set to work and through dressmaking, assemblage, embroidery, video, and photography, produced a body of work that we called *Cuttings 1820–2020*. Women and women's clothing are the focal point of the collaborative project, allowing an articulation of the female voices that history (both oral and written) has ignored.

Examining the complex relationship between female descendants of the Eastern Cape amaXhosa nation and those of the 1820 British settlers, we gave voice to our own interwoven experiences and those of our forebears. As we shared and processed the often painful personal stories, we came to see how these narrative threads could bind and unify rather than entangle us in the mess of history. We saw the exhibition not as a statement, suggesting static resolution, but as an expression of a dynamic, ongoing process, a conversational assemblage of sensuous objects, happenings, utterances, and symbolic motifs that allowed us to deconstruct and reconfigure, unravel and re-stitch stories from our collective past, against the historical landscape of the Eastern Cape in the time of the Frontier Wars between Xhosa groups and British settlers.

The material expression of this collective undertaking, based on trust, mutual respect, and transparency, was ten hand stitched garments using English-inspired fabrics in the genre of William Morris's famous designs, Dutch wax print (also called Ankara or African wax fabric), and South African-made isiShweshwe cloth. Also known as "blueprint", isiShweshwe's now iconic patterns are derived, like Dutch wax, from intercultural borrowing (from Europe, the East, and Africa) and its usage is steeped in history. Juliette Leeb-du Toit describes in *Isishweshwe: A History of the Indigenisation of Blueprint in Southern Africa* how German immigrants wore printed calico settler dress as *Blaudruck* after the 1850s when they settled on the seaboard of what is now the Eastern Cape. Due to German missionary influences, many Christianized amaMfengu, amaThembu, and amaXhosa women from the Eastern Cape used blueprint. "Originally associated with trade, coercion, colonization, Westernization, religious conversion and cultural marginalisation, and slavery," isiShweshwe, however, eventually "subverted its former history and alien origins and has come to reflect the authority of its users and their culture, conveying resilience, innovation and adaption and above all a distinctive South Africanness" (Leeb-du Toit 2017, jacket text).[1]

As Carrie Mae Weems expressed, "I'm interested in the tangled web of history, in the rough edges, and the bumpy surface, the mess just beneath the veneer of order" (2000: jacket text). Cutting, juxtaposing, and reassembling the different pieces of cloth into new configurations, we mixed and interpolated cultural signifiers and patterns. Through this process of stitching together contrasting, dissimilar patterns and motifs, we became intensely aware of the healing nature of the process: that it is only by opening up dialogue that one can salvage from ideology a more holistic and authentically human history. Sharing our attachment to isiShweshwe, for example, brought us into a place of shared or collective belonging and memory. As we punctured the cloth and threaded together the warp and the weft of our respective histories, top to bottom, selvedge to selvedge, we were rendering scars visible and piercing open old wounds. Hiding wounds does not lend itself to reparation. This is why the work was deliberately left unfinished. Threads were not cut, fabric not serged; by exposing the scars, the "rough edges, and the bumpy surface, the mess just beneath the veneer of order" (Weems 2000: jacket text), we were able to untangle the web of history and allow, in Derridean terms, the "different threads and different lines of meaning—or of force—to go off again in different directions . . . to tie [themselves] up with others" (Derrida 1982: 3).

> I insist upon the word sheaf for two reasons. On the one hand, I will not be concerned, as I might have been, with describing a history and narrating its stages, text by text, context by context . . . On the other hand, the word sheaf seems to mark more appropriately that the assemblage to be proposed has the complex structure of a weaving, an interlacing which permits the different threads and different lines of meaning—or of force—to go off again in different directions, just as it is always ready to tie itself up with others.
>
> **DERRIDA 1982: 3**

Nozeti Makhubalo weaves a similar sentiment into her thoughts on the symbolism of sewing. She says:

> The Europeans arrived and made boundaries. When you are sewing the materials you are breaking the boundaries and uniting the fabric. The cutting symbolizes the separation—the differences—but the sewing mends these differences. We are no longer interested in being separate.[2]

> Cutting the pieces of material to make the outfits felt like we were mending the wounds of history. The material representing two histories used to make one dress was like healing balm for the scars of a difficult history.[3]

This cathartic sense also came through in viewers' responses to the exhibition. Mbali Sikakana commented on the way this collective expression of reparation "[veered] towards the spiritual." Yet she perceptively noted how, simultaneously, the dresses referenced more of the European than the African [style] so that the "concept of erasure is [still] there . . . in an interesting nod to the history itself."[4]

Artist Nobukho Nqaba highlighted the importance of engaging female voices and perspectives: "I am particularly happy that [this body of work] has this very strong female voice and the production process . . . was driven by dialogue and ongoing conversations. [The] garments . . . are metaphoric . . . a representation of [the] different fragments of the complex narratives [of] Xhosa people . . . as well [as descendants of] the settlers."[5]

* * * * *

I was born and raised between rural farmland and the city of Johannesburg, witness to South Africa's natural beauty and the evil of apartheid spatial planning, still evident in disparities of extreme (white) wealth on the one hand, and desperate poverty in urban and rural black communities on the other. My English ancestors arrived in South Africa in the 1820s. Although they were Londoners with no farming background, they were allocated land on the southern bank of the Fish River in the Eastern Cape as a promise from the British government of greener pastures, a new future, and a way out of harsh living conditions in an economically depressed United Kingdom. However, upon arrival it became apparent that they were part of a cohort of recruits who had been strategically enlisted to act as a buffer between the amaXhosa north of the Fish River and the British-ruled Eastern Cape to the south. The soil was arid and impossible to farm, so cattle very quickly became an important local commodity.

My ancestors were allocated land between the Kap and Coombs rivers—a territory referred to by the British settlers as "Forlorn Hope." R. T. McGeogh writes that "[t]he broad design of the scheme was to people [populate] the Zuurveld with Europeans in close settlements. This would cover the vulnerable coastal sector of the official Fish River boundary beyond which lay the land between the Fish and Keiskamma Rivers which was misleadingly dubbed the 'neutral belt'" (1965: 6). (The Zuurveld was the Dutch name given to the vegetation in the area, meaning land producing grass that is sour and unpalatable to stock in winter, but that provides good grazing in summer.) Central to this harsh stretch of land was a clay pit. South African historian Noël Mostert writes that the "controversial Clay Pits, from which the Xhosa obtained the red ochre for their body ornament, were the earliest flashpoint between themselves and the British settlers" (1993: 669). The controversy over the clay pits sparked one of the biggest Frontier Wars—a series of nine intermittent clashes between the amaXhosa people, Boers, Khoikhoi, San, and the British that lasted 100 years.

The clay pits, a ridge of red oxide rock chips, had been excavated by the amaXhosa for generations. The site was enormously valuable to the amaXhosa because the chips could be ground into a fine powder and mixed with animal fat or water to make a clay or red paint traditionally used for body adornment, signifying a spiritual link to the ancestors, and to dye cloth (hence the British settlers' common designation of the amaXhosa as "the Red Blanket People"). The clay pits proved dangerous for the amaXhosa, their families living across the river, and for my predecessors: it was treacherous for the amaXhosa to illegally cross the river into British territory and dangerous for my family to interact with the "enemy." The British government laid down strict rules demarcating land ownership and denied the amaXhosa permission to access British-occupied land.[6]

For financial survival my great great-grandfather, John Stubbs, started trading cattle illegally with the amaXhosa on the other side of the river. He was killed in a botched trade agreement and his wife died of a broken heart a few months later. At the age of sixteen, their second-eldest son (my great-grandfather) Thomas Stubbs, was left to look after his younger siblings. The younger children were eventually fostered in different homes, but Thomas was sent to work as a blacksmith's apprentice. He was a rebel and a writer who fought for and against the British government and died a pauper.[7] This much I know. But what of those amaXhosa families living across the river? Where is their history to be found?

Michael Conway writes, "Currently, most students learn history as a set narrative—a process that reinforces the mistaken idea that the past can be synthesized into a single, standardized chronicle of several hundred pages" (2015: online). Conway references the relationship between history and memory: "People construct unique memories while informing perfectly valid histories. Just as there is a plurality of memories, so, too, is there a plurality of histories" (2015: online). Although Conway is writing about the problem with single-perspective narratives taught in Civil Rights American history classes, a similar lesson can be applied to the time of the Frontier Wars in South African history. Documented history is told in a linear way by the oppressor or the victor. But history is far more complex than this: a mesh of multivalent, criss-crossing threads that are impossible to disentangle. I am reminded of a 2009 TED talk by Nigerian writer Chimamanda Ngozi Adichie, where she speaks of the danger of the single story: "The single story creates stereotypes . . . make[s] one story become the only story . . . The consequence of the single story is this: it robs people of dignity. It makes our recognition of our equal humanity difficult. It emphasizes how we are different, rather than how we are similar" (2009: 18:43).

We are all tangled in the interwoven, multilayered, contested histories we come from. One of the most contested narratives in the oral and written histories of the Eastern Cape region is the story of Nongqawuse, a young Xhosa girl whose alleged prophecies led to large-scale destruction of the amaXhosa's cattle and crops between 1856 and 1857, resulting in widespread famine and hardship. Aware of the tensions between the amaXhosa and the colonial forces, Nongqawuse informed the elders that in exchange for destruction of their cattle and crops, the ancestral spirits had promised to drive the British settlers into the sea and bring back an abundance of grain and livestock. What happened instead was a form of self-immolation: starvation, poverty, and immense suffering.

Journalist and author Gregory Mthembu-Salter writes, "The relationship between South Africans and their cattle—and between one another over their cattle—is long-running and, at times, epic" (2019: 7). Like the clay pits, cattle were the catalyst for many clashes between the amaXhosa and the British settlers, particularly the mass cattle killing connected to the prophecy of Nongqawuse that led to devastation for the amaXhosa in an area known then as British Kaffraria (now the Eastern Cape) in 1850, which sparked the eighth and second last of the Frontier Wars. By the end of 1858, just two years after Nongqawuse's prophecy, the amaXhosa population was recorded at just 26,000. Mthembu-Salter writes, "An estimated 40,000 Xhosa people died as a result of the cattle killing, mostly from starvation" (2019: 18).

African National Congress Veteran, Sindiso Mfenyano remembers the strong colonial bias of his history textbooks in his Eastern Cape primary school in Noupoort in the early 1950s.[8]

> I recall that the textbook gave a very biased, colonial account of the Xhosa cattle-killing crisis of 1856 and 1857 . . . In 1856, Nongqawuse claimed that the spirits . . . appeared to her when she went to fetch water from a pool near the mouth of the Gxarha River. Their message to Nongqawuse was that . . . "two moons away, the sun will rise but stop at noon and return to the east. On that day the Ancestors

will arise from their graves and drive the British settlers into the sea. There will be abundant harvest and livestock. For this to happen, all households must destroy their existing livestock and consume all their grain and any other produce . . ." Her uncle and guardian, Mhlakaza, a Xhosa spiritualist, relayed this prophecy to the paramount chief, Sarhili, who authorized the mass slaughter of cattle, sheep and goats and destruction of crops and food supplies. The mass food destruction is recorded as lasting a whole year, from April 1856 to May 1857.

2017: 39

Reflecting on his school life and introduction to politics, Mfenyana recalls a trainee teacher giving his class "a new and—to us—highly plausible version" of the cattle killing.

> The wealth-seeking white capitalists entered into a mutually beneficial agreement with the Christianising missionaries and a sinister plot was conceived. A group of whites hid at the river bank where Nongqawuse . . . dutifully fetched water every morning. Speaking through a reed pipe, they delivered their fatal message from the "ancestors" to the frightened but gullible girl. This unofficial version of events was the earliest political education that I received. It planted a seed in my mind that would grow into a determination to regain our freedom.

2017: 40

Nozeti Makhubalo of KAP commented in a recent conversation how it saddens her that this "other" side of history has often been ignored:

> When I think of my history it makes me sad. My grandmother, a freedom fighter, told me that we come from the *amaMfengu* people who ran away from the Zulu King Shaka and settled on the banks of the Great Fish River in the Eastern Cape. She relayed my history in a political and painful way. She told me the true story of how Nongqawuse was tricked by the white people, making her believe that she had been delivered a message. This doubled the pain for me. It was a way of white people getting the black people to kill their cattle to make them poor.[9]

Mfenyana echoes this sentiment when he explains how the 1856–7 cattle killing eventually forced "the once proud and self-sufficient Xhosa tribes" to the colonizers' mine recruiting stations, and brought about the tragic demise of their independence as a people (2017: 40). As Makhubalo reflects on her grandmother's oral teachings she comments further:

> What Nongqawuse told our people made them suffer; they gave up their pride. But it was a long time ago and we are trying to mend and heal from the memories . . . to change our mindsets and understand that healing takes a long time . . . [I]t can be painful, but healing is possible. Stitching cows into our artwork is a way of healing as it brings the cows back into our lives as a way of restoration. Using fabric to heal also helps, mixing the old and the new.[10]

Over a century and a half after the prophecies of Nongqawuse, I found myself—a descendant of those very British settlers who should have been driven into the sea—interrogating the legitimacy of my own history and its Eurocentric presentation to me. Working with the remarkable amaXhosa female artists of the Keiskamma Art Project—documenting their embroidery, their lives, and their personal histories—I was struck by the contradictions between some of the British settler stories I had grown up with and the resilient counternarratives of these talented women.

In an exhibition called *Matereality*, curator Andrea Lewis posited that "A work of art can never be separated from its physical material and this inescapable truth has been subject to investigation for a long time."[11] Following a similar thought process, in *Cuttings 1820–2020* we chose mixed media to give expression to the multilayered complexities of the history of the Eastern Cape. These materials not only challenge traditional notions around what materials are suited to art making, they also challenge traditional symbolisms attached to material from the past. *Cuttings 1820–2020* uses physical materials to raise questions about history and memory, starting of course with the foundational cloth.

Journalist Catherine Del Monte interviews fashion curator and academic Erica de Greef, who explains that fashion is an ideological marker with the ability to carry meaning:

> It [fashion] is both ideological or symbolic and material or practical (making and wearing). This

dual quality also is both separable from the person—we see it in museums, in magazines, in shops and on other people—as well as an intrinsic part of ourselves and our own bodies. In this regard fashion becomes a powerful tool to create social (and cultural) orders as well as the means with which to navigate our place in the world in terms of belonging or in terms of standing out. In other words, fashion straddles the divide that excludes-includes, it marks the boundaries of our being in the world.

DEL MONTE 2021: online

While *Cuttings 1820–2020* is not a comment on fashion, it does show how we embody our histories using cloth and textile as metaphors, resonant with meaning. Our intention was to use clothing to bring history into the present, to wear our histories on our sleeve. Reflecting on how it felt to make the first dress and first skirt of the *Cuttings* collection of garments, Makhubalo says:

> It brings me hope of moving forward, especially after where I'm from . . . I was sad, but when we started the project I felt like a model and it sparkled me. It makes me proud of my sad history . . . When I think of Xhosa history, I think of how we . . . lost a lot of love, the love for each other . . . [T]here was hatred, but now we treat each other with love . . . The togetherness brings us closer; we were meant to be together and not to fight.[12]

From my initial workshop with the artists from the KAP I felt a deep desire to keep the conversation going, to keep it open and fluid and not allow the illusion of resolution through a one-off conversation. I realized it would need to be an ongoing, dynamic dialogue in which stitch by stitch, fabric by fabric, pattern by pattern, we could feel our way toward some kind of reparation.

So, on October 15, 2019 we began an intense residency in Cape Town where we lived, breathed, and shared the making of the garments. Diligently, we spent an hour every morning discussing the work we had made the day before and looked at historical material made of photos, writings, and shared oral history. Pain was often palpable, and conversations tricky, but we pushed through the discomfort. Stephanie Victor, Curator of History at the Amathole Museum in Qonce (formerly King William's Town), supplied us with some interesting imagery to work with. One of the hardest dialogues we had was around a government notice issued in Fort Murray on April 20, 1858 by Chief Commissioner John Maclean that read: "No Natives will henceforth be allowed to enter, or to remain in King William's Town, unless they are decently dressed in European clothing. The police have received instructions to remove from the town any Native not complying with this Notice."[13] Moved to silence while reading this, we found pause for remembering, pause for memory and hurt.

Asked to comment on how European clothing changed her ancestors' way of life, Keiskamma artist Nothandile Bopani reflects:

> [T]he history about European clothing makes me very sad because it was so cruel. We were the people who were making clothes from skins and ibayi (hessian) and using the ochre to dye it. We were walking bare-skinned and smearing ochre as adornment and sunblock. But the British changed that and we feel like we lost our humanity and dignity and our memory of who we are.[14]

Still showing ambivalence, Bopani adds, "Because the [fabrics were] . . . introduced to us we have ended up loving them, although today they are so expensive compared to our traditional material. We were not using [them] that much, but we are enjoying them amongst our communities now."[15]

Makhubalo offers a different, practical, perspective:

> [I]t feels like it brings dignity to women to cover ourselves with clothes. The creative process of making clothes brings self-esteem . . . [T]o take material and to make something that is useful . . . [A]part from the project it brings something that makes business . . . [S]ewing clothes for other people . . . brings food to the table.[16]

Makhubalo's comment encouraged us to explore further the meaning of some of the fabric pieces with which we were working. I had made photographs of the landscape where the Frontier Wars were fought and purposefully inverted the negatives to reverse light and dark, another way of subverting history, and printed them onto cotton. The use of the negative was a way of talking about a repository of memory. Riffing off the theme of using the photo negative as a metaphor for memory, we made some

Figure 12.1 *Cuttings 1820–2020 #7*, 2019. Textile, cyanotype, wire, 40 cm x 140 cm. © Pippa Hetherington and Keiskamma Art Project. Photography: © Pippa Hetherington.

cyanotypes on fabric and sewed them into a few of the pieces. As shown in Figure 12.1, fabric, embroidery, and wire, the cyanotype of an indigenous thorn branch sits on the belly of an apron with a scientific image of a human heart embroidered onto it, sewn on top of a piece of isiShweshwe. The use of isiShweshwe and indigo cyanotype cloth brought into focus the biased way historical "facts" were captured through photography's colonial lens in the nineteenth century.

We began observing how the different pieces of fabric and patterns were juxtaposed. Pieces uncomfortable on the eye were sewn together in an intended metaphor for the discomforting but important process of talking about our histories. In this context, Jessica Hemmings's quote frequently came to mind: "[T]extiles thrive under close reading in much the same way as a text can. The closer you look, the more detail you see, and the more information tumbles out" (Hemmings 2013: 25).

Pushing the process further, examining the landscape photographic negatives, Makhubalo and I felt compelled to embed ourselves in the same landscape physically. We chose to visit one of the most painful historical sites of our collective history, the clay pits.[17] Standing on a mound of ochre and yellow rocks in the Zuurveld, Makhubalo instinctively picked up a few pieces of the natural iron-rich oxide (resembling flints in shape and size) and started rubbing them together. This action produced a deep, astonishingly beautiful ochre, profound as blood, an ancient natural pigment. We both immediately had the same innate desire to use this rich pigment in our artworks. For an hour we collected the rocks, small enough to hold in the palm of a hand. Back in the studio, we crushed and pestled them into fine powder, mixed the powder with water, and dyed the pieces of cotton cloth that had the landscape negatives already printed on them. The result was staggeringly close to dried blood, yet exquisite.

Makhubalo's daughter, Sinovuyo Makhubalo, an undergraduate fine art student at Fort Hare University in the Eastern Cape, was drawn into our process. Not only did we exchange memories around history and the way it is told, but we entered into an intergenerational discussion about clothing, women's bodies, and agency in the context of the Eastern Cape Xhosa heritage. Sinovuyo spoke out about the male gaze, and the colonial gaze. As a gesture of working through some of these memories, thought processes, and feelings, Sinovuyo and I made a video performance piece—deliberately unchoreographed and filmed in one take. We agreed on three elements: ochre clay made from the oxide, a piece of red isiShweshwe fabric, and the sea. Out of it came a poignant performance of Sinovuyo walking down a sand dune, toward the sea. Laying down the cloth, she rubbed the clay over her body in a ritualistic manner, then walked into the ocean and let the clay wash off.[18]

When we sat down and watched and edited the footage, several symbolic themes emerged. The ocean referenced Nongqawuse's prophecies that the ancestral spirits would drive the British settlers into the sea if the amaXhosa killed their cattle and destroyed their crops. The sea also becomes a dual representation embodying both promise and loss. Ships transported European settlers across the sea to the Eastern Cape. Many were wrecked along the coastline, where relics from the vessels can still be found today, often in the form of small chips of porcelain and china washed up on the shores. The ships that made it safely into port were often serviced by amaXhosa, who carried the European passengers ashore. This performance piece is a translation of the female voice that has been lost in history. The sea is a symbol of hardship and hope, and rubbing ochre clay on to the body not only evokes a proud Xhosa tradition but symbolizes a memory of blood spilt. The female body allows an expression of grief, as well as an act of cleansing and restoration.

The thirteenth-century Islamic poet and scholar Rumi famously wrote: "The wound is the place where the Light enters you." Commenting on South African and African artists' ability to express suffering and pain through art, author of *Strange Cargo: Essays on Art* Ashraf Jamal writes, "Three things converge in Rumi's saying—pain, location,

Figure 12.2 *Cuttings 1820–2020. Clay #2*, 2020 Pigmented denim, cotton twill, embroidery. 123 × 82 cm. © Pippa Hetherington and Keiskamma Art Project. Photography: © Pippa Hetherington.

transformation. There is no change without suffering, no consciousness of change without an understanding of place. In South Africa, a country unerring in its commitment to suffering, Rumi's narrative is *de rigueur*" (Jamal 2021: 34).

In *Cuttings 1820–2020* the same three things converge: the pain of colonial subjugation and cultural erasure; the red oxide clay pits like a bleeding wound, a flashpoint of conflict on a now vanished British frontier; and, two centuries on, possibilities of transformation, of light entering that desolate place called "Forlorn Hope." Working with the Keiskamma artists Nozeti Makhubalo, Nomonde Mtandana, Nomfundo Makhubalo, and Nothandile Bopani, I wished to open up possibilities for forgiveness and mutual understanding through creative collaboration, and to initiate another kind of historical remembering. A history premised not on the wounded word "Forlorn" but rather on the strong, transformative noun "Hope."

Like all conversations around conflict, shared and withheld, this one is continuous. Producing the dresses together with the artists from the Keiskamma Art Project was an attempt at a reparation of my past and an embracing of my own imperfection. In many ways they are self-portraits too, a way of processing the weight of layers of memory, coexisting strata of joy and pain laid down by my family history. The layers still carry weight, speak of a burden, but through constant re-membering—making, unmaking and remaking, over and over—we are reinventing and unburdening ourselves and find, paradoxically, a sense of lightness and freedom. And I continue, in my practice, to cut, stitch together, unpick, re-stitch—I re-shape and re-form the dress/es. And the artists of Keiskamma continue to thread their stories of hope and pain.

There is something about *sharing* trauma that reduces its potent hold. The dresses are a worn channel to connect to others' pain and psychological conflict, a way of listening to the ways people from different backgrounds experience the weight of social and personal history. The juxtaposition of African shweshwe and colonial English fabric takes the personal into the communal and collective. We are a collage of shared stories—a matrix of past, present, and future. We are womb-like, interwoven.

Notes

1. Juliette Leeb-du Toit, *Isishweshwe: A History of The Indigenisation of Blueprint in Southern Africa*, 2017 (jacket text). Elsewhere Leeb-du Toit writes: "Rather than merely denoting the economic and cultural imposition of European hegemony and control, the colonial usage of cloth, clothing and beads by black South Africans undeniably suggests the presence of individual and collective preferences and choices, despite European oppression and the invasiveness of trader holdings from the nineteenth century onwards" (2017: 3).
2. Nozeti Makhubalo, in-person interview with Pippa Hetherington, February 10, 2020.
3. Nozeti Makhubalo, in-person interview with Pippa Hetherington, October 15, 2019.
4. In Conversation: Mbali Sikakana and Pippa Hetherington discuss how themes of family, cultural memory and displacement are articulated through *Cuttings 1820–2020* exhibition. August 20, 2021, on Zoom video call. https://www.youtube.com/watch?v=2BDyZLHvCcw
5. Virtual launch of *Cuttings 1820–2020*, Pippa Hetherington in conversation with Nobukho Nqaba, South African fine artist. https://www.youtube.com/watch?v=BqO04E95kXg&t=302s.
6. Disputes over land ownership and use in South Africa are inextricably linked to the country's colonial history. But they also predate it. The San and Khoikhoi people, the first inhabitants of southern Africa, suffered at the hands of every new wave of settlers, including amaXhosa groups whose gradual southerly migration led to conflict with the Khoisan over land and resources. The large-scale, bloody, and brutal land theft of the colonizing Dutch and British powers and the "divide and rule" ideology of the British exacerbated divisions within and between the black Nguni-speaking peoples and ultimately decimated the first nation groups.
7. His reminiscences were discovered generations later and published as *The Reminiscences of Thomas Stubbs*, by W. A. Maxwell and R. T. McGeogh (1978). The physical reminiscences are housed in the National Literary Museum in Makhanda (formerly Grahamstown), often referred to by the renowned late writer and English academic, Guy Butler, of Rhodes University.
8. The Eastern Cape was not only the site of successive Frontier Wars between the British and the amaXhosa, but also violent conflict between the Dutch settlers (Boers) and the British during the South African War of 1899 to 1902. It became the locus of impoverished native "reserves" following discriminatory Land Acts promulgated in 1913 and 1936, which dispossessed many black farmers of fertile farmland and forced them into artificially demarcated and scattered areas. The self-governing "Bantustans" created by the apartheid government were rooted in these colonial policies, whose legacy is still evident in widespread municipal mismanagement and malpractice in the Eastern Cape region in recent decades.
9. Nozeti Makhubalo, telephonic interview with Pippa Hetherington, March 9, 2022.
10. Nozeti Makhubalo, March 9, 2022.
11. Andrea Lewis, curator, commenting on *Matereality—a testament to the challenge of tradition*, an exhibition at Iziko

South African National Gallery, Cape Town, February 14, 2020–February 21, 2021: Accessed on March 16, 2022 at https://www.iziko.org.za/exhibitions/matereality.

12 Nozeti Makhubalo, in-person interview with Pippa Hetherington, September 12, 2019.
13 Stephanie Victor, Curator of History at the Amathole Museum in Qonce (formerly King William's Town), supplied this government notice from the Amathole Museum archive at a workshop on October 15, 2019.
14 Nothandile Bopani, in an in-person interview with Pippa Hetherington (translated by Nozeti Makhubalo), October 15, 2019.
15 Nozeti Makhubalo, in-person interview with Pippa Hetherington, October 15, 2019.
16 Ibid.
17 Nozeti Makhubalo and Pippa Hetherington research excursion to the clay pits in the Eastern Cape in Coombs Valley, November 24, 2019.
18 Virtual exhibition of *Cuttings 1820–2020* at GFI Art Gallery in Gqeberha. April 2020. http://gfiartgallery.com/virtual/ (accessed January 10, 2023).

References

Adichie, Chimamanda Ngozi. *"The danger of a single story."* Filmed July 2009 at TEDGlobal. Video. http://www.ted.com/talks/chimamanda_adichie_the_danger_of_a_single_story.

Del Monte, C 2021, "Sportswear: Decrypting the dress code", *Daily Maverick*, 22 August, viewed 14 March 2022, Available online: https://www.dailymaverick.co.za/article/2021-08-22-sportswear-decrypting-the-dress-code/ (accessed January 9, 2021).

Derrida, Jacques (1982). "Différance", essay in *Margins of Philosophy*. Translated by Alan Bass. Chicago: University of Chicago Press: 3.

Hemmings Jessica (2013), *Postcolonial Textiles: Negotiating Dialogue*. Published by Brill. Available online: https://brill.com/view/book/9789401210027/B9789401210027-s003.xml: 25 (accessed January 5, 2021).

Jamal, Ashraf (2021), *Strange Cargo: Essays on Art*. Edited by Christian, Sven. Italy: Skira editore S.p.A: 34.

Leeb-du Toit, Juliette (2017), *Isishweshwe: A History of The Indigenisation of Blueprint in Southern Africa*, Pietermaritzburg: University of Kwazulu-Natal Press: jacket text, 3.

McGeogh, R.T. 1965. *The Reminiscences of Thomas Stubbs: 1820–1877*. Thesis, Chapter 1.

Mfenyana, Sindiso (2017), *Walking with Giants: Life and Times of an ANC Veteran*. Cape Town: South African History Online (SAHO): 39, 40.

Mostert, Noël (1993), *Frontiers: The Epic of South Africa's Creation and the Tragedy of the Xhosa People*. First published by Jonathan Cape 1992. London: Pimlico edition: 669.

Mthembu-Salter, Gregory (2019), *Wanted Dead & Alive: The Case For South Africa's Cattle*, South Africa: Face2Face: 7, 18.

Weems, Carrie Mae (2000), *The Hampton Project*. New York: Aperture: Jacket text.

Artist Celia Pym in conversation with Lesley Millar

Part 1

LESLEY MILLAR

LM: You are known as an artist who mends cloth—clothing, blankets, bags, anything that is made from cloth that people bring to you for repair. This is cloth that already has some meaning for them. However, when you repair, there is a sense that you also change it don't you? And how do you feel about the change and how does the person who has brought you the item feel about the change—the act of repair?

CP: Hmm, I am only recently come to think about this. When I started, I wanted to become an expert in holes. I realized that to understand something, you have to do a lot of it, in my case mend a lot of clothing. When people first began to bring me a piece of clothing, we talked about what the problem was, how the hole occurred, why they want this particular thing mended, and then in what manner I would do the mending. And that was that; I mended the item and the person got it back. I didn't know if they were pleased or not, if they wore it or not. More recently, well, over the last ten years, I have heard back from people. For example, the (Freddie Robins') rug, she told me she felt I had made a painting out of her rug, that I had transformed it, made it into something different that she didn't know it could be. She decided the rug was not going to be used for picnics anymore and I was really pleased about that. I hadn't thought about the role I had in transforming the thing. I thought I was just doing a job and so I began to think about the emotional transformation, not that I thought I was being passive, but when I started to think about all the things I had mended, and where they are in the world and wondered if there was a way of re-gathering them or meeting them again, because they stay with me, I remember them but I have not had the practice of asking people how they feel when they get them back.

LM: Well, it is a visible mend and I am intrigued why people want visible mends rather than invisible ones. Clearly when you have done that, you are not giving them back the same thing.

CP: I do like that, the act of visible mending. And I have thought that the mend gives an additional story on top of the original one. Why do people want visible mending?

Figure CP1 *Freddie's rug,* 2022. © Celia Pym. Photographer: © Michele Panzeri.

Well, because they trust me and I think it is much more confident to see what has changed, to embrace what has changed, if the person is able to, if the garment or item is of importance to them and if you mend it visibly you are admitting the life of the thing. It's a kind of empathy with the person and the thing and by making it visible it becomes part of the story, the visibility says it's ok being part of the story, on the surface.

I've always loved, been attracted to the negative spaces in things, the holes, the dust marks where a chair used to be, that trace or evidence that something was there. That is how I've also thought about visible mending.

LM: But you do cover the hole . . . you don't see it anymore . . .

CP: You see it in outline maybe. Actually, the technique, the way in which I repair has changed a little over time. I now tend to go really wide with the reinforcement. I look at the weave, the holes in the weave where the edges are really fragile. If I am looking at a tear or something that is worn down, the edge isn't going to support my darn unless I go really wide. Then as I work and go into the hole, the stitch becomes denser and the edge becomes quite soft as the stitches spread out around the hole. I can see that the running stitch is trying to mesh itself with the structure of the cloth, so the original structure lends itself to the pattern of the stitch. For example, if it is a cable stitch on a sweater, that's a three-dimensional surface, so the reinforcing stitch as I approach the hole rolls over and under the cable and suddenly the cable looks more three-dimensional.

LM: Why do you always use a running stitch?

CP: I love a running stitch! I use it because I am attracted to making that looks straightforward and the running stitch has a kind of transparency—it is what it is. Over, under, in and out, and on knitted fabric it counts quite nicely, you can take a whole knit stitch with one running stitch and then you can go under a whole knit stitch . . . or you can go over or under two knit stitches . . . It is easy to go in and out. I don't mean easy in that I can't be bothered to find something more complicated. It is more that it just makes sense no matter what the base is in a way that something like chain stitch or couch stitch are almost too decorative for me, and the language of that kind of embroidery is very decorative. I like something much more straightforward. You know, my intention when I'm mending, it's not that I want it under the radar, but I think of it as part of life. It is there but you don't need to draw tons of attention to it, even though the visibility does draw attention to it and people often comment that my work on the cloth has turned it into a piece of art work. Which is fine but that is not where I began with this work.

LM: You say you want it to be almost unnoticed, but there is no ignoring it. You have chosen to make it visible.

CP: I know, I guess that is something I have to figure out. When I first started to notice repair was with my uncle's sweater, and I think I was startled to see my aunt in the repairs. And I was reminded how pragmatic she was in the care she took of all of us in our daily lives. My surprise was that I hadn't noticed how much I missed it, and I started to think about remembering and noticing the everyday. That's what I mean about being under the radar. It is about the quieter moments.

LM: Also, her mendings were not only about what she did for others but was in fact the trace she left behind.

CP: The most important aspect of that jumper was not about him, the wearer, but about her, the mender.

LM: But you call it "Roly's Sweater"?

CP: You're right, even though she knitted it! Until recently I didn't know that she had originally knitted that sweater for her husband. I think we assume that we know the stories of the lives of others, people who are close to us because we know them, but of course there is always stuff that has been omitted. Something that didn't get told because it wasn't considered significant, then if you ask you find things out that you didn't know. Her husband was a massive presence in her life, the photo was always there, but we never talked about it even though his loss must have been tremendous for her. It was never addressed and it really interested me that talking about the sweater opened up a whole area that I didn't know about. It is so much easier to talk through a thing than to speak directly about the story. So that is why I don't call it her sweater but her brother's, Uncle Roly, his sweater. But the more I looked at it the more I thought of her.

LM: What interests me is that her mending the sweater threaded their two stories together. It is all there in the sweater.

CP: I like that. Yes, literally. They were brother and sister and they were lifelong companions.

PART FOUR

Drafting the Future

This final section speaks of the physical and material form of cloth and the digitally rendered processes of production producing a very different relationship with embodied human experience. Through e-textiles technology, coding, and issues of material sustainability, cloth changes its relationship with the body and represents human experience as a site for constant reinvention. The cloth itself may never materialize, and ways of relating to cloth without sensation are discussed. E-textiles processes and technologies are described as refracting textile histories, processes, and tools by a group of e-textile practitioners (Perner-Wilson, Rose, Posch and Devendorf 2023, p.** of this volume) are seen in relation to the balancing of new digital processes and old analog techniques and the formal/cognitive with the felt-sense and visual aesthetics of cloth.

The dematerialized cloth in virtual fashion design challenges concepts of what it feels like to wear cloth. The use of textiles is described by Katharina Sand to convey and animate human experience reproduced in digital form in seen through the bodily motion of avatars of gaming worlds and the motion capture of human bodies in augmented reality. Digital textiles replicate the physical and material from inert to interactive and even generative renditions. These non-material versions force us to ask about the permanence of cloth as an enduring material record, what is "digital vintage" (Sand 2023, p.** of this volume) and what is durability of the digital?

The reproduction and visualization of scientific protein experiments into textiles, mediated through digital means, animates and generates meanings through the communicative capacity and material modality of textiles. Sonja Andrew working alongside scientists utilizes textile to articulate complex concepts across disciplines and their signification in a physical form. The cloth allows meaning to be tangible and to be taken "out into multiple real-world contexts" (Andrew 2023, p.** of this volume).

Many of the versions of textile in digital form, discuss this idea of real-world human experience, perceptions of value of what is not material. This connects with issues of sustainability, where if it doesn't exist there is no continuous production and disposal of textiles. Questions concerning finite resources of materials calls for constant translation and interpretation. The balance between technology, indigenous practices, socio-economic imperatives, and environmental concerns are all entwined and deeply implicated in the link between cloth and contemporary human experience.

In our final chapter, on an optimistic note, we hear about a model of circular economy, textiles as regenerative. In the Philippines, Carmen Hijosa is the founder of Ananas Anam Ltd, a company producing textiles as a sustainable operation. She is utilizing and preserving indigenous textile processes and materials that are adapted through new technologies to embrace local and overarching global environmental challenges. The community of human experience is served through understanding how textiles operates within it; "A restorative economy, co-evolves with the natural and human community it serves" (Hijosa, p.** of this volume).

"I am entangled in cloth. My cloths are my immediate everyday connection to an age-old, ever-changing technology. A material technology that I am involved in making, sharing, wearing, washing, mending, and wasting."

Hannah Perner-Wilson

13

Portraying a Practice: Communicating E-Textiles

HANNAH PERNER-WILSON, BECCA ROSE, IRENE POSCH, LAURA DEVENDORF

We are e-textile practitioners who often find ourselves confronting an ongoing tension between "new" and "old" technologies. We simultaneously craft with textile techniques and envision ways of translating those techniques to support electrical functions.

Hannah Perner-Wilson grew up making and improvising things out of household materials that surrounded her. Craft education in the Austrian school system introduced her to more traditional crafts such as embroidery, woodworking, and metalwork. She went on to study industrial design and media arts and sciences—which, in retrospect, she believes was driven by her interest in materials and production processes, but also the product object as a material prop for storytelling in the everyday— an opportunity for blurring usefulness/function with story/fiction. During her studies in Linz, she was exposed to the media arts scene and got sucked into a world of interactive/electronic/art, where she went looking to (re)make technologies from common/unusual materials in order to understand them as well as (re)imagine them differently.

Becca Rose started their artistic practice working in puppetry and costume and got into e-textiles through exploring how these craft practices could become interactive. Their performance work was in festival contexts, often improvising and working with artistic communities to put on large shows with small budgets. This has influenced their approach to e-textiles. They are drawn to the DIY aspects of it, where you can be resourceful with making electronics through repurposing everyday objects. This feels very playful and opens up new possibilities for the look and feel of electronics.

Irene Posch has a background in computer science and media studies and a passion for textile crafts since a young age. Working with digital fabrication techniques, specifically 3D printers, fascinated her for their ability to bridge the physical and the digital, but frustrated her for the limited accessible material spectrum. Turning to textile techniques as means to "fabricate almost anything" became her field of exploration of social, cultural, and aesthetic dimensions of technology production and use.

Laura Devendorf's interest in e-textiles emerged from a fascination in machines and practices of making that blend code and material. As a computer scientist and artist, e-textiles (specifically woven e-textiles) become a platform to think programmatically without sacrificing a kind of material negotiation and improvisation that she found to be a source of value in her art practice. It also made electronics approachable as materials that could be crafted and molded rather than simply purchased in black boxes.

We initially encountered each other's work through the internet; through attending workshops, conferences, and events aimed at teaching; and sharing and showcasing our practices in exhibition spaces. We found that meeting in person allowed us to share and discuss properties of our physical practices that we struggled to capture and communicate via online documentation. We learned so much from being together in person; however, because of the different countries and continents we live in, we continued to exchange ideas primarily through the internet. In 2013 we started creating and exchanging swatches so that our work could be read beyond the screen. These swatches, which were swapped through the E-Textile Swatchbook Exchange, enabled us to exchange our practices physically so that we could explore them with our hands, or with electrical tools such as multimeters. In this chapter we take a close look at the E-Textile Swatchbook Exchange through unpicking four of our swatches shared in this framework. We aim to give an insight into how the E-Textile Swatchbook Exchange communicates the complex relationships between electronics, textiles, individual or collective practices, process, and materials, which are some of the properties that characterize our e-textiles work.

An e-textile practice applies textiles techniques to electrically conductive materials. Through sewing, embroidering, felting, knitting, crocheting, weaving, and knotting, among others, e-textile practitioners produce electrical elements such as circuit traces and electrical connections, as well as components such as batteries, capacitors, sensors, and actuators. When circuitry is added to, knitted, woven, or crocheted into textiles, it often is transformed in scale; electronic components become large enough so that they can be manipulated by hand. Stitched electronics protrude out of fabric surfaces with style and draw attention to the patterning and materiality inherent in all technologies, as well as technology implicitly embodied in the textiles themselves. In the integration of circuits to textiles, e-textiles also grapple with questions about the politics of technological development. For example, in our practices we question who has access to the techniques to create e-textiles or who might benefit from e-textile inventions. We confront these questions in conversation with materials and use our work to try to uncover the physical nature of hardware that is mostly hidden away in black boxes. We draw from knowledge of textiles while paying attention to how electrons move across matter. Electronic know-how that might ordinarily be hidden inside a device such as a phone is not just broken out into the open, but sewn along in tracks that can be followed with a hand or an eye.

E-Textile Swatchbook Exchanges

A swatchbook traditionally contains a collection of fabric samples that can be distributed by textile producers to showcase their products or circulated among craftspeople to share new techniques for textile production (e.g., Unknown 1764). Textile historian Ellen Harlizius-Klück (2017) describes how swatchbooks were circulated among weavers at least since the seventeenth century. Used as essential record keeping of designs and a critical source of reference, swatchbooks are significant from an historic point of view as well as relevant for design reinterpretation and reproduction. They offer fabric references where a drawing or diagram would not illustrate the complex 3D nature of the fabric. Rather than an abstract representation of cloth, a swatch Is a record of how something was made, and it can be taken apart or reverse engineered so that makers or producers can understand its inner workings.

Swatchbooks are test beds for aesthetics, they store memories, and they become hosts for techniques that others can copy, and we borrow from historical swatchbooks to create platforms for archiving e-textiles designs. In our practice, a tangible way of archiving is especially important because of the complex nature of combining electronics and textiles. Hannah Perner-Wilson and Mika Satomi initiated the first E-Textile Swatchbook Exchange in 2013 by adapting the swatchbook format to communicate the complex set of properties to characterize our practices beyond the screen. In an E-Textile Swatchbook Exchange we represent our work through materials to offer a unique swatch of our practice to others, and in turn receive a collection of everybody else's practices. These books have helped to describe the properties of our work, and the E-Textile Swatchbook Exchanges have become a familiar format for our community to communicate the multiple approaches and configurations of e-textiles production that we collectively make (Hertenberger et al. 2014).

The E-Textile Swatchbook Exchange consists of physical swatchbooks, an online archive (E-textile Swatch Exchange 2013), and a collective moment where all participating makers gather in an exchange. Until now we have organized eight E-Textile Swatchbook Exchanges. Five E-Textile Swatchbook Exchanges (in the years 2013–2017) and one education-focused E-Textile Swatchbook Exchange (in 2019) were organized as part of the e-textile Summer Camp. A public E-Textile Swatchbook Exchange was organized in 2020, and a student-focused Swatchbook Exchange was organized as part of the International Conference of Tangible Embedded and Embodied Interaction (TEI) in 2021. All of these exchanges followed a similar process: a call for participation stating the concept, process, and guideline asks practitioners to submit a swatch idea that should relate to e-textiles and would mount on a 13×16 cm area. A collection of swatches is accepted by the community for participation, and then everyone accepted makes a swatch for everyone else who is participating.[1] All participants make as many multiples of their swatch as the total number of participants (see schematic in Perner-Wilson and Posch 2022), meaning that everyone contributes their physical sample of work in exchange for other participants' swatches (i.e., if there are twenty practitioners making a swatch, then everyone will make twenty swatches).

E-Textile Swatchbook Exchange participants have diverse e-textiles practices. Their backgrounds include diverse disciplines and approaches spanning research, design, art, craft, and engineering, among others. After finishing swatch multiplication, practitioners ship or bring their lot to an agreed central location (i.e., the organizer's studio, or a gathering), where the individual swatches are assembled into books. In addition to the physical swatch, there are spaces for makers to exchange the ideas behind the swatches through describing them at a gathering, through their online blog post, or in the text that accompanies the swatch in the book. Information alongside the swatch usually includes the creators' names, a title, a description of the materials, tools, and techniques used, schematic drawings, references and inspirations, and links to further information.

The E-Textile Swatchbook Exchange came into existence through the multiplication and exchange process we describe above. The communication between our practices is integral to the books, they describe what we are doing

Figure 13.1 A participant mounting their swatches as part of the E-Textile Swatchbook Exchange. Photographer: © Hannah Perner-Wilson.

between cloth and electrons in a way that digital images or text alone cannot. The exchange emphasizes the importance of the physical and textual quality of the work that is involved in e-textiles. Physical references are not only crucial for understanding swatches, but they are also used by practitioners to bring new ideas into their work by copying, integrating, or remaking a swatch, and therefore exploring textile form and electronic functionality under new material, pattern, or making conditions. Each successive swatchbook supports the creative re-making and repurposing of the earlier swatches, framing the book as both an archival text to be read, as well as an instructional text to be followed and reinterpreted. In this sense, the swatches bring the ethos of collectivity of textile craft to the practices associated with electronics.

There are many important aspects of practices, processes, materials entangled within the E-Textile Swatchbook Exchange. They enliven processes, techniques, or qualities of materials and they test ideas and concepts or directions for new practice. We want to reveal the stories behind swatches as we experienced them, and in what follows, we will unpick a selection of swatches that we have made, and discuss how the properties that characterize our practices are communicated. The following four swatches *Interested Sensor*, *Pin Probe*, *Darned and Mended*, and *Woven 2D Position Sensor* have been selected because they demonstrate a range of properties common throughout our e-textile practices. We selected our own swatch contributions so that we can include our perspectives, as their makers. To analyze our swatches, we discussed them between all the authors, helping us to understand how the swatch became meaningful or "read" within each of our personal practices.

SWATCH 1: ILLUSTRATING E-TEXTILES AS EMBODIED PRACTICE

The first swatch we highlight was created by Hannah Perner-Wilson as part of the 2020 E-Textile Swatchbook Exchange (Perner-Wilson 2020). She describes it as an "Interested Sensor #2," one of a broad class of sensors that

Figure 13.2 Interested Swatch #2, 2020. © Hannah Perner-Wilson. Photographer: © Becca Rose.

"express their interest in things without knowing in advance why the things are of interest" (pictured in the top row in the collage). Perner-Wilson describes details of this in the accompanying text:

> Interested sensors are made by crocheting a meshwork of electrically conductive yarn with varying electrical resistance between two things, in this case, fingers. The electrical resistance varies depending on forms of stress (stretch, pressure, twist, bend, squeeze . . .). Interested sensors are crochet because this technique is highly mobile, customizable and handmade, meaning interest can be expressed wherever you are, between all kinds of things and requires you to use your hands and let your mind wander while you make.

We chose to showcase the interested sensor to highlight the essential role of embodiment and play in the creation of e-textiles. Unlike many projects of technical development with clear aims and metrics for evaluation, e-textiles allow ideas of electrical functionality to meander along with the thread one crochets. Their outcome can be emergent, driven from the feel of the materials on the body and the desire to understand the relationship between sensing space and embodied space, in this case, the gaps between the fingers. Furthermore, just as crochet is a form of sculpting that can exactly fit a body, the swatch presents as an object meant to be embodied or designed for a body. It is a system whose meaning becomes evident through wear and play, there is more to be read here than first meets the eye. Flaunting the craft of circuitry is central to e-textiles design. Objects openly embed material qualities of electronic systems through the visual and tactile creations made possible through textiles. This embodied way of sharing the sensor through the swatch is a kind of un-blackboxing process. As a swatch, the interested sensor invites others to attach to their fingers and experience the material and sensations of the sensing.

SWATCH 2: THE SWATCH AS A READING TOOL

We picked *Pin Probe* by Irene Posch from the 2017 E-Textile Swatchbook Exchange as our second example (Posch 2017) because it demonstrates the variety of possible swatches in the book and how swatches may not only inspire new future work as explored above, but live out of the swatchbook (pictured in the second row). The way the swatch is mounted allows for easy removal, the page still containing an image of the swatch when the physical sample is removed. Posch (2017) describes the swatch in the accompanying text:

> The Pin Probe is a test lead to connect between a multimeter and conductive fabric or thread. The probe consists of a pin to make temporary but firm contact with textile materials without harming them. A soft and flexible textile cable then connects the probe to a banana plug to connect to a multimeter. The Pin Probe is designed to aid processes of textile electronic making, allowing to pin the probe to the textile material and have both hands free for the crafting routine. Directly while stitching the connection, the multimeter provides continuous information about its current electrical value. The immediate feedback allows instant action, facilitating an aesthetic-driven workflow to reach precise electronic results.

Her motivation for including such a swatch was to provide the community with new means to "read" their e-textile creations: to understand whether a connection is well made while making it, to read the values of a sensor while crocheting it—as well as to challenge the existing tools used so far—mostly connected to either an electronic or textile practice.

Tools specific to an e-textile practice allow turning attention from what is made toward how something is made (Posch and Fitzpatrick 2021). In this case, the tools, as swatches, invite others to take them up and literally probe the processes, values, and imagination embedded in our practice. Tooling, then, also becomes a form of communicating our collective values through practice. Put another way, our tools allow us to "tune in" to different material frequencies, to resonate with different qualities of the material, or to probe into the vocabularies of electromagnetism as though we were sensing the feel of cloth. By offering tools as swatches, we situate the things for making alongside the things made, the invention of a new tool alongside the invention of a new pattern. Here, we see material and process being read through the tooling. This reading may give form to imaginings of new technological futures, perhaps one where we probe, mend, and repair our electronics with thread. Thus, e-textiles offers a dimension to technology that is embedded in knowing about textiles, and brings with it the situated knowledge in storytelling, sociality, felt-sense, and ways of relating. In the words of Anusas and Ingold, "Far from reducing everything to objects, electrical wiring gives us a world that is more comparable to a woven textile" (Anusas and Ingold 2015).

SWATCH 3: THE SWATCH AS A WRITING

For the third swatch, we selected *Darned and Mended* by Becca Rose from the 2017 swatchbook (Rose 2017). It draws a bow between one of the oldest craft techniques, processes of darning and mending, to current body-worn electronic textile technologies (pictured in the third row). Rose describes this in the accompanying text:

> I am exploring sound and movement into the worn spaces of cloth through darning with conductive materials. Darned and mended swatches use conductive yarns to create pressure sensors around threadbare garments. The sensors can be connected to an Arduino or Pure Data circuit . . . and the feedback used to create musical or dance scores that are based on the worn areas.

Textile mender Celia Pym draws attention to "mak[ing] something new, but different" as a method of honoring the histories, stories, and memories held in fiber (Gibson 2021), Rose intervenes into these places by reimagining them as textile sensors. They use the precise places where garments have been worn down and thinned to reinforce them through e-darning techniques. Here, the growing thin represents a place where the body produces constant friction, the same kind of friction that enlivens technological sensors. Thus, e-darning maps the body's movement to ideal sensor locations. Rose's practice of mending combines care and repair of the cloth with a newfound functionality expanding beyond the visual form and into responsive sensors, sending electrons through the wear.

Written into the repair is the readily fixable nature of e-textiles. Presented as a swatch in the swatchbook, e-darning samples becomes a pointer to a practice of collecting, mending, and making the worn both new and electrical. It seeks to open new narratives of repairable electronics and new relationships with those we consider to be old or worn.

SWATCH 4: CROSS-REFERENCING SWATCHES

In our fourth example, we focus on two interrelated swatches, the first being the *Handwoven Waffle Sensor* (2012) submitted by Mika Satomi in the 2015 swatchbook (Satomi 2015) and the second being Laura Devendorf's *Woven 2D Position Sensor* from the 2020 swatchbook (Devendorf 2020) to tell the story of how the first swatch inspired the second (pictured in the bottom row). Many of the systems made with e-textiles have been developed within a culture of open hardware—making the processes available and transparent to people in ways that are not possible with proprietary electronics. This open ethos is what allowed Devendorf to take the concept presented by Satomi and develop it in new directions within her personal practices.

Satomi's 2015 swatch leverages the long-established waffle structure of weaving, and the ability for it to collapse and pop back out into 3D form, as a means for sensing pressure or the amount someone is "pressing" the swatch. This swatch, and the realization that fabric structures were mechanical systems, inspired Devendorf to launch a several-year inquiry into the sensing possibilities of several other woven structures. It was as though Satomi's swatch offered a lens through which Devendorf began to study woven structure and how integrating electrically conductive materials in various configurations within the structures could sense different body movements or interactions. The swatch, thus, planted a seed of possibility into Devendorf's brain that could be extended within her practice. It began with the simple desire to recreate Satomi's swatch, which introduced Devendorf to the mechanics of weave structure and practicalities of weaving on multishaft looms. It then continued with the exploration of the other possibilities of multilayer cloth, such as the position sensing offered through three-layer woven constructions represented in the 20202 swatch, the process of which Devendorf describes in the accompanying text:

The swatch leveraged multi-layer weaving, specifically triple weaving (where three layers are woven simultaneously) to create resistive, spacer, and conductive layers. Pressure causes the resistive and conductive layers to touch. Because a single resistive yarn winds continuously over the surface, the resistance change can be mapped to a position along the thread, and thus, a particular point on the 2D surface.

Here, one swatch inspires a second, illustrating a narrative whereby one practice branches into another, and the two evolve side-by-side. The open ethos of the swatchbook made this possible and allowed the two swatches to remain in correspondence with one another, the second as a variation or "sequel" of the first. While this narrative illustrates this direct connection, all swatches included are starting points for another project. As swatches have always been, they become mobile when taken up by other practitioners.

Diffracting E-Textiles Practice

For us, participating in E-Textile Swatchbook Exchange has manifested not only in the integration of electronics into cloth, but it also draws attention to other metallic components historically embedded in cloth or playful practices and rethinking of the technology we encounter in everyday life. While the swatches we selected reference various properties that we see as characterizing our e-textile practices, we specifically use the *Interested Sensors #2* to highlight the e-textiles process as embodied, the *Pin Probe* to show how an e-textiles practice can be read through tooling, *Darned and Mended* to write questions about the possibility of technological repair, and *Woven 2D Position Sensor* to demonstrate how practices are interrelated and communicate between each other. As we have mentioned earlier, there are complex properties that occur at the intersections of electrons and textiles. Some of the properties that characters the swatches we review above are:

embodiment—*wearability, movement, sensing,*
playfulness—*demonstrating "making" not only as problem solving but as opportunity for beauty and humor*

- **historical inquiry**—*practicing old techniques with new materials, new techniques with old materials*
- **tooling**—*new techniques, requiring new tools*
- **care/reuse**—*drawing attention to the value of textile material*
- **open-endedness**—*an invitation to continue to create, to collaborate*
- **sharing**—*building upon prior work and referencing this clearly and proudly*
- **documentation** *as a creative act, an opportunity for storytelling*

What becomes evident in our compilation of swatches is that they take forms and materialities beyond the traditional squares of cloth traditionally kept in swatchbooks. We present not only cloth, but tools to be used and documentation of events and stories. To some degree, all swatches can be seen as tools and documentation, but our collection makes evident that we are making a choice to call these swatches. By calling them swatches, we place the electronics within the vernacular of textiles: variations on a theme, circuits as patterns. The practice of "swatching" appeals to us because beyond being samples for distribution, swatches can also be read as stories. They are provisional, unfinished, open-ended bits of narrative intended to be integrated, or perhaps to infect, the creative ideation of others. Some stories focus on historical inquiry by retracing and refiguring a technology of the past. Some focus on other ways of knowing and making by making traditional computational components like buttons and swatches through processes of crochet or stitching. Others offer something in between: a new material or technique intended for new forms of engagement. Compiled collectively into a swatchbook, these objects are presented as material records, with any accompanying description or material list as supporting text only. The emphasis rests on implementation, allowing others to take up or rework the swatch into their own practice.

We'd like to suggest that the E-Textile Swatchbook Exchange is a way of diffracting e-textiles practice. In physics, diffraction is a meeting point between waves, they combine or overlap. Barad (2007) draws from concepts on quantum entanglement to describe a way of decentering one way of viewing things. The metaphor of diffraction provides a counter to reflection or the "logics of sameness" by focusing on the emergent and complex patterns of wave forms when mediated by different apparatuses. These waveforms do not produce sameness, they combine and entable to reveal something else and thus, are "attuned to difference" (2007: 5). This metaphor helps us understand that we are not reading E-Textile Swatchbook Exchange as a how-to book or a single recipe with concrete steps to take. Rather, we are looking to entangle multiple perspectives to reveal new approaches, ideas, and understandings. The outcome of a swatchbook is more than the sum of its parts, it animates through each reader's personal practice and artifacts, generating multiple trajectories for the ideas and techniques contained within.

The E-Textile Swatchbook Exchange demonstrates that e-textiles is more than electronics in textiles, and the swatchbook combines and overlaps multiple viewpoints to portray this. Like other textiles practices, it has become a network and point of exchange between people from various backgrounds across the arts and engineering. The process of collectivism and exchange that often function in textiles communities also function in e-textiles, as for example, shown in the cross-referencing of the Woven 2D Position Sensor. As a field, it explores the new forms of creative technological expression, as written into the *Darned and Mended* swatch, and a desire to understand the materiality of computing, as shown in *Interested Sensor #2* and the *Pin Probe*, and the swatchbook eloquently diffracts these stories allowing for an interwoven, overlapping story of technology, materials, processes, textile histories, and tools.

An Invitation

We would like to end with a new beginning, and invite you, the reader, to participate in or perhaps start your own Swatchbook Exchange practice using the process that we describe above. We invite you to keep your eyes open to metals and circuits contained in historic forms of embroidery and brocade cloth, to take a cloth or an old electronic object apart and explore how they might be mended, or to simply crochet around the body and explore the complex interplay when attaching different body parts together in a garment. Most importantly, we invite you to compile and share your material musings with a community of people who inspire you.

Notes

1. For most of the swatchbooks, the process for selection was that everyone who submits a swatch was able to vote on the final selection, but this was never implemented because there were never too many submissions to warrant a selection. The only swatchbooks that had a formal selection process was for the TEI version, where there was a panel made from people in the community.

References

Anusas, M., and Ingold, T. (2015) "The Charge against Electricity". *Cultural Anthropology* 30 (4): 540–54. https://doi.org/10.14506/ca30.4.03.

Barad, K. (2007) *Meeting the Universe Halfway: Quantum Physics and the Entanglement of Matter and Meaning*. Duke University Press Books.

Devendorf, L. (2020) "E-textile Swatch Exchange". *2d Woven Position Sensor* (blog). 2020. https://etextile-summercamp.org/swatch-exchange/woven-2d-position-sensor/.

"E-Textile Swatch Exchange". (2013) https://etextile-summercamp.org/swatch-exchange/category/2013/.

Gibson, L. (2021) "Damage and Repair". Harvard Magazine. December 7, 2021. https://www.harvardmagazine.com/2022/01/montage-celia-pym (accessed September 30, 2022).

Harlizius-Klück, E. (2017) "Weaving as Binary Art and the Algebra of Patterns". *TEXTILE* 15 (2): 176–97. https://doi.org/10.1080/14759756.2017.1298239.

Hertenberger, A., Scholz, B., Contrechoc, B., Stewart, B., Kurbak, E., Perner-Wilson, H., Posch, I., Cabral, I., Qi, J., Childs, K., Kuusk, K., Calder, L., Toeters, M., Kisand, M., Bhömer, M., Donneaud, M., Grant, M., Coleman, M., Satomi, M., Tharakan, M., Vierne, P., Robertson, S., Taylor, S., Nachtigall, T. (2014) "2013 E-textile Swatchbook Exchange: The Importance of Sharing Physical Work". In *Proceedings of the 2014 ACM International Symposium on Wearable Computers: Adjunct Program*, 77–81. ISWC '14 Adjunct. New York, NY, USA: Association for Computing Machinery. https://doi.org/10.1145/2641248.2641276.

Perner-Wilson, H. (2020) "E-textile Swatch Exchange". *Interested Sensor* (blog). 2020. https://etextile-summercamp.org/swatch-exchange/interested-sensors/.

Perner-Wilson, H. and Posch, I. (2021) "TEI2021 SWATCHBOOK—The Art of Interaction", 2021. https://tei.acm.org/2021/swatchbook/

Perner-Wilson, H. and Posch, I. (2022) "How Tangible is TEI? Exploring Swatches as a New Academic Publication Format", in *Sixteenth International Conference on Tangible, Embedded, and Embodied Interaction. TEI '22: Sixteenth International Conference on Tangible, Embedded, and Embodied Interaction*, Daejeon Republic of Korea: ACM, pp. 1–4. https://doi.org/10.1145/3490149.3503668.

Posch, I. (2017) "E-Textile Swatch Exchange". *Pin Probe* (blog). 2017. https://etextile-summercamp.org/swatch-exchange/pin-probe/.

Posch, I. and Fitzpatrick, G. (2021) "The Matter of Tools: Designing, Using and Reflecting on New Tools for Emerging eTextile Craft Practices". *ACM Transactions on Computer-Human Interaction* 28 (1): 4:1-4:38. https://doi.org/10.1145/3426776.

Rose, B. (2017) "E-Textile Swatch Exchange". *Darned and Mended* (blog). 2017. https://etextile-summercamp.org/swatch-exchange/darned-and-mended/.

Satomi, M. (2015) "E-Textile Swatch Exchange". *Waffle Fabric Sensor* (blog). 2015. https://etextile-summercamp.org/swatch-exchange/hand-woven-waffle-sensor/.

Unknown. (1764) *Swatch Book*. Silk, taffeta, linen, brocaded, leather bound, paper and ink, sealing wax. Victoria & Albert Museum Textiles and Fashion Collection. https://collections.vam.ac.uk/item/O134050/swatch-book-unknown/.

"Cloth moves me. Every day, I marvel at everything cloth records and resonates. I am shaped by cloth—and cloth is never still."

Katharina Sand

14

Cloth, Techné, and Traces in Digital Fashion

KATHARINA SAND

Introduction

While traditional cloth has served as a vessel for personal and cultural memories and knowledge, this review explores the experience of creators and wearers of dematerialized textiles used in virtual fashion design. In-depth qualitative interviews with four fashion designers and four wearers explore the bodily and emotional experiences of digital cloth manipulation. How does creating seams and silhouettes with the click of a mouse, computer screens, and Clo3D software change the experience and perception of textiles? What does the storage and care of digital cloth convey?

Cloth is brought into being by humans. In the case of physical cloth, through interactions with tools, machines, and fibers, and in the case of digital cloth, through human-machine interactions. The colors, textures, and patterns of fashion and textiles, in turn, transform the human embodied experience through their sensory perception. How does the experience of physical cloth's "capacity to receive the human imprint . . . to embody both a communal, historical moment and a local individual, specific story" (Hunt 2014: 207) compare to that of digital cloth? What do interactions with digital cloth reveal? This chapter explores the communication abilities of digital textiles throughout the process of designing, wearing, and storing digital cloth.

Context

Making is considered a practical art, requiring practical knowledge, in the tradition of *tékhnē*, the Greek term derived from "teks" (originating from the Proto-Indian verb "to weave, to fabricate"). The human practice of making is described by Tim Ingold as "itinerant, improvisatory and rhythmic" (Ingold 2010). This description conveys both the curiosity and play involved, and the harnessing and producing of knowledge through the repeating of tasks during textile *tékhnē*. The process of making of cloth is also deeply intertwined with the sociocultural context of makers and textiles, engrained with residues of colonialism in both agricultural and labor relations, reflecting kinship, exchanges, and reinterpretations of the past—and deeply anchored in the places in which it is made, as well as in the journeys of its makers (Crewe 2017; Kettle 2019).

Wearing cloth can be defined as an ongoing process of compositions, rearrangements, and interactions, which reach beyond the bodily sensation, engage in a constant dialogue with history, and enable redefinitions of the self amongst the many. Following a theoretical "material turn," fashion theory's "language turn" was heralded by the father of fashion semiotics, Roland Barthes, and established practices of "reading" fashion. Umberto Eco can be counted amongst the eminent scholars who solidified this perception of fashion as a semiotic communication practice. The relevance of communication theory for the domain of fashion and textiles is steadily increasing through the mediatization of the domain (Rocamora 2017), propelled by technological developments and digitization. As Malcom Barnard has pointed out (Barnard 2020), defining fashion as communication needs to consider different definitions of communication models. Communication theory is as multi-disciplinary as fashion theory, nourished by sociology, psychology, semiotics, linguistics and informatics, phenomenology, design, rhetoric, and marketing theory. This review takes an approach centered on medium theory, drawing parallels to cloth as a medium of communication (Sterne 2006), that is, a *form* of communication.

The experience of the medium of cloth has become central to embodied fashion research in the last twenty years (Entwistle 2000). Eloquent documentation of affect and worn cloth (Downes 2018; Millar 2013; Sampson 2020) and of the sensory perceptions of cloth (Ornati 2021) indicate that Ingold's description can be applied both to the making and to the wearing of cloth. Both are processes that intertwine form and matter.

What happens when this form is defined by computer code, and matter is immaterial? How is the medium of cloth experienced when it is "dematerialized" and mediatized? How is it stored and tended to? Storage and care have become central in the discussion of value transmission and consumption of cloth. The medium of digital cloth has yet to be addressed within the framework of wardrobe studies (Fletcher and Klepp 2017).

Physical Cloth

Traces are intrinsic to the making of traditional textiles, composed of natural or man-made fibers. Threads can store photosynthetic traces of local hours of sunlight, vestiges of the temperatures in which sheep grazed before their wool was sheared and spun, or the recipes of regional compounds and chemists. Seasonal and regional ebbs and flows in flora and fauna become interlaced in both fiber and dye compositions. Dyes and bleaching processes alter each strand's structures. Fibers are transformed into fabrics, in turn engrained with traces of making processes, of makers, and of their tools for netting, weaving, knitting, or looping. Cloth records the habits and errors of making, and is shaped by the savoir-faire, the characters, agility, bodies and moods of makers, and their dialogue with their surroundings.

As textiles travel from makers to their next owners, they absorb the way in which they are handled, wrapped, displayed, and often wrinkled. Depending on their use, they are sometimes steamed, cut, draped, tailored, embroidered, stitched, painted, or printed. Only later, when worn, do textile surfaces begin their interactions with new bodies. They embed body heat, sweat, perfume, and each wearer's unique body choreography. Bending elbows and knees create honeycombs of fine lines. Yarns are snagged, velvet bruised, cottons and silks stained.

Traditional textiles also record traces of care and storage: creases created from folding, the imprints of hangers, the fading of cloth exposed to sunlight. Dust and damp can transform fibers, while heat may melt others. Depending on the social, cultural, and geographical context, cloth structure will change as it is kneaded and rinsed in muddy rivers, or by Miele machines. It may absorb the scent of southern winds as it dries on gnarly tree branches. It can be transformed by rot as it slumbers in drawers, or change shape as it is squeezed into vacuum-sealed plastic. How cloth is cared for and stored both reflects and affects its use, and is embedded into its surface and structure.

Textiles communicate some of these traces visually—through regional motifs and color choices, hues, and saturations, through sheen or luster, through stitching or embroideries, or the fading or shape changes caused by distress. Their meaning is negotiated by individual visual perception, as well as by their social and cultural context. This is illustrated by the value given to distressed denim, or to antique Japanese Boro textiles. Resist-stitched indigo-dyed Ndop cloth, Flemish lace, or soprarizzi velvets can be appreciated visually by a layperson, and classified by experts. The intricate semiotics of sumptuous Kente cloth communicate stories through color and composition, transmitting geometric stories of historical events, political statements, and emotions. Scottish kilt motifs signify belonging to clans. Tais cloth of East Timor is intricately tied to social contracts, especially marriage, and communicates the status and age of its wearers through stripes. These symbolic meanings are encoded and decoded visually.

Yet textile topographies are also communicated by touch—their smoothness, temperature, texture, give, and weight of hand. While textile expertise allows for a deeper understanding and classification of cloth, some textile communication is tacit, especially in the case of sensory communication. The coolness of a fabric, its coarseness, or its elasticity are all understood through bodily sensations, through touch and wear. These are often unspoken—part of textile expertise is the knowledge of vocabularies, the ability to both understand and voice the bodily sensation of cloth. These sensory perceptions and experiences of cloth are negotiated by each individual, and enmeshed in social and cultural discourse. As David Howes and Constance Classen point out, they are accordingly attributed different social value (Howes and Classen 2014). Furthermore, since the value of cloth is not solely monetary, but highly symbolic, the act of transmission or trade is a communicative practice. The symbolic connection of cloth to national identity has, for example, frequently been employed for political and military purposes, as a communication tool for propaganda. The symbolic value of textiles also lies at the root of their use in ceremonial practices, ranging from cosmological balancing to the practice of athletes wearing a jersey for good luck.

Digital Cloth

Recent fashion industry and technological developments, accelerated by the digital shift of global pandemic lockdowns, have generated and increased the production of digital cloth to generate digital fashion designs. The practice has become central for prototyping in the garment manufacturing workflow. Digital cloth also envelops avatars in an exponentially growing gaming industry: the virtual platform Roblox alone has 50 million daily users (Condon 2022) and users are dressed in garment-like "skins." Several digital marketplaces, such as Dematerialized and DressX, offer and distribute digital designs that enswathe visuals of physical bodies via intricate photoshopping and hovering augmented reality filters. These can be shared on social media platforms or worn within a multitude of metaverse platforms. The rush toward the creation of digital garments by fashion brands includes industry leaders such as Balenciaga, Gucci, and Balmain, eager to claim their share of a market that has been estimated at $31 billion (McKinsey 2022).

While the use and impact of digital fabrication upon new design aesthetics and practices has been explored (Anderson and Weinthal 2021; Clarke and Harris 2012; Särmäkari 2020), the impact of digital cloth on both wearers and designers beckons to be documented. How do makers and wearers experience non-tactile cloth and its maintenance, storage, and care? How do they respond to shapes and surfaces that remain immaculate, which do not retain their bodily imprint of wear and time? *How does the body and the mind read digital cloth*? This chapter contextualizes and explores digital cloth's absence of material traces by using qualitative interviews with each four purposely selected makers and wearers of dematerialized cloth to explore meaning-making in the domain of digital cloth.

Physical fabrics continue to evolve and decay over time, storing unique sequences of temperature, moisture, light, and human interactions, whether they move through the world or slumber in closets. As cloth*ing*, they become shaped by wear, activated by bodily motions, infused with perfume and sweat. Textiles become tattered and torn over time. Their shape and surface records their wearers and their journeys until they disintegrate. In the words of Lesley Millar, "cloth is also the membrane through which we establish our sense of 'becoming', and formalise our relationship with the external world, while the fabric remorselessly records the evidence of those interactions" (Millar 2013). Its form evolves.

Digital cloth is designed and produced using computer-aided design (CAD). It is composed of code and displayed in pixels. While it is used as part of computer-aided manufacturing (CAM) workflows to enable more efficient mass-production, these technologies have also allowed fashion designers to create cloth and garments in the realm of fantasy. Särmäkari (2020) describes the creation of "real," "possible," and "impossible" garments: those recording existing garments, those enabling future garment production, and those that could not exist in the physical world, as they transcend rules such as gravity.

Digital fashion eliminates material production and distribution costs (Sand 2021), but requires hardware and software, as well as electricity, networks, and cloud-based computing servers. Wearers receive their purchases digitally, eliminating shipping costs and time. Although the production, wear, and maintenance of cloth consumes energy, digital cloth generates no textile waste and can be dispensed with instantly, by deleting its digital trace. Which different avenues of imprinting communication does digital cloth offer in comparison to traditional cloth?

Method

Participants for this qualitative case study were selected purposively to answer the research question. They were chosen over a two-year period of ethnographic and participative observation of the digital fashion Instagram community, supplemented by reviews of specialized press and industry events focused on digital fashion. The selection of digital fashion makers was chosen to represent differing degrees of physical fashion design experience, from zero to highly proficient, as well as a variety in design approaches. These approaches encompass designs for production-ready 3D patterns, "skins" worn and purchased in videogames, fashion layered over existing imagery for the purpose of distribution on social networks, hovering augmented reality filter garments, animation, as well as design experimentations bridging digital and physical worlds. The selection of wearers was chosen for their high levels of fashion knowledge and reflective wearing expertise, and their difference in perspectives: a fashion journalist, a model, a fashion curator, and an artist researching identity and clothing who is active in gaming worlds.

The semi-structured interviews ranged from 45 to 90 minutes and were held on Zoom, recorded, and transcribed. Their focus was on how designers and wearers of digital cloth experience digital cloth and construct meaning in relation to their interaction in the making or wearing process. The first interviews with digital makers were conducted in 2020, followed by an initial review of central themes. Parallel interviews for an EU project from July to October 2021 on the use of digital design tools for workflow and production purposes informed an intermediate

Figure 14.1 *Work in Progress*, 2022. Still image. © Alfatih.

coding process. A project creation with augmented reality fashion at the Université du Québec à Montréal (UQAM) from February to April 2022 informed a second range of interviews with wearers and makers during the month of August 2022, followed by an iterative literature review, and then more focused advanced coding.

Review

The iterative analysis revealed two central ways in which digital cloth records traces for both makers and wearers: bodily and emotional (experiential) traces, and archival digital practices and footprints. Makers used to handling physical cloth all pointed to similarities in the design process. Learning processes were described as equally strenuous. While software replaces traditional tools ("it's like a sewing machine for me") and elicited affect and emotion, it should be noted that unlike traditional tools, software requires updates and therefore is in constant evolution, requiring constant learning. Another key differentiator described by an interviewee is the plasticity of digital storage: "If something you've done doesn't work, or it messes up, you can go back in a lot of cases, versus in real life, if you've got something wrong, you've cut something wrong, it's cut, you can't uncut it." Storage of digital cloth thereby has a unique format, affecting the relation to cloth.

Bodily and Emotional Imprints

The traces of interaction between bodies and digital cloth differed significantly from that of makers. Wearers indicated a stronger disconnection with the body. One wearer, who was pictured in a Tribute Brand garment, layered over a previously taken photograph, commented:

> I think the verb to wear is not appropriate. It's not comparable at all. I didn't feel like I was wearing a garment—I felt like I was playing with my image. It loses the whole intimate aspect of the garment and everything that it can change in you, completely. For me, it's completely dissociated from my physical body and the relationship.

She also described missing the process of the act of wearing ("Does it feel good? Does it look like you? Does it feel like you? How does it move on your body?") and experiencing a sense of bodily disorientation: "It's . . . a little bit like in Hollywood, when you do a movie scene with dinosaurs, and you don't see them, only a greenscreen." Another indicated missing making the garment her own, with the help of mirrors, and interaction:

> Normally, you just wear the outfit. And then see how it feels. And then you just pose thinking of that . . . you feel it, you see in your mirror how it fits you . . . The biggest difference in between the digital textile was whether I was wearing them while seeing myself, like through an AR filter, through an Instagram filter, or in a Zoom meeting.

Strong visual tactility experiences were described by another:

> You are actually feeling, or you are imagining that you feel fur. I think if the material is something you have really strong memory of, like water or fire—then you really imagine how it feels to wear it.

For her, the process encouraged experimentation, and the choice of more playful outfits. For all cases, the activation of movement through seeing oneself on a screen improved the sensation of wearing the digital outfit. Another wearer who also creates garments was particularly attentive to the bodily movements and of the body in space, using wearing as a process for making:

> It gave me interesting movements in the process of modelling, I have to do multiple experiments until it works. You know, sometimes I move my arm, but then the speed doesn't follow. It is like trial and error, until you get it right. And because you have unlimited space, a way to kind of negotiate that as well.

One wearer was particularly attentive to cloth design in augmented reality (AR):

> AR is not adapted for fabric simulation. So it doesn't look natural. It's really important to know the media you're working on. There are designers who work WITH the media, and other designers that work against media. So clothing that is, for example, really bulky, a tunic for example, it's not going to work. It's not going to work because the fabric is not going to fall well, it will look like one of these images of a drawing pasted on a paperdoll.

For makers, all expressed a sense of abundance in digital design, and three out of four spoke of experiencing a sense of freedom, which generated emotions of joy: "everything is new"; "you have unlimited materials and limited things you can put on"; "the fun part is being creative and also discovering things." For one, the autonomy granted by digital design provided satisfaction: "It's so liberating to not rely on other people's artistic vision. I can do it all!" Furthermore, for makers, the impact of blending physical and digital experience was notable, with one describing how "it definitely changed my perception of color and lighting and how these two are affecting each other in real life."

Agency and the transgression of rules was described by both categories. A maker explained their practice as "finding other alternatives for ultra-digital spaces, beyond the control of the game masters in a way, and maybe finding a bit more agency in this space." A wearer stated:

> I try to produce glitches, I try to move in a way that an augmented reality app doesn't recognize my arm anymore. So I try to set up malfunctions and produce glitches. But then, if I notice that the app is really good, and it doesn't glitch, then I try to move accordingly to the dress.

Storing: Closets and Wallets

Archiving creates traces. The practice of preservation is bound to the advent of decay. Folds can break fiber strands over time, discoloration and degradation is linked to chemical compounds and interaction and evolves over time. How does the medium of dematerialized textile and its associated immediacy and perceived timelessness change our affect for cloth (Smelik 2016)? Wardrobe studies (Klepp and Fletcher 2017) have begun to unveil the affect and stories linking us to garments. Handwritten memories of physical cloth were collected during the seminal exhibition, *Cloth and Memory* (2013). The exhibition *Fashion Unraveled*, held at the Museum at the Fashion Institute of Technology (FIT) in 2018, used digital tools to crowdsource, record and transmit the "aberrant beauty in flawed objects" in fashion. Both exhibitions showcased cloth as a repository of emotions, and transmitted its tales intertwined with tattered threads. How does digital cloth communicate these narratives traces? How do we understand the medium of cloth when it is disassociated with traditional ways of storing and caring? Are digital garments reworn, and how are they stored?

It quickly becomes clear that terminologies are quite different to traditional cloth storage. Wearers posted worn digital designs on the social media platform Instagram, which can be situated in a performative "act" of memory (Palte and Smelik 2013) where the images are accessible as a public or private archive, depending on individual profile settings. Instagram posts can be individually archived and hidden from view, but also reposted or deleted. Some wearers keep the images of digital cloth on their smartphone photo archives, necessitating lengthy scrolling for retrieval. Another level of wearers purchased garments that they keep in *crypto wallets*—usually in multiple wallets. One wearer developed an app that allows her to wear a digital garment. Some makers save files on a USB stick or a zipped folder and use folder structuring for archives. Makers have more elaborate file management systems:

> I have a library of textile assets . . . it exists not only on my hard drive but on a backup drive, and on top of that I have a subscription to Substance, which is cloud-based. Which means all these assets, all these fabulous fabric textures, live on that online library for me. So, I have my library of textures and then a specific library for fabrics. And then I have an asset library for just Substance . . . things that you use constantly, like fabric, and looks. Those are things you want to have handy.

Figure 14.2 Judith Brachem in the *Puffed spacewalk.jumpsuit* by Caste.less in the Warburg Haus Hamburg, bought via DressX; altered by Judith Brachem. Photographer: © Paula Gropper.

While the space for storage of unused garments is a parallel to physical closets ("I just need places to put drives"), we can identify that clothes are managed as "files," kept in "live" libraries by makers and in "wallets" by wearers. The frequent use of fabrics and looks parallels the daily use of foundation garments in composing a daily outfit. Storage strategies show affect and attachment in terms of the fear of loss:

> I have projects that, once I'm done with them, time to get them off my computer. They're taking up too much space. And then what I do is I backup all my files onto the hard drives and just take them off and store them so that if I ever need them again, I come back to it. It's actually project-based. I mean, if you're the type of person that keeps live libraries, good for you. If I made a really good dress I obj export it and then put that obj in my Library on my iPhone model, and now I have a dress . . . And then it becomes like your base model that you can use again and again and again. But upkeep of your computer is obviously important and having enough drives . . . (I) will never have enough.

Computer memory, storage space, and backups are a central topic for all digital designers. Backups and updates can be seen as tending, upkeep, and care similar to washing:

> For my graduate collection I was really like obsessed with this idea of storage and . . . digital deterioration. In the same way that if you leave a garment in your closet and then there's . . . moths or something. You take it back out, and it'll be all damaged . . . like when you open a backup USB key and the file will be damaged. And I was playing a lot with this idea. So I store my files obviously on my computer and on an external drive, maybe sometimes a cloud, but usually with backups.

> We are also still using garments that the Fabricant created like three to four years ago, but . . . if you're opening a garment that is made in CLO3 and you're opening it now in CLO6, there will be flaws. So, there will be things that you need to reconstruct, because parts of the software are like missing or your file becomes corrupted or something . . . You need to update it to keep it up to date.

Correcting flaws when opening old files in new software thereby parallels mending. Backups and the saving of files are practiced daily, a practice of care and tending. While updates are not required daily, some updates are required every couple of months.

Repeated wear of digital designs was uncommon and practiced mainly within gaming platforms and Zoom. Each maker and each wearer had a different definition of digital vintage and practices of repeated wear. One maker mentioned having deleted older designs from her social media feed. By explaining, "I think I deleted them because I felt more ashamed before," she situated the idea of out-of-date clothing within the context of rapid improvements of software and of her own design skills, as well as gaining more confidence since then within her peer community. Another maker associated the concept of digital vintage with cryptocurrencies and limited editions. Two makers participated in the practice, which can enable "sartorial remembrance" as defined by Jenss (2015: 13), rendering historical styles virtually wearable and thus imbuing them with new meaning (though one described the work as "representational rather than historically correct"). One wearer, referring to a garment which is not an NFT, would not rewear the garment even if she could. Another would be willing to rewear a similar garment, but was discouraged by the extensive time necessary for a recreation on a different, more recent, image. One wearer referred to digital vintage as a nostalgia for digital items she has worn in the past, triggering memories of moods expressed through clothing at different times in her life. Yet another wearer described digital vintage as "more like sampling music," as software allows for reassembly and re-compositions. While this interpretation mirrors processes of upcycling, the "copy–paste" practice originated in 1970s software and is particularly significant in digital contexts as it evokes the reproduction of digital designs within questions of copyright. It is also relevant in the redefinitions of fashion time (Evans and Vaccari 2020). None of the interviewees referred to virtual archival practices such as *The Virtual Fashion Archive*, nor digital fashion collections by museums.

Contextualizing Digital Cloth

With physical cloth*ing*, the wearer becomes a co-designer, transforming textiles through creases created by friction, by repetition of movement, through body warmth, through care and repair over time (Entwistle 2000; Sampson 2020). The lack of physical feedback and imprint in digital fashion is experienced as a lack of agency by the wearers. Physical feedback of cloth also creates traces in the wearers' demeanor and posture: one example is elasticity, which allows for slouching. In static versions of digital fashion layered over a still image, bodily interaction can take place in the imaginary dialogue with the cloth: a pose is planned according to the outfit. In augmented reality cloth, physical feedback is enabled through the activation and repetition of movements, creating stronger bodily memories.

Just as in traditional craftsmanship, the act of digital designing is perceived as both strenuous and playful by designers. With the difference of ornately crafted physical cloth, the amount of effort, skill, and time invested is often undervalued. The interaction with, and mastering of digital tools elicits emotional memories of satisfaction, joy, and flow, equivalent to traditional fashion craftsmanship. For wearers, the highest amounts of bodily satisfaction were described for augmented reality filters, which blend physical and digital wear and allow for increased agency and participation. For makers, the main experiential difference to wearers is the higher degree of agency in creating a trace.

Results confirm that for both digital makers and wearers, the "understanding of fashion as image or text does not preclude bodily experiences" (Glikorovska 2020), and thereby digital fashion indeed remains a bodily practice. Technological tools including smartphones and computer mouses as well as software-generated materials all create specific sensory sensations—and sensory memories. Sarah E. Braddock Clarke and Jane Harris (2012) have described this interplay of humans, tools, and code in digital design processes, during which digital designers employ complex hand-eye coordination similar to traditional craftsmanship—a process intricately linked to creating traces of exploration and learning from processes and mistakes.

These learning processes in digital cloth design are based on community exchange. As one maker described,

> it's heavily influenced by internet culture . . . where people share the code, like open source, this kind of open-source mindset. There are so many help groups where people will ask questions, and other people will answer with expertise, or even on Instagram. There's a Facebook group where people will, you know, we'll help each other out on technical issues. I don't think there's this individualistic approach as much as in physical design, because of this internet culture. It's almost looked down upon, I think, to be hiding everything.

The multitude of traces of bodily and emotional memories they generate confirms the "inadequacy of a materiality-immateriality dualism dominating in discourses pertaining to digital" (Brachtendorf 2022). Drawing on media anthropology and Martin Seel's aesthetics theory, Charlotte Brachtendorf (2022) points out the haptic visuality of digital fashion images, and the concept of "cognition sensitiva" (sensuous knowledge), knowing through perception.

While differences such as drape, weight, or feel of cloth may be best expressed or remembered by fashion professionals (Ornati 2021), we all navigate through the world by relying on the firing up of sensory memories, rather than touching surrounding surfaces at all times. Most unworn physical cloth—whether displayed or worn in the immediate vicinity, on catwalks, in print, or online—is not perceived through direct touch, but through haptic memories and imagination. The interviews show that the strongest impact upon the scale of the digital experience of cloth was the level of cloth knowledge. However, surreal or surprising cloth activated stronger memories and traces across the board.

Traces in finished cloth can be circumstantial or voluntary. An example of the former are the new shapes fabrics can take at the last fabric mill in the historical center when waters rise during *aqua alta*, and "looms work in their own unpredictable ways" (Michelangelo 2019). Examples of the latter include embellishments and mending, or processes emulating wear and tear. That intentionally flawed or distressed techniques exist *per se* demonstrates our fascination with our imprint upon textiles. In the physical fashion domain, practices of distress are especially observed in the denim category, where they are as popular in the contemporary high street as they were in the niche subculture of the punk movement. Distressed and deconstructivist techniques have also been associated with the avant-garde uses of cloth, including fashion designers such as Rei Kawabuko, Martin Margiela, Susan Cianciolo, and Ottolinger. Within this canon, traces are used to question established beauty norms.

The historian Andrea Denny-Brown situates acts of cutting traces into cloth within Bourdieu's practices of *habitus*, namely the "minor rituals," which both "subvert and accompany a culture's normalizing discourse." Denny-Brown documents the popularity of medieval European practices of slashing, dagging (cutting or slashing the edges of fabric), and perforating garments, as well as vocal criticism generated against such "robes made of shreds" (Denny-Brown 2016: 227) and their associations with "loose morals" (Denny-Brown 2016: 223). As she points out, the practice of dagging and its visceral piercing of cloth nevertheless experienced several revivals. Intentional traces such as mending have a more contemplative character. Traditional Boro mending or the contemporary visible mending movement is viewed as an elaborate aesthetic practice of embellishment. Victoria Kelley (2015) examines repairing as imbuing objects with personal value, so that they may be passed on from one generation to the next. An expression of care and value, the practice can also be viewed as an "expression of resistance to the unmaking of our world and the environment" (Irvin 2018). Within the context of consumer culture, mending can be considered a radical act.

Both distressing and mending practices represent an *artisanal annotation of cloth*—a form of self-fashioning and agency of wearer. It attests to the understanding that textiles and garments are in fact never finished, but always "becoming," in the sense of Anneke Smelik's application of Deleuze's concepts to fashion materiality (Smelik 2016). In this context, circumstantial flaws may originate in code and in software updates, or in network or connection faults, creating glitches. The purposeful generation of glitches, however, creates voluntary traces. The interviews document two such instances, as well as an array of other traces of digital designs, namely the traces in bodily and emotional memories, new perceptions of the physical world, and the development of new vocabularies.

While technology in design processes is predominantly used to achieve functional results, the purposeful quest for the unexpected in the form of "bugs," malfunctions, and glitches is part of a creative "Glitch Design Culture," which aims for both imperfection and the use of chance. Glitch-generation challenges the conformity of controlled aesthetics, and through the intentional creation of error communicates failure and noise, rendering them acceptable and even desirable. This integration of the unforeseeable has roots in creative arts process such as DaDa and has found expression in a variety of woven and knit physical textile and fashion designs. In digital cloth designs, distortions or noise are predominantly integrated as an artistic element, generating surprising shapes. For wearers of interactive digital cloth, the creation of glitches when wearing digital designs is an intuitive bodily practice, similar to testing tension and elasticity of a garment, resulting in both the creation of movement sequences in relation to digital cloth as well as visual impact upon the cloth design.

The Future of Digital Cloth

Digital textiles can already follow bodily motion of avatars in gaming worlds and follow human bodies through motion capture in augmented reality filters. An example of adaptive design is the wide commercial application of garments that adjust to any avatar's shape, "Layered Clothing Studio," which was launched in 2022 by leading game company Roblox. While in the past, digital cloth was predominantly designed to be temporally static and did not evolve over time along with the body, several developments in generative design point toward possibilities of generative algorithmic textile designs in the near future. One is the experimentation with aspects of digital evolution (Sims 1994), namely the development of "digital evolution systems with complex, creative and surprising outcomes" (Lehman, Clune and Misevic 2018: 55). Just as physical textiles can age and develop according to interactions with the bodies and environments they interact with, new generations of software can enable responsive and evolving structures.

One maker mentioned Houdini software, which is mostly used in visual effects and allows for the creation of a pattern, to which "everybody can give their own story . . . The code stays, like a universal language. You can update it, but your code will stay the same." Another maker mentioned the concept of dynamic Non-Fungible Tokens (NFTS), which have the ability to change in response to data and events (Chainlink 2022). Traditional NFTs are static once they are "minted" to provide an identifier for verifiable ownership. The advent of dynamic NFTs (dNFTs) allows for digital designs to evolve *according to external conditions and data*. This feature is already used in video games for character progression through game levels. These code structures allow for digital cloth, which evolves over time. Combined with the rapid evolution of sensors and the increasing capacities to record movement and (body) temperature data in widely available devices such as smartphone, responsive digital textiles that evolve over time, as well as generatively, are potentially possible. One digital designer already projects a future in which designs are altered through livestreaming interactions. This vision of personalized digital co-creation was iterated by one wearer, describing a future in which "there will be traces of us in our digital wardrobe, but different from the traces in our physical wardrobe: there will be traces of us, as you can design your clothes in the morning before wearing them."

A new global study of 6,000 people by the Institute of Digital Fashion confirmed a desire for diversity in avatar "body type, gender identity, disabilities and types of clothing" (Institute of Digital Fashion Diversity Report 2021). The acceptance of wrinkles of our avatars may provide an indicator for whether aging and increasingly creased digital textiles could catch on in the virtual world. While many virtual avatars have shown and idealized youthfulness (Gligorovska 2020), Second Life does allow for the different levels of wrinkles (Schultz 2022). Zepeto, one of Asia's largest metaverse platforms and virtual fashion marketplaces, allows for the creation of an avatar by taking a selfie, and offers "senior" customization options. The platform, which features fashion labels such as Gucci and digital designs by DressX, boasts 2 million active users (McDowell 2022). It specifically states its aim to allow self-expression, "regardless of your skin color, nationality, age, interest, or gender" (Zepeto 2022). Aging processes in these platforms can be achieved by constant updates of avatars—a form of documentation that also extends to objects.

It should be noted that while this study accounted for a variety of gender, practices, and nationalities, this research only included able-bodied participants from two continents in the age range 23–33, and it would benefit from a larger variety and breadth of case studies. Further research aims include the exploration of the variety of experiences of making and experiencing digital design. Additional explorations into the practices of digital storage and value giving would benefit from frameworks of socio-technical negotiations of the body (Mauss 1973), as well as cross-cultural digital inclusion and exclusion (Maynard 2014; Cottom 2019; Särmäkari 2020).

Conclusion

Which different avenues of communication does digital cloth offer in comparison to traditional cloth? How does the medium of digital cloth differ from that of physical cloth? The case studies indicate a surprising wealth of similarities. Both forms record traces of both makers and wearers: bodily and emotional (experiential) traces, and archival digital practices and footprints. Both traditional cloth and digital cloth communicate visually and through haptic sensation: they are observed and experienced. The contextualized case studies illustrate the ability of digital cloth to both create and archive embodied communal, historical, and individual imprints, as well as leaving experiential traces in both makers and users. Just as a drawing is "an archive of its maker's muscles" (Elkins 1997), digital designs and their wearing experience represent archival records of bodily, emotional, and mental effort and specific socio-technical environments. Their traces expand to the use of new visual and textual vocabularies, offering new frameworks for textile and fashion design. This includes not only the "enclothed" (Barry 2017) digital fashion experience, but also the exploration of storage of digital cloth and garments, which is an original research approach. Durability and duration are different in form, yet with a similar impact: digital storage strategies show similar affect and attachment in terms of the fear of loss. While the physical sensations of designing, wearing, and storing digital and traditional cloth differ, as do their vocabularies, all record and transmit communicative process.

I posit that voluntary glitching of immaculate digital surfaces parallels practices of distressing garments, situating purposeful glitching amongst transgressive "minor rituals" defined by Pierre Bourdieu. Voluntary glitching provides a sense of creative agency through bodily interaction, comparable to the experience of tension: this visible practice can nonverbally and playfully transmit both creative and critical processes. Furthermore, the performance of updates to repair flaws parallels cloth-mending practices. Both practices can be seen as imprinting digital designs with new traces, as artisanal annotations of cloth.

While creating glitches can be seen as resistance to the established parameters and therefore as a radical act, the act of updating is a choice induced by external parameters.

The need to update digital cloth however does not only foster notions of care and tending. It also opens doors for reinterpretations, similar to the re-composition of clothing that occurs during the act of getting dressed (Brachem and Stübbe 2022). Current developments such as dynamic NFTs point to an increased mutability of digital cloth. Digital tools enable acts of reinterpretation, variation, and co-creation, and are increasing the abilities of digital textiles to evolve from inert to interactive and even generative. While similarities can be found in the developments in physical interactive wearables (Muntean, Plate, and Smelik 2016), these inbuilt abilities for updates and annotations of cloth point toward a significant differentiation of this medium in comparison to traditional cloth.

Digital designs also frame cloth practices in a new light. Design authorship has formal links to design copyright, documented by sketches and patterns as much as in finished designs strutting on catwalks. Growing digital markets and their high financial stakes have created a rush toward NFT authentication of digital fashion, while digital cloth is a dynamic repository of communal knowledge, imbuing digital fashion design with the traditions of textile crafts passed down through generations. In conclusion, the medium of digital cloth is not only far from immaculate, storing a multitude of traces of interactions by makers and wearers; recent developments of its technological compounds also indicate that the medium fosters new forms of interactions and communication.

References

Anderson, J. and L. Weinthal (eds) (2021), *Digital Fabrication in Interior Design: Body, Object, Enclosure*, New York: Routledge, Taylor & Francis Group.
Barnard, M., ed. (2020), *Fashion Theory: A Reader*, Second edition, Abingdon, Oxon: Routledge, Taylor & Francis Group.
Barry, B. (2017), "Enclothed Knowledge: The Fashion Show as a Method of Dissemination in Arts-Informed Research", *Forum Qualitative Sozialforschung / Forum: Qualitative Social Research*, Vol. 18: No. 3 (2017).
Brachem, J. (2022), *Materialitäten virtueller Mode am Beispiel von The Fabricant* (together with Helga Behrmann), Jour Fixe Netzwerk Mode Textil, 21.06.2022. The abstract is available here : https://www.netzwerk-mode-textil.de/index.php?option=com_content&view=article&id=8051:virtueller-jour-fixe-21-06-2022&catid=12:meetings&lang=de&Itemid=95 (accessed June 18, 2023).
Brachem, J. and L. Stübbe (n.d.), "Ways of Wearing", *The Fashion Studies Journal*, Available online: https://www.fashionstudies-journal.org/digital-engagement-a/2022/8/15/ways-of-wearing (accessed September 11, 2022).
Brachtendorf, C. (n.d.), "Virtually Dressed: Towards an Anthropomedial Theory of Digital Fashion (Working Title)".
Chainlink (2022), "What Is a Dynamic NFT?", *Chainlink Blog*, Available online: https://blog.chain.link/what-is-a-dynamic-nft/ (accessed September 11, 2022).
Clarke, S. E. B. and J. Harris (2012), *Digital Visions for Fashion + Textiles: Made in Code*, London: Thames & Hudson.
Condon, J. (2022), "Everything You Wanted to Know About the Metaverse—But Were Too Afraid to Ask", *Robb Report*.
Cottom, T. M. (2019), "The Poor Can't Afford Not to Wear Nice Clothes", *ZORA*.
Crewe, L. (2017), *The Geographies of Fashion: Consumption, Space and Value, Dress, Body, Culture*, London: Bloomsbury Academic, An imprint of Bloomsbury Publishing Plc.
Denny-Brown, A. (2016), "Rips and Slits: The Torn Garment and the Medieval Self", in C. Richardson (ed), *Clothing Culture 1350–1650*, London: Routledge.
Downes, S., ed. (2018), *Feeling Things: Objects and Emotions through History*, First edition, Emotions in history, Oxford, United Kingdom; New York: Oxford University Press.
Elkins, J. (1997), *The Object Stares Back: On the Nature of Seeing*, 1st Harvest ed, A Harvest book, San Diego: Harcourt Brace.
Entwistle, J. (2000), *The Fashioned Body: Fashion, Dress, and Modern Social Theory*, Cambridge: Malden, MA: Polity Press; Blackwell.
Evans, C. and A. Vaccari (eds) (2020), *Time in Fashion: Industrial, Antilinear and Uchronic Temporalities*, London New York Oxford New Delhi Sydney: Bloomsbury Visual Arts.
Fletcher, K. and I. G. Klepp (eds) (2017), *Opening up the Wardrobe: A Methods Book*, Oslo: Novus Press.
Gligorovska, K. (2020), "Virtual Encounter with The Picture of Dorian Gray", 2020 Dress and Body Association Conference.
Howes, D. and C. Classen (2014), *Ways of Sensing: Understanding the Senses in Society*, New York: Routledge.
Hunt, C. (2014), "Worn Clothes and Textiles as Archives of Memory", *Critical Studies in Fashion & Beauty*, 5 (2): 207–32.
Ingold, T. (2010), "The Textility of Making", *Cambridge Journal of Economics*, 34 (1): 91–102.
Institute of Digital Fashion Diversity Report (2021), *My Self, My Avatar, My Identity*. Available online https://www.cfs.fashion/article/iodf-partners-with-cfs-by-lablaco-to-bring-inclusivity-and-diversity-to-the-fashion-nfts-and-metaverse (accessed June 18, 2023).
Irvin, K. (2018), "Repair and Design Futures | RISD Museum", Available online: https://risdmuseum.org/exhibitions-events/

exhibitions/repair-and-design-futures (accessed September 11, 2022).

Kelley, V. (2015), "Time, Wear and Maintenance: The Afterlife of Things", in A. Gerritsen and G. Riello (eds), *Writing Material Culture History*, Writing history, 191–8, London: Bloomsbury Academic.

Kettle, A. (2019), "Textile and Place", *TEXTILE*, 17 (4): 332–9.

Lehman, J., J. Clune and D. Misevic (2018), "The Surprising Creativity of Digital Evolution", *The 2018 Conference on Artificial Life*, 55–6, Tokyo, Japan: MIT Press.

McDowell, M. (2022), "It's not just gamers and crypto dudes buying fashion", *Vogue Business*, available online https://www.voguebusiness.com/technology/its-not-just-gamers-and-crypto-dudes-buying-digital-fashion (accessed September 11, 2022).

Mauss, M. (1973), "Techniques of the Body ☞", *Economy and Society*, 2 (1): 70–88.

Maynard, M. (2022), "Dressed in Time", Dress, Body, Culture, London: Bloomsbury Visual Arts.

Michelangelo Foundation (2019), "Crafting All Summer Long", Available online: https://www.michelangelofoundation.org/newsletters/EN-201908.html (accessed September 11, 2022).

Millar, L. (2013), "CLOTH & MEMORY » Salts Estates Ltd", *Cloth and Memory*.

Muntean, L., L. Plate and A. Smelik (eds) (2016), *Materializing Memory in Art and Popular Culture*, London: Routledge.

Ornati, M. (2021), "Touch in Text. The Communication of Tactility in Fashion E-Commerce Garment Descriptions", *Fashion Communication*, 29–40, Cham: Springer.

Plate, L., and Smelik, A. (eds) (2013). *Performing memory in art and popular culture* (Vol. 48). London: Routledge.

Rocamora, A. (2017), "Mediatization and Digital Media in the Field of Fashion", *Fashion Theory*, 21 (5): 505–22.

Sampson, E. (2020), *Worn: Footwear, Attachment and the Affects of Wear*, Bloomsbury Publishing Plc.

Sand, K. (2021), "Could Innovations Such as Augmented Reality, the Internet of Things, and Artificial Intelligence Render the Fashion Industry More Sustainable?", in J. Sun and E. Fischer (eds) *Spirit of Luxury and Design from a Perspective of Fashion and Jewellery*, ORO Editions.

Särmäkari, N. (2020), "Digital 3D-Fashion: Designing for Virtual Bodies and Spaces", *2020 Dress and Body Association Conference*.

Schultz, R. (2022), "Old Age in Virtual Worlds and Social VR—Why the Representation of Aging Matters in the Metaverse", Available online: https://ryanschultz.com/2022/02/14/editorial-old-age-in-virtual-worlds-and-social-vr-why-the-representation-of-aging-matters-in-the-metaverse/ (accessed September 11, 2022).

Sims, K. (1994), "Evolved Virtual Creatures by Karl Sims, 1994", Available online: http://www.karlsims.com/evolved-virtual-creatures.html (accessed September 11, 2022).

Smelik, A. (2016), "Gilles Deleuze: Bodies-without-Organs in the Folds of Fashion", in A. Rocamora and A. Smelik (eds), *Thinking through Fashion: A Guide to Key Theorists*, Dress cultures, 165–83, London: I.B. Tauris.

Sterne, J. (2006). Communication as techné. *Communication as. . .: Perspectives on Theory*, 91–8.

"The State of Fashion 2022" (2022), *McKinsey, The Business of Fashion*.

"Zepeto. Https://Zepeto.Me" (2022), Available online: https://support.zepeto.me/hc/en-us/articles/9061262913817--Update-News-THE-NEW-Avatar-2-0-Release-.

"Textile as a medium is both ordinary and extraordinary, in a dialogic pluralism it can animate concepts and their signification in a physical form, making meaning tangible and taking a message out into multiple real-world contexts."

Sonja Andrew

15
The Coded Lab

SONJA ANDREW

Introduction

This chapter explores the role of textile practice as an alternative form for audience engagement with science research and its coded meanings. It reflects on the author's arts–science collaborative projects with the Cancer Research UK (CRUK) Manchester Institute, and biophysicists in the University of Leeds Cultural Institute's Creative Labs: Biological Sciences 2nd Edition. Creating textile concepts and artifacts within a semiotic-based arts practice framework, the historical foundations and precursors to contemporary scientific discoveries were investigated during the projects. Aspects of scientific inquiry were examined and the concept of technology modifying reality was explored, engaging viewers in reflection on science imagery and how smaller experimental studies lead to, and from, major scientific breakthroughs.

Imaging in Science

In *Expanding Hermeneutics, Visualism in Science* (1998) and *Material Hermeneutics, Reversing the Linguistic Turn* (2021), Ihde notes that imaging in science has a truth function, it must truly represent what is there; that what is seen is not in any way a by-product of the technology used that could cloud interpretation. But he acknowledges, "technologies transform all possible representations and are never purely correspondent. In this way they are 'hermeneutic'" (Ihde 1998: 92). This understanding of the visually transformative role of technology to explore perceived realities, their representation and interpretation, is embedded within art and design thinking and practices, and it can be argued that the advancement of technologies across 2D, 3D, and 4D imaging in science also provides an enhanced truth; digital technologies enhancing pixel by pixel—technology modeling and modifying reality. The question is if this *enhanced truth* is still perceived as science fact, or a conversion of it, a transformation of reality through visual processes? Digital intervention to develop image data via color, for example, can be used to enhance key areas and highlight specific phenomena (see Hu, Peng and Xu, 2012). Through this, a hyperrealism can be introduced via the technology to make these areas more visually prominent to aid scientific interpretation. This type of visual enhancement has been steadily built-in as integral to scientific imaging, from the pseudo-color image processing of magnetic resonance imaging (MRI) scans (Blow 2009; Isa et al. 2021) to developments in hyperspectral imaging (Schneider and Feussner 2017), combined with chemical dyes to highlight cancerous cells (Luthman et al. 2017). The truth of the image is enhanced via color in order to better read its meaning, and through this a hyperreality (Baudrillard 1994, 2015) of science fact is created.

The Fabric of Research

The concept of technology modifying reality via color enhancement informed the textile print *Signalling Networks*. This was one of three designs the author developed for the Cancer Research UK (CRUK) Manchester Institute arts–science project, *The Fabric of Research*. In the project, five design academics with fashion and textile backgrounds explored different aspects of the Institute's work, culminating in an exhibition at Manchester Craft and Design Centre (July 23–29, 2016). Steve Bagley, Head of Advanced Imaging at the Institute, provided insights into the pivotal role of color within CRUK's scientific research. For example, in sections of tumor tissue, normal blood vessels can be stained brown, while vasculogenic mimicry (VM) tumor blood supply vessels can be stained pink, and tumors treated with chemotherapy can be stained green. This enables evaluation of the impact of chemotherapy drug delivery for tumors growing with and without VM tumor blood supply vessels. The twin aims of stopping tumor growth while still delivering drug therapies can then be examined (see Williamson et al. 2016).

The CRUK Manchester Institute Advanced Imaging department supplied digital images where color highlighted the outcomes of targeted precision therapies (see Waterhouse 2017), and this formed the basis for a series of trial textile designs for *Signalling Networks*. One of the prerequisites for the design was incorporation of accurate imagery of the science direct from the source to communicate research being undertaken at that point in time. As an artifact, the final textile could be considered as a form of visual preservation of knowledge. This put specific parameters to the development of the textile as a representation rather than an interpretation of the scientific research, cloth as a literal record, the visual enhancement already built into the scientific imaging presented as a truth via the textile. During the design development stages, imagery was enlarged, and repeat compositions digitally trialed with coloration adaptions explored, but fundamentally the visual content of the textile had to accurately present the scientific image data provided.

In semiotic terms, it can be argued that the more literal and realistic an image is, the greater its redundancy. However, this is very much dependent on the way the image is rendered in the composition, the knowledge base of the audience, the physical and cultural context in which the image is viewed, the viewer's familiarity with any form/object that carries the image, and also the material it is made from (Andrew 2013). These multiple factors bring additional influences to how the image is read. When a viewer reads groups of image-based signifiers within a composition in combination, the interconnected communication relationships generated from these images, "micro visual syntagyms" (Andrew 2014), can also have significant impact on a viewer's reading of the work. The codified meaning of one image is interpreted in relation to another. These meanings are assigned to specific paradigms by the viewer to shape how the overall work is read, with the textile medium as an active contributing component to this reading. However, representation of woven cloth and knitted fabric within virtual reality now also bring new influencing factors to our reading of "textile," forming new definitions of what we understand as materiality.

The final *Signalling Networks* design (digitally printed on silk twill, 1 × 1 meter square) was based on a research image of lung squamous cell carcinoma provided by the Signalling Networks in Cancer lab at the CRUK Manchester Institute. The image itself was literal, yet not redundant in its communication; it involved highly entropic codes, in that only a very specialized scientific audience would be able to interpret the image content accurately. To a non-specialist audience, the image would most likely be read as "microscopic," "cellular," and "scientific," based on similar images previously seen in the media or educational contexts. A description was added in the exhibition to explain the visual content of the textile design, and the CRUK research undertaken to help combat the disease to aid viewers' understanding beyond their initial interpretations of the imagery.

Textile is an unconventional medium for science communication, and not normally associated with narratives of science experimentation and results. Textiles within science and medicine are utilitarian; they are often technical, aid healing, and provide barriers, the meanings they carry are defined by their use. However, artifacts that would attract audiences and create new forms of public engagement with the CRUK Manchester Institute research were key factors in the project, with a remit to use textiles as a bridge between the science and the public. The tactile qualities of woven cloth and knitted fabric, their physicality and relationship to everyday lives as protection, warmth, and adornment, humanize textile as a medium above all others. Textiles are close to us at all points in our existence; they are at our beginning and at our end. We have an inherent subconscious affinity with textiles and understanding of them through their place in our daily lives. As a medium textile was an ideal conduit to help extend public knowledge of the scientific research and make this more accessible to a range of audiences. Each designer's response was informed by the Institute's research and dialogue with one or more cancer patients and their lived experience of the disease. This discussion led to the author designing the textile pieces *Signalling Networks*, *We've Come a Long Way*, and *Writing an End to Cancer* as scarves. This utilized the unique position of cloth to carry its message on the body into a range of contexts in the future, humanizing the research, and becoming conversation pieces to enable the future wearer to explain the meaning held in the artifact. This would extend its dissemination beyond the exhibition, changing contextual paradigms of meaning by moving the science from the laboratory/consultation room, into the gallery, and onto the street. As scarves, they could be kept as both live everyday objects and as archival pieces and heirlooms for future generations.

Across the exhibition the textiles acted as catalysts to activate conversations in a different way to other media; their surfaces, folds and stitches could be observed but also handled. Making links between the research and the artifacts, a viewer could bring sight, knowledge, and touch together to inform their interpretative response to each work.

The author's second print design *We've Come a Long Way* (Andrew 2016) incorporated imagery to communicate the advances made since the early days of medicine through to discoveries made by CRUK researchers leading to more personalized cancer treatments. The design

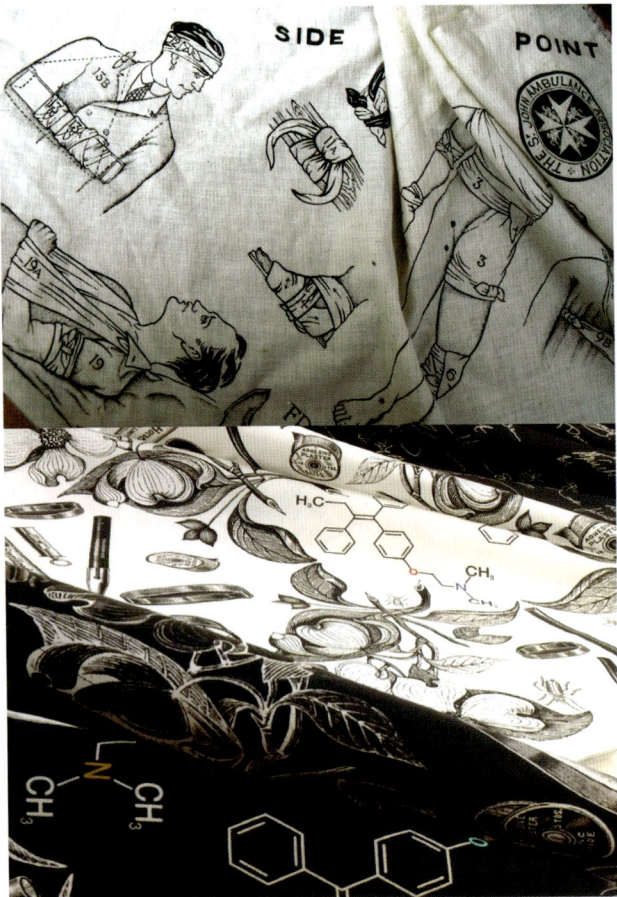

Figure 15.1 Above: detail from St John's Ambulance printed textile sling (First World War). Below: detail from "We've Come a Long Way", 1 × 1 meter square reactive dye digital prints on silk twill. © Sonja Andrew.

incorporated a range of images from medical history; from the days of using sterilized horsehair for suture, to the chemical structure for the breast cancer drug Tamoxifen, with compositional parallels to printed instructional slings used in the First World War.

The scope of the design and its figurative content enabled the textile to be a less literal but also a less entropic record, with potential for wider communication through the visual content of the cloth alone. It contained figurative imagery such as test tubes, adhesive plaster rolls, and petri dishes that were communicatively "redundant," operating via well recognized cultural codes of science and medicine recognizable to a non-specialist audience. These were incorporated into the composition alongside other historical laboratory, diagnostic, and surgical equipment that were more specialized, such as albuminometers and pulse glasses. These images had a greater degree of semiotic entropy but contributed to the connotations of "history of medicine" and "history of science" when viewed in conjunction with the more contemporary laboratory equipment incorporated in the design. During the textile development, an investigation of "Materia Medica" led to medicinal plants and insects also forming part of the composition. The chemical structure for Tamoxifen was positioned at the center of the black-and-white design and was the only element of the composition that incorporated any color. Alongside information from CRUK about the history of Tamoxifen development and their ongoing research to combat breast cancer, a full description of the meaning of each image component in the composition was included. Descriptive text, links, and supporting information on the scientific research from the CRUK Manchester Institute accompanied all the exhibition artifacts by each artist. Due to the complexities of the science informing each piece, the cloth could not stand alone as a record in an exhibition aimed at public engagement with the science and developing the public's understanding of CRUK's research. Juxtaposing textiles based on individual patient narratives with pieces designed to trigger dialogue on the discoveries made to improve cancer diagnosis and treatment, the traditional combination of artifact accompanied by explanatory exhibition text had to be maintained to fulfill the Institute's aim of highlighting the science of cancer treatments, and individual experiences of cancer. A "meet the artist and scientist" public engagement event was also arranged during the exhibition period, so the relationship between the textile artifacts and the science that informed them, could be explained further. *The Fabric of Research* exhibition was held as part of Manchester's European City of Science (ECOS) events, forming part of the Science in the City festival that aimed to encourage people to explore the connections between science and their lives via a range of activities and exhibitions. This wider context also primed the public with an expectation of learning about science through the artifacts on display at *The Fabric of Research* exhibition.

In both the CRUK and the Creative Labs projects, several trial textile samples were created, but digital design was prioritized over physical sampling to develop a range of textile concepts to share with the science teams. On a practical level, this enabled multiple image and color modifications and also scaling up ideas to digitally present the textiles in images of physical contexts for discussion. This approach reduced cloth usage and the environmental impacts of multiple screen-printing processes that would usually have been trialed as samples in several colorways over digitally printed base cloths, prior to production of final artifacts. Time that would have been spent on physical sample production could also be reallocated to digital design trials, designing prints and simulating fabric manipulations. Digital development also enabled a layering process. Proposals for textiles were developed whereby a digitally printed base cloth would be the carrier for the first layer of meaning, over which further communicative elements could be added via methods such as stitch, screen printing, bonding, heat transfer, or image projection.

As much of the practice existed in a digital-only format, this created its own form of hyperreality, a digital "simulacra" (Baudrillard 1994). And this approach relied on tacit knowledge of the physical textile processes and their likely outcomes in order to digitally articulate the results of layering image, color, and surface treatments effectively as design proposals for textiles that could eventually be physically produced. This was particularly relevant in the Creative Labs project. Knowledge of the likely contraction of the fabric surface if print media was applied to stretch fabrics under tension was needed, and the parameters for heat setting to achieve regular undulating surfaces, before embarking on digital simulations of these effects. Prior knowledge of how digitally printed base colors would show through overprinted translucent dye pastes and semi-opaque pigments informed the transparency levels of image layers in the digital rendering as design concepts were developed.

Creative Labs: Biological Sciences 2nd Edition

In 2012 the University of Leeds Cultural Institute established the Leeds Creative Labs "through a belief that both artists and academics would benefit from the space and time needed to collaborate, and working without expectations leads to playful, creative exploration" (https://medium.com/cultural-institute). As an ongoing catalyst for arts–science collaboration, the Creative Labs process has led to new concepts and outcomes, with over 100 academics connected with creative professionals via the initiative. In the 2019 Creative Labs: Biological Sciences 2nd Edition, four artists were paired with science academics to engage in an initial meeting, three lab days and a sharing event, to explore how their divergent research and practice backgrounds might lead to new collaborations. It enabled both parties to discuss ideas without an agenda, gradually establishing the focus of their engagement. This open agenda, without expectation of a concluded outcome, has enabled the Creative Labs process to be one of true exploration, where ideas emerge, grow, diverge, and reconfigure through dialogue, observation, and sharing of ideas and practices between artist and scientist.

Paired with biophysicists, the author developed initial ideas for creative work in response to their protein experiments, positioning textiles within a communication paradigm to explore how the scientists' research could be visualized in 2D and 3D form. To inform this process, the author considered Thomas Kuhn's theories of episodic paradigm shifting in relation to revolutionary science (originally published in 1962), where the accepted model of diligent sequences of closed parameter laboratory experiments as a route to major scientific discovery are questioned. Were these dichotomous? Would collaboration with scientists working toward scientific breakthroughs enable an expression of both positions on the nature of scientific inquiry, within a textile practice framework? While the science formed the catalyst for the textile practice, the biophysicists were also "viewers" within the communication context of the textile explorations. They fulfilled a dual role of content provider and "informed audience," becoming part of the cycle of "reflection in action" (Schon 2000; Getzel and Csikszentmihalyi 1976) that informed the author's design explorations. Their reactions to the aesthetic results that evolved from the creative interpretation of their research provided intermediate perceptions on the meanings generated, enabling reflection on the communicative, material, and aesthetic components of the textile practice, to inform development of the work.

Artist Meets Scientist

In the first Creative Labs meeting between artist and scientist, Professor Lorna Dougan, based in the School of

Physics and Astronomy, introduced proteins as the building blocks of biological systems, and how they could be assembled to create new materials with existing or new functionality. This had parallels with textiles in that connections in networks were being examined, their architectures, and their mechanical properties (such as response to stretching). This initial meeting informed a series of experimental visual responses by the artist following origami principles, using paper and cloth to explore the concept of individual building blocks to create network structures. Experiments with printing stretch fabrics under tension were also trialed to create undulating surfaces of concave/convex patterns and concertina-like formations as components that might form a starting point to visually articulate the response to stretch in protein architectures. A sketchbook practice was initiated to record these initial physical experiments and the subsequent digital manipulations that demonstrated their potential for rescaling and application as installations within public spaces.

Kuhn (1996: 210) notes, "Scientific knowledge, like language, is intrinsically the common property of a group or else nothing at all. To understand it we shall need to know the special characteristics of the groups that create and use it." This became clear in practice when participating in the first full lab day with the biophysics team. Observing their experiments, listening to their explanations, and watching aspects of scientific hypotheses incrementally tested, some of the verbal and visual languages common to their discipline were demonstrated. A deeper understanding of the kinetic nature of proteins was formed—their shape and their movement, folding, and unfolding. Microfluidics and hydrogels were explained, alongside the role of amino acids, thermophilic (heat-loving), and cold-shock proteins and energy landscapes. The everyday experience of the scientists became clearer—estimations then experiments as a series of tests to eliminate a myriad of possibilities that edge slowly closer to narrowing down solutions to specific aspects of much larger interconnected problems. Due to the pace of the day and the array of experiment, demonstrated, the labs were documented using photography, thumbnail sketches, and written notes on site. These were translated into the sketchbook in the days that followed, transcribing information on the science and reflecting on its potential visual and tactile articulation through textile practice. The first day had revealed a plethora of multifaceted biophysics investigations and revealed some of the history of science that led to the development of the biophysics discipline. Fundamentally, a simplified 3D printed model of a 1G6P monomeric protein and links to modeling of protein structures (www.rcsb.org) presented their visual complexity, models that might be translated through combinations of intertwined ribbons, stitch, shibori, trapunto, or intricate light installations. Several of these processes were trialed digitally and the biophysics team responded well to the idea of digital design experimentation as a series of tests of creative concepts. As knowledge of the work of the biophysics team grew, this necessitated a rethink on the organized pattern formations of the folding/unfolding origami structures and sculptural printing experiments generated in response to the initial meeting conversations. More significantly, the question remained as to which of the diverse range of biophysics experiments would form the focus for further textile exploration in the Creative Labs process, or if aspects of contemporary biophysics and their historical antecedents could be communicated through a final textile artifact? If this was the aim, what communicative record could cloth form that traced the historical experiments and breakthroughs underpinning contemporary biophysics? Kuhn's writing on the structure of scientific revolutions would suggest that any attempt to visualize these connections would inevitably misrepresent the complexity of the growth of scientific disciplines.

Paradigms of Science

Kuhn (1996: 145) states, "Few philosophers of science still seek absolute criteria for the verification of scientific theories. Noting that no theory can ever be exposed to all possible relevant tests, they ask not whether a theory has been verified but rather about its probability in the light of the evidence that actually exists." He discusses how one science paradigm is replaced by another, as new theories create new paradigms and alignment to them. He suggests, "to be accepted as a paradigm, a theory must seem better than its competitors, but it need not, and in fact never does, explain all the facts with which it can be confronted" (Kuhn 1996: 18). He questions whether scientists really do "*see* different things when *looking at* the same sorts of objects" (Kuhn 1996: 120) or differ in their *interpretations* of the phenomena in question. He offers Galileo and

Aristotle as an example; noting that when viewing a swinging stone, "the first saw a constrained fall, the second a pendulum" (Kuhn 1996: 121), suggesting that the data scientists collect from the same object may vary, due to the interpretation of the data being contextualized within a predetermined scientific paradigm. There are parallels here with how a viewer might read art and textiles; the extent of the viewer's predetermined knowledge of different types of art/textile object, their expectations of how it may fit into a specific genre or predetermined history, and the contextual parameters imposed on where and how the viewing takes place (including virtual in addition to actual), influencing how the art/textile object is read. Kuhn notes:

> Science does not deal in all possible laboratory manipulations. Instead, it selects those relevant to the juxtaposition of a paradigm with the immediate experience that that paradigm has partially determined. As a result scientists with different paradigms engage in different concrete laboratory experiments. The measurements to be performed on a pendulum are not the ones relevant to a case of a constrained fall.
>
> **KUHN 1996: 126**

Questions about the likely outcomes of specific laboratory manipulations depend upon the existence of a paradigm, and "presuppose a world already perceptually and conceptually divided in a certain way" (Kuhn 1996: 129). Kuhn (1996: 189) notes that there are "time tested and group-licensed ways of seeing." This has commonality with art broadly, and "art textiles," where canons of practice are built, and their boundaries and the ways of reading the codified work within them, soon become firmly established. Kuhn (1996: 150) argues that for scientists to communicate fully, "one group or the other must experience a paradigm shift." Paradigm change is likely to result in receiving different answers, and it is this, he suggests, that brings about scientific revolutions and the growth of new disciplines.

Cloth as a Record of Developments in Biophysics?

Based on Kuhn's reflections on processes of discovery in science, a multitudinous interconnected network of historical and contemporary scientific experiments and advances led to the current investigations undertaken by the biophysics team. A single textile artwork could not form the plural text that would be required to create cloth as a communicative record reflecting this. Barthes describes an ideal text as a plural text, a "galaxy of signifiers" where "the networks are many and interact, without any one of them being able to surpass the rest . . . we gain access to it by several entrances, none of which can be authoritatively declared to be the main one, the codes it mobilizes extend as far as the eye can reach, they are indeterminable" (Barthes 1990: 5–6). Even a series of textile artworks to be read sequentially as interconnected visual narratives would not necessarily solve the problem, as Kuhn (1996: 140) notes there is an impression that "science has reached its present state by a series of individual discoveries and inventions that, when gathered together, constitute the modern body of technical knowledge" and there is a "persistent tendency to make the history of science look linear or cumulative, a tendency that even affects scientists looking back at their own research" (Kuhn 1996: 139). Kuhn also argues that this is not the way a science develops: "Many of the puzzles of contemporary normal science did not exist until after the most recent scientific revolutions. Very few of them can be traced back to the historic beginning of the science within which they now occur. Earlier generations pursued their own problems with their own instruments and their own canons of solution" (1996: 140). Through discussion with the biophysics team during the Creative Lab days, it became clear that while the field of biophysics emerged from the paradigm shifts that lead to a revolution in science thinking and approaches, one of the roots of contemporary biophysics *could* be traced back to a specific science history, one within the field of textile physics; notably William Astbury and his X-ray diffraction experiments with silk and wool.

The Impact of Astbury

On the second lab day the biophysics team explained the links between Astbury's early X-ray diffraction crystallography studies on the configuration of stretched and unstretched proteins in silk and wool, and their work on the functionality and properties of protein architectures in new materials. This link formed a new direction in the Creative Labs collaborative process—a tangible historical connection between biophysics and textiles that became the focus for further creative exploration. Science historian Dr. Kersten Hall (2018) notes that Astbury's investigations established him as an international authority on the study of biological fibers using X-rays, leading to molecular biology as a new scientific discipline to understand living systems and the shape of the giant molecules they were made from. Following up on Astbury's work via the University of Leeds International Textile Archive (ULITA), a series of his academic publications from the 1930s in the journals of *Nature* and the *Textile Institute* were located, with figures including X-ray photographs of wool, silk, ramie and rubber, and photomicrographs of hair cortical cells. These images formed the basis for further design and print experimentation, the emphasis of the textile practice on the relationship between Astbury's historical work and the biophysicists' contemporary science experiments, to visually overlay the scientific present on its foundations from the scientific past. This would create cloth as an entropic record—one that incorporated highly specialized imagery to create links between past and present without conveying this relationship as a linear timeline. In the short time frame of the Creative Labs process (three full lab days on campus between January and March 2019) this made sense as a starting point that could be explored further through future collaboration. The Creative Labs process was more about building connections, speculative dialogue, and developing ideas than the development of tangible artifacts (with or without a communication agenda). The range of science presented by the biophysics team over the three lab days provided starting points for years of textile practice exploration, so a particular focus had to be established that could be explored within the collaboration period. Delving further into the history of Astbury at ULITA revealed that earlier designers had been inspired by the science of X-ray crystallography. This included Tibor Reich, who trained in the textile department where Astbury was undertaking his molecular biology experiments. A Hungarian designer based in Britain, Reich was part of the 1951 Festival of Britain Pattern Group. The group decided on a theme relating to crystal structures for the festival, exhibiting printed and woven designs influenced by scientific advances of the period (Powers, Hann and Cousens, 2009).

Before the final Creative Lab day, a series of digital experiments and printed textile samples were developed based on Astbury's work. Patterns based on the "pile of pennies" model (https://www.genome.gov/25520249) were trialed over digitally printed images of materials mounted in carriers for exploration by X-ray diffraction. The black-and-white images of X-ray photographs of wool, silk, ramie and rubber, and the photomicrographs of hair cortical cells were digitally enlarged, with gradual color adjustments to enhance the visual data in the image.

Further Outcomes

In addition to textile practice, the Creative Lab days provided opportunities to share and discuss ideas for science communication to the general public. By pairing science specialists with a designer in these conversations, new ways of communicating complex concepts to non-specialist audiences could be developed. A range of ideas evolved around public participation, such as joining together a range of component textile pieces in gallery/museum spaces to create interactive large-scale soft sculptures that followed the principles of protein formation. Specific ideas were also developed for work with primary schools, where the basics of protein formation could be demonstrated with pupils taking an active role by acting as the component parts in protein chains. This included activities for school assembly halls, outdoors, and also in the pool during swimming lessons, where other principles such as Brownian motion could also be explained, with pupils moving together through the water in different ways to explore this.

One of the unexpected outcomes of the Creative Labs process from the author's perspective was the amount of writing undertaken. A basic understanding of the science research information communicated at each lab day was recorded in the sketchbook, later following up links to research online, plus cataloguing and annotating digital material from the biophysics team, and the Astbury historical information from ULITA, to form a digital bank of text and images. Notes on ideas for textile practice in response to this information were made and then verbally shared with the biophysics team for feedback to inform the practice development. Digital composition methods helped to

Figure 15.2 Experiments with digital color adaptions and overprinting incorporating William Astbury's photomicrographs of hair cortical cells and X-ray crystallography images of silk, wool and rubber, 2019. © Sonja Andrew.

both with and beyond the scientific community" (https://medium.com/cultural-institute).

Summary

As scientists develop different methodologies within different paradigms on their paths to discovery, multiple readings are created within different sectors of science, and different approaches to communicating their work are established. Much like artists and designers, to progress forward, the scientists' explorations move to and fro between concrete and non-concrete—between fact, postulations, interpretations, and extrapolations. It can be argued that the scientists' modeling of a theory is a visualization that is not concrete; it is interpretive, and a new visual semantic is overlaid at any point a visual interpretation of science fact is created.

As an artist creating work based on each team's experimental explorations in the CRUK and Creative Labs projects, I was visually re-encoding evidence that had already been encoded via its original form of visual documentation. Scientists are still interpreters of their data, and that data may have already passed through several visual forms. When an artist then reinterprets this, they are developing a third or fourth generation translation with new layers of signification added through the medium and processes of making. Layers of meaning via material, aesthetic, realization as an artifact and contextualization in a space, are constructed beyond the relationship between the science imagery incorporated, developing further paradigms of signifiers from which viewers draw their cues to interpret the work. In the CRUK project there was an inbuilt redundancy to the work, due to being displayed with accompanying text and both artists and scientists being present at a public engagement event to discuss the work. The empiricism of the science was there, but also a visual narrative that engaged people with the science material, representing the facts via the visual to connect with the public—a view–read–talk engagement. The focus of the exhibition was on the science fact but included pieces in relation to people and their stories, with dialogues that brought in personal experience, and therefore subjectivity. In the Creative Labs collaboration the dialogue developed around our relative positions as scientists and artist, the visual practice as "findings" from the

visualize several concepts, without having to realize them physically via textile sampling. Due to the time constraints of the Creative Labs period, not every idea could be articulated visually (either digitally or via physical textile sample production), so writing then sharing ideas verbally also helped to work through possibilities. For example, a range of ideas for using thermochromic, photochromic, and UV printing were developed in response to information on thermophilic, cold-shock, and fluorescent proteins. Professor Lorna Dougan from the 2019 Creative Labs project notes: "Our collaboration with textile artist Dr Sonja Andrew began with Creative Labs and our mutual interest in materials design. This has grown into a powerful, curiosity-driven partnership with new projects continually emerging and exciting opportunities to engage dialogue, exploring what could be communicated. The ideas generated aimed to engage audiences with science via forms of visual crafting; material and form increasing accessibility to the science, rather than using more traditional forms of science documentation to communicate with audiences. In both projects, the materiality and mobility of textiles underpinned their communicative potential and ability to enable dialogue. Artifacts across *The Fabric of Research* exhibition particularly relied on the physicality of textiles to both engage audiences and function as a multimodal form of communication with them through the interplay of image, color, texture, and form.

Textile as a medium is both ordinary and extraordinary, in a dialogic pluralism it can animate concepts and their signification in a physical form, making meaning tangible and taking a message out into multiple real-world contexts. However, this physicality does not discount the increasing role of the digital in textile practice. As noted earlier in this chapter, working digitally in the development stages of projects that require physical textile outcomes can help navigate both time and production constraints. Where the likely outcomes of processes are already known through tacit knowledge and prior experimentation, the removal of raw materials, equipment and processing at the test stages can provide multiple sustainability benefits. Digital design can also allow concepts to be easily shared and alternative ideas to emerge, such as potential for projections of large-scale textiles as opposed to physical installations. While visual changes to textile concepts can be made quickly via design software, future advances in VR and the tactile and kinesthetic feedback technology in haptic gloves may soon be able to make the weight, drape and texture of fabric and cloth almost tangible. However, we do need to question if textiles lose any of their meaning in this simulation, becoming incidental not intrinsic through the hyperreality of digitization. Are we reducing the signification of physical textiles or are we transforming them via our readings of their virtual form, mediating our relationship with materials in a new way and adding another modality to textiles as a communicative medium?

Acknowledgments

Professor Lorna Dougan and her team, School of Physics and Astronomy, University of Leeds. Steve Bagley, Head of Visualisation Irradiation & Analysis, and Dr. Pedro Torres-Ayuso, Postdoctoral Scientist, Signalling Networks in Cancer Lab, Cancer Research UK Manchester Institute.

References

Andrew, S. (2013), "The Medium Carries the Message? Perspectives on Making and Viewing Textiles", *The Journal of Visual Arts Practice*, 12 (2): 195–221.

Andrew, S. (2014), "Image and Interpretation: Encoding and Decoding a Narrative Textile Installation", *The Journal of Textile Design Research and Practice*, 2 (2), 153–86.

Barthes, R. (1990), *S/Z*, Oxford: Blackwell. Originally published in French as *S/Z*, 1973, by Editions du Seuil, Paris. Translation 1974 by Farrar, Strauss and Giroux, Inc.

Baudrillard, J. (1994), *Simulacra and Simulations*. Originally published in French as *Simulacra et Simulation* by Editions Galilee, 1981. Translation by Sheila Faria Glaser, 1994, University of Michigan Press.

Baudrillard, J. (2015), *Jean Baudrillard: From Hyperreality to Disappearance: Uncollected Interviews*, Edinburgh: Edinburgh University Press.

Blow, N. (2009), "Changing the colour of MRI", *Nature*, 458: 926.

Getzel, J. and Csikszentmihalyi, M. (1976), *The Creative Vision: A Longitudinal Study of Problem Finding in Art*, New York: John Wiley and Sons.

Hall, K. (2018) *The Man in the Monkeynut Coat*, Oxford: Oxford University Press.

Hu, J., Peng, X. and Xu, Z. (2012), "Study of gray image pseudo-color processing algorithms, *6th International Symposium on Advanced Optical Manufacturing and Testing Technologies (AOMATT 2012)*", vol. 8415.

Ihde, D. (1998), *Expanding Hermeneutics, Visualism in Science*, Illinois: NorthWestern University Press.

Ihde, D. (2021), *Material Hermeneutics, Reversing the Linguistic Turn*, London: Routledge.

Isa, A. et al. (2021), "Pseudo-colour with K-means Clustering Algorithm for Acute Ischemic Stroke Lesion Segmentation in Brain MRI", *Pertanika Journal of Science & Technology*, 29 (2): 743–57.

Kuhn, T. (1996), *The Structure of Scientific Revolutions*, 3rd edn, Chicago: The University of Chicago Press.

Luthman, A. et al. (2017), "Fluorescence hyperspectral imaging (fHSI) using a spectrally resolved detector array", *Journal of BioPhotonics, Special Issue: In vivo Optical Imaging/Intravital Microscopy*, 10: 6–7.

Powers, K., Hann, M. and Cousens, J.A. (2009), Patterns of Culture, Tibor Reich: A Life of Colour and Weave', Ars Textrina, 39 (Monograph).

Schneider, A and Feussner, H. (2017), *Biomedical Engineering in Gastrointestinal Surgery*, London: Elsevier Inc.

Schon, D. (2000), *The Reflective Practitioner: How Practitioners Think in Action*, Aldershot: Ashgate/ARENA.

Waterhouse, D. (2017), "Beyond Colour Vision—spotting cancer when it hides between the red, green and blue", *Cancer Research UK: Cancer News,* March 14, 2017. Available online: https://news.cancerresearchuk.org/2017/03/14/beyond-colour-vision-spotting-cancer-when-it-hides-between-the-red-green-and-blue/ (accessed March 4, 2022).

Williamson, S. et al. Vasculogenic mimicry in small cell lung cancer. *Nat Commun* 7, 13322 (2016).

O: Sparking Innovation in Materials Research. Available online: https://medium.com/cultural-institute/sparking-innovation-in-materials-research-through-creative-collaborations-c3e5b0fd2e7a (accessed April 5, 2022).

O: 1G6P Solution NMR structure of the cold-shock protein from the hyperthermophilic bacterium Thermogata Maritima. Available online: https://www.rcsb.org/structure/1G6P (accessed January 25, 2019).

O: 1943: X-Ray Diffraction of DNA. Available online: https://www.genome.gov/25520249/online-education-kit-1943-xray-diffraction-of-dna (accessed April 13, 2022).

"The process of transformation can begin, at first within, for we cannot immediately change the world. We need to co-create a future based on values, people, and planet."

Carmen Hijosa

16

Piñatex®, A New Material for a New World

CARMEN HIJOSA

Introduction

This is a personal account of the ways in which the Piñatex® endeavor was gestated. The profound emotional and haptic response to making of cloth while working in Bolivia with weavers and spinners informed the subsequent development and focus of the Piñatex® project. This initiative developed a new material made from locally sourced agricultural waste materials in the Philippines and this invention formed the basis for the launch of the company Ananas Anam Ltd in 2010. The company seeks to promote the production and use of sustainable materials and support the local communities at the heart of the production process.

As I write, huge swathes of the planet are threatened under record-breaking heatwaves with wildfires that are visible from space, with a third of Pakistan flooded, affecting 33 million people. In the same year, 2022, the worst drought in forty years in Eastern Africa has the potential to propel 20 million people into severe hunger. Textile production and the appetite for Western consumption has contributed to these catastrophic events. It is in this context that the textile industry needs to examine more deeply how resources are extracted, how land is used and, most importantly, how to regenerate land that is severely damaged by over production and chemical use. As we enter this transition period to more sustainable methods, everyone in the textile world needs to ask some fundamental questions: How are we going to produce the number of natural fibers needed for our increasing population and decreasing land availability; What will it take to ease out the use of petroleum-based fibers in order to stop polluting our planet?

The challenge is great and the potential to change the world is greater. Partnerships, collaborations, sound policies and standards based on sustainability imperatives, building the right value chains, designing for disassembly, and land regeneration are key to this sustainable progress. We must start at a local and personal level by changing ourselves and our behaviors with regard to environmental challenges. Paul Hawken, using the lens of business, states, "To create an enduring society, we will need a system of commerce and production where each and every act is inherently sustainable and restorative. Business will need to integrate economic, biologic, and human systems to create sustainable methods of commerce" (Hawken 1993: xiv).

A restorative economy will have as its hallmark a business community that co-evolves with the natural and human community it serves. According to Hawken, not only do business and industry form the principal instruments of global destruction, they are also the only institutions large enough, wealthy enough, pervasive, and powerful enough to lead humankind out of the present situation.

In the 1990s I found myself working in the Philippines with the Product Development and Design Center Philippines (PDDCP). My mandate was to upgrade the design, quality, and manufacturing of leather-good fashion accessories "that would help to break into higher added value markets" and "possess some uniqueness that would be seen as 'Filipino' (Hijosa 2015: 53–4), making them ready for the export market. This role came about from the experience I had designing, manufacturing, and selling leather goods through my previous company in Ireland. I had a desire to research indigenous natural materials, traditions, and craftmanship and understand how local communities used their own resources. I discovered that the best quality bags being made in the Philippines "were manufactured using imported materials, especially leather" (Hijosa 2015: 54). It became apparent to me that what I could help with was not within the given brief and that natural indigenous fibers and textiles, not imported leather, were the path to new beginnings. It was then that I let go of working with leather and started to focus on natural fibers. My social and environmental awareness made this jump an obvious step, albeit not an easy one as sustainability was not yet in people's minds.

I started working with local communities, designers, researchers, weavers, and scientists to explore the potential of using alternative raw materials that would be suitable for international markets. Work with local leather tanneries and producers of leather goods highlighted "that there was a need to re-consider alternative sources of raw materials which would be local, readily available and not dependent on skills, chemical products and technology coming from outside the Philippines" (Hijosa 2015: 54). Slowly, a new world opened up, filled with natural fibers with names that were a mystery to me: buntal, abaca, rattan, pineapple leaf fibers; and natural dyes from trees like Sibukaw and Talisay, Annatto seeds, and indigo leaves.

BACKGROUND

I came into the textile world in my thirties while I was a consultant for the World Bank in the early 1990s, having built a small but successful leather fashion accessory brand in the late 1980s in Ireland. As part of this consultancy, I worked with indigenous communities, such as the Quechua and Aimara in the Altiplano in Bolivia, where I first came into close contact with natural fibers. The women would make threads and cords with a spindle from bundles of brown, soft llama wool. Considered the first art form in the region, cloth has possessed unparalleled importance in the Andes since the second millennium BCE.

My contribution was to develop products for the market in collaboration with these communities, which drew upon sustainable methods and supported the sustenance of the rich culture in textiles. The emphasis was on the use of natural materials, traditions, craftmanship, and how the locals used their own resources. On one of my trips to visit the weavers and dyers I wrote in my notes: "Design is a connecting tool between people, economics and the environment—and out of this communion, understanding and respect, new ideas and products with integrity can come about." Reflecting on my in-situ experiences during this time, I came to realize that the fundamental question was: How can we evolve as designers, makers, manufacturers without destroying and undervaluing local traditions and skills, without taking away their integrity and connection with their very founders: the people who brought these traditions, values, and knowledge this far into the twenty-first century? I was conscious that we needed to do this with respect for what has been developed already, sustaining dignity, livelihood, and cultures, while adjusting to the needs of today's commercial and ever-growing materialistic societies. To realize this vision there was a need for understanding, empathy, and admiration for what has been developed at a local, regional, and national scale, while guiding this transformation into a contemporary expression that does not violate the makers' acquired abilities, but helps to bring them, alongside their livelihood, into the demands of our present times. These accumulated experiences of deep respect for people and the natural world prepared the ground for Piñatex®, a new textile that would become a pioneer plant-based textile in the natural fiber and textile world. It grew out of these perceptions and collaborations. Piñatex® opened the door to a new sustainable approach to textile manufacture by introducing alternative plant-based, agricultural waste fibers into the global fiber markets and led to the formation of the company Ananas Anam in 2010.

ANANAS ANAM'S MISSION STATEMENT

> Ananas Anam is a company oriented to an ethical, human responsible and environmentally smart business growth.
>
> Ananas Anam aims to meet the challenges of our times by developing products in which commercial success is integrated with, and promotes, social, environmental and cultural development.
>
> **HIJOSA, 2015: 166**

The company and its goals were further developed through an incubator program, Innovation RCA, which was supported by the James Dyson Foundation within the Royal College of Art and Design, London, for which I was awarded a Ph.D. in 2015 (Ananas Anam website, n.d.). As stated in my doctoral thesis: "The mission statement of Ananas Anam is the result of my experience of working in the Philippines, where I first became aware of my responsibility as a designer, with design becoming a connecting tool between people, technology and the raw natural materials I was working with" (2015: 166). The vision for Ananas Anam came about as a direct result of these experiences, driven by a desire "to develop a business proposition that would encompass people, economy and the land" (Hijosa, 2015: 166). At the heart of these principles is this sentiment from philanthropist Jochen Zeist:

> Sustainability does not need to come at the sacrifice of economic prosperity. Through projects that balance conservation, community, culture, and commerce, I hope to encourage a new model for sustainable development: one that shows how working toward ecosphere safety can be commercially viable. I am convinced that if revenues generated by the success of these inclusive, holistic approaches are poured back into the Whole—the holistic system involving the entire sum of its parts—they can help to safeguard natural resources, enhance the livelihoods of communities, and promote sustainable economic development.
>
> **ZEITZ Foundation 2010: online**

This echoes the words of Hawken, who states that "[a] restorative economy will have as its hallmark a business community that co-evolves with the natural and human communities it serves" (Hawken 1993: 159). At the heart of Ananas Anam is a commitment to promote "a more sustainable lifestyle" through increasing the use of nature-based systems that positively impact communities (Hijosa 2015: 166).

In the development of Piñatex®, the use of a conceptual model based on "The Upstream and Downstream Model of Sustainable Design" (Wahl and Baxter, 2008), enabled the linking of personal experiences with more ethical considerations, including ecological and social values. It is the understanding of the flow along the *Upstream* and *Downstream* pathways, which express the sharing of knowledge across disciplines, that has underpinned this work. In the *Upstream* I "interacted with academics, scientists, researchers, chemists, visionary leaders and business mentors" (Hijosa 2015: 171). This "broadened my vision to encompass a varied sets of values, concepts and new knowledge" (2015: 171). This included harnessing different forms of knowledge from "scientific expertise on how to treat and process natural fibre" through to an increased understanding of the legal processes involved in protecting my own work, and recognizing "the importance of collaborative agreements amongst the different stakeholders" (2015: 171). In addition, realistic business proposals and routes to market were built through entrepreneurial skills learned through mentoring via the Imperial College Business School and Innovation RCA, London. Practical tools that linked "the economic side of the project to the social and ecological responsibilities" (2015: 171) were brought about through the practical knowledge offered through Cradle-to-Cradle design principles.

In the *Downstream*, interactions with farmers and farming cooperatives enabled insights into "what it means to grow and take care of nature" (2015: 172). I also connected with "fibre processors, makers and manufacturers, with whom I share the common language of making and material knowledge, through which the logistics of the value chain from fibre to product [became] clear and real" (2015: 172). Finally, "potential clients in this business-to-business model" (2015: 172) validate the process through bringing the product to the end users and customers.

THE BIRTH OF PIÑATEX®

Throughout my doctoral thesis are reflective segments that draw upon personal thoughts and experiences, all of which shaped my ongoing interactions with the world, my personal and professional life. Here I share some of those reflections on my experiences in the Philippines:

> During my consultancy work with the Product Development and Design Center Philippines (PDDCP), we did a lot of travelling around the Philippines, mainly to source and see natural fibres and work with weavers. Fe Gonzalez, head of the R&D department in the Centre, was my constant companion. In one of the trips and while visiting some weavers, we had to walk through a path cut in the jungle. At one point and while keenly observing our surroundings, Fe bent down and picked up what looked like a grass to me. Twisting it around her fingers and seeing that it had good flexibility and strength she commented: Carmen, I wonder what we can do with this? Let's bring some back to the laboratory and see if we can extract some fibres from it. This keen observation and comment from my colleague brought to me a new way of thinking; nothing is just a grass, everything may be used, we are surrounded by potential, we just have to learn to see things through their inherent qualities and what it may bring to the communities living in those surroundings. Ever since, I have become a keen observer of nature, not just for its beauty, but for the potential it carries to become our ally and sustainer. The seed planted by Fe in my mind that hot and humid day in the middle of the jungle in the Philippines has sprouted and given fruit; my reverence to local intelligence and skills, admiration for the potential that nature has to offer has been with me ever since.
>
> **HIJOSA 2015: 83**

Through my work with the Design Centre Philippines, we used to travel and visit different weaving communities to work and co-develop textiles made from natural fibres, one of these being PALF [Pineapple leaf fibres]. In one of our trips, we visited the weavers of Aklan, the birthplace of the hand-extracted pineapple fibres and of piña hand-woven textiles. India de la Cruz Legaspi, owner of one of the main weaving centres, showed me some of her heirloom clothing made with piña cloth—this was the first time I heard pineapple textiles called this way. Ms Legaspy made a comment: "It was your ancestors the Spanish that showed us how to do it!"

I felt at once that this piña cloth was somehow the link between the past and the present, between the weavers in Aklan and my own professional life. Little did I know at that time that years later I would end up concentrating on this fibre for quite a different use—but somehow that first impression of beauty, fluidity and sheen characteristic of the piña cloth remained with me and started the thinking process to what was to become Piñatex a few years later. (2015: 105)

THE CRADLE-TO-CRADLE APPROACH

The development of Piñatex was rooted in "Cradle-to-Cradle [C2C] design principles, which support ecological, intelligent and innovative design within today's economic environment" (Hijosa 2015: 155). These principles have been employed throughout the design and development stages "taking into account the consequential effects of such designs" (2015:159), both within the natural world and society, and have been put into practice when planning production processes as the product became commercially viable. "The evolution of Piñatex thus is the result of the interdependence of several resources and processes along its life cycle ... from the farm to the products made, to the final disposal of these products" (2015: 159).

Piñatex® is a pioneering plant-based textile made from pineapple leaf fibers, a by-product of the pineapple harvest. It can be used as a sustainable and natural alternative to leather and petroleum-based textiles for use in the fashion, accessory, interior, and automotive markets. "Piñatex® was born out of teamwork, sensory experiences, human experiences, and a close and deep respect for nature. Nature is the common denominator in all. The inspiration is rooted in nature, 'steeled' so to speak by science and C2C design inspiration. It is then interwoven into a rich tapestry, which includes people, places, and experiences" (2015: 153). Piñatex® opened the door to a new dimension in the world of textiles by introducing alternative plant-based, agricultural waste fibers into the global fiber production market. Today this market is still dominated by non-renewable, fossil-based synthetic fibers, with a cotton monopoly in the global fiber production as evidenced stated by the Fibral Material Alliance,[1] with over 26 million tonnes of global fiber production being derived from cotton in 2020.

This new world of alternative textile materials and processes is rapidly—and excitingly—opening up to much-needed change. A new wave of material innovation, and new chemical compounds, is bringing about new solutions and new processes, driving the need for change in today's fashion and textile worlds. Plant-based and agricultural waste-based new textiles, which come under the biobased materials category, are being joined by textiles grown from live microorganisms, such as bacteria, yeast, algae, and fungi root structures, widening this new door to alternative materials, which, in turn, are opening up and delivering new products into the marketplace, such as biofabricated textiles (Biofabricate and Fashion for Good 2020). This next wave of materials innovation is strengthened by Engineering Biology (industrialized synthetic biology), with companies such as Cambrium,[2] which is harnessing nature's protein building blocks to create plant-based collagen and engineering proteins at scale. The list and complexity of materials grows every day!. It is the hope of all material innovators that this common ground and drive will further enhance innovation partnerships between different stakeholders, driving forward the adoption of much needed solutions in the textile world.

For this brave new textile world to grow, time is needed. Perseverance is another quality also needed, but most important, in my experience, is the development of close collaborations and partnerships. Material innovators with established brands, have the power and responsibility to encourage and support needed changes and bring them to the end consumer. In these collaborations, transparency and trust is critical. Most times there is a "David," bringing innovation, ideas and a vision for a better world into the market place, and there is a "Goliath," needing new ways, new materials, but caught up in complex value chains, led by obsolete and unsustainable systems, which, in many cases, puts profit before people and planet. In this ever expanding and complex textile world of "sustainability" mired with green washing, a change is needed, and a change is coming.

The next and critical stage of any manufacturing, the elephant in the room of sustainability, is value chains and systems. Piñatex®, as a natural and versatile material, provides alternative to leather within fashion, accessory, and upholstery markets, and its ability to be mass-produced makes it a "cost-effective textile proposition" (Hijosa 2015: 154). The pineapple leaves from which it is produced are a by-product of pineapple harvesting for the food industry. Fibers from these leaves (PALF) are extracted from the Ananas Comosus plant of the Bromeliaceous family "by hand scraping, decortication or retting" (2015: 106)—the former two methods more generally. The qualities of PALF make it suitable "for making the nonwoven substrate, which forms the base" (2015: 106) of Piñatex®. A patented technology is then used to protect both the process and the finished material. As a by-product, pineapple leaves are "available in abundance for industrial purposes without any additional use of land, water, fertilizers and/or pesticides. However, extracting fibre from the leaves requires space, water and energy" (2015: 106).

Natural fibers can be defined as "long, thin strands which are directly obtainable from an animal, vegetable, or mineral source and convertible into nonwoven fabrics such as felt or paper" or woven into cloth after being spun into yarn (Hijosa 2015: 65).

Cellulose fibres are categorized by the part of the plant used: seed, stem or leaf. Cotton is a seed fibre, a fibre that grows within a pod or boll from developing seeds. Flax, hemp and ramie are bast fibres, from the stem of the plant. Leaf fibres are removed from the veins or ribs of a leaf. Pineapple leaves or piña fibres, sisal (a type of agave plant) and abaca (from the banana tree family) are examples of leaf fibres.

2015: 66

When I invented and developed Piñatex®, pineapple leaf fibers had been traditionally used in the Philippines from the eighteenth century, made into exquisite hand-woven textiles. Piña cloth made from pineapple leaf fibers has been part of the most precious heirlooms in Filipino

Figure 16.1 *No. 1 Piñatex® production line in Acabados Gonzalez*, 2019. © Carmen Hijosa, Founder, Ananas Anam. Photography: © Ananas Anam archives.

families for generations.³ At one point during my research I realized that these fibers could be used in a different way than the traditional manner used for centuries. The question: "What if . . . I make a mesh, not unlike leather and our skin with this fibre?" became the next threshold for the new to materialize.

THE PRODUCTION

The production of Piñatex® starts with the gathering of the pineapple leaves at the farm, "which is carried out by designated farming cooperatives" (Hijosa 2015: 154). As the harvest of the pineapples is already geared toward the food crop, the gathering of the leaves requires "no additional land, water, fertilizers or pesticides" (Hijosa 2015: 154). Production of the Piñatex substrate "goes from decortication of PALF fibres" to a degumming process and the consequent making of a nonwoven mesh or substrate" (2015: 154). A by-product of the decortication process is biomass, which can be "further converted into organic fertilizers and/or bio-gas" (2015: 154). This nonwoven substrate is "made into a versatile material, using specific coatings to meet the market requirements" (2015: 155).

Initially the Piñatex® range was divided into collections based upon the physical properties and aesthetic attributes achieved. Since its launch through Ananas Anam Ltd (www.ananas-anam.com), Piñatex® has expanded onto several more collections and extend onto different markets, improving its technical characteristics and haptics in response to increasing market demands. Some the original collections included *The Pinackpuck* Collection⁴, which used the symbol of a pineapple in its pattern using a traditional printed format, and *The Gamussa* Collection,⁵ which was soft and pliable with a flat finish. The latter came about through "experiments done with colour and texture" at the Royal College of Art and Design (RCA), London, "with the final finishing carried out at the Northampton Leather Technology Centre" (Hijosa 2015: 161). I envisaged the full project as a blueprint for bringing the knowledge developed to other pineapple-growing countries in the world such as India, Costa Rica, China, etc.

It took more than a decade to develop this new material from a mere idea to a prototype, a proof of concept, a working prototype to, eventually, a production prototype

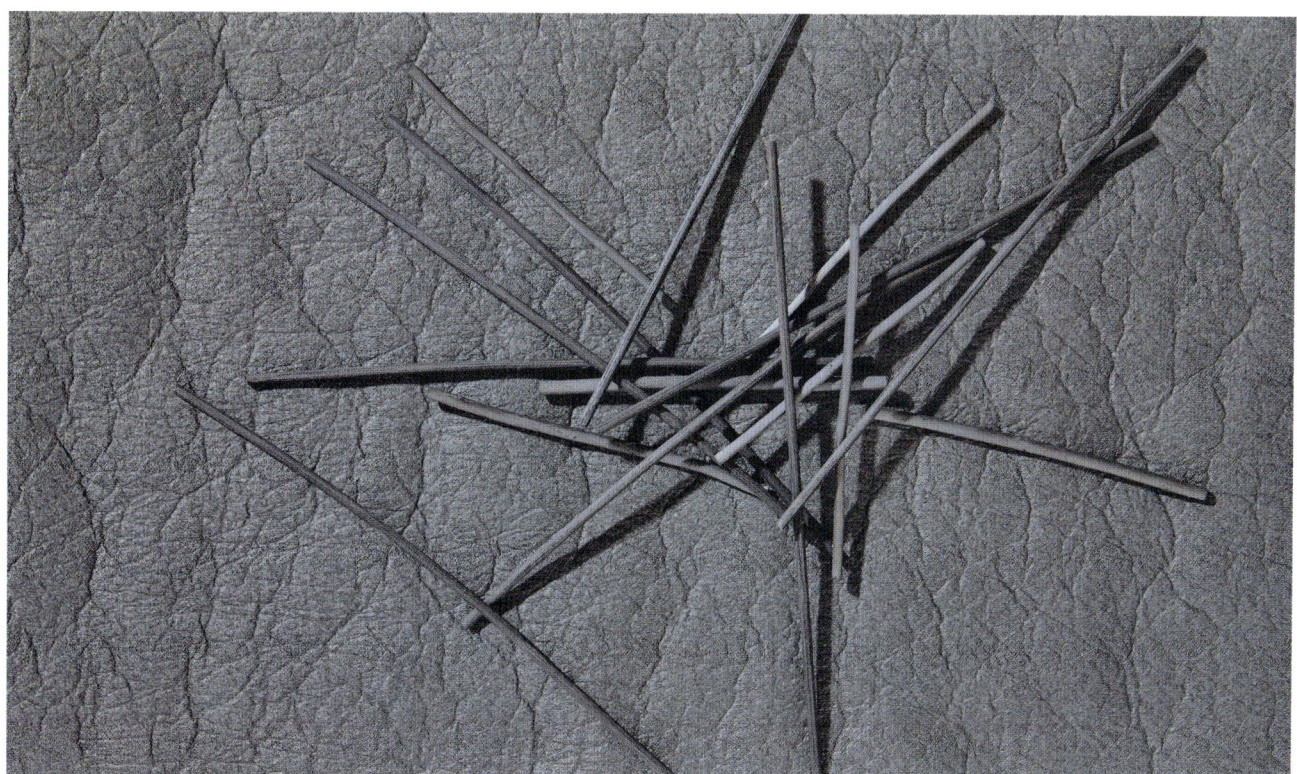

Figure 16.2 *Piñatex, charcoal (colour).* Photography: ©Ananas Anam UK Limited.

with scalable potential. The main reason for this length of time has been that there was no value chain in place to develop this new material industrially. Not only had we to develop a new material, but we also had to adapt and invent fiber extraction processes, build connections and collaborations with pineapple farming cooperatives, train workers, develop systems and quality control measures, and slowly we built a new value chain in an established industry: the textile industry.

The above experience gave us an insight and profound understanding into what it takes to develop a value chain, while becoming aware of the profound impact that a value chain has on people and planet. Every stage of a value chain is key to understanding, assessing, and taking on board as a personal responsibility, from small to big enterprises alike.

The days of shutting our eyes, ears, and hearts to the impact of value chains; the days of hiding behind obscure data, not easily understood by the end consumer with a lot of green washing going on, in the name of "sustainability," need to be over. Collaboration, mutual respect, and understanding is key. Textile companies and the fashion industry need to and are starting to grasp the responsibility we all have in the most critical part of a textile development: its value chain.

According to Textile Exchange La Rhea Pepper, co-founder and CEO (n.d.), engaging the full value chain from the field to the retailer is imperative because it truly takes everyone working in partnership to create transformative change. The whole model needs to be addressed. Trying to fix only one piece of it really does not address the interconnected and diverse problems. Businesses having collaborative relationships with their supply partners is imperative to bring about the necessary changes. A quote from George Monbiot sums up the challenge:

> With the exception of all-out nuclear war, all the most important issues that confront us are environmental. None of our hopes, none of our dreams, none of our plans and expectations can survive the loss of a habitable planet. And there is scarcely an Earth system that is not now threatened with collapse. . . . Above all, climate breakdown is gathering at shocking, unanticipated speed, with disasters occurring at 1.2°C of heating that scientists did not expect until we hit 2 or 3°.
>
> **2022: online**

We need to feel our responsibilities as members of planet Earth. The referenced data is shockingly true and with the enormity of the task, combined with the daily bombardment of data, it is easy to become blasé and overwhelmed. How can we become sympathizers and take action? In my view, we must learn to feel this as our individual responsibility and in the world of textiles, it should be an easy task, since we are clothed in them from the time we are born to the time we die.

FINAL REFLECTION

Ananas Anam's vision is to develop textiles and related products using processes that enhance the well-being of the Earth and its people through the entire life cycle of the products. Our inspiration was and continues to be the Cradle-to-Cradle approach, which supports ecological, intelligent, and innovative design policies within today's economic environment. In this light, Ananas Anam is a for-profit company with strong social responsibility and low environmental impact. The belief that I had at the start of this journey is the same today:

> [W]e must endeavor to open ourselves to humanity with the inner trust and conviction that what we do for the world has vast consequences in the world and in ourselves. The transformation we seek to better a particular world reality has also the potential to better ourselves. Let us find our own voices from within and then, with inner clarity and strength, move out into the world.
>
> **HIJOSA 2015: 184**

I would like to share the urge I feel to be more aware toward what is coming to us, a new threshold that needs to be adopted today if we are going to heal the rift between people and planet, and as a result continue holding our planet sacred, for it is the only home we have.

> Sustainability is not enough
> We must go further
> We must expand our vision to regenerative systems, regenerative industries, and regenerative policies.
> And we must achieve this by developing the inherent potential in every human and every living system.

We must only create initiatives, systems, and products with a humane agenda and a deep connection with the natural world and its preservation.

The task of everyone here is to envision this bold future in which the world turns on regenerative principles.

This is the new threshold.

And we must cross it together now.

Tackling these global and complex issues requires more than a shift in an individual's shopping habits, but it is a good start. It requires a system change to try to provide a circular, scalable fiber industry. Textiles made using leaves, fruits, or discarded agricultural waste may sound strange, but mountains of discarded clothing waste will hopefully become a memory from the past with the beginning of an environmental and social clothing shift (West 2021). For this to happen, businesses must take responsibility for their actions; governments need to provide incentives to allow companies to research alternative methods to create valuable products from their waste. The process of transformation can begin, at first within, for we cannot immediately change the world. We need to co-create a future based on values, people, and planet together, for evolution is a process of interaction.

At the outset of my research, I asked myself two questions: "What are the challenges in seeking to make a new and sustainable material from the waste products of pineapple agriculture in the Philippines?" and "How can a design practice link elements of materiality (artifacts) with immaterial elements (value systems) in order to improve sustainable social, ecological and economic development?" These questions are still the leading questions I live by as a textile designer, maker, and user. The looking in, and then outside ourselves and the consequences of our actions must lead the way, as we shift from sustainable practices to a regenerative world, as we create whole systems of mutually beneficial relationships.

WHERE IS ANANAS ANAM NOW?

It feels as though it is a long way from 2016, when the first Piñatex material was launched. Today, as I write at the close of 2022, Ananas Anam has grown from a thought process and a start-up to a well-known pioneer textile material company with an established value chain. It has subsidiaries in the Philippines and Spain while further expanding our value chain to enable us to work with pineapple growers in Bangladesh and Ivory Coast, as we cater for the increasingly growing market demands from fashion, interiors, and the car industry.

Ananas Anam and its subsidiaries give employment to over 320 people in the Philippines, mainly in the farming communities, and 130 in Bangladesh, directly having an impact on their livelihood and on the future of their communities. Our markets continue to expand, selling in eighty-two countries, with new products on the way, ongoing product research and development, and the improvement of technologies, both at the product level and at the supply-chain level.

In 2020 Ananas Anam become a B-Cop certified company and since then, we have published our *Impact Report*[6] annually, which echoes our commitment to the vision that ethics and business can be combined successfully. Winning international awards gives recognition to both the company and the product. Gaining key collaborations at local and international levels helps us to have a wider, positive social and economic impact among farming communities while continuously reducing our environmental footprint, valorizing waste at scale.

My personal commitment to share my vision and experiences remains high on my agenda. I spend a good part of my time doing this and explaining the purpose of my company via conferences, workshops, podcasts and media. The wish is to inspire others, in particular the younger generations, to understand that despite the challenges we encounter when we embark on a regenerative path, with determination and a clear vision and belief, we can make a difference in the world.

Notes

1. Fibral is an international Material Alliance that brings together companies and individuals working with ancient underrepresented and newly used plant-based fibers. See www.fibral.org.
2. See more at https://www.cambrium.bio/
3. Piña fabric was a luxury export from the Philippines during the Spanish colonial period and gained favor amongst European aristocracy in the eighteenth and nineteenth centuries.
4. "Pinackpuck means beaten cloth in Tagalog. This is in reference to the traditional technique employed in the Philippines to soften and make the hand-woven cloth more pliable by beating it with wooden mallets" (Hijosa 2015: 160).
5. "Gamussa in Tagalog means very soft leather cloth such as chamois or suede" (Hijosa 2015: 161).

6   Ananas Anam's 2021 *Impact Report* can be viewed via this link https://www.dropbox.com/s/kv3ft4q28yt5039/Ananas%20Anam%20Impact%20Report%202021.pdf?dl=0

References

Cambrium (n.d.) https://www.cambrium.bio/ (accessed August 20, 2022).

Biofabricate and Fashion for Good (2020) "UNDERSTANDING 'BIO' MATERIAL INNOVATION: a primer for the fashion industry". [Online] https://reports.fashionforgood.com/wp-content/uploads/2020/12/Understanding-Bio-Material-Innovations-Report.pdf (accessed December 18, 2022).

Hawken, P. (1993) *The Ecology of Commerce: A Declaration of Sustainability*, New York: Harper Collins Publishers, Inc.

Hijosa, C. (2015) "Piñatex, The Design Development of a New Sustainable Material", unpublished Ph.D. thesis, Royal College of Art, London https://researchonline.rca.ac.uk/1677/1/1.%20CARMEN%20THESIS%20FINAL%202015%20%281%29.pdf (accessed November 10, 2022).

Monbiot, G. (2022) "Earth is under threat, yet you would scarcely know it", *The Guardian*, September 30. [Online] Available at: https://www.theguardian.com/environment/2022/sep/28/guardian-climate-crisis- (accessed March 8, 2023)

Pepper, L. R. (n.d.) https://textileexchange.org/

West, A. (2021) "FIBER WORLD: Sustainable Alternative Plant Fibers for Textiles", Textile World, April 15. [Online] Available at: https://www.textileworld.com/textile-world/features/2021/04/fiber-world-sustainable-alternative-plant-fibers-for-textiles/ (accessed November 12, 2022).

Zeitz, J. (2010) "The Zeitz Foundation for Intercultural Ecosphere Safety", The Zeich Foundation. [Online] Available at: https://legendsandlegaciesofafrica.org/jochenzeitz.php (accessed May 7, 2023)

Artist Celia Pym in conversation with Lesley Millar

Part 2

LESLEY MILLAR

LM: When I look at your work, particularly with the clothing, I am reminded of the deep relationship between cloth and skin. It seems to me that the invisible mend is like the invisible tuck in the skin, the maintaining of the illusion of youth/being new. Whereas the visible mend, what you are dealing with, is so closely related to what happens to the body—every mark on the skin is a mark of life. What you do with the worn cloth is make that transparently visible.

CP: I completely agree! I've been thinking about this a lot. The thing about the skin is that it ages and we are often startled by aging. One day you wake up and look in the mirror and realize you look different. And it has happened without you noticing. And I think that is what cloth does . . . Of course it is different if it is an accident. I have seen people where the garments have been cut off them after a car crash or something and the damage is very different. That is not aging, that is an accident. A scar is a sharp line.

LM: I think it is most apparent in the Vivienne Leigh dress that you mended.

CP: Yes, when I researched the dress I was looking at pictures of her as a young, glamorous woman. Yet when I received the dress it was, well, dowdy. Of course, the fabric was gorgeous and the cut had an elegance to it, but the dress was so dark and so . . . un-fun . . . And so I thought of course when she had this dress she would have been an older woman. And I started looking at pictures of her as an older woman and there was a kind of mismatch. At that time movie stars were trying to fix themselves and hold on to their youth because once they were seen to be too old they disappeared. But I think cloth ages particularly beautifully, much in the same way that skin ages. And I think that is one of the reasons people can find textiles emotional, particularly clothing. You can see that relationship between the skin and the cloth, and that is what the mending brings to the forefront.

LM: I wonder how much does the idea of sustainability influence your way of working?

CP: Well, because of what I do, I often get invited to stand on platforms with, or give workshops alongside, those who are involved in sustainability. However, the conventional understanding of sustainability is not really what I am about. The way I think is that my work is concerned with emotional sustainability. The problems of mass consumption and all that goes with it are huge and I don't think that mending or fixing things is the solution. But I do think mending something enhances your relationship with that thing. And I believe there is a ripple effect, in that if you establish an emotional relationship with a thing, something, then you may find you have a different relationship with what you buy, and eventually, with the planet.

LM: How so? It seems a big leap.

CP: Because of that relationship, which has been slowly established between you and the thing. The way I work is very slow, very slow—and I think that act of slowing down shifts your perception of things, of time and how you use your time and that time potentially creates a different understanding about sustainability. Maybe shift people away from fast fashion and the quick fix. I love new things, I am not against new things, however what I am interested in, this emotional sustainability—actually I made the term up, I'm not sure if it exists—is that you are trying to pay attention, trying to make a relationship with what you already have, and you are doing it through the mending of what you have. And if you slow down you are forced to pay attention, be less speedy . . .

LM: How much have you thought about the current interest in the Japanese technique of mending ceramics: kintsugi? It is a very visible repair, as is your repair, but using gold, therefore the value lies as much in the gold as in the pot itself. In contrast, you use a very humble yarn to mend the things people bring to you.

CP: Yes. I often get paired up with someone giving a talk on kintsugi and I think as a technique it is absolutely stunning. But it is completely different from what I do. I find beauty in the ordinary, the everyday. I guess it comes back to the question of embellishment. The repair I make is not to make the thing precious in a monetary, gold kind of way. For me the joy lies in the wool thread, which I do select carefully. For example, the wool for Shetland jumpers has been specially bred for the purpose and it is my favorite wool. It is hairy and oily and the colors fit perfectly. If it is a bit scratchy at first, it becomes softer and comfortable with wearing. The hairy-ness is so practical as it keeps wind out. And I am attracted to that, to things that can withstand a bit of nature. I don't want my work, my mends to be held delicately. I like things that can go for a walk! Although I must confess that I did mend Vivienne Leigh's dress with a cashmere yarn! It was really nice to stitch with

Figure CP2 *Fraser's jacket* (detail), 2022. © Celia Pym. Photographer: ©Michele Panzeri.

that … and it felt like it matched the dress and the story of the dress: her, it being left in India at Ismail Merchant's house. I do like to find out where threads I use come from, what narrative they carry.

When I went to India for a conference a few years ago I made a point of learning about the Indian repair technique of Rafoogar. And those who practice this technique are called Rafoogari—Menders. Rafoogar is the most invisible mending of all, only for cashmere shawls, and I became thrilled by the specificity of this. Not that I wanted to become a Rafoogari or wanted to use their technique. But when I said that I was also a Mender I was introduced to these Menders. As we know, textiles—an interest, a personal practice—opens doors to places and people you might not otherwise meet. I love that when I visit a place and say I am a Mender then that is a further connection, thread of communication between practitioners, people, communities.

INDEX

Numbers in italics indicate figures. (724 lines)

abalungaana [Swahili-Arab traders] 108
Acabados Gonzalez, Piñatex production line 212
Access Hollywood comment (Trump), and *Pussyhat Project* 133
Adire
    cloth 57–58
    Yoruba clothes 56–58
Afetosyntesis (Nepomuceno) *114*
Agbada [tunic coveralls] 56, 59
    clothes men 56
AIDS Quilt 133
åkle [cover] 85
Akpang, Clement Emeka 15, 50
    biography x
Al Quran Festival, Alor Besar *19*
Albers, Anni *9*, 10
Albert (king) 42
Aldrich, Winifred 94
álfar [fairies] 86–87
Alhajis 58
All Things Fashion: Fashionista Catwalk Runway, London Fashion Week *111*
Alor Besar, Al Quran Festival *19*
Alurung clan
    culture 20–21
    history 19–20
    language 19
    tenapi 17–18, 22–27
    textile production 21–22
    weaving 21–22
Alurung men
    culture 20

tenapi 21, 24, *25*, 26
tenapi patola *25*
Alurung women, tenapi *19*, 24
amaMfengu 159
Amathole Museum, Qonce 160
Andrew, Sonja 169, 194, 197, *198*, 203, *203*
    biography xi
Ankara fabric 58
aqua alta 189
AR *see* augmented reality
Armstrong, Helen 94
arpilleristas 133
Art as Experience (Dewey) 10
art textiles, and science theory 200
artisanal annotation, of cloth 190
Aso Ibile, clothes women 56
Aso-Oke
    cloth 56–59
    Yoruba clothes 56–58
Astbury, William Thomas 201–202
Atampa fabric 58
augmented reality (AR) 169, 184–186, 189–190
Avila, Susan T. 10, 117
    biography xi

Babbar Riga [King of Clothes], clothes, wealthy 56, 58–59
Baganda 104
bakembuga [royal women] 104
banners, *Ribbon International, The* 133
bao lolong [banyan tree leaf] motif 23

bao lolong sambung [connecting banyan tree leaves] 23
bark cloth artisan [*mukomazi*] 107
bark cloth [*olubugo*] 53, 104–112
    in Buganda culture 104–107
    changing meaning 108–109
    cultural restoration 110
    ponchos 60
    processing 107
    refashioning 110–112, *111*
    in Uganda culture 110
    and Western missionaries 109
    workshop 107–108
Barnett, Pennina 34
Barthes, Roland, *Camera Lucida* 32
Bassett, Lynne Z. 71
Battle of Britain 45
    lace memorial 40, *40*, 42–43, 45–46, 48
Bauchi 58
Belgian Relief Fund, lace memorial 44–45
ben [second room] 88
Bhabha, Homi 54
bhunga [house] 95
Bight of Benin, Niger River, Kano, Katsina, Sokoto (Clapperton) 52
Billinghurst, May 125
biophysics, record in cloth 201–202
Black Friday 122
Blaudruck 156
blouses [*Buba*] 56
    [*Zani*] 58
body traces, digital cloth 185–190
bogus trousers [*Shokoto*] 56

Boise Peace Quilt Project (BPQP) 132
Brachem, Judith, puffed spacewalk jumpsuit (Caste.less) 187
Bradford Industrial Museum 35
Broca de Babbar Riga, *Hausa* 58–59
Buba [blouses/shirts]
    clothes men 56
    clothes women 56
Buganda culture 104
    bark cloth [*olubugo*] 104–107
burial ceremony 105–106
Burrell Collection, Glasgow 72
Burton, Robert 28, *33, 35*
    biography ix
but [main room] 88

CAD *see* computer-aided design
Caftan 58
Camera Lucida (Barthes) 32
Cancer Research UK (CRUK), Manchester Institute Advanced Imaging 196–198, 203
Cantour, Sarit 10
ceremonies
    burial 105–106
    okubikka akabugo 105
charcoal, Piñatex *213*
cheen-bandha [feather stitch] 97
child initiation ceremony [*okwalula abaana*] 105
chula [earthen gas fire] 94
Churchill, Winston 42–43
Cinématographe 144
Clapperton, Captain Hugh 52
cloth
    artisanal annotation of 190
    as biophysics record 201–202
    digital 183–191
    mutuba/mituba (*ficus natalensis*) bark 104
    physical 182–183
Cloth Called Witness, A (Cantour) 10
Cloth and Human Experience (Weiner and Schneider) 2
Cloth and Memory 186
Cloth, Memory, and Loss (Barnett) 34
cloth seller [*pheriwala*] 95
clothes, Yorubas 56
clothes, men
    Agbada 56
    Buba 56
    Dandogo 56
    Esiki 56
    Ewu Awoleke 56

Gbariye 56
Oyala 56
Sapara 56
Sulia 56
clothes, wealthy, *Babbar Riga* [King of Clothes] 56
clothes, women
    Aso Ibile 56
    Buba 56
    Ibante 56
    Kijipa 56
commemorative lace panel, Battle of Britain 40
Commission for the Relief of Belgium (CRB) 44–45, 47
computer-aided design (CAD) 184
computer-aided manufacturing (CAM) 184
Cool Stuff to Sew with Sara (Trail) 137
coronation, Kanaka Muwenda Mutebi II *106*, 110
CRB *see* Commission for the Relief of Belgium
Creative Labs 199–200, 202–203
crypto wallets 187
cultural dance troupe, *Onyonyo* dress 56
cultural identity, Nigeria cloth 54–59
cultural restoration, bark cloth [*olubugo*] 110
culture, Alurung clan 20–21
cutting room, Pathé Frères Production Studios 145, *146*, 147
Cuttings 6
Cuttings 1820-2020 156–163, *161–162*

Dan Kwali, wrapper/wrapper skirts [*Iro*] 58
Dandogo, clothes men 56
Darned and Mended swatch 174, 176–178
dematerialized textiles 169, 182–184, 186
designers, lace memorial design 45–46
Devendorf, Laura 177
Dewey, John 10
digital cloth 183–186
    body traces 185–190
    in context 188–190
    future of 190–191
digital composition methods 202–203
digital fashion 184–185
diplomatic gifts [*khila*] 108
Discipline and Punish: The Birth of the Prison (Foucault) 120
Dobson and Browne, Nottingham 40, *40*, 45–46
Doris Hainsworth née Wilson *33*

drapery 40–42
dress
    Onyonyo 55, *55–56*, 59
    Vivienne Leigh *ii* 218
dress T.1-1967, Victoria and Albert Museum *75*
dress T.854-1974, Victoria and Albert Museum *73*
Duvernay, Ava 138

E-textiles 171–178
    diffracting practice 177–178
    Swatchbook Exchanges 173–175
earthen gas fire [*chula*] 94
East Indonesia 18–27
ECOS *see* European City of Science
Efik ethnic group 54–55
Efik style, *Onyonyo* dress 55, *55*, 59
ekiwu [royal carpet] 110
ekyano [open area] 107
Elisabeth of Hungary (saint) 43
Elisabeth (queen), needlelace tablecloth *41*, 42–43
embroidered panel 120, *121–122*, 127
enhanced truth 196
ensamo [mallet] 107
enzo (*teclea nobilis*) mallet 107
Esiki, clothes men 56
ethnic groups
    Efiks 54–55
    Hausa 58
    Ibadan 56
    Ibibios 54–55
    Ijaws 54–55
    Ijebu-Ode 56
    Ikweres 54–55
    Ile Ife 56
    Ilesha 56
    Ilorin 56
    Isokos 54–55
    Itsekiris 54–55
    Kalabaris 54–55
    Nupe 58
    Okrikas 54–55
    Oyo 56
    Urhobos 54–55
European City of Science (ECOS) 198
European silk 70–71
Ewu Awoleke, clothes men 56
Expanding Hermeneutics, Visualism in Science 196

Fabric of Research, The exhibition 196–199
fairies [*álfar*] 86–87

fashion, *Virtual Fashion Archive, The* 188
fashion design, virtual 182–183, 188, 191
Fashion Institute of Technology (FIT) Museum 187
Fashion Unraveled 186–187
feather stitch [*cheen-bandha*] 97
figures, lace memorial design 43
film as fabric 144–145
Film as Fabric 144–151
    Radio Revolten festival 144, 148, *149*, 150
filmmaking, and textile practice 144
First World War 15, 40, 42, 44, 47, 198, *198*
    Blitz 42
FIT *see* Fashion Institute of Technology
floral borders, lace memorial design 43–44
Fort Hare University 161
Foucault, Michel 120
Fraser's jacket 219
Freddie's rug 166
Freud Museum 35
From Man to Man (Schreiner) 128

Gamussa Collection, The 213
Gandaness 110
Gauntlett, David 11, 141
Gbariye, clothes men 56
George (saint) 43
Ghai, LOkesh 67, 92
    biography x
Ghana, *Kente* cloth 52
Gliddon, Katie 122
Gothic to Goth: Romantic Era Fashion and its Legacy (Bassett) 71
GROUND, Thread Bearing Witness project *4*
Guillemot, Agnès 146

Haiku (Albers) 9
hair cortical cells, photomicrographs *203*
Handwoven Waffle Sensor swatch (Satom) 177
hari 20, 22
Hausa
    Broca de Babbar Riga 58–59
    ethnic group 56
Hetherington, Pippa, biography xi
hidden people [*huldufólk*] 86–87
Hijosa, Carmen, biography xii
history, Alurung clan 19–20
Hodgson, Ruby 67–68, *73*
    biography x

Holloway Prison 120
house [*bhunga*] 95
huldufólk [hidden people] 86–87

I want Great Climate, Tiny Pricks Project *136*
Ibadan, ethnic group 56
Ibante, clothes women 56
Ibibio ethnic group 54–55
Idaho and Peace quilt 132
If Walls Could Talk: The Last Yarn (Leighton-Boyce) 8
IFC *see* International Fiber Collective
Ijaw ethnic group 54–55
Ijebu-Ode ethnic group 56
ikat 22–26
Ikwere ethnic group 54–55
Ile Ife, ethnic group 56
Ilesha, ethnic group 56
Ilorin, ethnic group 56
imaging, in science 196
Impact Report 215
In Search of Lost Time (Proust) 34
Insibidi/Nsibidi symbol 53
Interested Sensor swatch 174, *174–175*
Interested Sensors #2 177–178
International Fiber Collective (IFC) 133
Interwoven Stories project (Weaver) 135
Intolerance (Guillemot) 146
Iro [wrapper/wrapper skirt] 56
Isishweshwe: A History of the Indigenisation of Blueprint in Southern Africa (Leeb-du Toit) 156
Isoko ethnic group 54–55
Itsekiri ethnic group 54–55

Jalaba 58
Jamal, Ashraf 162
Jamnaben
    stitching kediyun *96*
    wearing a kediyun *99*
Joint Soviet–American Peace Quilt 132
Jones, Denise 10, 117–118
    biography x

kago no eking [intertwining snakes] patterns 23
Kalabari ethnic group 54–55
Kanaka Muwenda Mutebi II, coronation *106*
Kano 58
kanzu [Uganda cultural wear] 109
Katsina 58
Kebbi 58
kediyun 94–100, *99*

chaar 97
cloth cutting 96
cloth measurements 95
cloth wastage 96–97
Jamnaben Ahir 96–98, *96*, *99*
stitching 95–98, *96*
traditional making 95
Kente cloth, Ghana 52
Kettle, Alice 4, 5, 12
    biography ix
    and Maria Nepomuceno 64–65, 114–115
khila [diplomatic gifts] 108
Kijipa, clothes women 56

lace
    Niger delta 54–56
    twentieth century 42
lace industries
    commercial success 47–48
    reviving 46
lace memorial design 42
    designers 45–46
    figures 43
    floral borders 43–44
    manufacture 46
    places 43
    text 42–43
lace memorials
    Battle of Britain 40, *40*, 42–43, 45–46, 48
    Belgian Relief Fund 42, 44
    origins 44–45
Lafia 58
language, Alurung clan 19
Last Yarn, Cloth and Memory, The (Leighton-Boyce) 8
Latour, Bruno 32
layers of meaning 105
Leeb-du Toit, Juliette 156
Leeds Creative Labs 199–200, 202–203
Leigh, Vivienne 218–219
    dress *ii* 218
Leighton-Boyce, Hannah 8–9
lending library, protest banner *140*
Les Amies de la Dentelle 42, 45
Lewis, Andrea 159
Littler, David 150
Location of Culture, The (Bhabha) 54
London Fashion Week, runway *111*

McIntosh, Linda 15–16
    biography ix
magnetic resonance imaging (MRI) 196

Making is Connecting (Gauntlett) 11, 141
mallets
    enzo (*teclea nobilis*) 107
    omusaali (*garcinia buchananii*) 107
    omusaali (*mimusops ugandensis*) 107
malu gilu [broken sirih fruit] patterns 23
Man with a Movie Camera (Svilova) 145–146
manufacture, lace memorial design 46
Mara barriers [*muruspjeld*] 89
marriage rug, non-pile side 84
Marsh, Jennifer 133
masiro 105
Matereality (Lewes) 159
Material Hermeneutics, Reversing the Linguistic Turn 196
meaning, layers of 105
men's shirts [*Buba*] 56
Metamorphoses (Ovid) 132
Metric Pattern Cutting (Aldrich) 94
Metropolitan Museum 72
Millar, Lesley 184
    biography ix
    and Celia Pym 166–167, 218–219
Mitchell, Victoria 33
motifs
    bao lolong [banyan tree leaf] 23
    ufe kotong [head of the sea hare] motif 23
    ula naga [snake Naga] 23
Moving Pictures: How They Are Made and Worked 145
MRI *see* magnetic resonance imaging
mukomazi [bark cloth maker] 107–108
Murch, Walter 145
muruspjeld [Mara barriers] 89
Museum 1000 Moko 18
Museum of Art 11
Museum of London *121*
mutuba/mituba (*ficus natalensis*) bark cloth 104
mythmaking, *Powerful Whispers* project 32–33

Nakazibwe, Venny Mary 67, 102, 110
    biography x
NAMES Project 133
napery 40–42
Nature (journal) 202
needlelace tablecloth, Queen Elisabeth *41*
Negarakertagama 19
Nepomuceno, Maria 12, 64–65, *64*, 114–115, *114*
    biography x

NFTS *see* Non-Fungible Tokens
Ngonge [otter] clan 104
Nicolson, Annabel 144, 147–148, 151
Niger delta, lace as opulence 54–56
Nigeria
    diverse ethnic indigenism 52
    Yorubas clothes 56
Nigeria cloth
    context 52–54
    cultural identity 54–59
Nigerian National Museum 55
Nigerianness 59
Nnamulondo [royal stool] 110
No. 1 Piñatex production line, Acabados Gonzalez *212*
Non-Fungible Tokens (NFTS) 190
Norway 85, 89
Nsibidi symbol 53
Nupe ethnic group 58
nura [boat] patterns 23

Okrika ethnic group 54–55
okubikka akabugo ceremony 105
okwalula abaana [child initiation ceremony] 105
olubugo [bark cloth] 104–112
olwebagyo [sash] 104
omusaali (*garcinia buchananii*) mallet 107
omusaali (*mimusops ugandensis*) mallet 107
omutuba/emituba 104
Onyonyo dress 55, *55*, 59
    cultural dance troupe *56*
open area [*ekyano*] 107
Other 53
otter [*Ngonge*] clan 104
Oyala, clothes men 56
Oyo, ethnic group 56

Pankhurst, Emmeline 120
Pankhurst, Sylvia 120
Parker, Rozsika 120, 124, 128, 150
participant, mounting swatches *174*
Pathé Frères Production Studios, cutting room 145, *146*, *147*
patolu/patola, imported 22
patrilineages (*uma*) 20
patrilineal identity markers, tenapi 22–25
Pattern Making for Fashion (Armstrong) 94
patterns
    kago no eking [intertwining snakes] 23
    malu gilu [broken sirih fruit] 23
    muruspjeld [Mara barriers] 89
    nura [boat] 23

    plinta [bursting kapok] 23
    utam pei [candle nut] 23
PDDCP *see* Product Development and Design Center Philippines
Pele [shawls] 56
pheriwala [cloth seller] 95
photomicrographs, hair cortical cells 128, 202, *203*
physical cloth 182–183
Pin Probe swatch 174, 177–178
Pinackpuck Collection, The 213
Piñatex 208–215
    charcoal *213*
    production line *212*
places, lace memorial design 43
Plants That Hold Us, The 11
plinta [bursting kapok] patterns 23
ponchos, bark cloth [*olubugo*] 60
Powerful Whispers project 30–36, *35*
    mythmaking 32–33
    remembered images 31–32
    remythologizing memory 33–36
printed textile sling, St John's Ambulance *198*
Procession, The 2, *3*
Product Development and Design Center Philippines (PDDCP) 208, 210
production, tenapi 25–27
production line, Acabados Gonzalez *212*
Protest Banner Lending Library (Sifuentes) 132, 139–141, *140*
    social justice textiles 139–141
Proust, Marcel 34
puffed spacewalk jumpsuit (Caste.less), Judith Brachem *187*
punctum, quality of 46
Pussyhat Project 10, 133
    and *Access Hollywood* comment (Trump) 133
Pym, Celia 166–167, 218–219
    biography xi

qamis [Swahili-Arab shirt] 109
Quarini, Carol 15, 38, *40–41*
    biography ix, x
quilt
    AIDS Quilt 133
    Idaho and Peace 132
    Joint Soviet–American Peace Quilt 132

Radio Revolten festival, *Film as Fabric* 149
RAF *see* Royal Air Force
Reading the Thread 8

Reel Time (film) (Nicolson) 144, 147–148, 151
refashioning, bark cloth [*olubugo*] 110–112, *111*
remembered images, *Powerful Whispers* project 31–32
remythologizing memory, *Powerful Whispers* project 33–36
Ribbon International, The banner 133
Rice Dreams 13
Robins, Freddie, *Freddie's* rug 166
romantic-era fashion 71–77
    silk 70–71
rooms
    ben [second room] 88
    but [main room] 88
ropes and beads (Nepomuceno) *64*
Rose, Becca 172, *175*, 176
    biography xi
Rosen, Andrew 120, 122
Royal Air Force (RAF) 48
royal carpet [*ekiwu*] 110
Royal Museum of Art and History, Brussels *41*, 42, 46
royal stool [*Nnamulondo*] 110
royal women [*bakembuga*] 104
rubber, X-ray crystallography images 202, *203*
rug, Shetland Taatit 67, 83–86, *83*, 89–90
rya
    bedcovers 89
    rugs 82, 84–86, 89–90

St John's Ambulance, printed textile sling *198*
St Paul's Cathedral 43
Sampler-Culture Clash (Littler) 150
Sand, Katharina 169, 180
    biography xi
Sapara, clothes men 56
sash [*olwebagyo*] 104
Satomi, Mika 177
Schneider, Jane 2
Schreiner, Olive 128
science research, and textile practice 196–204
science theory, and art textiles 200
Second World War 15, 30, 40, 42, 44–45, 47–48
Serres, Michel 32
Sew with Sara (Trail) 137
shawls [*Pele*] 56
Shetland Museum and Archives *83*–84

Shetland Taatit rug 82–90, *83*
Shokoto [bogus trousers] 56
Sifuentes, Han 139–141
Signalling Networks textile design 196–197
silk 125–126, 128
    European 70–71
    X-ray crystallography images 201–202, *203*
silk twill 197, *198*
silks, romantic-era fashion 70
SJSA *see* Social Justice Sewing Academy
sling, St John's Ambulance *198*
Smyth, Ethel 120
Social Justice Sewing Academy (SJSA) 132, 137–139
    social justice textiles 137–139
social justice textiles 132–141
    Protest Banner Lending Library 139–141
    Social Justice Sewing Academy 137–139
    Tiny Pricks Project 135–137
    25 Million Stitches 134–135
society role, tenapi 24–27
Sohn, Kim 132–135
Sokoto 58
Solomon's seal 43
Soviet Women's Peace Committee 132
Ssekabaka Ssemakiro 104
Stark, Mary *8*, 142, *149*
    biography xi
Stitch For Time, A (film) 132
Strange Cargo: Essays on Art (Jamal) 162
Sturlunga saga 88–89
Subversive Stitch: Embroidery and the Making of the Feminine, The (Parker) 120, 124, 128, 150
Suffragette signatures 122, 125
suffragette-embroidered cloths 10, 120, 126–128
    context 120–122
    embroidering 124–126
    Holloway Prison 122–124
    material processes 126–128
suffragettes 122–124
Sulia, clothes men 56
Svilova, Elizaveta 145–146
Swahili-Arab shirt [*qamis*] 109
Swahili-Arab traders [*abalungaana*] 108
swatches 174
    Interested Swatch *175*
    participant mounting *174*
Sweden 85

symbols
    Insibidi (Nsibidi) 53
    Uli 53

Tangible Embedded and Embodied Interaction (TEI) 173
Taylor, Mary Ellen (Nellie) 125
technology, modifying reality 196
TEI *see* Tangible Embedded and Embodied Interaction
tékhne 184
tenapi
    Alurung clan 17–18, 22–27
    Alurung men *25*
    Alurung women *19*
    patrilineal identity markers 22–25
    production 25–27
    society role 24–27
    use 25–27
tenapi matang karing, features 23
tenapi patola
    Alurung man *25*
    features 22–24
tenapi sonto raja, features 24
Tennessee Valley Authority (TVA) 132
Terrero, Janie 120, 124
text, lace memorial design 42–43
Textile Institute (journal) 202
textile practice
    and filmmaking 144
    and science research 196–204
textile production, Alurung clan 21–22
textiles, dematerialized 169, 182–184, 186
Textiles, Text and Techné (Mitchell) 33
The Women's Library (TWL) 120, *122*, 125–126
Thingification 53
13th (documentary) (Duvernay) 138
Thread Bearing Witness project 5
    GROUND (Kettle) *4*
Thread and Cloth—Thread as Way Finder 2–8
Tiny Pricks Project (Weymar) 132–133, 135–137
    I want Great Climate 136
    social justice textiles 135–137
Trail, Sara 133, 137–138
Trump, Donald 11, 133, 135, 137
truth, enhanced 196
tunic coveralls [*Agbada*] 56
TVA *see* Tennessee Valley Authority
25 Million Stitches project (Sohn) 132–135
TWL *see* The Women's Library

ufe kotong [head of the sea hare] motif 23
Uganda 104
    bark cloth *see* bark cloth
Uganda cultural wear [*kanzu*] 109
Uganda culture, bark cloth [*olubugo*] 110
ula naga [snake Naga] motif 23
Uli symbol 53
ULITA *see* University of Leeds International Textile Archive
uma see patrilineages
Université du Québec à Montréal (UQAM) 185
University of Leeds Cultural Institute's Creative Labs 196, 199
University of Leeds International Textile Archive (ULITA) 202
Upstream and Downstream Model of Sustainable Design, The 210
UQAM *see* Université du Québec à Montréal
Urhobo ethnic group 54–55
utam pei [candle nut] patterns 23

V&A *see* Victoria and Albert
vasculogenic mimicry (VM) 196
Victor, Stephanie 160
Victoria and Albert Museum (V&A) 70, 72–77
    cream dress T.854-1974 72–74, *73*, 76–77
    striped dress T.1-1967 74–77, *75*
Virtual Fashion Archive, The 188
virtual fashion design 182–183, 188, 191
VM *see* vasculogenic mimicry
Votes for Women (Rosen) 120, 122

Warp and Weft, Cloth and Memory 7
weaving, Alurung clan 21–22
Weiner, Annette B. 2
Western missionaries, and bark cloth [*olubugo*] 109
We've Come a Long Way textile design 197–198
Weymar, Diana 132–133, 135–137
What is Made, Now and Before 2
Where Things Enter into Collective Society (Serres and Latour) 32
Wilcox, Cissie 120, 125
Women's Social and Political Union (WSPU) 120
wool 85, 94, 125, 183, 209, 218
    X-ray crystallography images 201–202, *203*
Work in Progress 185
World Bank 209
World Reclamation Art Project (WRAP) (Marsh) 133
Woven 2D Position Sensor swatch (Devendorf) 174, 177
WRAP *see* World Reclamation Art Project
wrapper/wrapper skirts [*Iro*] 56
    Dan Kwali 58
Writing an End to Cancer textile design 197
WSPU *see* Women's Social and Political Union

X-ray diffraction crystallography 201–202
    rubber 202, *203*
    silk 201–202, *203*
    wool 201–202, *203*

Yobe 58
Yoruba clothes 56
    Adire 56–58
    Aso-Oke 56–58

Zani [blouse] 58
Zaria (Clapperton) 52